W9-AAK-979

CHAUCER AND THE
UNIVERSE OF LEARNING

ALSO BY ANN W. ASTELL

Job, Boethius, and Epic Truth

The Song of Songs in the Middle Ages

CHAUCER
AND THE
UNIVERSE
OF
LEARNING

ANN W. ASTELL

CORNELL UNIVERSITY PRESS

ITHACA AND LONDON

34410358
DLC

10-23-96

First published 1996 by Cornell University Press.

Printed in the United States of America

∞ The paper in this book meets the minimum requirements
of the American National Standard for Information Sciences—
Permanence of Paper for Printed Library Materials, ANSI Z39.48–1984.

Library of Congress Cataloging-in-Publication Data

Astell, Ann W.
    Chaucer and the universe of learning / Ann W. Astell.
        p.   cm.
    Includes bibliographical references and index.
    ISBN 0-8014-3269-3 (alk. paper)
    1. Chaucer, Geoffrey, d. 1400—Knowledge and learning.
2. Learning and scholarship—History—Medieval, 500–1500.
3. Christian pilgrims and pilgrimages in literature.   4. Chaucer,
Geoffrey, d. 1400. Canterbury tales.   5. Knowledge, Theory of, in
literature.   6. Philosophy, Medieval, in literature.   7. Cosmology,
Medieval, in literature.   8. Astrology in literature.   I. Title.
PR1933.K6A88   1996
821'.1—dc20   96-2315

CONTENTS

PREFACE

This book advances a bold argument on several fronts. Beginning with the layout of the Ellesmere manuscript, which interprets the *Canterbury Tales* as an encyclopedic *compilatio*, with Chaucer's early reception as a philosophical poet, and with his own poetic ambitions as articulated in the *House of Fame*, it positions Chaucer's work within the newly "clerical" lay culture of his time, emphasizing the catalytic role played by the universities in the redefinition of the feudal estates. It stresses the close correlation between societal divisions and hierarchies and the divisions of the arts and sciences and goes on to argue (1) that the *Canterbury Tales* represents both a social *summa* (in the General Prologue) and a philosophical *summa* (in the groupings of exemplary tales) and (2) that the storytelling contest and quarreling among pilgrims mirror current scholastic *quaestiones* and academic competitions.

Against the dominant scholarly view that the Ellesmere tale-order is not authorial, but merely editorial, this book argues that the Ellesmere arrangement of story-blocks logically continues a pattern of planetary descent that is initiated by Chaucer himself in Fragment I when he places "The Knight's Tale" under Saturnine influence and introduces into that first story all seven of the Ptolemaic planetary deities. Chaucer uses an astrological sequence, which becomes evident in the rapidly descending order of the first three tales, to structure the pilgrimage to Canterbury as a philosophical soul-journey, which subsumes under the successive *influentia* of the seven planets a topical survey of the arts and sciences, arranged according to the same outline used by Gower in Book VII of *Confessio Amantis*.

These two planetary and philosophical outlines establish remarkable and hitherto unnoticed correspondences between Chaucer's *Tales* and the works of Gower and Dante. Multiple Chaucerian *cruces* that have previously been treated in isolation all become explicable in the structural terms of this intertextual dialogue. Most important, the close parallels to Dante's work which emerge reveal the *Canterbury Tales* to be Chaucer's entry in an astonishing storytelling contest with the Dante of the *Paradiso*.

This book probably began some years ago in San Francisco during a job interview at the MLA Convention. The room was full of faculty members from the University of Chicago. Christina Von Nolcken asked me a question about my general approach to Chaucer's *Canterbury Tales*, to which I spontaneously replied, "Oh, I think of it as a kind of *Consolation of Philosophy*." After that bold beginning, I found myself unable to offer much in the way of elaboration. This book, then, may be regarded as a delayed answer to Christina's question.

On the way to its completion, I have been accompanied by many more fellow-travelers than Chaucer's nine-and-twenty pilgrims. Many of them are quoted in the pages of this book and named in my bibliography. My closest companions, however, as the dedication to this book indicates, have been my teachers and students. It has been my privilege to study under a number of truly "didascalic" teachers, among them, Jerome Taylor, to whom we are all indebted for his translation and edition of Hugh of St. Victor's *Didascalicon* and for his work on Chaucer's *Boece*; Fannie LeMoine, who has helped make Martianus Capella accessible to us; Donald W. Rowe, who opened my eyes to Dante's *Commedia*; and the late Judson Boyce Allen, who first encouraged me to become a medievalist and to whose memory this work is gratefully dedicated.

Over the years I have also been privileged to teach a number of bright, dedicated, and talented young people, who have taught me more than they will ever know. It was my dream to co-author this book with the graduate students who enrolled in my Chaucer seminar ("Chaucer's *Universitas*") in the fall of 1993, and their enthusiasm supported and increased mine in the early stages of this project. They agreed to play by my rules, however much they may have seemed at times like Harry Bailly's, and they wrote seminar papers that approached the various story-blocks from the perspective of particular branches of learning. In the process, we all learned a great deal. In the end, however, mainly because of the Dantean direction in which the major thesis developed in the years following the seminar, co-authorship in the usual meaning of that word proved impossible. In the broad meaning of the word, however, my students—D. Scott Bowers, Thomas E. Clemens, Mark L. Derdzinski, Steven P. Frye, Eric C. Link, Mary C. Olson, and Colleen Reilly—have all co-authored this work with me, because the seminar proved to be a fertile soil for the "seed" of this book, because I have benefited from the exchange of ideas and from their bibliographies, and because I have shared the work-in-progress, chapter by chapter, with them. As the dedication indicates, this book is with and for them. Without them, the book may never have come to be.

I am grateful to Eric C. Link and Steven Frye, in particular, for bringing my attention to bear on the question: "How were the various estates affected by the rise of the universities, and how does Chaucer's work reflect the societal impact of the university as an institution?" Thomas Clemens encouraged me to think about the ramifications of Chaucer's own education, especially his possible legal studies and attested courtroom experience. D. Scott Bowers prompted me to consider the possible significance of the different orderings of the deadly sins in the tales of the Pardoner and the Parson. Mark Derdzinski's interest in medieval medicine contributed to my treatment of the plague in Chapter 7. Mary C. Olson's careful research into medieval alchemy instructed me, and I was inspired by her particular interest in female agency, both alchemical and Chaucerian. At my suggestion, Colleen Reilly developed in her seminar paper the idea of a Macrobian planetary descent in the descending order of tales in Fragment I. Her essay stands as an important background to Chapter 1 of this book, where I contextualize that narrative descent in medieval astrological controversies and in Chaucer's dialogue with Dante. I am particularly indebted to her, not only for references to primary and secondary source materials, but also for her insightful interpretation of the "logic" of "The Knight's Tale" and of the "action" of "The Miller's Tale." In several passages, cited in the notes to Chapter 3, I have echoed the actual language of her paper.

There are others to whom I am greatly indebted. The Center for Research in the Humanities at Purdue University afforded me a semester's leave (spring 1995) for research and writing, and that fellowship was awarded, in turn, at the generous recommendation of Mary Carruthers, Dolores W. Frese, Lisa Kiser, and Christina Von Nolcken. My friends and colleagues in the Department of English gave me their moral support. Among them, I wish to name with special gratitude Thomas Adler, Marianne Boruch, Wendy Flory, Shaun F. D. Hughes, Thomas Ohlgren, Charles Ross, and Margaret M. Rowe.

Winthrop Wetherbee read the entire manuscript, gave me valuable directives for revision and encouraged me to take the extra steps that have greatly improved this book. To him, another of my "didascalic" teachers, I owe a heartfelt debt of gratitude. At Cornell University Press, Bernhard Kendler has been a constant source of support. I am thankful, too, to Lisa Turner and Teresa Jesionowski for copyediting the text with great care.

A I worked on this book, *The New Ellesmere Chaucer Facsimile* and *The Ellesmere Chaucer: Essays in Interpretation,* ed. Martin Stevens and Daniel Woodward (Tokyo and San Marino, Calif.: Huntington Library, 1995) were being prepared for publication. Due to the kindness of Mary Robertson, curator of manuscripts, I was able to consult a microfilm of the Ellesmere manuscript (San Marino, Huntington Library, MS.EL.26.C.9).

I gave an earlier version of Chapter 5 as a paper at the 1992 Meeting of the Medieval Academy of America in Columbus, Ohio. At that time, John Alford read it and offered me encouragement. Some classicist friends and colleagues—Patricia Curd, Keith Dickson, and Martin Winkler—kindly read versions of Chapters 2, 6, and 5, respectively, and gave me valuable suggestions for improvement. Lee Patterson read a version of Chapter 6, which was subsequently published as an article ("Chaucer's 'Literature Group' and the Medieval Causes of Books") in *ELH* 59.2 (1992): 269–87, copyright 1992 by The Johns Hopkins University Press. I thank the editors for permission to include it here.

In the end, however, I owe the greatest debt of gratitude to the

Holy Spirit and to an inner circle of special people who have communicated God's love to me: my parents and brothers and sisters, my fellow Schoenstatt Sisters of Mary, my spiritual father, and a few close friends. Without them, I would have no access to the universe of life and learning and no wings on which to fly.

ANN W. ASTELL

West Lafayette, Indiana

ABBREVIATIONS

C&M	*Classica et Mediaevalia*
EETS e.s.	Early English Text Society, extra series
EETS n.s.	Early English Text Society, new series
EETS o.s.	Early English Text Society, original series
ELH	*English Literary History*
ELN	*English Language Notes*
ES	*English Studies*
JEGP	*Journal of English and Germanic Philology*
MLN	*Modern Language Notes*
MLR	*Modern Language Review*
MP	*Modern Philology*
PL	Patrologiae Cursus Completus, Series Latina. Ed. J.-P. Migne. 221 vols. Paris, 1844–64.
PMLA	*Publications of the Modern Language Association*
PQ	*Philological Quarterly*
RS	Rolls Series: Rerum Britannicarum Medii Aevi Scriptores. London, 1858–96.
SAC	*Studies in the Age of Chaucer*
SP	*Studies in Philology*
UTQ	*University of Toronto Quarterly*
YES	*Yearbook of English Studies*

In addition, the following abbreviations are used to refer to works by Chaucer, Gower, and Dante:

BD	*Book of the Duchess*
CA	*Confessio Amantis*
CT	*Canterbury Tales*
GP	General Prologue
HF	*House of Fame*
Inf.	*Inferno*
LGW	*Legend of Good Women*
Par.	*Paradiso*
PF	*Parliament of Fowls*
Purg.	*Purgatorio*
TC	*Troilus and Criseyde*

CHAUCER AND THE
UNIVERSE OF LEARNING

Others commend Chaucer and Lidgate for their witt, pleasant veine, varietie of poetical discourse, and all humanitie. I specially note *their Astronomie, philosophie,* and other parts of *profound* or *cunning art.* Wherein few of their time were more exactly learned. It is not sufficient for poets to be superficial humanists: but they must be exquisite artists, and curious uniuersal schollers.

—Gabriel Harvey (1585)

The frontiers of a book are never clear-cut.

—Michel Foucault (1969)

INTRODUCTION

The scribe responsible for the sumptuous Ellesmere manuscript of the *Canterbury Tales* concluded his work with the solemn colophon: "Heere is ended the book of the tales of Caunterbury, compiled by Geffrey Chaucer, of whos soule Jhesu Crist have mercy. Amen."[1] The word "compiled" has long been taken to mean "composed"— one of its attested meanings in Middle English—and the colophon itself interpreted as a simple attribution of authorship.[2] Its appearance in the specific, material context of the Ellesmere manuscript has, however, led many scholars recently—following the magisterial lead of Malcolm B. Parkes, A. I. Doyle, and Alastair J. Minnis— to interpret the word "compile" in a second, more technical sense, to mean "to collect and present information from authentic sources, as in an encyclopedia or a comprehensive treatise."[3]

---

[1] Unless otherwise indicated, I use Larry D. Benson, ed., *The Riverside Chaucer,* 3d ed. (Boston: Houghton Mifflin, 1987).

[2] The "C" volume of *The Middle English Dictionary,* ed. Hans Kurath and Sherman M. Kuhn (Ann Arbor: University of Michigan Press, 1959) uses the Ellesmere colophon to illustrate this basic meaning of the word: "to compose or write." It dates the colophon c. 1390, attributing it to Chaucer's own lifetime—a dating that has been contested by scholars who argue that the manuscript was produced during the decade after Chaucer's death, 1400–1410.

[3] *The Middle English Dictionary* gives this second definition of the verb "compilen," along with multiple examples of its use in this sense.

In using the word "compile," they argue, the scribe actually interprets Chaucer's book as belonging to a specific literary genre, the
structural conventions of which correspond to the material design and
formal layout of the *Canterbury Tales* as they appear in the Ellesmere
manuscript. As Doyle and Parkes explain in an oft-quoted passage:

> The *compilatio* was developed as a genre in academic and legal circles
> during the course of the thirteenth century to make inherited material
> excerpted from the writings of established *auctores* accessible in a more
> systematic and convenient form. . . . The *ordinatio* of the Ellesmere man-
> uscript interprets the *Canterbury Tales* as a *compilatio* in that it emphasizes
> the role of the tales as repositories of *auctoritates—sententiae* and apho-
> risms on different topics which are indicated by the marginal headings.[4]

Indeed, according to Parkes, the Ellesmere manuscript of the *Canterbury Tales* stands, in comparison to manuscripts of thirteenth-century
compilations such as the tripartite *Speculum majus* of Vincent of Beauvais, as "the most spectacular example" of a late-medieval work presented so as to highlight features of order:

> Here we find almost all the trappings of *ordinatio*: sources and topics
> are indicated in the margins, and the word '*auctor*' is placed alongside
> a sententious statement. The text is well-disposed in its sections, and
> each section is carefully labelled by means of full rubrics. There are
> running titles, and the final touch is the introduction of pictures of
> each of the pilgrims (the basis of the division of the work) in order to
> assist the reader to identify them with the General Prologue.[5]

---

[4]   A. I. Doyle and Malcolm B. Parkes, "The Production of Copies of the *Canterbury Tales*
and the *Confessio Amantis* in the Early Fifteenth Century," in *Medieval Scribes, Manuscripts,
and Libraries: Essays Presented to N. R. Ker*, ed. M. B. Parkes and Andrew G. Watson (London: Scolar, 1978), p. 190. R. H. Rouse and M. A. Rouse have argued that the *compilatio*
is directly descended from the *florilegia* of the early Middle Ages and not an invention
of the thirteenth century, but they concede that the scope and complexity of the *compilatio* as an ordering resource kept pace with the growing sophistication of the universities. See their "*Ordinatio* and *Compilatio* Revisited," in *Ad litteram: Authoritative Texts and
Their Medieval Readers*, ed. Mark D. Jordan and Kent Emery, Jr., Notre Dame Conferences
in Medieval Studies (Notre Dame: University of Notre Dame Press, 1992), 3:113–34.
[5]   Malcolm B. Parkes, "The Influence of the Concepts of *Ordinatio* and *Compilatio* on
the Development of the Book," in *Medieval Learning and Literature: Essays Presented
to R. W. Hunt*, ed. J. J. G. Alexander and M. T. Gibson (Oxford: Oxford University Press,
1976), p. 134.

The historical reception of the *Canterbury Tales* as a *compilatio* by at least one notable interpreter—the Ellesmere scribe—and its apparent (subsequent, if not simultaneous) reception by other medieval readers as belonging to that same compendious genre have prompted and/ or supported a series of revisions in various, interrelated aspects of Chaucerian scholarship—in particular, studies of the composition of Chaucer's historical audience; Chaucer's image as a poet among his earliest readers; Chaucer's own authorial self-image and declared poetic ambitions; and, more narrowly, critical discussions of the *Canterbury Tales*, especially those focused on issues of genre and theme and related matters of textual scholarship, such as the ordering of the individual tales and fragments.

Chaucer's Early Reception: A Clerk among Clerks

The academic origins of the *compilatio* as a genre and its marked popularity in educated circles have raised new questions about Chaucer's real and intended audience for the *Canterbury Tales*. There has been considerable research into the library holdings, reading, and writing of the English royal family, and their patronage of poets and scholars in the fourteenth and early fifteenth centuries.[6] As Jeanne Krochalis observes, however, "though Chaucer's first audience is usually assumed to be the English royal court," royal ownership can only be proven for a single extant Chaucer manuscript, Henry V's copy of *Troilus and Criseyde*.[7]

Recent research into Chaucer's historical audience has, in fact, tended to undermine the previously accepted view of Chaucer as a prince-pleasing, courtly poet, adept at entertainment in oral performance (a view inspired by the portrait of a declaiming Chaucer in the familiar *Troilus* frontispiece)[8] and to affirm instead his close ties to a second circle or tier of bookish readers with an education, income, and interests similar to Chaucer's own. The current scholarly debate

---

[6]   See, for instance, Richard Firth Green, *Poets and Princepleasers: Literature and the English Court in the Late Middle Ages* (Toronto: University of Toronto Press, 1980).

[7]   Jeanne Krochalis, "The Books and Reading of Henry V and His Circle," *Chaucer Review* 23 (1988): 50.

[8]   See Margaret Galway, "The *Troilus* Frontispiece," *MLR* 44 (1949): 161–77; Derek Pearsall, "The *Troilus* Frontispiece and Chaucer's Audience," *YES* 7 (1977): 68–74.

centers on the dominant makeup of that second circle. The " 'tiered' conception of Chaucer's public," as Paul Strohm explains, distinguishes a range of readers "with gentlemen at one extreme and clerks at the other," and places Chaucer at the middle of an emergent social class constituted by "nonknightly gentlepersons and the bourgeoisie."[9]

Strohm's own analysis puts major emphasis on the gentlemen rather than the clerks in Chaucer's audience. Drawing on personal references in Chaucer's own poetry, on the one hand, and poetic tributes to Chaucer by his contemporaries, on the other, Strohm argues that Chaucer's "immediate public or 'point of attachment' " included "several knights in royal and civil service whom Chaucer knew in the 1370s and 1380s, including William Beauchamp, Lewis Clifford, Philip la Vache, John Clanvowe, William Nevill, and Richard Stury; London acquaintances of the 1380s, including Ralph Strode and (with certain qualifications) John Gower; and newcomers of the 1390s, including Henry Scogan and Peter Bukton."[10] All of these figures, according to Strohm, were *gentil* (with the exception of Strode), and all of them belonged to the "affinity" of Richard II and participated in his affairs "not just as an expression of political sympathy but as a source of livelihood and a way of life."[11]

Although his analysis characterizes Chaucer's friends as "educated bureaucrats" and admits lawyers like Strode and clerks like Thomas Usk (d. 1388) and Thomas Hoccleve (d. 1430) at the "lower tier" of Chaucer's audience, Strohm conspicuously underplays Chaucer's Oxford ties and Inns of Court connections, and insists that both Chaucer and Gower were "more gentleman than clerk."[12] His approach to Chaucer's historical audience centers, in the end, principally on the king, the court, and the lesser nobility as represented in the so-called Lollard knights. According to Strohm, "Chaucer's realization of himself as a social being occurred primarily within the supple bounds of

[9] Paul Strohm, "Chaucer's Fifteenth-Century Audience and the Narrowing of the 'Chaucer Tradition,' " *SAC* 4 (1982): 14; *Social Chaucer* (Cambridge: Harvard University Press, 1989), p. 4. Strohm translates here the description of the fourth estate given by Philippe de Mézières.
[10] Strohm, *Social Chaucer*, p. 42.
[11] Ibid.
[12] Strohm, *Social Chaucer*, p. 22; "Chaucer's Fifteenth-Century Audience," p. 14. The words "Inns of Court" and "Oxford University" do not appear in the index to *Social Chaucer*.

the King's affinity," a circle characterized by "literary proclivity" and "coextensive with his principal literary audience."[13] Indeed, Strohm characterizes the real audience of Chaucer's *Canterbury Tales* (unlike its fictional, pilgrim audience) as consisting almost exclusively of *gentils*, as that class was defined by the 1397 Poll Tax.[14]

Other scholars differ from Strohm in placing emphasis on the clerks, rather than the gentlemen, in Chaucer's audience and in the emergent "Fourth Estate" as a whole. They stress the catalytic role of the emergent class of lay clerks, educated at the Inns of Court and the Inns of Chancery, but also at the universities, in the changing makeup of an upwardly mobile and increasingly bureaucratic English society, and point to the tension between the "lerned" and the "lewed" in Chaucer's life and work as it complicated the (basically feudal) relationship between "gentils" and "cherls." As Malcolm Richardson insists,

> While at one time we generally accepted that Chaucer wrote for a group of nobles centering around the improvident but artistically sophisticated court of Richard II, now we are more likely to see Chaucer's immediate audience as being more of the "new men" of his age, an audience more suspicious of the heroic pretenses of the immediate past, more alienated from the court and its archaic concerns.[15]

As Thomas F. Tout explains, prominent among the "new men" of the English civil service were lay chancery and exchequer clerks who had made their way into posts "hitherto regarded as the exclusive preserve" of clerics who had taken minor or holy orders.[16] Well-educated, they had "the training that enabled [them] to befriend literature and science, and in some cases, to make personal contributions to them."[17] Chaucer himself was one of only two laymen to serve as Clerk of the King's Works during the reign of Richard II.[18]

---

[13] Strohm, *Social Chaucer*, p. 46. Strohm's analysis is indebted to K. B. McFarlane, *Lancastrian Kings and Lollard Knights* (Oxford: Clarendon Press, 1972).

[14] Strohm, *Social Chaucer*, pp. 9–11, 68–71.

[15] Malcolm Richardson, "The Earliest Known Owners of *Canterbury Tales* MSS and Chaucer's Secondary Audience," *Chaucer Review* 25.1 (1990): 17.

[16] Thomas F. Tout, "Literature and Learning in the English Civil Service in the Fourteenth Century," *Speculum* 4 (1929): 367.

[17] Ibid., pp. 369–70.

[18] *Chaucer Life-Records*, ed. Martin M. Crow and Clair C. Olson (Austin: University of

As Controller of Wool Customs in the Port of London (1374–86), Chaucer worked closely with the clerks of the collectors and the exchequer,[19] and as "clericus operacionum regis," Chaucer probably had his own clerical staff.[20] The poet Thomas Hoccleve (d. 1430), one of the four clerks of the privy seal, is but one of Chaucer's attested clerical readers and imitators.[21] As Richardson has shown, the two earliest-known owners of a *Canterbury Tales* manuscript, Richard Sotheworth and John Stopyndon, were, in fact, chancery clerks with possible ties to Thomas Chaucer through Thomas Haseley (d. 1448), a married layman and a prominent civil servant.[22]

Joining his voice to Richardson's and objecting to Strohm's courtly emphasis, John Fisher has argued that "Chaucer and the rest of London's bureaucratic and merchant society had an existence that was independent of the court," and that "most of [Chaucer's] verse and prose was addressed to the new bourgeoisie," including men like John Gower, Ralph Strode, Sir Philip de la Vache, "Maister" Bukton, and Henry Scogan, all of whom were "friends of the Inns of Court crowd."[23] As Fisher affirms, Chaucer's own education at the Inns of Chancery and Court and his professional duties as Controller of Customs in the port of London (1374–86), Justice of the Peace in Kent (1386–89), and Clerk of the King's Works (1389–91) brought him into close and lasting contact with the clerks of the new civil service, some of them university-trained.

Like Fisher, Janet Coleman points to a fluid interchange between and among the universities, the grammar schools, and the Inns of Court, especially through the "large number of students" that "came

---

Texas Press, 1966), p. 412. The other layman was Roger Elmham, whose term (6 January 1388–July 1389) immediately preceded Chaucer's.

[19] Unlike the controller, "who was required to write his records in his own hand (except when allowed a deputy)," the collectors regularly employed clerks. See *Life-Records*, pp. 208, 151, 169, 185.

[20] The names of Chaucer's clerks have not survived (with the possible exception of a clerk named John Wilton), but his successor as Clerk of Works, John Gedney (d. 14 October 1396), employed at least three clerks: William Caldecot, Otto Blundell, and John Chamberlain (*Chaucer Life-Records*, p. 419).

[21] See Malcolm Richardson, "Hoccleve in his Social Context," *Chaucer Review* 20.4 (1986): 313–22; R. T. Lenaghan, "Chaucer's Circle of Gentlemen and Clerks," *Chaucer Review* 18.1 (1983): 155–60.

[22] Richardson, "Earliest Known Owners."

[23] John H. Fisher, *The Importance of Chaucer* (Carbondale: Southern Illinois University Press, 1992), pp. 179n16, 56.

to Oxford only to learn the techniques of writing formal letters," left
the university after a brief stay, and then proceeded to instruct others
in grammar and *dictamen*.[24] According to Coleman, this "anonymous
force" was a potent factor in "the spread of current ideas and controversies raging at Oxford" (p. 29) among the London populace, as
the discussions of academic and theological issues in vernacular
works—notably *Piers Plowman*, but also the *Canterbury Tales*—bear witness.[25] Similarly, William Courtenay has argued that Chaucer and
William Langland were "influenced by [Oxford's] personalities and
ideas far more than has been recognized," but that the "major point
and place of contact between scholars and poets" was not Oxford
itself, but "London, with its own scholastic institutions, with its inter-
locking network of social and professional groups."[26]

In London the spread of vernacular literacy and lay education
served to produce a new audience for poets. Coleman, like Fisher,
deemphasizes the courtly element in Chaucer's audience, asserting
that "Chaucer's poetry, his own creations and his translations, were
intended for a wider audience than that of the nobility at Richard's
court, and he shared this public with Gower" (p. 21). Gower's audience, moreover, "must have included those learned in Latin, like the
hundred-odd Chancery clerks, who would be edified by his *Vox Clamantis*" (p. 22). Pointing in particular to the Ellesmere manuscript of
the *Canterbury Tales*, Coleman sees in it a clerical interpretation, and
consequent presentation, of Chaucer's work as a learned *compilatio*.
She speculates that the frequent reading, copying, and circulation of
the *Tales* in "discrete units" or fragments "suggested to the Ellesmere
editor that the work was in fact structured as a *compilatio*" (p. 199).

---

[24] Janet Coleman, *Medieval Readers and Writers, 1350–1400* (New York: Columbia University Press, 1981), p. 29.
[25] Coleman emphasizes that Langland himself belonged to "the graduate academic
proletariat" (p. 33), and that he must have expected his audience to consist, at least
in part, of university arts students" (p. 30) who would recognize, for example, the
specific allusions to Priscian's *Institutes* in B.XIII, lines 150–56. The audience of *Piers
Plowman* is generally understood to be the clerical laity. See Tim William Machan, "Language Contact in *Piers Plowman*," *Speculum* 69.2 (1994): 359–85; A. V. C. Schmidt, *The
Clerkly Maker: Langland's Poetic Art* (Cambridge: Cambridge University Press, 1987); Anne
Middleton, "The Audience and Public of *Piers Plowman*," in *Middle English Alliterative
Poetry and Its Literary Background: Seven Essays*, ed. David Lawton (Cambridge: Cambridge
University Press, 1982), pp. 101–23; J. A. Burrow, "The Audience of *Piers Plowman*,"
Anglia 75 (1957): 373–84.
[26] William J. Courtenay, *Schools and Scholars in Fourteenth-Century England* (Princeton:
Princeton University Press, 1987), pp. 376, 378.

At any rate, the *ordinatio* that the Ellesmere copyist perceived and/or imposed as a result of this structural understanding "sets the *Canterbury Tales*, in a startling manner, into the tradition of ordered and indexed preaching handbooks" and other *compilationes* familiar to a clerical audience (p. 199).

Coleman's analysis of the production of the Ellesmere manuscript as a symbolic act whereby the Chaucer of the *Canterbury Tales* (and especially of the Pardoner's and Parson's tales) is perceived to be, and appropriated by a clerical audience as, a "clerk among clerks" gains support from a survey of the earliest commentary on Chaucer. Caroline Spurgeon's interpretation of the data is, as I hope to show, misleading in its delineation of three distinct and successive images of Chaucer during the Middle Ages and Renaissance. According to Spurgeon, "Chaucer is golden-tongued, eloquent, 'ornate,' for about the first 150 years after his death (1400–1550)," whereas he is largely a "moral poet" and a "learned poet" for his readers from 1530 to 1660.[27] While it is certainly true, as Spurgeon indicates, that John Lydgate (d. 1451?) "again and again dwells on the rhetorical powers of his master" (p. xciii) and thus epitomizes an early emphasis on Chaucer the Rhetor, Lydgate does so within the context of a larger view of Chaucer as a philosophical poet, a view that persists from the fourteenth century through the sixteenth century. When Thomas Speght entitled his edition of 1598 "The Workes of our Antient and lerned English Poet," he did not so much react against an earlier image of Chaucer as "golden-tongued," as he reincorporated Lydgate's rhetorical Chaucer into an encyclopedic Chaucer, who was master of all the divisions of knowledge. This sixteenth-century Chaucer is remarkably similar to the Chaucer of the fourteenth, who, as Paul Olson puts it, appeared "in his own time . . . to be a great rhetorician, philosopher-poet, and master of the study of ethics."[28]

As Russell Peck has reminded us, the earliest tributes to Chaucer praise him for his encylopedic learning.[29] Already in 1385 the French poet Eustache Deschamps (1340–1410?), impressed by Chaucer's

---

[27]   Caroline F. E. Spurgeon, *Five Hundred Years of Chaucer Criticism and Allusion, 1357–1900*, 3 vols. (Cambridge: Cambridge University Press, 1925), 1: xciii–xcv.

[28]   Paul Olson, *The "Canterbury Tales" and the Good Society* (Princeton: Princeton University Press, 1986), p. 15.

[29]   Russell Peck, "Chaucer and the Nominalist Questions," *Speculum* 53 (1978): 745–60, esp. p. 745n2.

translation of Jean de Meun's compendious *Roman de la Rose*, sent to Chaucer via their mutual friend, Lewis Clifford, a ballade lauding "noble Geffroy Chaucier" as a new Socrates, replete with philosophy in its various speculative, ethical, and linquistic branches:

> O Socratès plains de philosophie,
> Seneque en meurs, Auglius en pratique,
> Ovides grans en ta poëterie,
> Briés en parler, saiges en rethorique,
> Aigles treshaulz, qui par ta theorique
> Enlumines le regne d'Eneas.

[O Socrates, full of philosophy, Seneca for morality, for practical life an Aulus Gellius, a great Ovid in your poetry, brief in speech, wise in the art of writing, lofty eagle, who by your science enlighten the kingdom of Aeneas.][30]

Similarly, the London official Thomas Usk in his *Testament of Love* (c. 1387) praises Chaucer, the author of *Troilus and Criseyde* and the translator of Boethius's *Consolation of Philosophy*, as "the noble philosophical poete in Englissh."[31] Henry Scogan (1361?–1407?), tutor to the sons of Henry IV, honors his "mayster Chaucer" in verse for his Boethian wisdom.[32] Thomas Hoccleve in the *Regement of Princes* (c. 1412) calls Chaucer not only the "flour of eloquence," but also a "vniversal fadir in science," the successor to M. Tullius Cicero in rhetoric, the "hier in philosophie / To Aristotle," and the follower of "virgile in poesie."[33] Even Lydgate, whose repeated references to Chaucer honor him chiefly as a "noble Rethor" and laureate poet, praises him in the *Fall of Princes*, in company with Virgil, Dante, and Petrarch, for prudence, "wisdam and science."[34] William Caxton (1422?–1491) prefaces his 1484 edition of the *Canterbury Tales* with "a synguler laude

---

[30] Quoted in *Chaucer: The Critical Heritage*, ed. Derek Brewer (London: Routledge and Kegan Paul, 1978), 1:40–41.

[31] Ibid., p. 43.

[32] Ibid., p. 60.

[33] Ibid., pp. 62–63. See also *Hoccleve's Works: The Minor Poems*, ed. Frederick J. Furnivall and I. Gollancz, rev. Jerome Mitchell and A. I. Doyle, EETS e.s. 61 and 73 (1892 and 1925; repr. rev. London: Oxford University Press, 1970), stanzas 281 and 299, pp. xxxi–xxxii.

[34] *Lydgate's Fall of Princes*, ed. Henry Bergen, Part II: Books III–V, EETS 122 (London: Oxford University Press, 1924, repr. 1967), lines 3858–64, p. 436.

vnto that noble & grete philosopher Gefferey chaucer," and he includes in his 1479 edition of Chaucer's *Boece* the Latin epitaph composed by Stefano de Surigone, which attributes to Chaucer "the
genius of Socrates or the springs of philosophy": "Socratis ingenium.
vel fontes philosophie."[35]

This view of Chaucer as a learned and philosophical poet reached
a certain peak during the heyday of English Renaissance humanism.
Supporting the work of William Thynne (d. 1546), Sir Brian Tuke (d.
1545), secretary to Henry VIII, recommended the king to read the
books of "that noble & famous clerke Geffray Chaucer, in whose
workes is manyfest comprobacion of his excellent lernying in all
kyndes of doctrynes and sciences" and to whom may be attributed
the marvelous "ornature" of the English language.[36] Shortly later,
John Leland (1500–1552), a graduate of Cambridge University, ac-
counted for Chaucer's remarkable erudition by inventing for him a
biography, long thereafter accepted as factual, according to which
Chaucer "studied at Oxford University with all the earnestness of
those who have applied themselves most diligently to learning" and
"left the university an acute logician, a delightful orator, an elegant
poet, a profound philosopher, . . . an able mathematician," and also
"a devout theologian," whose brilliance earned him the friendship of
John Gower and "a certain Strode, an alumnus of the college of Merton at Oxford."[37] Leland's biography then became the basis for subsequent accounts of Chaucer's life, such as the 1720 biographical
sketch by John Lewis, who numbered Chaucer as a proto-Protestant
among the erudite supporters of John Wycliffe: "He is said to have
been educated in *Canterbury* or *Merton* College with *John Wicliffe* &
thereupon to have commenced an accute [*sic*] Logician, a sweet Rhetorician, a pleasant Poet, a grave Philosopher, and an ingenious Mathematician, and an holy Divine."[38]

Although this brief survey accentuates the persistent, early view of
Chaucer as a philosophical poet, I do not thereby mean to deny that
the fifteenth and sixteenth centuries also witnessed a "narrowing" of

[35]   *Chaucer: The Critical Heritage*, 1:76–79; *The Prologues and Epilogues of William Caxton*,
ed. W. J. B. Crotch, EETS 176 (London: Oxford University Press, 1928, repr. 1956),
pp. 90, 37.
[36]   *Chaucer: The Critical Heritage*, 1:88.
[37]   Ibid., pp. 91–92.
[38]   In Spurgeon, ed., *Five Hundred Years of Chaucer Criticism and Allusion*, 1:350.

the Chaucer tradition—that is, a tendency to continue Chaucer's work through Lydgatian imitations and a related tendency on the part of reformist readers to favor the more serious and overtly moral of Chaucer's tales.[39] To such a puritanical "narrowing" the readers of the seventeenth and eighteenth centuries reacted, as Spurgeon indicates, with an equally narrow, but compensatory and contrastive view of Chaucer as a "jovial, facetious, merry poet" (p. xcvi). What I do want to refute, however, is the idea that "Chaucer the Clerk" was a latter-day Renaissance invention. Rather, as Seth Lerer has expressed it, Lydgate's "writing like the Clerk" is a direct response to clerical elements in Chaucer's own work that defined for him a clerical self-image as a poet and thus served to create for him a clerical audience, both in his own time and thereafter:

> Throughout Chaucer's major fictions, appeals to clerks and clerkly authority motivate the apologias of his narrators and help define their relations with future readers. The pleas for "correccioun" that close the *Troilus* and the Prologue to the *Parson's Tale* flesh out their narrators' personae as writers to and for the clerk in the audience. This distinctive idiom . . . will constitute the raw materials of Lydgate's public voice and will define much of the relationship of fifteenth-century writing to Chaucer's own clerkly *auctoritas*.[40]

Chaucer's Clerical Self-Image

Chaucer's clerkly *persona* has many aspects that, as Lerer argues, define "a complex set of literary relationships among author, source, and audience" (p. 25). Both Chaucer and his real and implied audiences, for instance, seem to have shared the expectation that a great poet must possess *auctoritas*—an expectation that affected both authorial self-representation and contemporary critical response. Alastair J. Minnis has emphasized in particular that although Chaucer, unlike the anonymous English poets before him, actually names him-

---

[39] See John M. Bowers, "*The Tale of Beryn* and *The Siege of Thebes*: Alternative Ideas of *The Canterbury Tales*," *SAC* 7 (1985): 23–50; Charles A. Owen, Jr., "The *Canterbury Tales*: Early Manuscripts and Relative Popularity," *JEGP* 54 (1955): 104–10; Paul Strohm, "Chaucer's Fifteenth-Century Audience."

[40] Seth Lerer, *Chaucer and His Readers: Imagining the Author in Late-Medieval England* (Princeton: Princeton University Press, 1993), p. 25.

self and thus boldly claims authorial status as a vernacular writer, he simultaneously softens that claim by assuming the modest pose of a mere translator of older works by Latin *auctores*, such as Virgil, Ovid, and Lollius (as in the *Legend of Good Women* and *Troilus and Criseyde*); a naive rehearser of others' words (as in the *Canterbury Tales*); and a "lewd compilator of the labour of olde astrologiens" (as in the *Treatise on the Astrolabe*, lines 61–62).[41]

As Minnis stresses, however, the humble appellation "compilatour" commanded considerable respect in an age when the production of *compendia*—theological, historical, moral, and scientific—gave proof of encyclopedic knowledge. Not only collections of ordered sets of *exempla* and *sententiae*, but also long narrative works, such as Virgil's *Aeneid* and Ovid's *Metamorphoses*, the *divisio* and *ordinatio* of which were held to be governed allegorically by topical categories, were regarded as compilations both through their use of older sources (in Virgil's case, Homer) and through the scholastic commentaries that uncovered their veiled truths and universal lore. If in the late Middle Ages even "Virgilius" was not ashamed to be called "a compiler of olde thinges,"[42] Chaucer, following Virgil's "lanterne" (*LGW* 926), could claim the title "compilatour" as a title of honor.

As Minnis points out, Gower, like Chaucer, explicitly names himself a "burel clerk" (line 52) and a compiler in the Prologue to *Confessio Amantis* (c.1390), indicating in a Latin side-note "that he has compiled [*compilavit*] extracts from chronicles, histories and the sayings of (pagan) philosophers and poets."[43] He has, moreover, ordered this material conveniently under the topical headings of the seven deadly sins and made the compilatory quality of the *Confessio* as a whole unmistakable by including in Book VII a summary of the whole of Aristotle's teaching to Alexander the Great.[44]

[41]   Alastair J. Minnis, *Medieval Theory of Authorship: Scholastic Literary Attitudes in the Later Middle Ages* (London: Scolar Press, 1984), pp. 190–210.
[42]   *Polychronicon Ranulphi Higden*, ed. C. Babington and J. R. Lumby, RS 41 (1865–86), 1.13; see also *Lydgate's Troy Book*, ed. H. Bergen, EETS e.s. 97 (London: Oxford University Press, 1906), 2.344: "Virgile . . . þat boke in worschip of Enee Compiled hath."
[43]   Alastair J. Minnis, " 'Moral Gower' and Medieval Literary Theory," in *Gower's "Confessio Amantis": Responses and Reassessments*, ed. A. J. Minnis (Cambridge: D. S. Brewer, 1983), p. 71. Minnis translates the Latin marginalia from *The English Works of John Gower*, ed. G. C. Macaulay, EETS 81 (London: Oxford University Press, 1900, repr. 1969), 1: 3–4.
[44]   According to Mahmoud A. Manzalaoui, the "Aristotelian excursus outside the 'registre of Venus' . . . is more central to Gower's grand system of thought than is the main

Gower thus belongs among the "great compilers of the later Middle Ages." In this category Minnis mentions Vincent of Beauvais, Bartholomaeus Anglicus, Brunetto Latini, John of Wales, and Ralph Higden, who "fitted classical antiquity into such organizing frameworks as universal history, the hierarchy of the sciences, the social and moral hierarchies of the Christian state, and so forth" and thus "presented in a convenient way the sum of received knowledge on any given topic to readers eager for historical and scientific facts."[45] These compilers looked backward to late-antique works of the fifth and sixth centuries, such as Macrobius's *Commentary on the Dream of Scipio*, Martianus Capella's *Marriage of Mercury and Philology*, Boethius's *Consolation of Philosophy*, and Isidore of Seville's *Etymologiae*. The encyclopedic allegories of the twelfth century—the *Cosmographia* of Bernard Silvestris and the *Anticlaudianus* and *De Planctu Naturae* of Alan de Lille—drew their inspiration from these same early sources and, as Minnis suggests, both the didactic allegories of Alan and Bernard and the scholastic *compilationes* of the thirteenth and fourteenth centuries inspired the compendious dream-visions of the late Middle Ages: Jean de Meun's *Roman de la Rose*, Dante's *Commedia*, Langland's *Piers Plowman*, and John Gower's *Confessio Amantis*.

Chaucer's familiarity with, and participation in, this tradition is indisputable, albeit difficult to assess. He translated the *Roman de la Rose* and Boethius's *Consolation*. He alludes to Martianus Capella and Vincent of Beauvais, draws upon Macrobius, translates Virgil and Ovid, imitates and paraphrases Dante, and competes with his friend Gower. There is, moreover, as Peter Dronke indicates, "evidence that Chaucer had read the three most outstanding Latin epics of the twelfth century: the *Cosmographia* of Bernard Silvestris (also known as *De Mundi Universitate*); the *De Planctu Naturae* and *Anticlaudianus* of Alan de Lille."[46] The extent of the influence of the medieval Latin epics on Chaucer's work as a whole has, however, never been studied in depth, and approaches to Chaucer's *Canterbury Tales* in particular have

---

body of the *Confessio*." See " 'Noght in the Registre of Venus': Gower's English Mirror for Princes," in *Medieval Studies for J. A. W. Bennett*, ed. P. L. Heyworth (Oxford: Clarendon Press, 1981), p. 164.

[45] Minnis, " 'Moral Gower,' " pp. 58–59, 70.

[46] Peter Dronke, "Chaucer and the Medieval Latin Poets, Part A," in *Geoffrey Chaucer: Writers and Their Backgrounds*, ed. Derek Brewer (London: G. Bell and Sons, 1974), p. 154.

ignored this critical perspective. Nor have there been any successful attempts to compare Gower's *Confessio* and Chaucer's *Tales* structurally as compilations.[47]

There are multiple, obvious reasons for this neglect. Derek Brewer has, to be sure, grounds for his complaint that Chaucerians have expended more energy on "an often unduly self-contained, unhistorical, literary criticism" than on gaining "knowledge about *Chaucer's* knowledge."[48] Beyond that, however, problems arise first from the qualities peculiar to Chaucer's clerkly persona which, bookish as they are, seem frankly at odds with the gravitas of Cicero's Scipio, the earnest quest of Alan's Prudence, the zealous instruction of Gower's Genius, and the sublimity of Dante's Virgil and Beatrice. The much admired, homely "realism" and dramatic quality of Chaucer's dream-visions and, even more, of his *Canterbury Tales* have little, seemingly, to do with the philosophical Realism investing the allegorical figures of the Latin cosmological epics—so much so that it appears wrongheaded to compare them, even in passages where direct allusion occurs. The *Canterbury Tales*, moreover, seems far removed in its basic literary kind from visionary works in general, including Chaucer's own *Book of the Duchess, Parliament of Fowls,* and *House of Fame.* Finally, the multiple textual and editorial controversies surrounding the *Canterbury Tales* make any study of the work as such exceedingly problematic, given the close link between the order of the individual tales and fragments and the "unity" of the work as an (unfinished) whole. To compare the *Canterbury Tales* as a *compilatio* with Gower's *Confessio Amantis,* for instance, virtually identifies Chaucer's *Tales* with the *Tales* as the Ellesmere manuscript presents them.

Although at first sight these difficulties seem to prohibit an approach to the *Canterbury Tales* from the direction of scholastic *compendia* and encyclopedic allegory, Chaucer himself opens a way for us through a conspicuous gap in the unfinished *House of Fame* (1379–80). An important, early, and enigmatic work, the *House of Fame* gives

[47]   Frederick Tupper's interpretation of the whole of the *Canterbury Tales* as organized, from the summary perspective of "The Parson's Tale," according to the seven deadly sins may be seen as such a comparative attempt. See "Chaucer and the Seven Deadly Sins," *PMLA* 29 (1914): 93–128; "Chaucer's Sinners and Sins," *JEGP* 15 (1916): 56–106.

[48]   Derek Brewer, "Editor's Preface," in *Writers and Their Backgrounds,* p. x. The classic study of Chaucer's general knowledge is and remains Walter Clyde Curry's *Chaucer and the Mediaeval Sciences* (London: Oxford University Press, 1926, repr. 1966).

direct and programmatic expression to Chaucer's own ambitions as an aspiring poet, names his chief poetic models, indicates the direction of his artistic departure from them, and breaks off in an imaginary *locus* to which he will later return in the *Canterbury Tales*. As Richard Neuse has argued (with special reference to Chaucer's reading of and response to Dante), "The poem as a whole ... serves as Chaucer's announcement or preparation for the new departure that is to be *The Canterbury Tales*."[49]

Commenting on the unfinished poem, Robert O. Payne has written about an "interesting idea," advanced "infrequently, but with some persistence": "the theory that the *House of Fame* ... may have been intended to introduce a collection of tales."[50] In Payne's view, such a theory imagines an artistic solution "to the problem of various and apparently irreconcilable values and perspectives in Chaucer's earlier poems" through the creation of "a variety of different narratives" within the "reconciling structure" of a "single frame" (p. 147). In other words, it anticipates the actual direction of Chaucer's development as he moved away from the "books-dreams-experience" paradigm governing his early work.

More recently, Piero Boitani and Richard Neuse have moved beyond Payne's gentle musing to renew the bold thesis, originally put forward by John M. Manly, that the *House of Fame* directly anticipates the *Canterbury Tales*. Calling attention to the " 'tidings' which fill the House of Rumour and which are spoken or carried around by messengers, pardoners, shipmen and pilgrims," Boitani links the fragmentary finish of the *House of Fame* with the beginning of Chaucer's Canterbury collection: "It will eventually be Geoffrey's task to put these very messengers, pardoners, shipmen and pilgrims on the way from the Tabard Inn to Becket's tomb, to make them tell their 'tidings,' their tales, in short, to write a book of tales told orally—the *Canterbury Tales*."[51]

Linking the ending of one work with the beginning of another in

---

[49]   Richard Neuse, *Chaucer's Dante: Allegory and Epic Theater in "The Canterbury Tales"* (Berkeley: University of California Press, 1991), p. 26.

[50]   Robert O. Payne, *The Key of Remembrance: A Study of Chaucer's Poetics* (New Haven: Yale University Press, 1963, repr. 1964), p. 147.

[51]   Piero Boitani, *Chaucer and the Imaginary World of Fame* (London: D. S. Brewer, 1984), p. 206. See also Neuse, *Chaucer's Dante*; J. A. W. Bennett, *Chaucer's Book of Fame* (Oxford: Clarendon Press, 1968), esp. pp. 178–87; John M. Manly, "What Is Chaucer's *Hous of Fame*?" *Anniversary Papers by Colleagues and Pupils of George Lyman Kittredge*, ed. Fred N.

this fashion (albeit across a significant discursive gap, to which we will return in Chapter Two) not only incorporates the pilgrim-journey of the *Canterbury Tales* into what F. N. Robinson calls the "intellectual or mental flight" of the *House of Fame* as part of a single, unfolding metaphor of artistic development;[52] it also allows us to trace through the fluid modulation of one literary genre into another Chaucer's relationship to his chief literary models, his theory of poetry, and his sense of himself as a philosophical poet. As Boitani puts it, "this December dream is a vision of the poet's literary universe—past, present and future."[53]

In the *House of Fame* Chaucer begins the story proper by identifying himself as a pilgrim-dreamer, who falls asleep quickly "As he that wery was forgo / On pilgrymage myles two / To the sorseint Leonard" (lines 115–17). Chaucer thus draws a parallel between his imaginary eagle's flight from "a temple ymad of glas" (line 120) to the magnificent castle of Fame and the wicker house of Rumor and his waking-life walk to and from the shrine of a saint, the etymology of whose name, as B. G. Koonce has noted, is "the odor of good fame."[54]

Like Dante, whose *Commedia* he echoes and parodies throughout the poem, Chaucer places his poetic and visionary journey initially under the aegis of Virgil. Finding himself in Venus's temple, Chaucer reads "on a table of bras" (line 142) his own English translation of the opening lines of the *Aeneid* and proceeds to retell Virgil's story as he "saugh" it on the wall, correcting it along the way with Ovidian strokes and supplementing it with allusions to fuller accounts given "On Virgile or on Claudian / Or Daunte" (lines 449–50). Calling attention to Vigil's own reference to the personified, public "fama" surrounding the love affair between Dido and Aeneas—"O wikke Fame! For ther nys / Nothing so swift, lo, as she is!" (lines 349–50)— Chaucer sees the fame of Virgil the Poet to be resting uncomfortably on Dido's ruined reputation and discovers behind the literary *aucto-*

Robinson, William A. Neilson, and Edward S. Sheldon (Boston: Ginn, 1913; repr. New York: Russell and Russell, 1967), pp. 73–82.

[52]   F. N. Robinson, ed., *The Works of Geoffrey Chaucer*, 2d ed. (Boston: Houghton Mifflin, 1957), p. 778.

[53]   Boitani, *Chaucer and the Imaginary World of Fame*, p. 191.

[54]   B. G. Koonce, *Chaucer and the Tradition of Fame* (Princeton: Princeton University Press, 1966), p. 71.

ritas of the *Aeneid* its own first origins in a complex and contradictory oral tradition; in rumor, repetition, and hearsay.[55]

Entering the desert outside, Chaucer's prayer for guidance to the "Lord . . . that madest us" (line 470) and to Christ (lines 492–94) is answered by the sudden descent of an eagle "with fethres as of gold" (line 530) who transports him at Jupiter's command through the air to "Fames Hous" (line 882). On the way the gregarious bird instructs his captive listener about sound physics in the context of a long discussion about the "propre mansyon" to which every thing tends, according to a familiar "sentence" pronounced by "every philosophres mouth / As Aristotle and daun Platon, / And other clerkys many oon" (lines 754, 757–60). From the heights Geoffrey enjoys a view of earth and heaven comparable to Scipio's, praises the Creator (lines 970–71), recalls the flight of Boethius "Wyth fetheres of Philosophye" (line 974) through and beyond the elements, echoes Saint Paul in his rapture (lines 980–82), and thinks "on Marcian, / And eke on Anteclaudian," whose "descripsion / Of alle the hevenes region" (lines 985–88) his own visionary experience (albeit within a fictionalized dream) now confirms to be true.

When they arrive at the House of Fame, Chaucer finds it to be built on a "roche of yse" (line 1130) into which many names have been engraved, only to be melted away. The house is populated with harpers such as Orpheus and Orion; pipers and trumpeters; "mynstralles / And gestiours that tellen tales" (lines 1197–98); magicians, and clerks learned in incantations and "magic naturel" (line 1266)—all those, in short, upon whose artful mediation the fame or infamy of others depends. The praises of Fame herself are sung by Calliope, "the myghty Muse," and her eight sisters (lines 1399–1400); and great poets, who have themselves gained fame by celebrating the deeds of others, stand on separate pillars—Josephus and seven others bearing up "the fame . . . of the Jewerye" (line 1436); Statius supporting the matter of Thebes; Homer, Dares, Dictys, Lollius, Guido delle Colonne, and Geoffrey of Monmouth keeping alive the memory of Troy; Virgil carrying Aeneas; Ovid serving Love; Lucan supporting

---

[55] John M. Fyler memorably describes the *House of Fame* as a poem "teetering on the brink of formless energy and flux" that mirrors the poet's art in Ovidian terms as a repeated creation out of Chaos (*Chaucer and Ovid* [New Haven: Yale University Press, 1979], p. 24).

Rome on his shoulders; Claudian responsible for "the fame of helle, / Of Pluto, and of Proserpyne" (lines 1510–11).

Chaucer has not yet reach his final destination, however, for the "tydings" that take the form of art in the House of Fame have their first origin elsewhere, in the airborne gossip, whispering, and noisy tale-telling that fill the House of Rumor in the valley below. There, waiting for him, Chaucer finds his guide, the eagle, who assures him that here indeed he will learn the "newe tydynges" (line 1886) that Jupiter has promised to him, and discover fecund subject matter for the "bookys, songes, dytees, / In ryme or elles in cadence" (lines 622–23) that he longs and labors to write. Inside the revolving wicker house the buzzing voices of "shipmen and pilgrimes, / With scrippes bretful of lesinges" (lines 2122–23); of pardoners, couriers, and messengers; of people telling of "love-tydynges" (line 2143) rise to a cacophonous pitch, and the poem ends abruptly with the sudden appearance of a mysterious "man of gret auctorite" (line 2158).

Central to the *House of Fame* in its extant form (and, I would argue, to Chaucer's entire *oeuvre*) is the Book II flight of Geoffrey in the "clawes starke" (line 545) of Jove's eagle. As we have seen, it explicitly evokes major poetic works narrating a philosophical *via mentis*: Dante's *Commedia*, Martianus Capella's *Marriage*, Boethius's *Consolation*, and Alan's *Anticlaudianus*. Framing Book II are the descriptions of the temple of Venus in Book I and of the House of Fame in Book III, both of which give prominent place to Virgil's *Aeneid* and Ovid's *Metamorphoses*, works which the Middle Ages commonly interpreted as allegories veiling philosophical truth, especially the truths of ethics and physics. The "love-tydynges" in the House of Rumor recall the "fama" of Dido and other disgraced women in Venus's Temple, and the "man of gret auctorite" (line 2158) at the end of Book III harkens back, as Boitani argues convincingly, to Virgil and all the poets and philosophers inhabiting Dante's castle of Limbo—a place which early commentators on the *Commedia* interpreted as "the seat of philosophy or 'sapientia' surrounded by the seven walls of the liberal arts."[56]

If the *House of Fame* indicates—as does the invocation of "Virgile,

---

[56] Boitani, *Chaucer and the Imaginary World of Fame*, p. 83.

Ovide, Omer, Lucan, and Stace" (V.1792) at the conclusion of *Troilus and Criseyde*—Chaucer's conscious ambition to join the company of the renowned poets, it emphasizes in particular the ideal of the philosopher-poet and the Boethian narrative of an earthly pilgrimage to one's true home or "kindely stede" (*HF* 731). Chaucer shared this ideal and pilgrimage path with Dante and Gower. His relationship to the tradition of the magisterial poet, however, differs significantly from theirs. Whereas Dante and Gower could assume a clerical position with relative ease, Chaucer finds himself both caught uncomfortably in the "clawes starke" (*HF* 545) of the eagle and carried by them. In general, he identifies himself directly with learned clerks only to the extent that he can claim them either as his *auctores* or as his audience and thus rely on their authority, correction, and commentary to supply what he lacks. For Chaucer, the only way to claim clerkly *auctoritas* is to deny that he possesses any, to evoke *quaestiones* without supplying their *determinatio*, to imagine a nameless "man of grete auctorite" (*HF* 2158) and then leave the space allotted to him empty and occupiable.[57]

As lay clerks, all three writers—Dante, Gower, and Chaucer—occupied a novel status in late medieval society. As Mariateresa Brocchieri has shown, the rise of the European universities in the twelfth and thirteenth centuries created a new, sacerdotal or quasi-sacerdotal (because celibate), intellectual elite, who, as professional *magistri*, "waged a two-pronged battle" that extended "downward, against the *rustici* and the plebians; upward, against the landed proprietors and nobles. In the first case, their chief weapon was verbal distain; in the second, it was equating nobility with virtue."[58]

The fourteenth century saw a significant complication of this "dual polemic" as the universities directly and indirectly affected wider social circles. Pointing to lay scholars such as Brunetto Latini, Raymond Lull, and Dante, Ruedi Imbach speaks of an "Entklerikalisierung der Wissenschaft" and emphasizes that the vernacular translation of

---

[57] See Karla Taylor, *Chaucer Reads "The Divine Comedy"* (Stanford: Stanford University Press, 1989), for an insightful comparison of the authorial stances taken by Chaucer and Dante.

[58] Mariateresa Fumagalli Beonio Brocchieri, "The Intellectual," in *Medieval Callings*, ed. Jacques Le Goff, trans. Lydia G. Cochrane (Chicago: University of Chicago Press, 1990), p. 202.

Latin philosophical works, such as Boethius's *Consolation of Philosophy* and the pseudo-Aristotelian *Secretum secretorum*, as well as the production of vernacular compilations, worked to undermine the definition of the laity as illiterati.[59] Others have charted the increasing numbers of laymen, single and married, working as clerks in civil administration.[60] According to Courtenay, the tremendous "growth of lay literacy" in England after 1350 "provided a new audience and a new market" for Latin and vernacular works, a development that encouraged scholars to produce "scriptural, homiletical, and devotional writings" to meet the interests and needs of "audiences primarily found outside of universities and composed of clerics, lawyers, civil servants, merchants, and, among the latter groups, their wives and older children."[61] The dispersion of knowledge, as Brocchieri points out, introduced "variety . . . into the panorama of the intellectual citadel, and a new intellectual stratum began to emerge that included jurists and, in Italy, notaries, flanked by the new figure of the artist."[62]

To illustrate what she terms a "proliferation in the typology of the intellectual," Brocchieri points in particular to John Wycliffe and Dante. A professor of logic and theology at Oxford, but also a major polemicist whose vernacular works reached a wide popular audience, Wycliffe left the university milieu, at first by choice in 1372, when he entered the royal service, and later unwillingly in 1381, when his scholarly activity was suspended by decree and his teaching on the Eucharist condemned as heretical. Whereas Wycliffe suffered at having to leave his proper place in the university setting, Dante suffered under the continual, painful awareness "of not being in his 'natural seat'—of being elsewhere, 'out of place' " (p. 196). The author of the *Convivio*, Dante was a man who "labored with his intellect and with the spoken or written word, but not in a setting conceived for the purpose," and whose sense of intellectual exile actually led him to enroll "in the corporation of the doctors and druggists . . .

[59] Ruedi Imbach, *Laien in der Philosophie des Mittelalters: Hinweise und Anregungen zu einem vernachlässigten Thema* (Amsterdam: B. R. Grüner, 1989), esp. pp. 158, 134, 43–46.

[60] See T. F. Tout, "Literature and Learning in the English Civil Service in the Fourteenth Century"; *Chapters in the Administrative History of Medieval England*, 6 vols. (1920–33; repr. New York: Barnes and Noble, 1967), 5:75–112; Richardson, "Hoccleve in His Social Context."

[61] Courtenay, *Schools and Scholars*, p. 373.

[62] Brocchieri, "The Intellectual," p. 203.

signing the register of a professional organization in which he was essentially an outsider."[63]

Judging by his clerkly persona, Chaucer too felt himself to be awkwardly out of place as an intellectual—not learned enough to be a *magister* himself, not situated by training or profession at a university, lacking a vocation to celibacy, but yet irredeemably bookish, well versed in astronomy, alchemy, and letters, conversant in the current academic debates, and the admiring friend of men like "moral Gower" and "philosophical Strode" (*TC* V.1856–57). Not unlike Dante, Chaucer addressed this problem in part by casting himself in his poetry as a childlike pupil in need of instruction by superior guides, as a bumbler in need of "correcioun." Chaucer, however, employed other strategies that simultaneously marked his distance from, and his closeness to, the academy of his day, thus creating a gap that he invited a clerical audience to fill.

As Chapter One of this book argues, Chaucer introduces the Clerk of Oxenford as one of four ideal pilgrims in the General Prologue to the *Canterbury Tales* to represent the university community as a catalytic fourth estate in late medieval England. As the universities struggled for independence from municipal and ecclesiastical control, they became a direct and indirect force for a complex clericalization of the previously existing estates. Through the spread of literacy among the laity, an ever more diverse group claimed clerical status and its accompanying privileges for themselves. Chaucer's estate satire gives an original expression to this social transformation through the readiness of his pilgrims to speak for and as clerks.

Although Chaucer occasionally draws upon the *sententiae* of "wise clerkes" in support of particular views, he seldom does so unambiguously, outside of a dramatic context. More often he refers to "the opinioun of certein clerkis" (*CT* VII.3235) without endorsing it, or he highlights matters of clerical contention and authoritative disagree-

---

[63] Ibid., p. 196. To Brocchieri's examples of suffering, "out of place" intellectuals, one must add Petrarch. The son of a notary, Petrarch studied civil law at the University of Montpellier and law and literature at the University of Bologna before becoming a permanent cleric in minor orders in 1330. Petrarch left the university in order to pursue an intellectual career as an ecclesiastic in service to Cardinal Giovanni Colonna, and the choice left him open to the charge, later lodged against him by four young Venetian Averroists, that he was a "good but uneducated man," to which he replied in his *Invectiva de sui ipsius et multorum ignorantia* (1367), wherein he gives priority to moral and religious wisdom over science and natural philosophy.

ment without attempting to take a position himself. At the start of the *House of Fame*, for instance, after a long survey of contradictory medieval dream lore, Geoffrey declares:

> Wel worth of this thyng grete clerkys
> That trete of this and other werkes,
> For I of noon opinion
> Nyl as now make mensyon,
> But oonly that the holy roode
> Turne us every drem to goode!
>
> (lines 53–58)

In doing so, Chaucer draws a significant parallel between the true and false tale-telling of the gossips in the House of Rumor, the competitive fictions of poets like Virgil and Ovid, and the "greet altercacioun" and "greet disputisoun" (*CT* VII.3237–38) of scholars. Indeed, Chaucer's work as a whole suggests that the "parfit clerk" (*CT* VII.3236), like the truly great poet, knows about and portrays the existence of "altercacioun"; of multiple perspectives, opinions, and views; of various versions of a single story and of different possible interpretations of words and events. As Lisa Kiser has put it, "Chaucer raises very real doubts about any poetic project that claims to have discovered, recorded, or in any way represented truth."[64]

Much has been made of what Sheila Delany calls Chaucer's "skeptical fideism," of the possible impact of nominalist philosophy, ecclesial schism, and theological dissent on his world view and artistic creation.[65] The closest connection Chaucer himself draws between fiction and philosophy is, however, explicitly Boethian and Platonic. As we have seen, the *House of Fame* sharply delineates and opposes celestial and terrestrial perspectives—the world below, composed of shadows, whispering, fiction, and *fama*; and the starry heavens above, through which Geoffrey takes his eagle-borne flight and about which, he says, Boethius, Plato, Martianus, and Alan have written something "sooth" (line 987) that his own visionary experience allows him to

---

[64] Lisa Kiser, *Truth and Textuality in Chaucer's Poetry* (Hanover: University Press of New England, 1991), p. 113.

[65] Sheila Delany, *Chaucer's "House of Fame": The Poetics of Skeptical Fideism* (1972; repr. Gainesville: University Press of Florida, 1994). See Courtenay's cautionary word about the attribution of a nominalist aesthetic to Chaucer (*Schools and Scholars*, pp. 376, 378).

believe. Similarly, the so-called epilogue to *Troilus and Criseyde* juxta-
poses the view of Troilus's ascendant ghost, looking down from the
eighth sphere, with the view "Of hem that wepten for his deth"
(V.1822) on the earth below—a company that includes Chaucer's
own weeping narrator.

At the same time, however, Chaucer casts real doubt on our access
to the truth that that heavenly perspective provides, since we see it
only in dreams, dream-visions, and fictions reflecting earthly experience, human preconceptions, and book-reading. The eagle-borne
Geoffrey tells us that he "kan . . . now beleve" (*HF* 990) the authoritative accounts he has read, but only because he has experienced
their truth in a comic vision inside a confused dream. Chaucer's narrator relates Troilus's whole history, including his soul's ascent, on the
basis of legendary accounts, as "the storie telleth us" (*TC* V.1051).
And as the F Prologue to the *Legend of Good Women* affirms, our knowledge of "joy in hevene and peyne in helle" (Dante's supreme subjects) depends on what we have "herd seyd, or founde . . . writen"
(lines 2, 8).

A similar duality of earthly and heavenly perspectives informs the
Canterbury Tales, but there too Chaucer offers no simple, literal representation of heavenly truth and earthly fiction. Instead he juxta-
poses in opposed contexts that elicit divergent interpretations two
citations of the same *sententia* from Plato's *Timaeus*, which he knew
from the *Consolation of Philosophy* and translated in his own *Boece*, "the
sentence of Plato that nedes the wordis moot be cosynes to the thinges
of whiche thei speken" (III.pr12.205–7). This sentence appears in
only three places in Chaucer's writings—once in *Boece*, and twice in
the *Canterbury Tales*.[66]

In the original Boethian context, Lady Philosophy uses this "sentence" to defend herself against the sufferer's reproach that she has
constructed the universe into a "hous of Didalus" (III.pr12.156)
through serial syllogisms and circular arguments, at the center of
which is God, whose super-Real being, goodness, and power make
"evel nothing" (III.pr12.151)—a conclusion her patient is unwill-
ing to accept. Within the "compas" of the "devyne substaunce" that

---

[66] For treatments of this passage, see P. B. Taylor, "Chaucer's *Cosyn to the Dede*," *Spec-
ulum* 57 (1982): 315–27; Marc M. Pelen, "The Manciple's 'Cosyn' to the 'Dede,' "
Chaucer Review 25.4 (1991): 343–54. Pelen emphasizes the importance to Chaucer of
Jean de Meun's variation on this theme in *Roman de la Rose*, lines 15158–62.

turns the world she has, she says, spoken what is true by definition. But she does not deny that there are "resouns" outside of that "compas," and she goes on to illustrate that inside/outside contrast with the story of the archetypal poet, Orpheus, for whom the shadowy experience of human love and grief is so real that he cannot "unbyden hym fro the boondes of the hevy erthe" and consequently turns his gaze away from the celestial "cleernesse of sovereyn good" (III.m12.3, 63).

Unlike Lady Philosophy, the pilgrim Chaucer of the *Canterbury Tales* draws his "resouns" from within a distinctly Orphic "compas."[67] In the General Prologue he draws on the authority of a Boethian Plato to justify his witless performance as a mere rehearser of the words actually spoken by the pilgrim tale-tellers: "Eek Plato seith, whoso kan hym rede, / The wordes moote be cosyn to the dede" (GP 741–42). Rather than tell a "tale untrewe" (GP 735), he will repeat exactly what he has heard and seen. In short, he will play the artless part of the inspired poet, who speaks just as he is prompted, without really knowing what he says and without bearing responsibility for it. In assuming this part, of course, Chaucer departs from Plato in substituting an earthly source of inspiration—the pilgrims—for the heavenly influx that possesses Platonic poets, fools, and lovers.[68] Nonetheless, the authoritative "sentence" provides a theoretical justification for his narrative fiction and an actual starting point for the tale-collection that follows, which is—again in Platonic fashion—an imitation of imitations, a representation of representations, and therefore at least twice removed from the truth of things and likely to be its "cosyn" not in the sense of a match, but of a counterfeit.[69]

The quotation appears yet a third time in an opposed rhetorical context that militates against the telling of both fables and truth. The Manciple, who uses the "knavyssh speche" (IX.205) conventional to a fabliau to refer to Apollo's wife and her lover, justifies his breaking of decorum by repeating the Boethian sentence: "The wise Plato seith, as ye may rede, / The word moot nede accorde with the dede" (IX.207–8). As the Manciple goes on to explain, taking the dictum

[67] On the Boethian myth of Orpheus and Chaucer's use of it in *Troilus and Criseyde*, see my *Job, Boethius, and Epic Truth* (Ithaca: Cornell University Press, 1994).
[68] The key Platonic passages dealing with poetry and poets are, of course, the *Ion* and Books 2–3 and 10 of the *Republic*.
[69] Cf. P. B. Taylor, "Chaucer's *Cosyn to the Dede*," p. 324.

literally is antithetical to storytelling, since romance shapes its matter into ideal forms, turning a "lemman" into a "lady," an "outlawe" into a "captayn," lust into love. The reverse case is also implied, however—namely, that the Manciple's reduction of Ovid's heroine to an unnamed, she-wolfish whore in the name of truth may indeed be less true than Apollo's romantic idealization of her as a gemlike "deere wyf . . . so sad and eek so trewe" (IX.274–75). At any rate, telling a tale untrue—that is, not as a tale but as truth—brings poetry and fiction symbolically to an end with the breaking of Apollo's "mynstralcie, / Bothe harpe, and lute, and gyterne, and sautrie" (IX.267–68), the violent death of Apollo's birdlike spouse, and the transformation of the white crow, whose song had been "lyk a nyghtyngale" (IX.294), into a black caw-caw.

Thus the same Apollo whom Chaucer invokes as the "god of science and of light" and to whom he entrusts the manifestation of "art poetical" in the Book III descriptions of the Houses of Fame and Rumor (HF 1091, 1095) reappears near the conclusion of the Canterbury Tales as a symbol not of poetry's origin, but of its end. Unlike the "love-tydynges" and amatory gossip in the House of Rumor that nourish Chaucer's poetry, the crow's report of adultery leads to the silencing of song and inspires the Manciple's warning, "My sone, be war, and be noon auctour newe, / Of tidynges, wheither they been false or trewe" (IX.359–60).

Taken together, the three uses of Boethius's Platonic adage describe an understanding of poetry that is, like Plato's own, dual in its separation of shadow and light, fiction and truth, and paradoxical in its claim that the inspired poet arrives at truth precisely by remaining twice-removed from it, by humbly imitating imitations, by creating fictions *as* fictions, and by adhering to the Boethian principle that things can never be known directly according to the truth of their own nature, but only indirectly, according to the limited nature of the knower (cf. *Boece* V.pr6.1–8). Thus even "The Parson's Tale," while not a "fable" (X.31), is still "a myrie tale in prose" (X.46), limited in its grasp of truth and subject to supplementation and correction:

> "But nathelees, this meditacioun
> I putt it ay under correccioun
> Of clerkes, for I am nat textueel;

I take but the sentence, trusteth weel.
Therefore I make protestacioun
That I wol stonde to correccioun.''
                    (X.55–60)

Here and elsewhere the repeated appeal to learned clerks for correction invents a particular kind of readership for the *Canterbury Tales,*
actively engages its members in the work of co-authorship, and elicits
from them a scholarly apparatus of interpretive and critical commentary to serve as the other-speaking of the *Tales.* A wise fool and a
philosophical poet, Chaucer insists that the truth of his fictions must
be discovered outside of them and represented, if at all, extra-textually
and by others more learned than he, even as "this litel spot of erthe"
(*TC* V.1815) stands parallel to, but far below, the stars of heaven and
the extra-terrestrial truth they symbolize.

The Clerkly Tales *of the Ellesmere Manuscript*

In the Ellesmere manuscript we find the clearest evidence of a
clerkly response to Chaucer's appeal for the study and "correccioun"
of his work. Looking to Chaucer as a "clerk among clerks," the editor
presented his book of tales "in the manner which was presumed to
be intended by Chaucer," giving it (to echo Derek Pearsall) "the
dignified and ordered treatment that was associated with learned
works in Latin."[70] As we have seen, the formal layout resembles that
given to scholarly *compilationes.* The scribe has carefully rubricated the
text in both Latin and English, supplying headings and marginal
glosses. More importantly, he has rendered Chaucer's own Latin notes
in a large script and accorded them a prominent position at the side
of the text proper, so that Chaucer is represented as playing the part
of a learned commentator, explicating his own authoritative text,
much as Gower does in the Latin commentary that frames his *Confessio
Amantis.*[71]

---

[70] Derek Pearsall, *The Canterbury Tales* (London: George Allen and Unwin, 1985), p.
18.
[71] On Gower, see Tim William Machan, "Language Contact in *Piers Plowman,*" pp.
380–81. Chaucer's authorship of most of the Latin side-notes has been convincingly
argued by Robert E. Lewis, "Glosses to the *Man of Law's Tale* from Pope Innocent III's

In addition, the Ellesmere editor has perceived in Chaucer's collection of tales a definite *ordinatio,* and he has arranged them accordingly. Whereas the aesthetic rationale supporting the Ellesmere order has been much discussed by critics, the logical principles informing its arrangement as a clerical compilation have remained uninvestigated.[72] That logic, according to Judson B. Allen, involved two steps. First of all, the interpreter of Chaucer's book observed its literal division into discrete parts—that is, into fragments or story-blocks of linked tales—and assumed that that division was meaningful. Second, in accord with the regular practice of medieval commentators, he sought to draw a correspondence between the literal parts or divisions of the *forma tractatus* and a matching *distinctio* or external outline of topics in the public domain, "in terms of which the author's literal material has its full significance."[73] Having perceived such a correspondence, the clerk saw the poem's unity emerge as the logical outcome of a "dialectic between a poem's textuality" and an independent categorical set—the seven deadly sins, for instance, or the cardinal virtues, or the ages of man.[74]

This book is an extended exercise in reading "like a clerk." It recalls the actual social contests in which the clerks of Chaucer's time participated and within which they had a catalytic function, and it goes on to draw a link between that historical divisiveness and the literal and logical *divisiones* of the *Canterbury Tales.* In particular, it

---

De Miseria Humane Conditionis," SP 64.1 (1967): 1–16; Daniel S. Silvia, "Glosses to the *Canterbury Tales* from St. Jerome's *Epistola adversus Jovinianum,"* SP 62 (1965): 28–39; Graham D. Caie, "The Significance of the Early Chaucer Manuscript Glosses (with Special Reference to the *Wife of Bath's Prologue),"* *Chaucer Review* 10 (1975–76): 350–60.

[72] For an aesthetic reading of the Ellesmere unity, see Donald R. Howard, *The Idea of the Canterbury Tales* (Berkeley: University of California Press, 1967).

[73] Judson B. Allen, *The Ethical Poetic of the Later Middle Ages: A Decorum of Convenient Distinction* (Toronto: University of Toronto Press, 1982), p. 90.

[74] Ibid., p. 150. Allen's own attempt to recover the medieval "logic" of order in the *Canterbury Tales* failed because Theresa Moritz and he began, against his own procedural recommendation, not with an extant manuscript of the *Tales,* but rather with a fourfold *distinctio* of transformations used to interpret Ovid's *Metamorphoses,* and then proceeded to invent a tale-order (unattested in any surviving manuscript of Chaucer's work) to fit that *distinctio.* See their *A Distinction of Stories: The Medieval Unity of Chaucer's Fair Chain of Narratives for Canterbury* (Columbus: Ohio State University Press, 1981). This book, in contrast, takes its orientation from a particular manuscript, the Ellesmere, the material layout of which witnesses to the generic reception of the *Tales* as an ordered *compilatio* with appropriately marked divisions.

attempts to recover the underlying *distinctio* or topical outline that determines the *ordinatio* of the Ellesmere *Canterbury Tales* by approaching that tale-collection from the generic perspective of the didascalic literature familiar to both Chaucer and his clerical audience—the works of Macrobius, Martianus Capella, Boethius, Bernard Silvestris, and Alan de Lille, among others.

Building on the treatment of fourteenth-century school culture in Chapter One, Chapter Two concerns itself with the definition of didascalic literature as a genre, traces its development from antiquity through the fourteenth century, and discusses the divergent responses to this tradition given by Dante, Gower, and Chaucer. I argue that salient features of this literary kind serve to illumine the Ellesmere *Canterbury Tales*: (1) the drawing of explicit analogies between the various social estates and the divisions of the arts and sciences, (2) the hierarchical competition between and among the disciplines as reflected in the different *arbores scientiarum*, and (3) the tendency of didascalic writers to incorporate the encyclopedic survey of the divisions of knowledge into the imaginative plot of a cosmological pilgrimage, the soul's planetary descent and ascent.[75]

Taking the individual fragments or story-blocks as logical units corresponding to a preexistent outline in the public domain, the remaining chapters pair the fragments of the Ellesmere *Tales* within the structural scheme of an overarching chiasmus governed by (1) direct literal analogies; (2) the systematic exemplification of different divisions of knowledge: speculative (theology and physics), logical, and practical; and (3) an allusive, circular pattern of planetary descent from Saturn to the sublunar earth and back again.

At a literal level, the delineation of the story-blocks in a chiastic arrangement recalls Robert Jordan's general emphasis on "inorganic form" and discerns within the Ellesmere *Tales* as a whole the same operative principles of analogy and chiasmus that close-reading critics such as Penn R. Szittya and, more recently, Jerome Mandel have de-

---

[75] Cf. Neuse's intuitive comparison of the *Canterbury Tales* to a philosophical symposium and his suggestion that the *Tales* displays a "roughly circular" and "philosophical" plot (*Chaucer's Dante*, pp. 85–87). The notion of the soul's *descensus* into the body is, of course, a Neoplatonic commonplace. See, for example, *The Commentary on the First Six Books of Virgil's "Aeneid" by Bernardus Silvestris*, trans. Earl G. Schreiber and Thomas E. Maresca (Lincoln: University of Nebraska Press, 1979), pp. 32–33.

scribed at a micro-level within the individual fragments or story-blocks.[76] At the level of topical exemplification, the analysis of the individual tales and fragments in relation to the divisions of knowledge brings the Ellesmere *Tales* into close dialogue with Gower's *Confessio Amantis* as a whole and with the encyclopedic treatment of "Theorique, Rhetorique, and Practique" in Book VII, in particular. Finally, at the more allusive level of planetary reference, it establishes a connection between pilgrims' journey to Becket's Shrine and Chaucer's Dantean, philosophical flight in the *House of Fame.*

Whereas Geoffrey's waking pilgrimage to the Shrine of St. Leonard merely occasions his dream-journey among the stars in the earlier poem, in the Ellesmere *Canterbury Tales* the opposite is the case. There the daytime journey is foregrounded while, as we shall see, key astrological allusions work to determine the *ordinatio* of the story-blocks through what J. D. North terms a "higher syntax, . . . a syntax on an architectonic scale," and thus prepare the way for the Parson's comparison of "this viage" of the pilgrims to "thilke parfit glorious pilgrymage / That highte Jerusalem celestial" (X.49–51).[77] Unlike earlier, allegorical epics of learning and unlike Dante's *Paradiso,* the Ellesmere *Canterbury Tales* includes no direct account of an ascent to the heavens, but its exemplary stories are nonetheless among those "ywriten . . . / With sterres" in the "large book / Which that men clepe the hevene" (II.190–92), as the Man of Law, echoing Bernard Silvestris, declares.

Responding in a clerkly fashion to the Ellesmere *compilatio* (a response that is invited by the very layout of the manuscript and by the early history of Chaucerian reception) allows us to see what has hitherto escaped notice—namely, that the Ellesmere tale order logically continues a conventional series that is initiated by Chaucer himself in Fragment I when he introduces Saturn, in company with all the Ptolemaic planetary deities, into "The Knight's Tale" and places that tale's characters and action under a pronounced and all-pervasive

---

[76] Robert M. Jordan, *Chaucer and the Shape of Creation: The Aesthetic Possibilities of Inorganic Structure* (Cambridge: Harvard University Press, 1967); Penn R. Szittya, "The Green Yeoman as Loathly Lady: The Friar's Parody of the Wife of Bath's Tale," *PMLA* 90.3 (1975): 386–94; Jerome Mandel, *Geoffrey Chaucer: Building the Fragments of the "Canterbury Tales"* (London: Associated University Presses, 1992).

[77] J. D. North, *Chaucer's Universe* (Oxford: Clarendon Press, 1988), p. 499.

Saturnine influence. "The Knight's Tale," in short, offers a topical heading for the tales that follow, beginning with the Jovian tale of the Miller and the Martian tale of the Reeve. The rapidly descending order of narratives in Fragment I, which commences the horizontal pilgrimage to Canterbury, thus begins at the same time a soul-journey for which Chaucer had definite literary models in the didascalic tradition.

Those models provided astrological and philosophical markers with which to plot the soul's itinerary from beginning to end, an itinerary to which the Ellesmere tale order adheres and which it exemplifies topologically, fragment by fragment. In contrast to Harry Bailly's plan of a two-way trip from London and back again, Chaucer's planetary scheme charts the two-way progression of the soul into and out of the world of sensory experience and imaginative fictions on its way homeward to God. The saint's shrine at Canterbury stands, finally, as the earthly analogue for the soul's homegoing, but that endpoint is only reached after a systematic pilgrimage from one planetary and topical "place" to another. Indeed, in the Ellesmere manuscript, this sequential, planetary placement overrides in importance the geographical signposts that the pilgrims pass on their way to Canterbury.[78]

As we hope to demonstrate, the sequence of tales and tale- groups in the Ellesmere arrangement is not arbitrary, but rather conforms to two preexistent outlines that were frequently configured to one another in didascalic literature: namely, the list of seven planets and that of the branches of philosophy. Taken together, these two outlines enable us literally to locate Chaucer's *Canterbury Tales* in relation to the works of Gower and Dante in unprecedented ways. In particular, the use of a planetary scheme aligns Chaucer's tales and tale-groups with Dante's planetary cantos in the *Paradiso* and enables the discovery of an astonishing series of correspondences that serve not only to resolve multiple Chaucerian *cruces*, but also to redefine Chaucer's storytelling contest among pilgrims as an amazing poetic contest between Chaucer and Dante.

The argument of this book, then, moves from the historical reception of the *Canterbury Tales* by a clerical audience to a focus on the poem itself as the *compilatio* of a clerkly Chaucer in conscious dialogue

---

[78] On the question of geographical reference and the Bradshaw Shift, see Allen and Moritz, *Distinction of Stories*, pp. 103–5.

with "moral Gower" (*TC* V.1856) and "the wise poete of Florence, / That highte Dant" (*CT* III.1125–26). To be sure, reading the *Tales* "like a clerk" necessarily leads one in that direction. The invitation to do so, however, comes from Chaucer himself, who has put his work "ay under correccioun / Of clerkes" (X.56–57).

"Learning" is an ambiguous word.

—Thomas Lounsbury

1

CHAUCER AND THE

DIVISION OF CLERKS

In an attempt to account for the considerable learning displayed in Chaucer's poetry, scholars have advanced various hypotheses about his education. According to one such reconstruction, Chaucer as a "litel clergeon" (*CT* VII.503) attended the cathedral school at St. Paul's in London, studying under the university-educated schoolmaster and almoner, William de Ravenstone.[1] A second hypothesis, which does not necessarily exclude the first, emphasizes that Chaucer's education as a page in the household of the Countess of Ulster (1356–59) probably included formal instruction in grammar sufficient to have afforded him access to the "bokes olde and newe" (*LGW* G Prologue.273) to which he so frequently alludes.[2] Other scholars, trying to fill a significant gap in Chaucer's life-records from 1360 to 1366, have speculated that he was preparing for his subsequent ambassadorial and administrative career by studying either at the Inns of Chancery and Court in Lon-

---

[1] Edith Rickert, "Chaucer at School," *MP* 29 (1931–32): 257–74; Derek Brewer, *Chaucer in His Time* (London: Thomas Nelson, 1963), pp. 127–28.

[2] Richard F. Green, *Poets and Princepleasers: Literature and the English Court in the Late Middle Ages* (Toronto: University of Toronto Press, 1980), pp. 71–91; Nicholas Orme, *From Childhood to Chivalry: The Education of the English Kings and Aristocracy, 1066–1530* (London: Methuen, 1984), esp. pp. 48–60.

don or at one of the two major English universities, Oxford and Cambridge.[3]

Barring the discovery of new evidence, these explanations must remain hypothetical additions to what Thomas Lounsbury calls "the Chaucer legend."[4] Taken together, however, they not only offer a topology of the most important educational sites in late fourteenth-century England, but also make possible a typology of clerkhood in Chaucer's life and work. The threefold definition of "clerk" given in the *Middle English Dictionary* distinguishes the clerk who is a clergyman in minor or major orders from both the clerk who is a "learned person" or "scholar" and the clerk who is a "secretary, amanuensis, recorder" or "an official in charge of records and accounts." This semantic scheme, as we hope to show, sorts out with deceptive simplicity a variety of overlapping and competitive clerical states in Chaucer's time that powerfully affected his own status as a clerkly poet and worked to shape his original view of the emergent fourth estate. Unlike many of his contemporaries who singled out the merchants as representatives of the new social order, Chaucer placed a surprising spotlight on the retiring Clerk of Oxenford and thus on the universities as a hidden catalyst for far-reaching societal change. As Chaucer recognized, directly and indirectly the universities contributed to the widespread secularization of a literacy previously reserved to clergymen. That literacy was gradually effecting a "clericalization" of previously existing estates, from the *gentils* to the *cherls*, even as its secular uses were producing an ever-widening division among ecclesiastics themselves.

The Clerkly Gentils

Medieval social theory, following the tripartite scheme first enunciated in Adalberon of Laon's *Carmen ad Rodbertum regem* (1030), distinguished three estates in Christian society: *oratores*, *bellatores*, and

---

[3] Edith Rickert, "Was Chaucer a Student at the Inner Temple?" in *Manly Anniversary Studies* (Chicago: University of Chicago Press, 1923), pp. 20–31; D. S. Bland, "Chaucer and the Inns of Court: A Reexamination," *ES* 33 (1952): 145–55. For a recent spokesman in favor of the university hypothesis, see John Gardner, *The Life and Times of Chaucer* (New York: Alfred A. Knopf, 1977), pp. 135–37, 140, 149, 285.

[4] Thomas R. Lounsbury, "The Chaucer Legend," in *Studies in Chaucer*, 3 vols. (1892; New York: Russell and Russell, 1962), 1:129–224. See pp. 164–73 for a discussion of the university thesis. The epigram above is taken from 2:174.

laboratores—those who pray, those who fight, and those who work.[5] Military action, rather than reading, writing, and praying, was thus the proper province of the feudal nobility and, as Nicholas Orme affirms, there was "no simple transition from the unlettered warrior to the learned statesman."[6] That gradual transition was propelled by both cooperation with, and competition between, church and civil leaders, a complex interaction that altered considerably with the rise of the European universities in the twelfth and thirteenth centuries.

Beginning in 1140, the University of Bologna offered its students a specialization in canon law studies. Between 1150 and 1170 the University of Paris grew up out of three cells: the monastic school of St. Victor, the cathedral school of Notre Dame, and the collegiate church of St. Genevieve. As a result of an exodus of English masters and scholars from Paris in 1167, Oxford University had its first beginnings, gained official recognition as a *studium generale*, and was formally organized under the chancellorship of Robert Grosseteste (1215–17). In 1209 Cambridge University had its inception. Subsequent continental foundations included the universities at Padua (1222), Toulouse (1229), Orléans (1309), and Vienna (1365).[7]

A striking coincidence aligns the growth of kingly literacy with the establishment of these universities. The famous maxim "*rex illiteratus, asinus coronatus,*" which implicitly contrasts the crown of the asinine-because-illiterate king with the tonsured scholar's *corona*, begins to appear in texts by Englishmen in the twelfth century. In Orme's view, it "seems to indicate for the first time an idea of obligation that kings at least should be able to read," and inaugurs the spread of literacy "from a few of the lay aristocracy to most of the order between about the middle of the twelfth century and the middle of the thirteenth."[8] The "exercise of arms, social accomplishments and the ability to read" gradually became essential elements in the education of the

---

[5] See Jacques Le Goff, Introduction to *Medieval Callings*, ed. Jacques Le Goff, trans. Lydia G. Cochrane (Chicago: University of Chicago Press, 1990), p. 11; Georges Duby, *The Three Orders: Feudal Society Imagined,* trans. Arthur Goldhammer (Chicago: University of Chicago Press, 1980), esp. pp. 13–20.

[6] Nicholas Orme, *English Schools in the Middle Ages* (London: Methuen, 1973), p. 21.

[7] For an excellent brief introduction to the medieval universities, see Friedrich Heer, "Intellectualism and the Universities," in *The Medieval World,* trans. Janet Sondheimer (London: George Wiedenfeld and Nicolson, 1962), pp. 235–60.

[8] Orme, *From Childhood to Chivalry,* pp. 143–44.

nobility, although, as Orme notes, "Exactly when the study of letters became a normal part of this curriculum is difficult to define."[9]

Clearly the official introduction of the works of Aristotle to the university curriculum in Paris in 1255 did much, both directly and indirectly, to promote the clericalization of European kings and aristocrats. As Mariateresa Brocchieri observes, it bolstered the polemical claim of scholars to the "true aristocracy" that is attained through the contemplation of truth and the exercise of moral virtue.[10] Side by side the older ranks of the chivalric order, the new order of philosophers established their own "bachelor," masters, and doctoral degrees; conducted tournament-like *disputationes*; and granted their "knightly" services alternately to the king or the pope, who vied for their loyalty.

These professional intellectuals actively played the part of an Aristotle to more than one contemporary Alexander and invited the *nobiles* in turn to impersonate a philosopher-king. John of Salisbury, who began his studies in Paris under Peter Abelard in 1136 and continued them under masters in Chartres (1137–40) and Paris, established an important precedent in composing his *Metalogicon* and *Policraticus* in 1159 for Thomas Becket, then Chancellor of England under Henry II. As Jean-Philippe Genet emphasizes, however, the recovery of Aristotle's *Ethics* and *Politics* led to the composition of a new type of pedagogical literature for rulers in the latter half of the thirteenth century, as illustrated by the following works: the *Eruditio regum et principum* (1259) of the Franciscan Gilbert de Tournai, composed for Louis IX; the *De eruditione filiorum regalium* and *De moralis principis instructione* (c. 1259) by the Dominican Vincent of Beauvais; the *De eruditione principum* attributed to the Franciscan Guillaume Perrault; the *Liber tertius de informatione regiae prolis*, composed by the Dominican Bartholomeus Vincentinus for Queen Margaret of France; the *De regimine principum* of Egidius Colonna, written for Philip the Fair; and the *Liber de informatione principum*, dedicated by an anonymous author to the future Louis X. All these works, as Genet points out, evince a distinctly "Aristotelian bias." They are probably the work of friars, who "willingly adopt a didactic tone" in dealing with pedagogical problems and whose approach to politics reflects the current practice

---

[9] Orme, *English Schools*, p. 33.
[10] Mariateresa Fumagalli Beonio Brocchieri, "The Intellectual," in *Medieval Callings*, p. 195.

at the universities of treating the topic in moral terms, under the heading of practical theology rather than rhetoric.[11]

Strictly speaking, as Genet insists, "no English tract qualifies entirely for the appelation of *Miroir*," which remained "a Capetian speciality."[12] Nonetheless, the English too participated in, and contributed to, this Aristotelian tradition, albeit in ways more varied than their European counterparts. Roger Bacon edited the pseudo-Aristotelian *Secretum secretorum* in the thirteenth century, and Walter Burley produced his widely circulated *Exposicio super libros octo politicorum Aristotelis* in the fourteenth. Walter de Milemete composed for the young Edward III a Latin mirror, *De nobilitatibus, sapientiis et prudentiis* (1326–27), based on the *Secretum secretorum.*[13] The *III Consideracions right necesserye to the good governance of a Prince*, a fifteenth-century English translation of a French text written in 1374, exhorts a king, in true Aristotelian fashion, to bear in mind first self-knowledge and self-control, then the proper management of his family and household, and finally the government of the state. It begins with an allusion to "thopynyons, sentences and diffinicions of wyse Philosophers and other sage persoones auncient and autentike," including the biblical books of Solomon, Aristotle's *Poetics* and *Nicomachean Ethics*, Vegetius's *De re militari*, and Egidius Colonna's *De regimine principum.*[14] The *Quadripartita regis specie* was written in Ireland for Richard II, probably either by Richard White, who served as Treasurer there from 1388 to 1391, or by the Cambridge *magister* and royal official, John Thorpe.[15] It too imitates the pseudo-Aristotelian *Secretum* in its emphasis on moral virtue ("sapiencia, prudencia, providencia, et aliis virtutibus") and scientific knowledge: "Phis[i]onomiam Ar[i]stotelis, quam composuit ad opus Alexandri conquestoris, presenti adiunxi libello."[16]

Multiple English translations of the *Secretum* survive in fifteenth-century manuscripts. In the *Secretum*, as in Book VII of John Gower's *Confessio Amantis*, King Alexander the Great plays the part of a pupil to the Prince of Philosophers, who answers his zeal for learning with a compendium of the sciences:

[11] Jean-Philippe Genet, Introduction to *Four English Political Tracts of the Later Middle Ages*, Camden Fourth Series (London: Royal Historical Society, 1977), 18:xii–xiv.

[12] Ibid., p. xiv.

[13] Orme, *From Childhood to Chivalry*, p. 99.

[14] *Four English Political Tracts*, p. 180.

[15] Ibid., p. 26.

[16] Ibid., pp. 37, 39 ("I have appended to the present book the *Physiognomy* of Aristotle, which he composed at the urging of Alexander the Conqueror" [translation mine]).

þe wilke booke Aristotel þe wyseste Prynce of Philosofers made at þe askynge of kynge Alexander his disciple þat askyd of him þat he sholde come to him or elles þat he sholde shewe to him þe preuyeȝ of diuers craftes, þat ys to say þe sterynge of wirkynges and power of sternes in astronomy, þe craft of alkenamy in kynde, and þe craft of kennynge kyndes & of wirkynge eschauntemenȝ in piromancye & gewmatry.[17]

From a historical perspective, however, the most important use of the *Secretum secretorum* is that of John Wycliffe, who draws upon that pseudo-Aristotelian source repeatedly in his *De officio regis* (1379) to assert an essential relationship between virtue and authority, to argue for the supremacy of the king over the pope and the Church in temporal matters, and to urge the king's support of scholars, especially reformist theologians like himself: "Et hinc Aristoteles in secretis secretorum capitulo xii sic alloquitur Alexandrum, 'Studia in civitatibus regni tui permitte et precipe tuis hominibus ut doceant filios suos sciencias litterarum et faciant eos studere in nobilibus liberalibus scienciis.' "[18]

To a remarkable extent, the English *gentils* of the fourteenth century were willing to play the part of a studious Alexander opposite the Aristotle impersonated by contemporary clerks. As William Courtenay has argued, the "scholastic and court worlds" of fourteenth-century England "blended in other ways than through patronage and careers" and actually "impinged on one another, sometimes shaping the content of thought and letters."[19] The records indicate that the households of nobles became schools in which they were instructed by both knightly tutors and clerical tutors.[20] In 1395, for instance, a collection of seven Latin books was purchased for the eight-year-old boy who was destined to become Henry V. As Jeanne Krochalis notes, it was "probably some version of the standard collection of *Auctores*

---

[17] *The Gouernaunce of Prynces*, in *Three Prose Versions of the "Secreta Secretorum,"* ed. Robert Steele, EETS e.s. 74 (London: Kegan Paul, Trench, & Trübner, 1898), p. 41.

[18] John Wycliffe, *De officio regis*, ed. Alfred W. Pollard and Charles Sayle, in *Wyclif's Latin Works*, 21 vols. (1887; London: Trübner, 1966), 8:73–74 ("And Aristotle therefore in the *Secret of Secrets*, Chapter 12, speaks thus to Alexander, 'Establish schools in the cities of your realm and urge your people to teach their sons to read and write and to see to it that they study the noble liberal arts' " [translation mine]). Other mentions of the *Secretum* appear on pp. 53–55, 57–58, 77–78, 96–97.

[19] William J. Courtenay, *Schools and Scholars in Fourteenth-Century England* (Princeton: Princeton University Press, 1987), p. xi.

[20] Nicholas Orme, *Education and Society in Medieval and Renaissance England* (London: The Hambledon Press, 1989), pp. 160–61.

Octo: Donatus; the fables of Aesop, Avianus, and Phaedrus; the proverbs of Alain de Lille and the Distichs of Cato; a collection of tales ascribed to St. Bernard; and the *Eclogue of Theodulus*."[21] An extant book list reveals that Sir Simon Burley, Richard II's beloved tutor, owned "a book of the government of kings and princes" in French in 1387–88.[22] In 1397 the arrest and execution of Thomas of Woodstock, duke of Gloucester and son of Edward III, led to the confiscation and catalog of the 123 books belonging to him.[23] Woodstock's love of books places him, along with men like Sir Lewis Clifford and Sir John Clanvow, in the midst of what Orme terms "a whole literary circle of noblemen and gentlemen centred on the [Ricardian] court, owning books, keeping company with poets, and writing prose or verse themselves."[24]

The educated English aristocracy, moreover, as Richard F. Green insists, "maintained strong links with the universities."[25] In 1337 Edward III formally established King's Hall in Cambridge, and records attest to "the regular practice of support for the children of the chapel who had the ability and the desire to attend the university."[26] King Henry V willed his volumes of law and scholastic theology to the university library at Oxford.[27] From the universities, moreover, as we shall see, the court and the great magnates drew a considerable number of well-educated men into administrative and judicial service.

Noblemen who intended to become clerics in minor or major orders actually enrolled in the universities themselves. As Orme points out, Henry Beaufort resided at Peterhouse, Cambridge, and then at Queen's College, Oxford, between 1388 and 1393; and "men like William Courtenay and Lionel Wydeville at Oxford, and Henry Beaufort and Richard Scrope at Cambridge, served as chancellors of their universities, gave benefactions, and after becoming bishops were in a position to promote poor students to ecclesiastical benefices."[28] Only

---

[21] Jeanne E. Krochalis, "The Books and Reading of Henry V and His Circle," *Chaucer Review* 23 (1988): 61. See also George A. Plimpton, *The Education of Chaucer Illustrated from the Schoolbooks in Use in His Time* (London: Oxford University Press, 1935).
[22] Orme, *From Childhood to Chivalry*, p. 97.
[23] Krochalis, "Books and Reading," p. 50.
[24] Orme, *English Schools*, p. 33.
[25] Green, *Poets and Princepleasers*, pp. 90–91.
[26] Ibid., pp. 87–88.
[27] Krochalis, "Books and Reading," p. 68.
[28] Orme, *From Childhood to Chivalry*, pp. 68–70.

in the 1430s and 1440s, however, do we find "clear cases of noble boys at Oxford and Cambridge who were definitely intended to follow secular careers," most of whom attended only for a short period during which they "can scarcely have studied more than grammar," probably as a preparation for "studying the common law in London" at the Inns of Court.[29]

Long ago Thomas F. Tout speculated that "the London law schools . . . owed their very existence to the fact that the university had no place for the lay student or for the student of common law."[30] His surmise rightly suggests that the Inns of Chancery and Court stood in a position parallel to the older institutions at Oxford and Cambridge, collaborated and competed with them, and derived their sense of identity from the "otherness" of the universities. As Courtenay has observed, "the inns resembled halls of medieval universities," and they did so "more closely . . . than is generally recognized."[31]

Sir John Fortescue's *De laudibus legum Anglie* (c. 1468–71), our major source for reconstructing the earlier history of the London Inns, takes the form of a dialogue between the exiled Edward, Prince of Wales, and Fortescue himself, fictionalized as "a certain aged knight, chancellor" of King Henry VI, and thus continues the tradition of Aristotle and Alexander in a new vein.[32] The wise old man, observing the young prince at swordplay, wishes him "to be devoted to the study of laws with the same zeal as [he is] to that of arms" (p. 3). His ensuing remarks are filled with references to Aristotle, whose *Politics, Ethics, Physics, Posteriora,* and *Topica* are cited by name.[33]

In the discussion that follows, the prince wonders why the laws of England are not taught in the universities, to which his learned interlocutor replies that English common law differs from the Roman civil and canon law of the continent, and "since the laws of England

---

[29] Ibid., pp. 71–73. As Alan B. Cobban emphasizes, however, "In general, sons of the nobility did not enter the English universities on any scale before the latter half of the fifteenth century" (*The Medieval English Universities: Oxford and Cambridge to circa 1500* [Berkeley: University of California Press, 1988], p. 313).

[30] Thomas F. Tout, "Literature and Learning in the English Civil Service in the Fourteenth Century," *Speculum* 4 (1929): 369.

[31] Courtenay, *Schools and Scholars,* p. 98.

[32] Sir John Fortescue, *De laudibus legum Anglie,* ed. S. B. Chrimes (1942; Cambridge: Cambridge University Press, 1949), p. 3. Subsequent citations are parenthetical by page.

[33] According to Chrimes, Fortescue drew upon "one or other of the compilations of classical quotations known as *Auctoritates Aristotelis*" (p. lxxxix).

are learned in three languages [English, French, and Latin], they could not be conveniently learned or studied in the Universities, where the Latin language alone is used" (p. 117). Fortescue's chancellor goes on to describe the location near the king's courts of "ten lesser inns . . . , which are called the Inns of Chancery," where students learn "something of the elements of law" before enrolling in "the greater inns of the academy, which are called the Inns of Court" (p. 117). There are four such inns, he says—an oblique reference to the Middle Temple, Lincoln's Inn, the Inner Temple, and Gray's Inn.[34]

The implicit and explicit comparison of the inns to the universities continues as the dialogue progresses. The chancellor informs the prince that the young men attending the inns, unlike the students of the universities, are almost exclusively "the sons of nobles" (p. 119), some of them being instructed not in legal science, but rather in a liberal arts course aimed at inculcating "all the manners that the nobles learn," including music, dancing, and the reading of Scripture and of chronicles.

When the prince asks "why the degrees of bachelor and doctor are not given in the laws of England, as they are customarily given in both laws in the Universities," the chancellor draws a strong analogy between the achievement of the doctor of law and the sergeant-at-law: "I want you to know that, though degrees of this kind are not conferred at all in the laws of England, yet there is given in them, not only a degree, but also a certain estate, not less eminent or solemn than the degree of doctor, which is called the degree of serjeant-at-law" (p. 121).

Like Chaucer, who places the portrait of the "Sergeant of the Lawe" (GP 309–330) immediately after that of the Clerk of Oxenford in the General Prologue to the *Canterbury Tales*, Fortescue compares the Sergeant's accomplishments to that of a university clerk, describing him as "dressed in a long robe, like a priest's, with a furred cape about his shoulders, and above that a hood with two tappets, as doctors of law customarily wear in certain Universities" (p. 129).[35]

---

[34]   See Orme, *From Childhood to Chivalry*, p. 75. Fortescue was Governor of Lincoln's Inn in 1424–26 and again in 1428–30.

[35]   Fortescue was elevated to sergeant-at-law in 1430 and became chief justice of the king's bench in 1442.

Fortescue's rhetorical attempt to establish a separate-but-equal status for the students of the inns obscures the amount of contact between them and the universities. University-trained teachers undoubtedly taught *dictamen* in the Inns of Chancery. By the fifteenth century, as we have seen, students from the gentry participated briefly in the arts course at Oxford and Cambridge in preparation for study at the inns. Already by the mid-fourteenth century, however, many young boys studied at Oxford or Cambridge, "not . . . in the universities, but in the grammar and business schools which also flourished there and over which the university authorities exercised a loose control"—commercial schools such as that run by Thomas Sampson at Oxford between 1350 and 1409, where boys learned "to write letters, cast accounts, and convey property as a training for lay careers."[36] Among these boys was Chaucer's ten-year-old son (or godson), "lyte Lowys," to whom he in 1391 offered "a suffisant Astrolabie as for oure orizonte, compowned after latitude of Oxenforde" (*Treatise on the Astrolabe*, lines 1, 10–12).

Sixteenth-century biographies of Chaucer place him at the London inns and hold that he studied there in company with Ralph Strode, whose name appears in Chaucer's life-records and whom he praises as "philosophical" in *Troilus and Criseyde* (V.1857).[37] Strode's career as an Oxford logician and a London lawyer bears witness to the remarkable commerce between the two educational institutions. As John Fisher observes, "Recent scholarship accepts the identity of the fellow of Merton College (1359–60) and the London lawyer (1373–87). Strode's Oxford records end in 1360, the same year that Chaucer's end in Prince Lionel's household. Presumably they both entered the inns of chancery in that year and proceeded to the inns of court."[38]

Like the so-called Lollard knights associated with the *Conclusions* of 1395—Richard Sturry, Lewis Clifford, William Nevill, John Clanvow, Thomas Latimer, and John Montagu—Strode was apparently a friend not only of Chaucer but also of John Wycliffe, who addresses him as

---

[36]   Orme, *From Childhood to Chivalry*, p. 70.
[37]   Chaucer stood surety with Ralph Strode for London draper John Hend in 1381. See *Chaucer Life-Records*, ed. Martin M. Crow and Clair C. Olson (Austin: University of Texas Press, 1966), pp. 281–84.
[38]   John H. Fisher, *The Importance of Chaucer* (Carbondale: Southern Illinois University Press, 1992), pp. 51–52. See also *Chaucer Life-Records*, p. 284.

a "friend of truth" ("amicus veritatis") in his *Responsiones ad 18 argumenta Radulfi Strode.*[39] In it Wycliffe defends his controversial views regarding the Church, predestination, priestly celibacy, and benefices; refers to himself as a man whom Strode once knew in the schools ("homo quem novistis in scolis"); and confesses that his zeal for reform has led him occasionally to speak out in an arrogant and presumptuous way.[40] As Johann Loserth affirms, the pointed content of the *argumenta* necessitates a late dating of the *Responsiones*—certainly no earlier than 1377, when Strode was no longer "in scolis," but rather a practicing lawyer in London.[41] John Capgrave's *Abbreuaicion of Cronicles* (1462–63) assigns to 1376 the first publication of Wycliffe's "straunge opiniones," which were to be condemned by the Curia on May 22, 1378:

> In þis tyme on Jon Wiclef, maystir of Oxenforth, held many straunge opiniones: that þe Cherch of Rome is not hed of all Cherchis; that Petir had no more auctorité þan þe oþer aposteles, ne þe pope no more power þan anoþir prest; and þat temporal lordes may take awey þe godes fro þe Cherch whan þe parsones trespasin. . . . [42]

Whatever Strode's doctrinal differences with Wycliffe may have been, his choice of a legal career accords with Wycliffe's own predilection for English common law, rather than Justinianean civil law and the canon law embodied in Gratian's *Decretals.* As S. B. Chrimes indicates, "Wycliffe was a precursor of Fortescue" in his assertion of "the sufficiency [and superiority] of English case-law as developed by the common law courts."[43] In Wycliffe's Oxford, as Alan Cobban has

[39] John S. P. Tatlock calls attention to the "numerous adherents and supporters of Wyclif . . . among [Chaucer's] friends and associates" ("Chaucer and Wyclif," *MP* 14 [1916]: 259). See also K. B. McFarlane, *Lancastrian Kings and Lollard Knights* (Oxford: Clarendon Press, 1972), pp. 182–83; Paul Strohm, *Social Chaucer* (Cambridge: Harvard University Press, 1989).

[40] John Wycliffe, "Responsiones ad argumenta Radulfi Strode," in *Opera Minora,* ed. Johann Loserth, in *Wyclif's Latin Works* (London: C. K. Paul, 1913; repr. 1966), 21:197. The "Responsio ad decem questiones magistri Ricardi Strode" (*Opera Minora,* pp. 398–404) may also have been addressed to Ralph (not Richard) Strode.

[41] Ibid., p. xxxi.

[42] *John Capgrave's Abbreuiacion of Cronicles,* ed. Peter J. Lucas, EETS 285 (Oxford: Oxford University Press, 1983), p. 181.

[43] S. B. Chrimes, ed., *De laudibus legum Anglie,* p. xvii.

shown, the students of the two laws outnumbered those studying theology—a condition deplored by Gower in *Vox Clamantis* and more forcibly by preachers such as John Bromyard, Thomas Wimbledon, and Wycliffe himself.[44] In *De officio regis* Wycliffe urged the English universities to follow the example of the University of Paris and ban the teaching of civil law altogether ("ne ius civile legatur in Anglia"), since it includes measures contrary to both English and Church law.[45] In addition, he suggested that the study of canon law also be dispensed with, since it tended to detract from the simpler and more wholesome "lex Christi" embodied in the Scriptures.[46]

Beginning as early as 1374, Wycliffe argued on the double basis of English common law and the "lex Christi" revealed in Christ's submission to Pilate and Caesar (Matt. 17:24–27, Matt. 22:19–21) in favor of the king's right to conscribe the Church's wealth and punish possessioners and against the king's obligation to levy a tax in support of the papacy—a twofold position that won for him the initial protection of lay *gentils* like John of Gaunt, duke of Lancaster.[47] Echoing the opening of *De officio regis*, the Wycliffite *Tractatus de regibus* expresses "Goddus Lawe" thus: "Crist payed taliage to þo Emperoure, Crist tauȝt to pay to þo Emperoure þat was his, Crist ... commyttid his chirche to governaile of knyghttes. . . . Mony syche wordis spekis Goddus lawe of kyngus, but it spekis not of popis."[48]

In general, Wycliffe's pseudo-Aristotelian counsel to the English king takes the "clericalization" of the aristocracy to an extreme conclusion. At issue is not only a share in clerical literacy, but also authority over the Church. In the face of schism and rampant abuse, Wycliffe exhorts the educated king to assume the spiritual and temporal leadership abdicated by the hierarchy. According to Wycliffe, the king reflects God's fatherly authority over laity and clergy alike, acts as God's vicar ("vicarius dei") within his kingdom, and bears

---

[44] See Cobban, *Medieval English Universities*, esp. pp. 213, 220–221, and 230; John Gower, *The Voice of One Crying*, in *The Major Latin Works of John Gower*, trans. Eric W. Stockton (Seattle: University of Washington Press, 1962), Book III.29, p. 164.

[45] Wycliffe, *De officio regis*, p. 189.

[46] Ibid., p. 190.

[47] Wycliffe entered the king's service in 1372. On April 7, 1374 Edward III appointed him to the rectory of Lutterworth. Wycliffe's political views gained their first systematic expression shortly thereafter in *De Dominio divino libri tres* and *Tractatus de civili Dominio.*

[48] *Four English Political Tracts*, pp. 6–7.

responsibility for the vigorous reform of the Church, especially the eradication of the various forms of simony.[49]

Asserting that a person can be a philosopher, a pontiff, and a priest without being ordained ("non importet quod quis sit clericus, licet sit philosophus, pontifex et sacerdos"), and that every faithful layman is also a theologian ("omnem fidelem eciam laicum esse theologum"),[50] Wycliffe insists that the king is bound to know and obey God's law himself and to guard his subjects against heresy by promoting the diligent study of Holy Scripture. In fact, Wycliffe carries his argument for the king's ecclesiastical responsibility and authority so far that, as he acknowledges, his position could be misconstrued to imply that the king vicariously celebrates the Mass and administers the sacraments through the clergymen under his temporal jurisdiction and is thus—by extension—"clericus" himself: "ut rex celebrat, conficit et ministrat omnia sacramenta."[51]

The Clerkly Commons

Wycliffe's doctrine of a universal priesthood appealed to the anti-clerical sentiments of both the aristocracy and the commons. His "Eighteen Theses" were condemned by the Curia in 1378, and his teaching on the Eucharist was judged to be heretical by the commission of theologians headed by the chancellor of the University of Oxford in 1381. He insisted, however, that the positions taken by the magisterium of the Church were themselves heretical, and he endeavored to oppose them in part through a program of popular education that involved not only the public preaching of "poor priests,"[52] but also the publication of vernacular translations of the Bible and of polemical tracts in English, many of them translations of Wycliffe's own Latin works. For example, the views expressed in De officio regis gained new expression in a shorter, English tract bearing

[49] See De officio regis, esp. pp. 4–5, 12, 14, 51–71.
[50] Ibid., pp. 149, 72.
[51] Ibid., p. 132.
[52] Wycliffe himself preached in London churches from September 1376 through February 1377. Many of these churches—St. Andrew's, for instance—had Oxford men as rectors.

the Latin title *Tractatus de regibus*, which begins with an apology for
the use of the vernacular:

> Sythen witte stondis not in langage but in groundynge of treuthe, for
> þo same witte is in laten þat is in Grew or Ebrew, and trouthe schuld
> be openly knowen to alle maneres of folke, trowthe moveþ mony men
> to speke sentencis in yngelysche þat þai hav gedirid in latyne, and her
> fore bene men holden heretikis.[53]

The translation process brought treatises "gedirid in latyne" and
composed in a university setting into the homes of literate, lay com-
moners. In order to gain a wider forum for his views, Wycliffe and his
Bohemian admirer John Hus were willing, as Mariateresa Brocchieri
emphasizes, to go so far as "to abandon Latin, the language that
defined and distinguished them as intellectuals,"[54] and in so doing,
they helped to create a commons that was clerkly not only in its literacy, but also in its direct access to theological reflection. In the
words of Peggy Knapp, "[Wycliffe] and his confederates developed a
recognizable 'linguistic dialect' inflected toward the social program
they hoped to bring into being."[55] Wycliffe's journeys from Oxford to
London, from London to Oxford, and finally from Oxford to his re-
tirement in Lutterworth, meant repeatedly crossing the physical, intellectual, and linguistic boundaries that separated the university from
the city and the country parish and the village, and that crossing by
Wycliffe and many others worked to effect an actual redefinition of
the clerical domain in fourteenth-century England.

Wycliffe's anti-authoritarian stance vis-à-vis the pope and vehement
calls for a return to apostolic poverty quickly transmuted into other,
more violent forms of dissent against the rich and powerful, whether
clerical or lay. As Brocchieri succinctly observes, "The revolt of 1381
made Wycliffe suspect in the eyes of the wealthy laity who previously
had supported him against the papacy, and the lords found the program of the 'poor priests' too similar to the demands of the rebels."[56]
John Ball sounded too much like John Wycliffe. The close coincidence
of Wycliffe's dismissal from Oxford in the spring of 1381 and the

---

53 *Four English Political Tracts*, p. 5.
54 Brocchieri, "The Intellectual," p. 200.
55 Peggy Knapp, *Chaucer and the Social Contest* (New York: Routledge, 1990), p. 63.
56 Brocchieri, "The Intellectual," p. 198.

outbreak of the Peasants' Revolt in June of that same year fixed itself so firmly in the minds of chroniclers such as Thomas Walsingham and John Capgrave that Wycliffe's sacramental heresy ("Wykbeleve") and the desecration of the Eucharistic Host by one of his alleged followers (John Montague or "Laurentius de Sancto Martino") that it supposedly inspired, were considered virtual causes of the riots that raged in Kent and London during the days surrounding the Feast of Corpus Christi. An attack on the Body of Christ, as they saw it, entailed an actual assault on the body politic that was all the more powerful because it was demonic.[57]

To counter the spread of Wycliffe's teachings by the Lollards, the king and the English bishops launched their own two-pronged pedagogical campaign. At Oxford itself, Archbishop William Courtenay called for the expulsion of anyone who subscribed to Wycliffe's views. As K. B. McFarlane points out, scholars representing various religious orders "led a shattering onslaught on [Wycliffe's] opinions during the 1380s and 1390s"— among them, "the Benedictines Ughtred Boldon, Adam Easton and John Wells, the Cistercian William Remington, the Dominican Roger Dymoke, the Franciscan William Widford, the Austin Thomas Winterton, and Stephen Patrington and Thomas Netter, Carmelites."[58] Finally, in 1406 a Lollard sermon preached at St. Paul's cross by William Taylor, an Oxford clerk, prompted Thomas Arundel, archbishop of Canterbury, to press for an episcopal visitation to scrutinize what remained there of Wycliffe's writings and to purge the university of heresy.

Outside the university, Wycliffe's educational opponents focused on the grammar schools as real and potential sites for the dissemination of false doctrine. As Leona Gabel observes, "various references to

---

[57] For accounts of the Eucharistic sacrilege, see Thomas Walsingham, *Historia Anglicana*, ed. Henry Thomas Riley, in *Rerum Britannicarum Medii Aevi Scriptores* (London: HMSO, 1863; repr. 1965), 28:450; *John Capgrave's Abbreuiacions*, p. 191. Using sexual imagery, Walsingham calls Wycliffe the father of monsters and virtually personifies him as the embodiment of evil through a telling pun on his name: "quanta mala bestia quae ascendit de abysso, collega Sathanae, Johannes Wyclyff, sive Wikkebeleve, seminavit in terra" (*Historia Anglicana*, p. 451). Similarly, Capgrave excoriates "Jon Wyclif" as "þe orgon of þe deuel, þe enmy of þe Cherch, þe confusion of men, þe ydol of heresie, þe merour of ypocrisie, þe norcher of scisme" (*Abbreuiacioun*, p. 188). For a useful compilation of chronicle accounts, see *The Peasants' Revolt of 1381*, ed. R. B. Dobson, 2d ed. (London: Macmillan, 1970, repr. 1980).

[58] K. B. McFarlane, *John Wycliffe and the Beginnings of English Nonconformity* (London: English Universities Press, 1952), p. 148.

schools kept by the Lollards during the reigns of Richard and Henry IV suggest that the sect constituted an agency for the spread of education, in the interest, no doubt, of extending their doctrines."[59] She cites as examples the parliamentary statutes against Lollard schools enacted in 1401 and 1414 and the 1406 petition of the Prince of Wales to safeguard the kingdom against the dangerous propaganda carried on in "lieux secretes appelez Escoles."[60] Orme calls attention to the 1408 constitutions issued by Archbishop Arundel for the province of Canterbury, which "included an order that masters and others who taught boys in arts, grammar, or the elementary subjects should not teach anything concerning the catholic faith or the sacraments against what had been determined by the Church."[61]

Judging by these and other attempts at control and suppression and by the number of extant Wycliffite manuscripts, the Lollards not only established their own clandestine schools, but also, and more importantly, capitalized on the existing system for elementary education. As Orme and others have demonstrated, the fourteenth-century English towns were veritable "nurseries of literacy": "By Chaucer's time, there was a school open to the male public in most English towns of any importance," where students could learn "to read French or English," as well as Latin.[62] Chaucer's London had three authorized public schools—St. Martin-Le-Grand, St. Mary Arches, and St. Paul—plus other, unauthorized schools.[63] The elementary curriculum advanced "from the alphabet through plainsong" (taught in the song schools) "to the various branches of Latin: its grammar, its composition, its oratory, and its elementary literature" (taught in the grammar schools).[64] According to Orme, "A well-taught youth who graduated from a medieval grammar school ought to have known enough Latin to embark on a career as a priest, lawyer, merchant, or secretarial clerk, or to undertake university studies, which were also carried on through the medium of Latin."[65]

[59]   Leona C. Gabel, *Benefit of Clergy in England in the Later Middle Ages*, Smith College Series in History, vol. 14, nos. 1–4 (1928–29; New York: Octagon Books, 1969), p. 86.
[60]   Ibid.
[61]   Orme, *English Schools*, pp. 253–54.
[62]   Ibid., p. 43; *Education and Society*, p. 231. See also Courtenay, *Schools and Scholars*, p. 19.
[63]   See "A List of Medieval English Schools," in Orme, *English Schools*, pp. 308–9.
[64]   Orme, *Education and Society*, p. 63.
[65]   Ibid., p. 232.

The relationship between the grammar schools and the universities was mutually enforcing. As Janet Coleman notes, "One effect of the proliferation of grammar schools was the turning out of a relatively large number of men for whom more opportunities [for study] had been created at Oxford and Cambridge."[66] A second effect was that the grammar schools provided employment opportunities for university graduates, students, and dropouts.

According to Orme, "The largest group of medieval schools—the fee-paying institutions of the towns—allowed their masters to be priests, clerks, or married laymen, without discrimination."[67] Since "it was not absolutely necessary [for a schoolmaster] to be a celibate cleric or a university graduate,"[68] the grammar schools could employ a large number of literate men who had attended the universities for a short time, if at all. Given the absence of formal entrance examinations, the youthful age of entry in the arts course, and the stringent curricular demands in written and spoken Latin, and motivational problems (not to mention the physical toll taken by recurrent outbreaks of the plague), the wastage rate of undergraduates at Oxford and Cambridge was relatively high, probably between 30 and 40 percent.[69] Those who left the universities to become schoolmasters were, in Coleman's words, "an anonymous force to be reckoned with in the spread of current ideas and controversies raging at Oxford."[70]

Tonsured students who left the universities without having taken minor or major orders reverted to lay status, as did clerics in minor orders (porters, acolytes, lectors, and exorcists) who married.[71] No longer "cleri" in the strict sense of the word, they remained "clerks" nonetheless by virtue of their general education and professional activity. The paradoxical existence of nonclerical or lay clerks led to two major social contests in late medieval England: the first, administrative; the second, judicial.

[66]   Janet Coleman, *Medieval Readers and Writers, 1350–1400* (New York: Columbia University Press, 1981), p. 31.

[67]   Orme, *Education and Society*, p. 53.

[68]   Ibid., p. 52.

[69]   See Cobban, *Medieval English Universities*, pp. 353–57.

[70]   Coleman, *Medieval Readers and Writers*, p. 29.

[71]   For a treatment of the meaning of tonsure, see Hastings Rashdall, *The Universities of Europe in the Middle Ages*, ed. F. M. Powicke and A. B. Emden, 3 vols. (Oxford: Clarendon Press, 1936), 3:393–97.

As we have already noted, the English crown supported King's Hall at Cambridge (founded 1337) and Queen's College at Oxford (founded 1341). These colleges, in Coleman's words, "were increasingly seen as the primary source for administrative and legal personnel," especially for positions at the higher levels.[72] Alan Cobban indicates that a "fairly substantial" proportion of King's Hall fellows came to be directly employed in the service of the crown":

> King's Hall fellows were employed in the chancery, the exchequer, the king's council and the diplomatic arena; they were employed in the queen's household, as royal bailiffs and keepers of the forest, and as judicial commissioners; at least three held the office of master of the rolls; one was a keeper of the privy seal; another a king's secretary; and one rose to the position of keeper of the great seal of England.[73]

The employment of tonsured clerics in secular professions such as these became the subject of increasing controversy as clerical abuses multiplied and as more and more lay men with a comparable education appeared on the scene. Orme summarizes the historical tug-of-war as follows:

> Until 1371 the great officers of state—chancellor, treasurer and keeper of the privy seal—were ecclesiastics to a man, except for a short period after 1340 when Edward III tried the experiment of appointing laymen. ... The laymen who took office ... in 1371 were no more successful than their predecessors, and by 1377 the clergy were again in control of the three great offices.[74]

Lay men, to be sure, occupied lower-level administrative posts, and they did so in increasing numbers in the latter half of the fourteenth century. As we have already noted, Chaucer was the second lay man to hold the office of Clerk of the King's Works during the reign of Richard II. Married clerks (Thomas Hoccleve among them) were, however, relatively rare and professionally disadvantaged. As Malcolm

---

[72] Coleman, *Medieval Readers and Writers*, p. 32.
[73] Cobban, *Medieval English Universities*, p. 397.
[74] Orme, *English Schools*, pp. 40–41. See also T. F. Tout, *Chapters in the Administrative History of Mediaeval England*, 6 vols. (1920–33; repr. New York: Barnes and Noble, 1967), 3:124–25, 266–82.

Richardson notes, "The *Ordinaciones cancellarie* contain several prohibitions against married clerks in the chancery . . . , and in the rolls we find occasional stern notes about married officials."[75]

Wycliffe termed the restrictions on married clerks a Pharisaical straining-at-the-gnat that diverted attention from the camel-swallowing of priestly simony. In his view, the governmental service that would be laudable for a lay man was disgraceful for a clergyman, whose divine calling bound him to pastoral service and to a life of poverty.[76] He wondered why "lordis myȝtten not fynde in alle here lordiscipe trewe worldly men to reule here houshold and worldly offices," instead of employing curates as "stiwardis & clerkis of kechene & resceyuoris & rente gedereris & hunteris."[77] Similarly, the Prologue to the B Text of *Piers Plowman* lists various secular functions fulfilled by ordained men at the expense of their priestly duties:

> Somme seruen þe kyng and his siluer tellen,
> In Cheker and in Chauncelrie chalangen hise dettes
> Of wardes and of wardemotes, weyues and streyues.
> And somme seruen as seruauntȝ lordes and ladies,
> And in stede of Stywardes sitten and demen.
> Hire messe & hire matyns and many of hire houres
> Arn doon vndeuoutliche. . . .[78]

In the view of reformers like Wycliffe, both such clerics and the lords who employ them are guilty of simony. The lords, for their part, are willing to purchase the service of priests through benefices and draw them away from the care of souls: "þei wolen not presente a clerk able of kunnynge & of good lif & holy ensaumple to þe peple, but a kechen clerk or a penne clerk or wis of bildynge of castelis or worldly doynge, þouȝ he . . . knoweþ not þe comaundementis of god ne sacramentis of holy chirche."[79] The clerics, on the other hand, are willing to sell what properly belongs to God and the Church. They go

[75] Malcolm Richardson, "Hoccleve in His Social Context," *Chaucer Review* 20.4 (1986): 319–20.

[76] Wycliffe, *De officio regis*, pp. 28–29.

[77] *The English Works of Wyclif*, ed. F. D. Matthew, EETS 74 (London: Trübner, 1880), pp. 247, 168.

[78] William Langland, *Piers Plowman: The B Version*, ed. George Kane and E. Talbot Donaldson (London: Athlone Press, 1975), Prologue, lines 92–98.

[79] Wycliffe, *The English Works*, p. 246.

to school and accept tonsure, as Thomas Wimbledon complains in a famous 1388 sermon, "for to gete hem grete auauncementis," rather than to "lerne reule of good lyuynge in þe book of Goddis lawe."[80] And, as Wycliffe laments, "þei ben more maad prestis for worldly honour & aisy lif and welfare of body þan for deuocion to lyue in clennesse & holynesse & penaunce."[81]

Education, especially at the universities, was in fact a key factor in the upward mobility of youth from the lower classes. The Church itself, as Cobban reminds us, was a "principal employer for university-trained personnel," who worked as schoolmasters, vicars, rectors, chaplains, and deans of secular cathedrals. "Between 1216 and 1499 Oxford supplied 57 percent of English bishops, compared with the 10 percent provided by Cambridge."[82]

The social ramifications of this kind of clerical advancement were unsettling to many. An oft-quoted passage from *Pierce the Ploughmans Crede* (c. 1394) laments a world turned upside down, where lords bow down before the literate sons of beggars and shoemakers, who have through book-learning become bishops:

> Now mote ich soutere his sone setten to schole,
> And ich a beggers brol on þe booke lerne
> And worþ to a writere & wiþ a lorde dwell,
> Oþer falsly to a frere þe fend for to seruen!
> So of þat beggers brol a bychop schal worþen,
> Among þe peres of þe lond prese to sitten,
> And lordes sones lowly to þe losells aloute,
> Knyʒtes croukeþ hem to & crucheþ full lowe;
> And his syre a soutere y-suled in grees. . . . [83]

Although this reactionary passage from the *Crede* was not penned by a member of the gentry, they certainly shared in the social unease it expresses. The universities and cathedral schools admitted and sup-

[80] *Wimbledon's Sermon*, ed. Ione Kemp Knight (Pittsburgh: Duquesne University Press, 1967), pp. 72–73. See, too, Book III.29 of *Vox Clamantis*, where Gower decries clerks who wear the "shaven tonsure" as the price for an easy life, clerical immunity from secular prosecution, and worldly preferment (*The Voice of One Crying*, pp. 163–64).

[81] Wycliffe, *The English Works*, p. 166.

[82] Cobban, *Medieval English Universities*, p. 394.

[83] *Pierce the Ploughmans Crede*, ed. Walter W. Skeat, EETS o.s. 30 (London: Kegan Paul, Trench, Trübner, 1867, repr. 1895), lines 745–52.

ported "poor scholars," and that category almost certainly included not only the sons of retailers and artisans, but also a smaller number of serfs and laborers. According to A. F. Leach, "the fourteenth-century manor rolls all over the country are dotted with fines for sending boys *ad scolas clericalis*, to schools to become clerks."[84] Leona Gabel notes that "as late as 15 Richard II [1391] the Commons were still petitioning that villeins be henceforth forbidden to send their children to school."[85] Although the language of the 1406 Statute of Apprentices seemingly removes all educational restrictions upon serfs, Orme insists that lords "continued levying fines on villeins who went to school without permission, and treatises on how to hold manorial courts went on enquiring 'if there be any bondman of blood that putteth his son unto the school to make him a priest or a prentice' until as late as 1552."[86]

Even the children of laborers became priests, but not every youth who received the clerk's tonsure and was subsequently ordained was well educated. The system of pluralities allowed the best-educated and well-connected men to hold benefices, enjoy their revenues, and reside elsewhere, while other priests performed the actual work of the parishes at a small salary. The result was, in Gabel's words, a "marked increase in the number of clergy, recruited largely from the lower classes."[87] Many of the parish priests were ill-equipped to act as pastors. Wycliffe complains, on the one hand, about "ʒonge childre vnable boþ of lif & kunnynge" who "presen faste to be prestis in name and not in ded, & aftirward wolen not bisien hem to lerne, But bete stretis vp & down & synge & pleie as mynystrelis, & vse vanytees & ydelnesse."[88] He deplores, on the other hand, the plight of holy curates who "ben stired to gone lerne goddis lawe & teche here parischenys þe gospel," but who fail to receive permission from their bishop for a leave for continued education.[89] Barely literate and poorly educated in theology, these parish priests represented in growing numbers the paradox of the unclerkly cleric.

Confronted with a panoply of clerical abuses, Wycliffe and others

---

[84] Quoted in Gabel, *Benefit of Clergy*, p. 80.
[85] Ibid. See also Orme, *English Schools*, p. 192.
[86] Orme, *Education and Society*, p. 13. See also *English Schools*, pp. 50–52.
[87] Gabel, *Benefit of Clergy*, p. 85.
[88] Wycliffe, *The English Works*, p. 166.
[89] Ibid., p. 250.

urged a pragmatic division between lay clerks (in secular professions) and ordained clerks (in pastoral service) as a means of separating "anticristis clerkis" from Christ's.[90] The contemporary resistance to such a division indicates, among other things, the complexity and breadth with which clerical status had come to be defined in fourteenth-century England. The administrative contest between lay and ordained clerks had its judicial double in the relationship between the lay and ecclesiastical courts, a relationship that hinged, as Leona Gabel has shown, on determining "the precise meaning of 'clerk' as applied to persons, and of 'clergyable' as applied to the offenses for which the privilege [of benefice of clergy] held, terms . . . capable of different constructions according to the angle from which they were regarded."[91]

A person under arrest for felony could obtain the transfer of his case from the lay to the ecclesiastical courts by claiming his "clergy." According to Gabel, whereas during the reign of Henry II the term *clericus* probably applied only to clerks in Holy Orders, its definition gradually broadened to include "all having first tonsure, and finally, all who [were] literate." The period from the thirteenth through the fifteenth centuries "witnesses the gradual introduction of the reading-test as a mode for ascertaining 'clergy,' at first merely to supplement older modes of proof, ultimately as proof competent itself."[92]

By the latter half of the fourteenth century, the spread of literacy among the laity was such that widespread abuses began to occur. Gabel's survey of Gaol Delivery Rolls shows "literate clerks described as 'quondam serviens,' 'mercer,' 'serviens,' 'taillour,' 'spicer,' 'fysshe-monger,' 'hosyer,' 'smyth,' 'fyssher,' 'shipman,' 'chapman,' 'yoman,' 'bucher,' 'husbandmen,' 'masun,' 'walker,' 'webster,' 'couper,' 'vestmentmaker,' and relatively numerous instances of literate laborers."[93] As Gabel observes, the variety of secular occupations on this list "points to a state of affairs in which the practical distinction between a 'clerk' and a layman in every-day affairs was in many cases negligible or even non-existent."[94] The clericalization of the commons—from

---

[90] Ibid., p. 246.
[91] Gabel, *Benefit of Clergy*, p. 8.
[92] Ibid., pp. 29–30.
[93] Ibid., p. 81. As Gabel explains, "The term 'laborer' meant the poor, unskilled worker as contrasted with the better paid workman or artisan."
[94] Ibid., p. 77.

Wycliffe's lay theologians and civil servants to felonious artisans, retailers, and laborers—was, in short, nearly complete.

Chaucer's Clerk of Oxenford and the Fourth Estate

The preceding discussion of the clericalization of fourteenth-century English society from its rulers to its laborers provides a new context for consideration of Chaucer's Clerk of Oxenford. Chaucerians, following the lead of Jill Mann and George Engelhardt, generally agree, in the words of Paul Olson, "that the pilgrims who represent the features of virtue are the Parson and the Clerk, the Knight, and the Plowman," and that these ideal pilgrims represent the three estates of medieval social theory: those who pray, those who fight, and those who work.[95] In order to accommodate four representative pilgrims to three estates, however, they either ignore the Clerk altogether or underplay his importance by treating him (as Olson does) as a double of the Parson, who merely "represent[s] the Parson's estate at study."[96]

There are, to be sure, grounds for such a subdivision of the priestly estate. As a university student, the Clerk has received first tonsure and thus, whether or not he has taken minor orders, enjoys privilege of clergy. In Book III of *Vox Clamantis* Gower first distinguishes the traditional three estates: "Sunt clerus, miles, cultor, tres trina gerentes; / Hic docet, hic pugnat, alter et arua colit." Later he subdivides the first estate to call attention to scholars: "Nomine sub cleri cognouimus esse scholares."[97] He prepares for this subdivision, moreover, by emphasizing teaching, rather than praying, as the primary function of the *clerus*: "Hic docet." In Gower's scheme, teaching presupposes learning; therefore, behind the *clerus* he discovers the student.

Chaucer's Clerk, however, enjoys an autonomy within the pilgrim

---

[95] Paul Olson, *The "Canterbury Tales" and the Good Society* (Princeton: Princeton University Press, 1986), p. 30. He cites George J. Engelhardt, "The Lay Pilgrims of the *Canterbury Tales*: A Study in Ethology," *Mediaeval Studies* 36 (1974): 283.

[96] Olson, *The Good Society*, p. 35. Paul Strohm, for his part, ignores the Clerk in his discussion of estates. See *Social Chaucer*, p. 85.

[97] John Gower, *The Latin Works*, in *The Complete Works of John Gower*, ed. G. C. Macaulay (Oxford: Clarendon Press, 1902), vol. 4, Book III.i, p. 105; III.xxviii, p. 162.

company and an equality among the ideal pilgrims that resists either a backgrounding behind the Parson or a close, representative pairing with him, comparable to the brotherhood between the Parson and the Plowman, whose portraits adjoin. The Clerk, as Jill Mann indicates, "performs the role of the ideal scholar" and stands as "an ideal representative of the life of study."[98] His portrait stands at a considerable distance from the Parson's, preceding that of the Sergeant of Law and following the Merchant's. Nothing in his portrait, moreover, orientates his studies toward theology or his future toward pastoral work. As Mann emphasizes, "The Clerk's studies, in so far as we hear of them, are secular ones; we hear of 'logyk,' of 'Aristotle and his philosophie,' but nothing of theology, the queen of sciences."[99] The Clerk, we are told, is reluctant to accept "worldly . . . office" (GP 292) in service to a magnate, but his unexplained lack of a benefice leaves us decidedly unsure whether "his desire was to take on the parochial duties of the Parson."[100]

The relative secularity of the Clerk's portrait accords with Chaucer's other depictions of scholars in the *Canterbury Tales*. By the count of J. Burke Severs, there are six or seven additional clerks: Nicholas (and possibly Absolon) in "The Miller's Tale," Aleyn and John in "The Reeve's Tale," Jankyn in the Wife of Bath's Prologue, the clerk at Orléans, and Aurelius's brother in "The Franklin's Tale."[101] As Orme observes, these scholars share certain common features: "Most appear to be secular clerks who have not yet committed themselves to the priesthood and are not members of religious orders." They are young, "of modest means, probably engaged in studying the arts course, and likely to have exploits of a non-academic kind." Unlike the Clerk of Oxenford, these other clerks "are all portrayed in their extracurricular moments, or when they have left the university."[102]

---

[98] Jill Mann, *Chaucer and Medieval Estates Satire* (Cambridge: Cambridge University Press, 1973), p. 74.

[99] Ibid., p. 83.

[100] Ibid.

[101] J. Burke Severs, "Chaucer's Clerks," in *Chaucer and Medieval English Studies*, ed. Beryl Rowland (London: George Allen and Unwin, 1974), pp. 140–52. For other treatments of Chaucer's clerks, see Nicholas Orme, "Chaucer and Education," *Chaucer Review* 16.1 (1981): 38–59; repr. in *Education and Society*, pp. 221–42; Muriel Bowden, *A Commentary on the General Prologue to the "Canterbury Tales"* (1948; New York: Columbia University Press, 1967); pp. 155–64.

[102] Orme, *Education and Society*, pp. 235, 237.

In the context of these related character sketches, the secular emphasis in the Clerk's portrait suggests that Chaucer's four ideal pilgrims are not simply a conservative bow to the three estates of feudal social theory, but rather an original vision of the new social order being shaped by the book-learning fostered preeminently at the universities. In a uniquely open-ended way, the Clerk of Oxenford represents an independent fourth estate, not a simple subdivision of the *cleri.* As Donald Howard argues, "The idealized Clerk represents an estate other than the traditional three, but by Chaucer's time the universities *were* a world unto themselves."[103]

The significance of Chaucer's choice of the Clerk as a fourth ideal pilgrim becomes apparent when we compare his work to other contemporary discussions that imagine an emergent fourth estate. Paul Strohm comments on "the fourteenth-century habit of recognizing a fourth social category, between the lords on the one hand and the peasants on the other."[104] He cites, for example, a 1375 sermon of Thomas Brinton, bishop of Rochester, who "divides society into four kinds of men ('genera hominum') according to vocation: prelates and ecclesiastics, kings and princes, merchants ('mercatores'), and workers ('operarii et laboratores')." Similarly, Philippe de Mézières refashions the older feudal scheme by demoting the knights and promoting certain categories of tradesmen to envision a fourth estate of "non-knightly gentlepersons and bourgeoisie."[105]

Chaucer, in distinct contrast to these formulations, portrays in ideal terms not a merchant but a clerk as representative of the new social order, even as he groups the Clerk, not with the Parson or the Monk, but with the Merchant and the Sergeant of the Law. In doing so, Chaucer articulated a vision that accorded to the use of books a greater and more fundamental power to effect or forestall societal change than that deriving from mercantile exchange. He shared that insight, albeit with different sentiments, with the Lollard translators and schoolmasters and the peasant rioters of 1381, who destroyed the records at Cambridge University, St. Alban's, and the Temple, "bren-

---

[103]   Donald Howard, *The Idea of the "Canterbury Tales"* (Berkeley: University of California Press, 1967), p. 52; see also Howard, "The *Canterbury Tales:* Memory and Form," *ELH* 38.3 (1971): 319–28.
[104]   Strohm, *Social Chaucer,* p. 3.
[105]   Ibid., pp. 3–4.

ning dedis and chartoris; all clausures of wodis þei distroyed, bokis and rolles of cortis and obligaciones þei rent and brent."[106]

Chaucer's maidenly, book-loving Clerk seems, to be sure, far removed from the violence of such real-world contests; indeed, as Mann has observed, the scholarly ideal he represents is and was "associated with an 'ivory tower.' "[107] As Chaucer recognized, however, carving out the societal space for that "ivory tower" involved a series of often violent confrontations and negotiations between opposed parties that accentuated the central importance of the universities as a novel institution within a changing society. The history of the universities describes their ongoing struggle for autonomy in relation to the municipalities, on the one hand, and the bishops, on the other—a struggle in which the king and Parliament repeatedly intervened.

As Cobban explains, the emergence of Oxford and Cambridge "as privileged institutions at the hearts of their respective towns provoked ambivalent responses from the burgesses," who recognized that the universities offered "a stimulus to the urban economy," but resented the economic and judicial privileges accorded to the members of the ever-extended university community.[108] The periodic Town and Gown conflicts that resulted culminated in Oxford in the bloody St. Scholastica Day riot of 1355; in Cambridge, in the riots of 1381. In each case, royal intervention led to a settlement in which the scholars gained at the expense of the townspeople: "From 1355 at Oxford and from 1382 at Cambridge, the chancellors, after previous stages of limited participation gained decisive control of the operation of market trading in the university towns and their suburbs through custody of the assize of bread, wine and ale, the supervision of weights and measures, and the regulation of other matters related to the disciplined conduct of urban commerce."[109]

The struggle for the autonomy of the universities within their municipal settings parallels their efforts to win independence from ecclesiastical control. Beginning in 1370, Oxford was no longer answerable to the bishop of Lincoln. By a bull of Boniface IX of 13 June

---

[106] *John Capgrave's Abbreuiacions*, p. 186.
[107] Mann, *Estates Satire*, p. 74.
[108] Cobban, *Medieval English Universities*, p. 258. See Rashdall, "The University and the Town," in *Universities of Europe*, 3:79–113.
[109] Cobban, *Medieval English Universities*, p. 260.

1395, the university claimed "full emancipation from all ecclesiastical jurisdiction, including that of the archbishop of Canterbury."[110] Charges of forgery subsequently brought the authenticity of the bull into question, and it was formally rescinded by John XXIII in 1411 at the urging of Thomas Arundel, who was enthroned as archbishop of Canterbury in 1397 and who, in Cobban's words, "was determined to assert archiepiscopal control over Oxford University and to carry out a thorough visitation in order to eradicate all lingering traces of Wycliffite and Lollard doctrines."[111]

As others have shown, Chaucer's *Canterbury Tales* gives expression to these two social contests. J. A. W. Bennett, in particular, has documented Chaucer's intimate knowledge of the contemporary university scene. He stresses that both "The Miller's Tale" and "The Reeve's Tale" revolve around the poles of Town and Gown and are controlled by the "theme of clerkly cunning, the 'sleightes of philosophye' pitted against plain men's practice."[112] Chaucer's all-pervasive anticlerical social satire, moreover, although not specifically Wycliffite, is so closely akin to it that the notable omission in the Ellesmere manuscript of the Host's casual reference to the Parson as "a Lollere" (II.1173)— and indeed, the apparent cancellation of the entire Epilogue to "The Man of Law's Tale"— may be seen as a clerical "visitation" of Chaucer's *Tales* analogous to Arundel's 1411 scrutiny of Oxford's library holdings.

In a letter Wycliffe compared his beloved "universitas Oxoniensis" to an insular world set apart and autonomous, calling it the protected vineyard of the Lord ("vinea Domini"), a paradisiacal "locus amenus fertilis," the house of God and the gate of Heaven.[113] Chaucer's Clerk of Oxenford would surely have approved that description. As Mann aptly describes Chaucer's Clerk, he is a "eternal student" who learns for the sake of learning, converting that "means" into its own "end" and postponing even the "end" of graduation.[114] We do not know why the studious Clerk "had geten hym yet no benefice" (GP 292),

[110] Ibid., p. 283. See also Rashdall, "The University and the Church," in *Universities of Europe*, 3:114–39.

[111] Cobban, *Medieval English Universities*, p. 284.

[112] J. A. W. Bennett, *Chaucer at Oxford and Cambridge* (Toronto: University of Toronto Press, 1974), pp. 11, 20. See also Derek S. Brewer, "The *Reeve's Tale* and the King's Hall, Cambridge," *Chaucer Review* 5 (1971): 311–17.

[113] John Wycliffe, "De Fratribus ad Scholares," Epistola 9 in *Opera Minora*, p. 18.

[114] Mann, *Estates Satire*, pp. 74, 76.

and the suggestion is strong that he has avoided procuring one in order to prolong his stay at Oxford.[115]

We do not know what the Clerk will be when and if he leaves the university, or even how old he is. Unlike the portraits of the other ideal pilgrims, the Clerk's depicts someone who is "unfinished," *in potentia*, and therefore uniquely potent. The Clerk could become another Parson or even a Friar; he could yield to the Wife of Bath's overtures and become a *clericus uxoratus* (as her previous husband did); he could become a schoolteacher, a secretary to a lord, a civil administrator, a physician, or even a lawyer. Wide-ranging and fanciful as these options are, they point to the seminal significance of the clerkly figure in fourteenth-century England. Retired from the world for a time of vocational and professional preparation, the clerk can reenter it at virtually every point.

The apartness of the Clerk, withdrawn into study and musingly silent, constitutes a kind of absence that allows the other pilgrims to impersonate him in multiple ways and thus render him present virtually everywhere. This is true not only in the sense of pilgrims such as the Miller, the Reeve, the Wife, and the Franklin, who vocalize the speech of clerks and tell their stories, but also in the sense of pilgrims who, in one way or another, ape the Clerk and lay claim to the learning that is properly his.   The Knight paraphrases Boethius; the Man of Law displays his astronomical and literary knowledge; the Wife of Bath delves into "scole-matere" (III.1272); the Monk summarizes the content of his library of tragedies; the Summoner cries "*Questio quid iuris*" (GP 646) and threatens with "*Significat*" (GP 662); the Pardoner uses a Latin text for his theme; the Physician touts his Galenic reading; the Nun's Priest alludes to the predestinarian doctrine of "Bisshop Bradwardyn" (VII.3242); Chaucer translates a sententious treatise full of *auctoritates*; the Squire and the Franklin bow to "Marcus Tullius Scithero" (V.722); the Merchant keeps his account books; and at a pinch, even the felonious Shipman may have laid claim to "clergy" by drawing on the "litel Latyn in [his] mawe" (II.1190) to save his life with a *legit*.

The diverse company of pilgrims speaking for and as clerks recalls the ever widening boundaries of the university community in Chaucer's time. As the universities gained increased autonomy and control

[115] Ibid., p. 83.

over their surroundings, the privileges accorded to their faculty members and students were gradually extended in application, as Cobban has shown, to "servants of scholars, bedels, parchment-dealers, illuminators, scribes and barbers, and any others who wore the livery or robes of clerks . . . the university bellringer, caterers, manciples, spencers, cooks, launderers."[116] Drawn into the ambit of the university, all were "clerks," at least by association.

As Orme emphasizes, Chaucer has drawn a clericalized society, "whose upper echelons are all literate," and where, apart from the clergy and the aristocracy, the "chief exponents of learning and literacy . . . are the professional men and the great traders."[117] The key symbolic figure in such a society is the scholar, whose "means" of learning, an end in itself within the university, is applied to multiple ends outside of it.

The four-estate model Chaucer employs in the General Prologue uniquely emphasizes the secular role of the universities, and it does so in a way evocative of the four Aristotelian causes. The Knight represents the temporal power of the aristocracy as an efficient cause; the Parson points to God and eternal things as the final cause; the Plowman's labor provides the material cause of social existence; and the Clerk, representing book-learning, stands as a formal cause to condition all the estates, transforming people at every rank—from kings to cobblers—into "clerks," the world into a *universitas*.

---

[116] Cobban, *Medieval English Universities*, p. 270. Compare Carl Lindahl's fine treatment of parish guilds as a social microcosm similar to Chaucer's pilgrim company in *Earnest Games: Folkloric Patterns in the "Canterbury Tales"* (Bloomington: Indiana University Press, 1987).

[117] Orme, *Education and Society*, pp. 238–39.

The parts of philosophy are equal in number to the different types of those things over which its extension has now been established.

—Hugh of St. Victor

2

THE DIVISIONS OF KNOWLEDGE

In keeping with the Platonic principle that "the constituent categories of a community and of any individual's mind are identical in nature and number,"[1] Western thought has tended to draw analogies between the hierarchical divisions or estates within a society and the various divisions of knowledge.[2] Focusing on the elite divisions, Macrobius points to a parallel between the theoretical and practical branches of philosophy, on the one hand, and the social division between scholars and kingly "leaders in public wel-

---

[1] Plato, *The Republic*, trans. Robin Waterfield (Oxford: Oxford University Press, 1993), 441c, p. 152. The rulers, Socrates argues, should be true philosophers and theologians, who embody the wisdom of the community; the fighters should represent its lawful courage or fortitude. In such a society, as in the life of the individual, "the rational part will do the planning, and the passionate part will do the fighting" (442b, p. 154). Isidore of Seville, citing Plato, lists the cardinal virtues as the subdivisions of moral or practical philosophy (*Etymologiae* II.xxiv, PL 82, c141).

[2] Depending on the context, I refer to either the "divisions" or the "parts" of philosophy. The terms are not, strictly speaking, synonymous, and the debate about which term is appropriate is ancient. "Divisio" implies the relationship between a genus and its species; "partitio," that of a whole to its parts. A genus can survive the extinction of a species, whereas the existence of a whole depends on that of all its parts. See Katerina Ierodiakonou, "The Stoic Division of Philosophy," *Phronesis* 38.1 (1993): 57–74, esp. 64–67.

fare," on the other.[3] More basically, as Hugh of St. Victor explains, the distinction between the liberal arts and the mechanical arts equivocates a difference between social classes, because "in antiquity only free and noble men [*liberi*] were accustomed to study [the liberal arts], while the populace and the sons of men not free sought operative skill in things mechanical."[4] Significantly, as R. Howard Bloch has shown, the genealogical interest of the medieval nobility expressed itself in grammatical terms and in diagrams not unlike the *arbores scientiarum*.[5] By extension, as Georges Duby has suggested, a complex relationship may be said to exist between the so-called three philosophies of the later Middle Ages—metaphysics, physics, and moral philosophy—and the trifunctionality of the three feudal estates: the *oratores*, *bellatores*, and *laboratores*.[6]

Through Saint Augustine, Boethius, Cassiodorus, and Isidore of Seville, the Middle Ages inherited a variety of antique schemes for the *divisiones* of philosophy.[7] Whereas twelfth-century writers sought to resolve the internal differences between and among authoritative sources through allegorical myth and numerical play, later writers had to confront the external relationship between the *partes philosophiae* and the social estates. The particular site of intersection between philosophical theory and social practice was the university, where the divisions of knowledge were literally embodied in diverse faculties, and the courses of study increasingly linked to lucrative, vocational ends. There the discrepancy between the branches of philosophy as the classical *auctores* had rendered them and the actual curricular divisions that developed occasioned repeated controversies and promoted a series of theoretical and pragmatic negotiations between opposed camps. These negotiations display a conscious awareness of

[3] Macrobius, *Commentary on the Dream of Scipio*, trans. William H. Stahl (New York: Columbia University Press, 1952, repr. 1990), II.xvii.4, p. 244.
[4] *The Didascalicon of Hugh of St. Victor: A Medieval Guide to the Arts*, trans. Jerome Taylor (New York: Columbia University Press, 1961, repr. 1991), II.20, p. 75. Subsequent citations are parenthetical by book, chapter, and page.
[5] R. Howard Bloch, *Etymologies and Genealogies: A Literary Anthropology of the French Middle Ages* (Chicago: University of Chicago Press, 1983), esp. pp. 87–90.
[6] See Georges Duby, *The Three Orders: Feudal Society Imagined*, trans. Arthur Goldhammer (1978; Chicago: University of Chicago Press, 1980), pp. 243–44.
[7] See James A. Weisheipl, O.P., "The Nature, Scope, and Classification of the Sciences," in *Science in the Middle Ages*, ed. David C. Lindberg (Chicago: University of Chicago Press, 1978), pp. 461–82.

the analogy between the divisions of knowledge and social classifications and preserve that analogy in ever more complex summations.

This book argues that Chaucer's Ellesmere *Tales* is such a *summa*, and that the rubricated *divisiones* in the Ellesmere manuscript reflect a discernible attempt to achieve an ordered analogy between social groups, tale groups, and the branches of schematic trees of the sciences (*arbores scientiarum*) within the larger narrative context of a pilgrimage that is simultaneously earthly and planetary. Chaucer's particular treatment of social and philosophical division is, moreover, not to be seen in isolation, but as part of a conscious dialogue between Chaucer and Gower, on the one hand, and Chaucer and Dante, on the other.

Confronted by violent social change and by scholastic challenges to the hierarchical unity of knowledge, Gower employs the exposition of the *partes philosophiae* in Book VII of his *Confessio Amantis* as a nostalgic emblem for an ordered society. Dante, by contrast, subjects the didascalic tradition to a searching critique, assigning a place in hell to his (and Gower's) encyclopedist teacher, Brunetto Latini. Like Dante, Chaucer sees the limitations of any philosophical system that represents itself as self-enclosed and complete. Whereas Dante explodes those limitations through an imaginative, theological transcendence, however, Chaucer takes an immanent route that dramatizes debate and rivalry, preserving *quaestiones* as *quaestiones* and using them as an avenue to a humble self-knowledge. In a sense, Chaucer answers the Dante of the *Paradiso* with a parody of Dante's own *Convivio*. In so doing, Chaucer provides an alternative way of interpreting, imitating, and revising the philosophical tradition that was the common inheritance of all three poets and which inspired their imaginary pilgrim's paths.

Playing the Parts of Philosophy: Epic and Encyclopedia

Important early works known to Dante and Chaucer had joined the image of a spiritual journey to the theme of education. Macrobius's *Commentary on the Dream of Scipio* explicates an oracular dream-vision, which includes a planetary ascent, in a compendious way that discovers in its enigmas the whole of philosophy in its various branches, arts, and sciences. Martianus Capella's *Marriage of Mercury and Philology* (fifth century) describes the ascent of the bride to heaven, where the seven liberal arts, personified as her handmaidens, entertain the assembled wedding guests with the wealth of their knowledge. In the *Consolation of Philosophy* (A.D. 525), Philosophia's gown is embroidered with the Theta and the Pi of theoretical and practical philosophy, as well as the seven-rung ladder of the liberal arts, when she descends from heaven into Boethius's prison cell, engages in an instructive dialogue with him, and invites his soul to fly on her pinions homeward to the eternal fatherland.

Only in the twelfth century, however, did poets systematically interweave the two, using allegorical protagonists and the plot of an epic journey between heaven and earth to represent the gradual acquisition of encyclopedic knowledge.[8] As Peter Dronke notes, Chaucer learned from Bernard Silvestris and Alan de Lille "how a meaning beyond fable—a philosophical meaning—could be embodied in a fabled matter."[9] The argument of their works corresponds closely to the outline of philosophy, as the *partes philosophiae* are literally given parts to play within a mythic drama of the educational process.

As M.-D. Chenu has observed, the subtitle of Bernard Silvestris's work, *De mundi universitate*, attests to "the spread of the word *universitas* employed independently and as a concrete noun (not *universitas rerum*) to designate the universe in descriptions or in systematic treatises" during the twelfth-century Renaissance.[10] The students of Plato's *Timaeus*, of hexaemeral commentaries on Genesis, and of Pseudo-Dionysius's *Celestial Hierarchies* perceived the universe freshly as an entity; as "an ordered aggregation of creatures" ("ordinata collectio creaturarum"); as a single, organic whole, composed of diverse, related parts.[11] Although the word *universitas* only later came to be

---

[8]   In a variation on this theme, Godfrey of St. Victor's *Fons philosophiae* (c. 1176) recounts Godfrey's own educational history in lively detail, using the allegory of a fountain with many streams. See *The Fountain of Philosophy*, trans. Edward A. Synan (Toronto: Pontifical Institute of Mediaeval Studies, 1972).

[9]   Peter Dronke, "Chaucer and the Medieval Latin Poets, Part A," in *Geoffrey Chaucer: Writers and Their Backgrounds*, ed. Derek Brewer (London: G. Bell and Sons, 1974), p. 157.

[10]   M.-D. Chenu, *Nature, Man, and Society in the Twelfth Century*, ed. and trans. Jerome Taylor and Lester K. Little (Chicago: University of Chicago Press, 1968, repr. 1983), pp. 5–6.

[11]   Ibid., p. 7n14. Chenu quotes from William of Conches's *Glossa in Timaeum*.

used to refer to the university as an academic institution composed
of various schools and colleges,[12] the logical relationship between the
two uses of the word is grounded in the medieval axiom that there
are as many parts of philosophy as there are kinds of things to be
known.

A natural theory of knowledge stands behind the production of
encyclopedias, the composition of diagrammatic *arbores scientiarum*,
and the rise of the universities. Perceiving the world to be a book, a
picture, and a mirror (to echo Alan de Lille), twelfth- and thirteenth-
century intellectuals literally converted those metaphors into books
and *specula*.[13] Indeed, as Jesse Gellrich has shown, "encyclopedias and
summae" best manifest "the medieval idea of the Book" and represent an "attempt to gather all strands of learning into an enormous
Text . . . that would mirror the historical and transcendental orders,
just as the Book of God's Word (the Bible) was the speculum of the
Book of his Work (nature)."[14]

Involving personifications of the parts of philosophy in the work of
creation out of primal chaos (in Bernard's *Cosmographia*) and in the
task of recreation out of moral chaos (in Alan's *Anticlaudianus*) gives
mythopoetic expression to the naturalness of encyclopedic knowledge. Most obviously, Bernard's Physis represents both physical nature
itself and physics, the speculative science devoted to its study. Dwelling
on earth, Physis is "occupied with the study of created life" and has
"taken as the subject of her thought the origins of all natural things,
their properties, powers and functions, and the whole range of Aristotelian categories."[15] Physis labors also as a physician to restrain and
correct harmful imbalance in animate creatures, drawing "curative
effects" not only from "herbs, plants and grasses," but also "from
metals and stones" (p. 112). Thus she combines theory and practice,
knowledge and application, in her function. To her Noys assigns the

[12] According to Friedrich Heer, the word "universitas" in the academic setting originally referred to an association of students or faculty members and only later acquired
its more general meaning. See *The Medieval World* (London: Wiedenfeld and Nicolson,
1962), p. 242.
[13] See Alan de Lille, *Rythmus alter*, PL 210, c579.
[14] Jesse M. Gellrich, *The Idea of the Book in the Middle Ages: Language Theory, Mythology,
and Fiction* (Ithaca: Cornell University Press, 1985), pp. 139, 18.
[15] *The "Cosmographia" of Bernardus Silvestris*, trans. Winthrop Wetherbee (New York:
Columbia University Press, 1973), p. 112. Subsequent citations are parenthetical by
page.

task of "the composition of a [human] body by the conditioning of matter" (p. 114). Similarly, in the *Anticlaudianus* (1179–82?), Alan's Nature, playing the part given to Physis in the *Cosmographia*, fashions for the soul of the New Man a "dwelling in the flesh" out of the "ideal matter" of the four elements, selecting the "purified parts" of earth, the "pure parts" of water, the "purer parts" of air, and "all the refined parts that purer fire keeps for itself."[16]

In both epics the plot presents the principal protagonists with the difficult task of creating humankind as a microcosm whose constituent elements span the full range of created things and who is therefore capable of knowing all things connaturally: "The body possesses the earth, the spirit the heavens" (*Anticlaudianus*, p. 60). This uniting of physical and spiritual opposites within humanity requires an analogous joining together of heaven and earth as a continuum, for which Bernard uses the Macrobian image of Homer's Golden Chain, which "unites the higher with the lower universe" (p. 105).[17]

Both poets narrate this joining together through a story of planetary ascent and descent. In the *Cosmographia*, Nature first ascends to the heavens to find Urania, whose glance is directed upward and whose starry habitation is close to the throne of Noys. She and Nature then descend together through the planetary spheres, beginning with the orbit of savage Saturn and ending with the circle of the moon, carefully trying to avoid their respective negative influences on the human soul. Similarly, in the *Anticlaudianus*, Phronesis first ascends through the heavens to the pinnacle of the world, where Theology assists her. Then, having received from God the soul of the New Man, she descends to earth, taking care "lest the soul, touched by Saturn's icy chill, experience excessive cold or be parched in Mars' heat, or affected with Dione's sweet itch, begin to dally or go to and fro before the moon's currents" (p. 171).

Natural harmony characterizes not only the goal, but also the method of Bernard's and Alan's protagonists, who cooperate with one another in a complementary fashion. As James Simpson observes, the epics of Bernard and Alan reflect "an intensely optimistic current of humanism" in which the various speculative and practical sciences are closely interrelated.[18] In the *Cosmographia*, the joint efforts of Ura-

---

[16] Alan of Lille, *Anticlaudianus*, trans. James J. Sheridan (Toronto: Pontifical Institute of Mediaeval Studies, 1973), p. 173. Subsequent citations are parenthetical by page.

[17] See Macrobius, *Commentary*, I.xiv.15, p. 145.

[18] James Simpson, *Sciences and the Self in Medieval Poetry: Alan of Lille's "Anticlaudianus"*

nia, Physis, and Nature (as images of Theology, Physics, and Astronomy, respectively) effect "the composition of a soul from Endelechia and the edifying power of the virtues; the composition of a body by the conditioning of matter; and the formative uniting of the two, body and soul, through emulation of the order of the heavens" (p. 114), in whose firmament the "Table of Destiny" is inscribed with stars.[19] Alan's epic involves a larger cast of equally harmonious coworkers, including the Seven Liberal Arts, who construct the chariot by which Phronesis takes her flight and who endow the New Man with their respective gifts.

Confirmed in the possession of gifts of grace, wisdom, and virtue by a Fortune who acts contrary to her own habitual fickleness, the New Man is miraculous. Alan portrays him as a chivalric figure, bound by moral virtues "to defend widows, console the unhappy, support the needy, feed the destitute and befriend orphans" (p. 184). Equipped with "impressive nobility, illustrious lineage, free-born parents, unrestricted liberty, noble birth" (p. 193), as well as all the erudition of Sophia, he stands not only as a model for the young French king, Philip Augustus (and thus, as an image of the philosopher-king), but also as an emblem of the "new aristocracy" to which the scholars of the recently founded European universities laid claim.[20] Indeed, the whole *Anticlaudianus* may be seen as a celebratory, twelfth-century myth of the intellectual as the "new creation" of the new urban centers of learning, in which reformers placed their hope for social change through an educated elite. The conclusion of Alan's work depicts the New Man as a spiritual Aeneas whose good *fama* is true (p. 175) and who leads the personified forces of good victoriously against a host of vices: "Virtue rises, Vice sinks, Nature triumphs, Love rules" (p. 215).

As Simpson has brilliantly demonstrated, the first six books of the *Anticlaudianus* take their shape from the Aristotelian speculative sciences; the last three books, from the practical sciences. Through *involucra*, the poem as a whole becomes a *Bildungsroman*, which begins

---

and John Gower's "Confessio Amantis" (Cambridge: Cambridge University Press, 1995), p. 133.

[19] For a glossator's identification of the three figures with the three speculative sciences, see *Cosmographia*, trans. Wetherbee, p. 162 n75.

[20] See Simpson, *Sciences and the Self*, p. 291; Pearl Kibre and Nancy G. Siraisi, "The Institutional Setting: The Universities," in *Science in the Middle Ages*, pp. 120–44, esp. p. 121.

at the center of the work with the creation of the soul of the New
Man and its descent through the spheres and ends with what Winthrop Wetherbee has called the Chartrian "ascent 'per creaturas ad
creatorem' " of Phronesis, the highest faculty of the New Man's
soul.[21] At the same time, however, as Simpson insists, the practical
and political emphasis of the literal ending of the poem has its own,
indispensable value in the (in)formation of both the New Man and
the reader, who is challenged to discover the allegorical connection
between the two halves of the poem, and thus between the theoretical and practical sciences. The literary form of the poem is "cor-
relative with the form of the soul whose integration is imagined"
and designed not only to represent, but also to effect, that formation.[22]

As cultural symbols, the epics of Alan and Bernard stand beside the
encyclopedias and the *arbores scientiarum* of the twelfth and thirteenth
centuries. The educational epic, the encyclopedia, and the *arbor* all
envision the various arts and sciences as parts within a single whole
and as counterparts of natural entities, which are in turn known connaturally by the integrated human being. The harmonious interaction
of the personified *partes philosophiae* in the works of Bernard and Alan
reflect the balance, number, and hierarchical arrangement of the
philosophical schemes that underlie and contextualize their fictions.
The argument of these epics as (re)creation stories derives, moreover,
from a pedagogical theory that associated the *partes* of philosophy with
definite stages in the educational process.

The *Didascalicon* (c. 1127) of Hugh of St. Victor is especially close
to the works of Bernard and Alan in its delineation of philosophical
partes and in its sense of learning as a soul-journey. Fascinated by the
possibility of conceiving the whole of philosophy as an architectonic
structure erected through the power of number itself to define proportion, balance, equation, weight, and counterweight, Hugh, like Augustine before him, sought to harmonize the threefold scheme of the
Neoplatonists (ethics, physics, and logic) with the Aristotelian division

---

[21]   See Winthrop Wetherbee, *Platonism and Poetry in the Twelfth Century: The Literary Influence of the School of Chartres* (Princeton: Princeton University Press, 1972), p. 213.
Simpson's *Sciences and the Self* addresses in a powerful way the apparent disjuncture and
anticlimax that Wetherbee and others have found so problematic in Alan's two-part
poem.
[22]   Simpson, *Sciences and the Self*, p. 272.

of philosophy into theoretical, practical (and productive) branches.[23] The end result is a fourfold scheme accommodated to Hugh's larger vision of the pursuit of wisdom as a salvific path leading to the redemptive restoration in body and soul of a fallen humanity. As Hugh summarizes,

> there are four branches of knowledge only, and . . . they contain all the rest: they are the theoretical, which strives for the contemplation of truth; the practical, which considers the regulation of morals; the mechanical, which supervises the occupations of this life; and the logical, which provides the knowledge necessary for correct speaking and clear argumentation. (I.11, p. 60)

Treating logic last, as the fourth and the latest of the sciences to have been discovered, allows Hugh to find in the branches of knowledge a proof of the Pythagorean doctrine of the "quaternary number" of the soul (I.11, p. 60). "Number itself teaches us the nature of the going out and the return of the soul," Hugh explains, referring to four, numerically encoded "progressions" (II.4, p. 64). The number three (1×3) governs the first progression, whereby the soul "flows *from* the monad *into* [the] threeness" of concupiscence, wrath, and reason. The number nine (3×3) controls the second progression, whereby the soul enters the body with its nine apertures. The number twenty-seven ($3 \times 3 \times 3$), a cube number, rules the third progression of the soul, when it pours itself out "through the senses upon all visible things." Finally, the number eighty-one ($3 \times 3 \times 3 \times 3$) governs the soul's return at the end of a long, full life ($80 + 1$) to the "unity of its simple state, from which it had departed when it descended to rule a human body" (II.4, p. 65).

The four parts of philosophy thus correspond exactly to the four progressions of the soul as it descends into the body and earthly existence and returns from it. The circle of life coincides with what Giuseppe Mazzotta has called "the circle of knowledge."[24] The eighty-one of the fourth progression repeats the one of the first, even as

[23] See St. Augustine, *The City of God against the Pagans*, trans. David S. Wiesen, Loeb Classical Library (Cambridge: Harvard University Press, 1968), vol. 3, VIII.iii–vii, pp. 11–37.
[24] See Giuseppe Mazzotta, *Dante's Vision and the Circle of Knowledge* (Princeton: Princeton University Press, 1993).

logic, the fourth of the sciences, reiterates (and, broadly understood, can be identified with) dialectics or metaphysics, the first of the speculative sciences, in its approach to universals. The last of the arts to have been invented, logic serves as a necessary corrective for the metaphysical and ethical errors of the ancients, who "lacked discrimination in the use of words and concepts" (I.11, p. 58) as they searched into the causes of things and actions. A matter of use before it became a matter of art, logic is thus both an instrument and a part of philosophy, putting rational and linguistic art (dialectic, grammar, and rhetoric) at the service of speculative and practical philosophy.[25]

Hugh's treatment of the parts of philosophy was enormously influential. The *Didascalicon* "enjoyed continuous circulation from the time that it was written" and inspired multiple imitations.[26] As James A. Weisheipl has shown, "The period between roughly 1170 and 1270 was the high watermark for treatises on the nature and division of the sciences" (p. 474). In Spain, scholars such as Dominic Gundissalinus and Gerard of Cremona translated al-Farabi's *De scientiis* into Latin. Vincent of Beauvais's *Speculum doctrinale* includes "at least ten definitions and divisions of the sciences, drawn from earlier and contemporary sources" (p. 475). In the mid-thirteenth century, Nicholas of Paris, Arnulph of Provence, and John of Dacia produced treatises "to show beginners the scope and nobility of each science, and why it should be studied with diligence" (p. 479). The "most ambitious and astute consideration of the nature, scope and classification of the then-known sciences" (p. 478) was, however, the widely circulated thirteenth-century *De ortu scientiarum* of Robert Kilwardby, an English master of arts at Paris.

After Kilwardby's work, as Weisheipl indicates, "philosophers ceased to write treatises on the nature, scope, and classification of the sciences" (p. 479).[27] Weisheipl attributes this cessation, on the one

---

[25]   The question whether logic belongs to theory or practice, or whether it stands as a separate branch of philosophy, instrumental to all the others, is often debated in didascalic works. Boethius's first and second commentaries on Porphyry's *Isagoge* raise the issue without resolving it. See James A. Weisheipl, O.P., "Classification of the Sciences in Medieval Thought," *Mediaeval Studies* 27 (1965): 54–90, esp. p. 60.

[26]   Weisheipl, "Nature, Scope, and Classification," p. 474. Subsequent citations are parenthetical by page.

[27]   An important exception to Weisheipl's claim is the original work of Henry of Langenstein (d. 1397). Commenting on St. Jerome's division of philosophy into "theory, method, and practice," plus the minor, manual arts, in his Prologue to the Bible

hand, to the masterful completeness of Kilwardby's treatise, which seems to offer a last word on the subject; on the other hand, to a simple loss of interest: "For some reason, scholastics of the fourteenth century were no longer interested in writing this type of literature."

There are, however, other possible explanations. As Mazzotta has argued, medieval encyclopedias "are certainly repositories of knowledge, but they are also, and fundamentally, emblems (both a fact and a metaphor) of the belief in a unified order of the sciences and of the unity of knowledge."[28] In the later Middle Ages that belief was undermined as the curricula rapidly expanded, as pedagogical method shifted, and as the universities underwent structural change.

Dramatizing the Divisions of Knowledge: Quaestio *and* Disputatio

As Chenu notes, "in the entire pedagogical method described by Hugh of Saint-Victor in his *Didascalicon,* there is barely an allusion to the *disputatio.*"[29] By the middle of the thirteenth century, however, formal disputation had become the keystone of the scholastic approach, and the *quaestio* as such gave voice to what Mark Jordan has termed "a symphony of competing *sententiae,* competing voices, each sounding a different instrument differently."[30] The method of proposing a question for debate, of entertaining objections, and of providing *responsiones* not only characterized the exploration of issues proper to specific disciplines, but also turned reflexively on the very definition of the disciplines themselves and on their relationship to other branches of knowledge.

During the thirteenth and fourteenth centuries, the scholastic method and the actual historical embodiment of the different branches of philosophy in the *Realpolitik* of the university setting increasingly brought to the fore the discrepancy between the author-

---

(*Epistola* 53), Henry devised a "strictly symmetrical and dichotomous breakdown" that has "no precedent" in earlier *arbores.* See Nicholas H. Steneck, "A Late Medieval *Arbor Scientiarum,*" *Speculum* 50.2 (1975): 245–69.

[28]   Mazzotta, *Vision and Circle,* p. 5.

[29]   Chenu, *Nature, Man, and Society,* p. 294.

[30]   Mark D. Jordan, *Ordering Wisdom: The Hierarchy of Philosophical Discourses in Aquinas* (Notre Dame: University of Notre Dame Press, 1986), p. 65.

itative *arbores* and the actual curricular divisions, as well as the incon-
sistencies between the abstract order of the sciences and the actual
order of study. These differences were exacerbated by the turf-fighting
of the faculties over overlapping fields of content and application, and
the various battles for disciplinary autonomy and preeminence.

Institutional historians and the historians of individual disciplines
have called attention to some of the most famous of these quarrels,
which literally set into motion the traditional classifications. At the
institutional level, as Louis John Paetow and others have shown, different universities specialized in different fields of study—a process
that created conflicting hierarchies and fostered competition among
the rival urban centers. In his *Poetria nova* (c. 1198–1216), Geoffrey
of Vinsauf bears witness to the fame of Salerno for medicine, Bologna
for law, Paris for the arts (especially logic), and Orléans for the study
of classical authors.[31] The subsequent decline of humanistic studies at
Orléans inspired John Garland, a professor of grammar at Paris, to
champion the losing cause of the classics in his *Morale scholarium*
(1240). In Henri d'Andeli's famous allegory, *Bataille des set arts* (1250),
Grammar, the champion of Orléans, supported by the classical authors, does spirited battle with the forces under the command of Parisian Logic, only to suffer defeat in the end.[32] Mentioned prominently
among the Parisian enemies of letters in d'Andeli's *Bataille* and other
contemporary sources are the physicians and the lawyers.[33]

Although the classical *arbores scientiarum* mention medicine, if at all,
as one of the lowly mechanical arts and give short shrift to jurispru-
dence, medicine, law (civil and canon), and theology were firmly established as the three "superior" or graduate faculties at the various
medieval universities practically from the time of their inception. The
recognition of these superior faculties and the lucrative, vocational
attractions of law and medicine, in particular, profoundly affected the
configuration of the arts course, which came to be seen as inferior
and merely preparatory to the course of the higher studies.[34] As Je-

[31] Geoffrey of Vinsauf, *The Poetria Nova*, ed. Ernest Gallo (The Hague and Paris: Mouton, 1971), lines 1013–1017, pp. 66–69.
[32] See Louis John Paetow, *The Arts Course at Medieval Universities, With Special Reference to
Grammar and Rhetoric*, University of Illinois University Studies, vol. 3, no. 7 (Urbana-
Champaign: University Press, 1910), p. 509.
[33] Ibid., p. 517.
[34] See Kibre and Siraisi, "The Institutional Setting," esp. pp. 132–41.

rome Taylor adroitly remarks, "learning itself was making secularist adaptations."[35] Unlike the preeminence of theology, which had a definite theoretical basis in the Platonic and Aristotelian traditions, the preferment of medicine and law derived from pragmatic societal needs. The manifest utility of the latter disciplines affected theology, in turn, in complex ways.[36] The stage, in short, was already being set for the distinction Immanuel Kant was later to make in *Der Streit der Fakultäten* (1798) between "scholars proper" and the doctors, lawyers, and clergymen, whom he termed the "businessmen or technicians of learning," because of their public service and governmental regulation.[37]

Judging by the evidence of late medieval disputations, the discrepancy between these historical configurations and the traditional *divisiones* of the metaphysicians did not pass unnoticed.[38] The contest over the definition and ordering of the *divisiones scientiarum* eventually came to a head in the battles for preeminence among the higher faculties of theology, law, and medicine.[39] What was at issue was the Platonic One and the multiple ways it informed hierarchies within both the *arbores scientiarum* and the university community.[40] Although

[35] Jerome Taylor, Introduction to *Didascalicon*, p. 4.

[36] Henry of Langenstein's unique, fourteenth-century *arbor scientiarum* differs from its predecessors in dividing each branch of philosophy into its theoretical and practical dimensions. He thus distinguishes between theoretical theology and practical theology (pastoral, judicial, and liturgical). A principle of utility governs the whole scheme and, as Nicholas Steneck observes, Henry conceives of "the fruits of the arts in corporate terms," judging each branch of learning by its societal effect (p. 268). See "A Late Medieval *Arbor Scientiarum*."

[37] Immanuel Kant, *The Conflict of the Faculties*, trans. Mary J. Gregor (Lincoln: University of Nebraska Press, 1992), p. 25.

[38] In his commentary on Chapter 2 of Boethius's *De Trinitate*, for example, St. Thomas Aquinas asks whether "speculative science [is] appropriately divided into these three parts: natural, mathematical, and divine" and proceeds to list, and to respond to, ten objections to this Aristotelian/Boethian scheme, none of which are specious. See *The Division and Methods of the Sciences: Questions V and VI of his Commentary on the 'De Trinitate' of Boethius*, trans. Armand Maurer, 4th rev. ed. (1953; Toronto: Pontifical Institute of Mediaeval Studies, 1986), Q5.a1, pp. 9–24.

[39] For the battles between the lawyers and the physicians, see Beryl Rowland, "The Physician's 'Historial Thyng Notable' and the Man of Law," *ELH* 40 (1973): 165–78.

[40] Weisheipl points to a key effect of the Aristotelian additions to the curriculum: "With the introduction of the new disciplines, the temptation became increasingly great to see a hierarchical gradation of the sciences after the manner of Plato" ("Nature, Scope, and Classification," p. 476). A particular quarrel arose between the metaphysicians (Aquinas and Albertus Magnus) and the mathematically inclined physicists (Robert Grosseteste and Roger Bacon) over the Platonic identification of God with the number One (pp. 476–77).

the participants in these debates continue to use arguments reflecting a natural theory of knowledge and its divisions, the public spectacle of theologians defending theology, of politicians defending policy, and of physicians defending medicine inevitably served to underscore the relationship between the sciences and competing societal groups.

Theologians argued for the foremost position of theology on the grounds that the object of their study was the highest thing, God himself. As Aquinas, citing Aristotle, puts it in his commentary on Boethius's *De Trinitate,* "the most excellent science deals with the most excellent beings. But the most excellent science is divine science. Therefore, since immaterial and immobile beings are the most excellent, divine science will treat of them."[41] Elsewhere, in his commentary on Aristotle's *Metaphysics,* he argues that the science that exercises a person's highest faculty, his intellect, with respect to "the most intelligible beings" must be "the most intellectual and the director or mistress of the rest" of the sciences.[42]

In opposition to this view, an increasing number of writers argued for the preeminence of practical or moral philosophy, which subsumes law (under politics) and medicine (under the mechanical arts), and thus reinforced the political position of the medical and legal faculties. Among these writers were Peter of Abano, Robert Kilwardby, and Brunetto Latini, who argued for the primacy of medicine, ethics, and politics, respectively.

Peter of Abano (d. 1316), who taught at the universities of Padua and Paris in the late thirteenth century, argued that medicine was the first of the sciences, because its discovery antedated that of all the speculative sciences, and because it deals with the noblest of creatures, humankind. As Charles H. Talbot summarizes the debate, which involved 210 public disputations on the subject, the philosophers and theologians countered with *ad hominem* attacks on the characters of physicians and objected that "medicine was reducible to a form of divination, that it was a servile craft which plied for money, and finally, that it dealt solely with the mortal and corruptible body, a subject less noble than the soul with its spiritual faculties."[43]

---

[41] Aquinas, *Division and Methods,* Q5, a4, p. 49.
[42] Ibid., appendix 2, p. 97.
[43] Charles H. Talbot, "Medicine," in *Science in the Middle Ages,* p. 404.

In *De ortu scientiarum*, Kilwardby argued for the primacy of ethics on a triple basis, asserting (1) that the volitional pursuit of the Good is greater than the mere knowledge of the True, (2) that the will, rather than the intellect, is the more noble of the human faculties ("sicut voluntas est principium nobilius quam natura"), and (3) that "all the speculative sciences are ordered to the service of ethics."[44] Since, moreover, the pursuit of the Good entails the gaining of happiness, all the active sciences are similarly ordered toward, and serve, ethics. Thus, ethics or practical philosophy stands as the end of the whole of philosophy, the end of all the other ends: "Et ita finis ultimus quodammodo totius philosophiae est ethica moralis et finis eius ultimus finis omnium finium intentorum in philosophia et partibus eius" (I.xliii.409, pp. 142–43).

Brunetto Latini in his *Li Livres dou Tresor* (c. 1256) also argued for the preeminence of practical philosophy, but he, unlike Kilwardby, elevated politics over ethics. Brunetto divided the whole of philosophy into a three-part scheme: theoretical (which explores the being of things), practical (which instructs one in proper actions), and logic, which he defined narrowly as the art of argumentation, not as encompassing the whole of the trivium.[45] As Ruedi Imbach emphasizes, Brunetto regarded "die Politik als die höchste Wissenschaft" and treated under the heading of policy both the *artes mechanicae* and the verbal arts, giving special importance to rhetoric.[46] Not surprisingly, Aquinas was to refute this claim for the preeminence of politics among the sciences on the basis of the order of being. No man, not even the greatest king, is God; therefore, "Inconveniens est si quis politicam vel prudentiam aestimet esse scientiam studiosam, idest optimam, inter scientias, quod quidem esse non posset nisi homo esset optimum eorum quae sunt in mundo."[47]

---

[44] Robert Kilwardby, O.P., *De ortu scientiarum*, ed. Albert G. Judy, O.P., Auctores Britannici Medii Aevi IV (Oxford: British Academy, and Toronto: Pontifical Institute of Medieval Studies, 1976), I.xliii.405, p. 141. Translation mine.

[45] Brunetto Latini, *Li Livres dou Tresor*, ed. Francis J. Carmody (Berkeley: University of California Press, 1948), I.ii–v, pp. 18–22.

[46] Ruedi Imbach, *Laien in der Philosophie des Mittelalters: Hinweise und Anregungen zu einem vernachlässigten Thema* (Amsterdam: B. R. Grüner, 1989), p. 56. Latini actually includes "dialetique" in his scheme twice, under both "Practique" and "Logike," the second and third sciences of philosophy.

[47] *Sententia libri ethicorum*, 6, lect. 6, Leonina, t. xlvii, 2, 3526, 35–45; cited and quoted by Imbach, *Laien*, p. 57 ("It is improper for anyone to esteem policy or prudence as the science-most-to-be-studied, that is, as the highest of the sciences, because that simply

Brunetto Latini's Tresor *as Literary Emblem*

The last mentioned title in the debate over the primacy of the sciences, Brunetto Latini's *Tresor* is a late work at the end of a dying encyclopedic tradition; it nonetheless proved to be extremely popular, perhaps because it was the first encyclopedia to be written in a vernacular language.[48] His *Tresor* provides us with a touchstone for assessing and comparing the respective stances taken by Gower, Dante, and Chaucer in relation to literature of its kind.

Gower accords a remarkable importance to the *Tresor*, using it, in addition to Giles of Rome's *De regimine principum* and the pseudo-Aristotelian *Secretum secretorum*, as a principal source for Book VII of his *Confessio Amantis*, where Genius, at Amans's request, ostensibly departs from his appointed role as Venus's priest to summarize the whole of Aristotle's instruction of Alexander. As Elizabeth Porter has suggested, Gower deliberately revises Brunetto's treatment of rhetoric and policy in order to secure an all-pervasive, ethical emphasis in his philosophical scheme, similar to that found in Kilwardby's.[49] Like Brunetto, however, Gower accords a special importance to politics.[50] He equivocates, moreover, about the primacy of theology by making speculative philosophy ("Theorique") first and practical philosophy ("Practique") last, as alpha and omega terms, with "Rethorique" (not logic, as in Brunetto) standing as a prominent middle term within a triadic division of philosophy.

Of "keystone importance" for the *Confessio* as a whole, Book VII "returns us consciously to the problems of the Prologue."[51] As an encyclopedic book, it affords us what R. F. Yeager has called "a spectacle of the whole" in its survey of the divisions of knowledge, the plenitudinous scope of which mirrors the overview of the social estates

---

cannot be, unless humankind is the best of those beings which exist" [translation mine]).

[48] See Introduction to Brunetto Latini, *The Book of the Treasure*, trans. Paul Barrette and Spurgeon Baldwin, Garland Library of Medieval Literature, vol. 90, Series B (New York: Garland, 1993), p. ix.

[49] Elizabeth Porter, "Gower's Ethical Microcosm and Political Macrocosm," in *Gower's "Confessio Amantis": Responses and Reassessments*, ed. A. J. Minnis (London: D. S. Brewer, 1983), pp. 135–62, esp. p. 154.

[50] See Simpson, *Sciences and the Self*, pp. 226–28.

[51] R. F. Yeager, *John Gower's Poetic: The Search for a New Arion* (Cambridge: D. S. Brewer, 1990), pp. 278, 276.

in the Prologue.[52] Given this double philosophical and social perspective, Yeager appropriately compares "the view from the seventh Book of the *Confessio*" to that of "Dante the pilgrim contemplating the Celestial Rose at the end of the *Paradiso*" (p. 278). Going one step farther, Simpson convincingly treats the scientific survey in Book VII as the actual "frame" of the *Confessio*, which reveals "the whole poem outside Book VII [to be a] discussion of ethics and economics" and thus a preparation for the extended treatment of politics in the seventh book.[53] Gower's educational method, in short, challenges the reader to discover the hidden connection between the apparent digression and the subject matter of the other books, and thus the interrelationship among the three practical sciences.

In Book VII the relationship between the orders of knowledge and society is carefully drawn. Because "the lores been diverse" (VII.23), Genius begins to declare "the Scole ... / Of Aristotle" (3–4) to Amans with a *divisio* of philosophy into three branches: "Theorique," "Rethorique," and "Practique."[54] As Genius defines and unfolds their properties and subdivisions, he suggestively aligns them with separate social estates. "Theorique," Genius explains, is grounded on the Creator and his creation (31–32), and therefore concerns both things "noght bodely" (75) and "bodiliche thinges" (138). It includes "Theologie," "Phisique," and "Mathematique" (70–72), the latter of which is divided, in turn, into the quadrivium: arithmetic, music, geometry, and astronomy. The chief of the theoretical sciences, Genius emphasizes, is theology, which he associates with the clergy, the *oratores* of feudal social theory: "To this science ben prive / The clerkes of divinite, / The whiche onto the poeple prechen / The feith of holi cherche and techen" (121–24).

Genius then proceeds to illustrate the domain of theoretical philosophy by telling an extended story of creation out of chaos, which begins with a macrocosmic account of the four elements: earth, water, air, and fire (203–392), followed by a microcosmic treatment of the four humors (melancholic, phlegmatic, sanguinic, and choleric) in nature's constitution of the human body (393–489). God's creation

---

52 Ibid., p. 278.
53 Simpson, *Sciences and the Self*, pp. 223, 220.
54 Quotations from Book VII of Gower's *Confessio* are all taken from *The Complete Works of John Gower*, vol. 3, ed. G. C. Macaulay (Oxford: Clarendon Press, 1901). I cite line numbers parenthetically.

in the divine likeness of the soul, which governs the senses, establishes man, in turn, as steward over the earth, which is divided into three parts: Asia, Africa, and Europe (490–632). The earth and humankind are both governed (or at least influenced) by what stands above them—the seven planets, the stars, and the constellations. The main part of Genius's theoretical discussion, therefore, focuses on astronomy and astrology (633–1506), the natural counterpart of the heavenly science, theology.

Whereas theology is the province of the clergy, "Practique," the third of the philosophical divisions, "stant upon thre thinges / Toward the governance of kinges" (1649–50): ethics (self-rule), economy (household rule), and policy (rule of the kingdom). Genius thus explicitly associates practical philosophy with the aristocratic *bellatores* of feudal estates theory, especially the king himself, who governs the lower, "mechanical" classes, exercising his rule

> "In time of werre, in time of pes,
> To worschipe and to good encress
> Of clerk, of kniht and of Marchant,
> And so forth of the remenant
> Of al the comun poeple aboute,
> Withinne Burgh and ek withoute,
> Of hem that ben Artificiers,
> Whiche usen craftes and mestiers,
> Whos Art is cleped Mechanique."
>   (1685–93)

In these few telling lines, which sketch a societal, ruler-ruled analogue for the pairing of moral philosophy and mechanical art in abstract *arbores scientiarum*, Genius prepares the way for a lengthy discussion of the five virtues of policy—truth, liberality, justice, mercy, and chastity—each of which he illustrates with exemplary tales, among them, the tale of Virginia (5131–5306).

Between the extended treatments of theory and practice, Genius offers a relatively brief treatment of rhetoric as a separate branch of philosophy (1507–1640). The discussion departs radically from Brunetto's, substituting rhetoric for logic and emphasizing ethical rather than argumentative concerns. It presents rhetoric in such an unusual way that James Murphy has concluded that Gower knew little of Cicero.[55] The main point of Genius's treatment is that words are "vertuous" (1548), possessing a greater power ("vertu") than the "ston and gras" (1545) with which physics concerns itself, and that they have potent results in history, "wher so it be to evele or goode" (1549), stirring up discord among people or effecting their reconciliation:

> "Word hath beguiled many a man;
> With word the wilde beste is daunted,
> With word the Serpent is enchaunted,
> Of word among the men of Armes
> Ben woundes heeled with the charmes,
> Wher lacketh other medicine."
>
> (1564–69)

Using an incantatory anaphora to describe the verbal art of persuasion in quasi-magical terms, Genius creates a bridge between the material elements of natural philosophy and the moral realm of virtuous, kingly governance. Even more important, perhaps, Genius describes the rhetor and evokes the creative and destructive power of words in a way that harkens back to Gower's own pose in the Prologue as a new Arion, whose song brings about the reordering of the physical and societal world, recalling to virtue the clergy, the king, and the commons. If theology belongs to the *oratores* and policy to the *nobiles*, then rhetoric in a special way belongs to the poets.

If not to the poets, then to the peasants. Gower knew that unless the prophetic *vox clamantis* of social reformers were heeded, the voice of God would speak through the voice of the people in accord with the maxim, *vox populi, vox dei*—not, to be sure, in eloquent pleas, but in the shrieks of riot and rebellion.[56] The laborers who make up the third estate of feudal social theory have, in fact, no correspondent field of knowledge in Gower's pseudo-Aristotelian *arbor scientiarum*. The "mechanical" artisans are mentioned briefly, but they are described as skilled urban workers, not *agricultores*. The men of toil are

---

[55] James J. Murphy, "John Gower's *Confessio Amantis* and the First Discussion of Rhetoric in the English Language," *PQ* 41 (1962): 401–11.

[56] See my "Peasants' Revolt: Cock-crow in Gower and Chaucer," in *Four Last Things: Death, Judgment, Heaven, and Hell in the Middle Ages*, ed. Allen J. Frantzen, Essays in Medieval Studies 10 (Chicago: Illinois Medieval Association, 1994), pp. 53–64.

without education, without a voice, without a place. Thus, in the *Confessio* three estates may be said to remain, but the new "third estate" of literate merchants and urban "mechanicals" has pushed the original last estate off the scale. As Georges Duby puts it, "The three estates . . . [sit] high above an enormous mass of men bowed down in silence—forgotten."[57]

Written not long after the Peasant's Revolt and intended primarily as "instruction for the king," Gower's Book VII devotes disproportionate attention to policy, the treatment of which, as Yeager notes, "is more than twice the length of all the other sections combined."[58] The five points of policy offer, as Russell Peck observes, "remedy for all vice" and thus "reach magnetically into [the] preceding tales" and back to the Prologue's depiction of societal disarray.[59] Cast imaginatively into the part of Alexander, Amans begins to rediscover himself as a king who is called to order the kingdom of his own soul and thus to bring harmony into the world around him. The antiquity and all-inclusiveness of his instruction, for which Brunetto Latini's *Tresor* stands as an emblem, harkens back to the Golden Age that Gower depicts in the Prologue as a distant, and perhaps irrevocable, ideal of social and scientific unity.

Brunetto Latini and his *Tresor* have a very different emblematic function within Dante's *Commedia*. Dante the pilgrim encounters and immediately recognizes "ser Brunetto" (*Inf.* 15.30) among the sodomites in the third ring of the seventh circle of hell.[60] Brunetto greets Dante affectionately, calling him "my son" (15.31, 37: "o figliuol mio," "o figliuol"). Dante, for his part, treats Brunetto with reverence, walking beside him with "head bent low," honoring the memory of his "kind, parental image" (15.44, 83), and thanking him for all that he has taught him. Dante's first words to Brunetto, which describe his "going astray within a valley" (15.50–51), echo the beginning of both Dante's *Commedia* and Brunetto's *Tesoretto*. Brunetto's last words to Dante name his *Tesoro* and identify the work with his

57   Duby, *The Three Orders*, p. 356.
58   Yeager, *John Gower's Poetic*, pp. 275, 269.
59   Russell Peck, *Kingship and Common Profit in Gower's "Confessio Amantis"* (Carbondale: Southern Illinois University Press, 1978), p. 142.
60   Here and throughout I use *The Divine Comedy of Dante Alighieri*, trans. Allen Mandelbaum (New York: Bantam, 1982).

own immortality as an author: "Let my *Tesoro*, in which I still live, be precious to you; and I ask no more" (15.119–20).

The whole encounter is carefully staged to make Brunetto, not unlike the Ulysses of *Inferno* 26, an alter ego for the Dante of the *Convivio*, who, guilty of intellectual presumption, had fallen in love (to echo Patrick Boyde) "with a fully elaborated system of thought which was at once philosophical and theological, and which claimed to be universal and certain."[61] Brunetto's company in hell includes clerics "and men of letters and of fame" (15.107: "e literati grandi e di gran fama") representing various disciplines, among them, the grammarian Priscian and Francesco d'Accorso (d. 1293), who had been a professor of law at the universities of Bologna and Oxford. Brunetto prophesies that Dante, the most gifted of his students, will achieve a similar fame and honor (15.70), and Dante credits Brunetto with having taught him "how man makes himself eternal" (15.85) through writing learned books.

As Mazzotta remarks, however, the aim of Brunetto's education, "to teach man how he can make himself eternal, is at odds with the whole point of Dante's own journey."[62] Dante's poetry sets the literary afterlife of Brunetto's *Tesoro* against Brunetto's own afterlife in hell, and that juxtaposition not only undercuts Brunetto's concept of immortality as vain and self-deluding, but also exposes the latent, intellectual sodomy in encyclopedic thought. "Patently enough," as Mazzotta observes, "the claim of a total knowledge is a logical contradiction, because it reduces knowledge to a static and sterile ensemble and excludes the possibility of augmenting it" (p. 31). Such a claim, moreover, makes the educational process narcissistic by definition, because it leads the pedagogue to fashion his student into a clone of himself, a mere repository of his own imparted knowledge.

Brunetto evidently views Dante in this way. He not only begs Dante to hold his *Tesoro* dear and prophesies fame for his student; but he also predicts for Dante an exile from Florence like his own.[63] Mazzotta

---

[61] Patrick Boyde, *Dante: Philomythes and Philosopher* (Cambridge: Cambridge University Press, 1981), p. 26.

[62] Mazzotta, *Vision and Circle*, p. 176. Citations hereafter are parenthetical by page.

[63] Brunetto, a prominent figure in civil affairs, was exiled from Florence from 1260 until 1267, when he returned to the city. Dante was banished from Florence in 1301, never to return.

aptly characterizes Brunetto "as a figure who narcissistically stresses his priority over his disciple, who can come to terms with his disciple's destiny only as a version of his own, and who believes that Dante's extraordinary adventure is already written in Brunetto's own script" (p. 32). Dante, however, insists upon the open-endedness of Brunetto's prophecy, submitting it as a "text" to be commented upon, and interpreted by, Beatrice (*Inf.* 15.88–90),[64] and asserting his readiness to accept whatever Fortune has prepared for him.

As critical as Dante is of Brunetto's encyclopedic program, he does not and cannot disassociate himself from it completely. Brunetto is and remains a father-figure for him, and Brunetto's love for knowledge and quest for fame have their counterparts in Dante's own intellectual formation and poetic ambitions. To Dante, however, as Mazzotta remarks, "Brunetto's and the encyclopedic texts of the thirteenth century were bound to appear . . . as a symptom of mere nostalgia for a unified culture at a critical time when that spiritual unity was about to disintegrate" (p. 32).

In the end, Dante's response to Brunetto Latini is as complex as his treatment of his own philosophical pursuit. Dante the pilgrim greets Brunetto and Ulysses eagerly, but leaves them behind him in hellish torment; at the entrance to Purgatory, he takes momentary comfort in hearing Casella sing his own canzone in praise of Lady Philosophy (*Purg.* 2.112), only to be rebuked by Cato for doing so; finally, in the Earthly Paradise, a chastened and penitent Dante answers Beatrice's demand by confessing his former enslavement to the false pleasures of *temporalia* (*Purg.* 31.34–36) and the seductions of secular philosophy (33.85–87). Yet, despite this strong pattern of philosophical critique, there is (in Boyde's words) "no escaping the fact that the author of the *Comedy* is a repentant sinner but an unrepentant intellectual."[65] Charles Martel recites for Dante in the sphere of Venus the canzone "Voi che 'ntendendo il terzo ciel movete" (*Par.* 8.37) upon which Dante comments in the second book of the *Convivio*. The Beatrice who guides the pilgrim Dante "from heaven to heaven in the *Paradiso* . . . delivers no less than five major philosophical discourses in the first seven cantos,"[66] and, as Mazzotta and others

---

[64] Cf. Mazzotta, *Vision and Circle*, p. 176.

[65] Boyde, *Philomythes and Philosopher*, p. 39.

[66] Ibid.

have argued, the *Commedia* as a whole "is organized by a steady pattern of references to the disciplines of the curriculum."[67]

Dante's poem thus both is, and is not, an encyclopedia. Most obviously, Dante counters the static categories of the *divisiones philosophiae* by dramatizing through dialogue and journey the subjectivity and historicity of the learning process. "The intrusion of subjectivity," as Mazzotta observes, "contradicts the idea of a mere objective, forever fixed knowledge arranged according to the arbitrary principle of alphabetical order and/or the neatly divided juxtaposition of entries" (p. 13). In this respect, Boethius and his *Consolation of Philosophy* were Dante's teachers.[68] Beyond this, Dante's radical solution to the problem of the impossibility of confining knowledge within any sort of *summa* is to explode those confining limits along a vertical axis extending beyond the merely rational into the imaginative, the visionary, and the divine. In this regard, Dante's *Commedia* recalls the epic poetry of Bernard and Alan. It literally subsumes all of knowledge into poetry and thus suggests, in Mazzotta's words, "that all knowledge may be imaginary" (p. 33).[69]

In so doing, however, Dante actually creates another kind of philosophical *summa*, at the peak of which is the poetry of mystical language that, by definition, both asserts and breaks its own limits and stands as an emblem for the supreme knowledge that is love. The Celestial Rose that Dante beholds at the close of the *Paradiso* is at once both a vitally alive *arbor scientiarum* and an organic image of a celestial society, whose ranks and rows of saints both exhibit perfect order and hierarchy and transcend those divisions through ecstacy. As Gellrich and others have noted, Dante explicitly likens the Rose to an encyclopedic book, in whose depths he sees "—ingathered, and bound by love into one single volume [*legato con amore in un volume*]—what, in the universe, seems separate, scattered" (*Par.* 33.85–87).[70] Dante's open, voluminous Rose thus answers to the closed book of Brunetto by simultaneously imitating and surpassing its comprehensiveness.

---

[67] Mazzotta, *Vision and Circle*, p. 33. See also *The "Divine Comedy" and the Encyclopedia of Arts and Sciences*, ed. Giuseppe Di Scipio and Aldo Scaglione (Philadelphia: John Benjamins, 1988).

[68] See "Dante's Boethian Beatrice," in my *Job, Boethius, and Epic Truth* (Ithaca: Cornell University Press), pp. 156–60.

[69] See Simpson's treatment of "The Place of Poetry Among the Sciences" in *Sciences and the Self*, pp. 230–71.

[70] See Gellrich, *Idea of the Book*, pp. 160–61.

The Ellesmere Tales: *Planetary Pilgrimage and the*
Divisions of Knowledge

Whereas Gower in the *Confessio* looks backward to classical "tyme passed" (Prologue, line 94) for an emblem of social and scientific plenitude, Dante looks down to hell and up to heaven, juxtaposing the *Tresor* of Brunetto and the Rose of Beatrice and Bernard as opposed images of summation. Chaucer's encyclopedic vision, on the other hand, tends to be horizontal, rather than vertical; immanent, rather than transcendent; focused on the present, rather than on the ancient past or the paradisaical afterlife. All three poets exhibit an impulse toward plenitude. Less optimistic than Gower, Chaucer shares Dante's sense that encyclopedias like Brunetto's offer a false picture of the order of knowledge and of things; he takes a critical view, however, of Dante's eschatological solution, which makes enormous truth-claims for a transcendent poetry that absorbs every other discipline, including theology, into itself.[71] In the *Canterbury Tales* Chaucer answers Dante, in effect, by challenging the extent of Dante's supposed disavowal of philosophy. Adapting the planetary paradigm Dante himself sketches in the *Convivio*, Chaucer systematically exposes the philosophical underpinnings of Dante's *Paradiso*, and on that basis Chaucer reopens the world of Dante's seemingly all-inclusive vision to commentary and debate. Whereas Dante the pilgrim submits Brunetto Latini's "text" to Beatrice's commentary, Chaucer submits Dante's text to interpretation by his assorted pilgrims. Chaucer, in short, brings Dante's heaven back to earth.

In the *Convivio* (a work certainly known to Chaucer, probably already at the time when he composed the *House of Fame*),[72] Dante declares, "By 'heaven' I mean knowledge, and by 'heavens' the various sciences."[73] He proceeds to elaborate on the following general analogy:

---

[71] Karla Taylor emphasizes that "the *Commedia* carries traditional truth-claims to a unique extreme," whereas Chaucer's *House of Fame* and *Troilus and Criseyde* display a marked "ambivalence toward authentication" (*Chaucer Reads "The Divine Comedy"* [Stanford: Stanford University Press, 1989], p. 45).

[72] See Howard H. Schless, *Chaucer and Dante: A Revaluation* (Norman, Okla.: Pilgrim Books, 1984), esp. pp. 75–76. Scholars most frequently point to Chaucer's elaboration of the theme of "gentilesse," which is the subject of *Convivio* IV.

[73] Dante, *The Banquet*, trans. Christopher Ryan (Saratoga, Calif.: ANMA Libri, 1989), II.xiii, p. 66. Subsequent citations are parenthetical by book, chapter, and page.

To the first seven heavens correspond the seven sciences making up the Trivium and the Quadrivium: Grammar, Dialectic, Rhetoric, Arithmetic, Music, Geometry, and Astronomy. To the eighth sphere (the Sphere of the Stars) corresponds natural science, called Physics, and the first science, called Metaphysics; to the ninth sphere corresponds moral science: and to the heavens at rest corresponds the divine science, called Theology. (II.xiii, p. 67)

Dante thus associates the seven Ptolemaic planets—the Moon, Mercury, Venus, the Sun, Mars, Jupiter, and Saturn—with the seven liberal arts, respectively, and he does so in two imagistic contexts. The first, announced in the opening lines of the *Convivio*, is that of quest and pilgrimage: "As the Philosopher says at the beginning of the *Metaphysics*, all men naturally desire to possess knowledge. This can, and should, be traced to the fact that every human being has a drive inherent in its own nature directing it toward its own perfection" (I.i, p. 13). The second context, signaled in the title of the work, is that of a banquet in which knowledge is shared among people, even as bread is broken: "Since every man is by nature a friend of every other man, and every friend is grieved by a deficiency in the one he loves. . . . I now intend to respond to their want by providing a full-scale banquet of the food I displayed before their eyes" (I.i, p. 14).

Chaucer's Ellesmere *Tales* engages Dante's *Paradiso* systematically from the threefold perspective that Dante suggests in the *Convivio*. Using an outline closely resembling Gower's in Book VII of the *Confessio*, Chaucer effects a topical matching of the branches of philosophy to the planetary spheres in his exemplary stories and story-blocks. He aligns the succession of topics with a path of philosophical and geographical pilgrimage. Finally, he establishes a convivial context for the whole in the exchange between and among pilgrims, for which the promised reward is "a soper at oure aller cost" (GP 879).

Unlike the Dante of both the *Convivio* and the *Paradiso*, however, Chaucer embraces the open-endedness of debate, *quaestio*, and competition as a means of testing the limits of closed systems of knowledge and of knowing, at last, how little we know. Although both Dante (in the figures of Brunetto and Ulysses) and Gower (in those of Ulysses and Nectanabus) acknowledge, in the words of Simpson, that knowledge of the sciences can be "inimical, or at least obstructive" to self-knowledge, fostering pride rather than humility,[74] they nonetheless share an optimistic belief in the compatibility of the two through the assistance of the proper guide (a Beatrice or a Genius instructed by Aristotle) and the establishment of an appropriate hierarchy of the sciences that gives primacy either to a theological poetics (Dante) or to an ethical politics (Gower).

Chaucer, too, affirms the compatibility of science and self-knowledge, but in an ironic way that calls for multiple, comically misleading teachers, representing all the branches of philosophy, whose fullsome, often contradictory instruction ultimately disappoints and thus readies the soul to learn in silence from the Augustinian *magister internus*—a learning that depends less on the active desire to know and to be filled with information than on the passive longing to be known by God and others in one's emptiness, limitation, and need. In the end, Chaucer's pilgrims listen to the Parson, and Chaucer himself models repentance in his "retracciouns." Whereas Gower points to ethics and politics, both Dante and Chaucer point toward theology, albeit in divergent ways. Dante's theology, like Alan's, is mystical, speculative, and poetic; Chaucer's, on the other hand, is moral, practical, and prosaic. Whereas the Dante of the *Commedia* aspires to see God, the Chaucer of the *Tales* asks in the end only to be seen and judged mercifully by him.

To that humble self-knowledge, all have access. Like Gower's Prologue (in its survey of Rulers, the Church, and the Commons) and like Dante's description of the Celestial Rose, Chaucer's General Prologue presents an array of learners and teachers. A social *speculum*, Chaucer's colorful "compaignye / Of sondry folk" (GP 24–25) includes ideal representatives of all the traditional estates and pays appropriate attention to the "condicioun," "degree," and "estaat" of its members (GP 38, 40, 716). As we have seen, Gower's assembled estates mirror the Aristotelian divisions of knowledge in Book VII; and Dante's Rose, peopled with saints, both offers a review of Dante's previous learning in the spheres of Paradise and finds its infernal antitype in Brunetto's infernal *Tresor*. Similarly, Chaucer's *compilatio* of tales represents a philosophical *summa* analogous to the societal one presented in the General Prologue. Reading the *Tales* "like a clerk," we see that the Ellesmere arrangement of story-blocks reflects

[74] Simpson, *Sciences and the Self*, p. 204.

and exemplifies traditional philosophical *divisiones* and is keyed to a chiastic pattern of planetary descent and ascent from Saturn to the sublunary earth and back again.

There are, as we have seen, important precedents for such a pattern in didascalic works known to Chaucer and his clerical audience: Scipio's dream-flight among the stars, Philologia's celestial ascent, Boethius's homeward journey on Philosophia's wings, Hugh of St. Victor's fourfold progression of the soul, the journeys of Nature and Urania in the *Cosmographia* and of Phronesis in the *Anticlaudianus*, and Dante's planetary voyages in the *Convivio* and the *Paradiso*. Each of these literary precedents, moreover, somehow connect a heavenly journey with the educational process and the *partes philosophiae*.[75]

"The Knight's Tale" suggests and inaugurs such a sequence through its pronounced employ of planetary deities, the original rulership it grants to Saturn (the highest and most distant of the seven planets), and its Boethian echoes. In particular, its lengthy evocation of the "faire cheyne of love" (I.2988), which corresponds to the golden chain of Homer in Macrobius's *Commentary* and Bernardus's *Cosmographia*, sets into motion a pattern of planetary and narrative descent that plays itself out in the linked tales of the first fragment. "The Miller's Tale" stands under the influence of Jupiter—the god who in Ovid's *Metamorphoses* orders the Hesiodic equivalent of Noah's flood, and the planet whose sphere, according to Macrobius, imparts to the descending soul a concupiscence and a power to act (*praktikon*) correspondent to Nicholas's handyness.[76] "The Reeve's Tale," told by a rancorous pilgrim, illustrates the wrathfulness of Mars and the "bold spirit" (*thymikon*) his planetary influence imparts. The "Cook's Tale" (unfinished in Fragment I and unspoken in Fragment IX) dissolves in a drunkenness that corresponds to the "intoxication" that Macrobius associates with the soul's approach to, and exit from, the Apollonian sphere of the Sun, which imbues the soul with sense perception and imagination (*aisthetikon* and *phantastikon*).

---

[75] See Myra L. Uhlfelder, "The Role of the Liberal Arts in Boethius' *Consolatio*," in *Boethius and the Liberal Arts: A Collection of Essays*, ed. Michael Masi (Las Vegas: Peter Lang, 1981), pp. 17–34. She discerns a circular structure in the work, keyed to educational levels.

[76] For Macrobius's discussion of the planets' influence on the soul, see *Commentary* I.xii.13–14, pp. 136–37. Stahl notes that the doctrine was "very popular in the Middle Ages" (p. 137 n23).

The overt Boethian and astrological concerns of "The Knight's Tale"—divine foreknowledge, predestination, human freedom, the eternity of the Creator, and the mutability of creation—are the familiar topics of a Christian "first philosophy." Even the Miller, who voices an initial response to "The Knight's Tale," singles out and comically continues the theme of "Goddes pryvetee" (I.3164), using a phrase that aptly sums up that branch of philosophy. Metaphysical concerns are especially appropriate to the tales under the influences of Saturn, Jupiter, and Mars, the planets farthest from the earth, which are grouped together in Neoplatonic texts to mirror the triadic unfolding of the monad into reason, concupiscence, and wrath prior to its emanation into matter.[77] The earthy Town and Gown conflicts in "The Miller's Tale" and "The Reeve's Tale" highlight, by way of contrast, the esoteric nature of metaphysical inquiry and underscore the epistemological questions that return in the dramatized truth-telling of the Manciple's Prologue and Tale.

Whereas Fragments I and IX engage metaphysical concerns, Fragments II and VIII, on the other hand, may be said to exemplify physics, the "second philosophy," especially as it concerns the science of matter and its particular subtopics: the four elements, activity and passivity, elemental combination and alteration, and the related question of the conversion of spiritual substances. The tales in these story-blocks, paired through chiasmus, are the only tales in the collection that deal overtly with the conversion of pagans to Christianity, pagan/Christian marriage, and alchemical processes. Such physical, alchemical, and spiritual concerns are, as we shall see, especially appropriate to the sphere of the fourth planet, "the brighte sonne" (II.1), to which the introduction to "The Man of Law's Tale" calls special attention.

Fragments III–IV–V and Fragment VII, also paired through chiasmus in the Ellesmere order, both concern themselves with the verbal arts—in particular, the trivium (in the "Marriage Group") and the Aristotelian causes of books (in the "Literature Group"). Positioning the "logic" of these story-blocks between the speculative concerns of first two sets of tales (metaphysics and physics) and the practical concerns of Fragment VI recalls Gower's tripartite *divisio* ("Theorique, Rethorique, Practique"), as well as Kilwardby's treatment of the verbal

---

[77]   See *Didascalicon* II.4, p. 65; Macrobius, *Commentary* I.vi.42, p. 108.

arts as a "neutra pars philosophiae," with both speculative and practical aspects.[78] The tales in these fragments are appropriately and explicitly associated with the crossing orbits of Venus and Mercury, the fifth and sixth planets, to which the Wife of Bath calls special attention as she charts her quarrel with clerks in the Prologue that initiates the first sequence of tales. Passage near these planets, according to Macrobius, impresses upon the soul amatory passion (*epithymetikon*) and the ability to speak and interpret (*hermeneutikon*), respectively.

The pattern of descent ends in the sublunary realm of Fragment VI, which begins with a speech by Nature reminiscent of Alan de Lille; which features a virginal heroine akin to the moon goddess; and whose paired stories share a unique focus on disease and death. In the Macrobian scheme, the moon imparts *phytikon*, which empowers the soul to mold and enliven the mortal body into which it enters as a temporary dwelling. The tales that comprise Fragment VI, at the sublunar center of the pattern of descent and ascent, exemplify the practical concerns of the "third philosophy," as it was embodied in the superior faculties of the university: law, medicine, and pastoral theology. In this story-block, as in Gower's Book VII, the tale of Virginia exemplifies an aspect of policy. "The Physician's Tale" and "The Pardoner's Tale" depict the administration of unjust justice and impotent physical and spiritual remedies, and they do so appropriately in the sublunar sphere.

Against this fragment, and indeed the whole of the philosophical journey leading to and from it, stands "The Parson's Tale," grounded not on human reason but on revealed truth, whose systematic exposition of the seven deadly sins and of the remedies appropriate to each offers a wholesome pastoral theology and a divinely normed moral philosophy. Paradoxically, the movement away from the lunar center of the Ellesmere *Tales*, and the analogous movement away from the corrupt "practique" of legal, medical and clerical practitioners, ends not in a return to Saturn and Neoplatonic metaphysics, but beyond it, in the higher, plainer truth of "Cristes gospel" (GP 481), as it was taught and lived by a humble pilgrim. "The Parson's Tale" and the imminent arrival of the pilgrims at Becket's tomb thus bring together the circular, planetary soul-flight and the linear earthly journey at a common point of heavenly home-going.

---

[78] See Kilwardby, *De ortu scientiarum* I.lxii.623, p. 212.

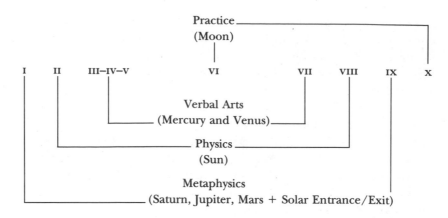

That the Ellesmere tale-order and its division into fragments accommodate such a philosophical scheme and support an overarching pattern of planetary pilgrimage helps to explain the clerical
reception of the *Tales* as a *compilatio* which could fittingly be attributed to the Chaucer whom Deschamps had praised as an English
Socrates. Whether such an order comes about purely as a learned,
editorial response to the Parson's plea for "correccioun" by "textueel" clerks (X.56–57), or whether it results from correctly naming
the parts Chaucer himself had arranged, the very existence of the
Ellesmere *compilatio* depends on an elided act of co-authorship that
allows Chaucer actually to accomplish what he had imagined himself doing in the *House of Fame*—namely, following in the traces of
philosophical poets such as Alan de Lille, Martianus, Boethius, and
most importantly, Dante.

As we shall see, Chaucer's pilgrim's progress through what Chauncey Wood has called the "country of the stars"[79] and his simultaneous
passage through the divisions of knowledge place him in especially
close company with Dante, with whom he carries on a lively, intertextual dialogue that includes points of agreement, exposition, amplifi-
cation, inversion, and disagreement. Indeed, the planetary and
philosophical itinerary we have just sketched in broad outline allows
us literally to locate Chaucer's *Tales* in relation to both Dante's *Pa-*

[79]   Chauncey Wood, *Chaucer and the Country of the Stars: Poetic Uses of Astrological Imagery*
(Princeton: Princeton University Press, 1970).

radiso and Gower's *Confessio Amantis* in unprecedented ways that reveal the high stakes involved in the Canterbury story-telling contest as a contest of poets, each of whom confronts and continues the tradition of encyclopedic poetry in a different way.

Darker in his epistemological assumptions than his philosophical predecessors, Chaucer leaves the stars and the eternal truths they symbolize still visible, but at a greater distance from his pilgrims than they were for Bernard's Urania and Dante's Beatrice. Arguably nominalist in his aesthetic, he gives individual examples rather than personifying abstractions and allows others to specify the categories they illustrate. Playfully skeptical, he entertains the *quaestiones* and admits among his clerical pilgrims the very rivalries that were undermining the authority of the *arbores scientiarum* at the universities. In so doing, however, he evokes precisely those encyclopedic structures of thought whereby the fragments he creates become meaningful precisely as *partes*, as units to be numbered, dramatized, divided against one another, and ultimately added together to form a *summa*.

There is no doubt that the rising and the aspect of the stars have a great effect on the works of nature and art.

—Saint Albert the Great

3

FROM SATURN TO THE SUN:

PLANETARY PILGRIMAGE

IN FRAGMENTS I AND IX

A commonplace of Chaucerian criticism regards the closely linked tales in the first fragment of the *Canterbury Tales* as patterned by a rapidly descending order—generic, stylistic, thematic, quantitative, and societal.[1] Although Chaucer's addition of Saturn in "The Knight's Tale" has excited considerable commentary, no one has drawn a correlation between the descending narrative order in the Fragment and the Ptolemaic order of the planets.[2] Interpreting the first story-block "like a clerk," this chapter argues that Chaucer connects the journey of his pilgrims to that of the soul by linking each stage in the soul's descent to a separate tale.[3] As we shall see, the dominant planet in each of the first four spheres significantly shapes the narrative action and themes of the tale with which it is associated. The planetary pattern is, in fact, so firmly established in Fragment I that it provides the key for the entire Ellesmere arrangement.

[1] For a summary statement, see Donald Howard, *The Idea of the "Canterbury Tales"* (Berkeley: University of California Press, 1967), p. 265.
[2] For a useful critical overview, see Alan T. Gaylord, "The Role of Saturn in the *Knight's Tale*," *Chaucer Review* 8 (1974): 171–90.
[3] As I indicate in the Preface, Colleen Reilly's seminar paper, which argued this Macrobian thesis at my suggestion, has served as an important background to this chapter. With her kind permission, I have drawn several passages and references from it.

According to Macrobius, the soul's journey involves its initial descent from the Supreme One to the Mind to the World-Soul, and from there, through the seven celestial spheres to the earth, and finally into the human body.[4] In this process, the soul is exposed in turn to the influence of each sphere's governing planet: Saturn, Jupiter, Mars, the Sun, Venus, Mercury, and the Moon. From them, the soul "acquires each of the attributes which it will use later" (I.xii.13, p. 136):

> In the sphere of Saturn, it obtains reason and understanding, called *logistikon* and *theoretikon*; in Jupiter's sphere, the power to act, called *praktikon*; in Mars' sphere, a bold spirit or *thymikon*; in the sun's sphere, sense-perception and imagination, *aisthetikon* and *phantastikon*; in Venus' sphere, the impulse of passion, *epithymetikon*; in Mercury's sphere, the ability to speak and interpret, *hermeneutikon*; and in the lunar sphere, the function of molding and increasing bodies, *phytikon*. (I.xii.14, pp. 136–37)

As William H. Stahl notes, the Neoplatonic doctrine expressed in this passage "became very popular in the Middle Ages."[5] Chaucer certainly knew it from Macrobius and other sources, notably Alan de Lille, Bernard Silvestris, and Dante.

In using a planetary pattern of descent to order the narratives in Fragment I (and, by clerical extension, the whole of the Canterbury collection), Chaucer endeavored to make his "book of the tales of Caunterbury" a literal reflection of "thilke large book / Which that men clepe the hevene," in which everyone's life-story has been "ywriten . . . / With sterres" (II.190–92), and thus to link the progress of his pilgrims with that of the wandering stars. Not without irony, Chaucer allows his worst literary critic, the Man of Law, to suggest unwittingly the very scheme that he employs. Paraphrasing a passage from Bernard Silvestris that Chaucer's own Latin gloss provides in the margin, the Man of Law finds the "strif of Thebes"—a partial subject of "The Knight's Tale"—to have been "writen" in the "sterres" long

---

[4] I use Macrobius, *Commentary on the Dream of Scipio*, trans. William H. Stahl (New York: Columbia University Press, 1952, repr. 1990), I.xii, pp. 133–37. Hereafter citations are parenthetical.

[5] Ibid., p. 137 n23. Among other sources, see Dante, *Purgatorio* 18.46–75 and 16.67–81 and *Paradiso* 4.49–63.

ago, along with many other tales that the dullness of "mennes wittes" prevents them from reading (II.197–203).

Chaucer's imagistic and structural use of "the book of the heavens" in the *Canterbury Tales* puts the work as a whole, and Fragment I in particular, in dialogue with major controversies in the closely related fields of late medieval speculative science. Indeed, interpreted from a clerical point of view, the tales in Fragment I may be said to exemplify those controversies through the philosophical *quaestiones* that are first raised by the overt astrological *influentia* in "The Knight's Tale," and then responded to, in turn, by the tales of the Miller, Reeve, and Cook.

The Fictions of Astrological Debate

As Paola Zambelli explains, the thirteenth-century translations of the *libri naturales*, which included Aristotle's astrological treatises, as well as numerous other Greek and Arabic works, gave rise to a serious conflict between the astrologers and the theologians. At first a commonly accepted discipline, astrology was regarded as a special branch of astronomy, the highest of the mathematical sciences, and thus a "middle science" between physics (natural philosophy) and metaphysics. In 1264 Gerard of Feltre, a Dominican, wrote his *Summa de astris*, in which he attacked astrological doctrine as blasphemously incompatible with Christian teaching on free will. In opposition, his fellow Dominican, Albert the Great, penned his famous *Speculum astronomiae* in defense of astrology as a legitimate science beneficial to Christian belief.[6] The controversies between the theologians and the astrologers escalated, leading in 1277 to the condemnation of numerous astrological doctrines by Bishop Étienne Tempier. The matter was far from closed, however, and as Lynn Thorndike has shown, the contest came to a head a second time in the later fourteenth century when Nicolas Oresme (d. 1382) joined forces with Henry of Hesse to attack the astrological arts of their time.[7] At issue in these disputations

---

[6] See Paola Zambelli, *The "Speculum Astronomiae" and Its Enigma: Astrology, Theology, and Science in Albertus Magnus and His Contemporaries* (Dordrecht: Kluwer Academic Publishers, 1992), esp. pp. xiv, 3, 51–59.

[7] Lynn Thorndike, *A History of Magic and Experimental Science*, 8 vols., History of Science Society Publications, n.s. 4 (New York: Columbia University Press, 1934), 3:398.

were weighty theological matters: in the words of Tullio Gregory, "God's foreseeing vs. freedom, fate vs. contingency, universal order vs. evil and disorder."[8]

These astrological debates were widely known outside of university circles. William Langland's Dame Study refers to Albert the Great in connection with astronomy and alchemy and calls the former subject a "hard þing and euil for to knowe."[9] John Gower's treatment of astronomy in Book VII of *Confessio Amantis* offers a virtual epitome of the debate. The Latin quatrain heading the section affirms both the principle of planetary influence ("Lege planetarum magis inferiora reguntur") and the wise man's ability through grace to master the stars: "vir mediante deo sapiens dominabitur astris."[10] The English verses that follow outline the various positions taken on the subject. The natural philosopher, "which is an Astronomien" (650), holds that the stars determine the "stat of realmes and of kinges" (646), "Bot the divin seith otherwise" (651), defending free will. On the other hand, barring a miraculous suspension of the laws of nature, there can be "non obstacle" (661) to the working of natural "lawe original" (658) in God's creatures.[11] The difficulties involved in upholding both free will (human and divine) and natural causality are reflected in Gower's use of the adversative conjunction "bot" three times in only eleven lines.

Beginning with the Saturnine "Knight's Tale," Chaucer's Fragment I transforms the logic of astrological debate into a narrative series and thus exemplifies it. Like Dante in the *Convivio*, Chaucer makes "the heaven of Saturn" a symbolic *locus* for the sciences of astronomy and astrology.[12] Like Oresme and Gower, Chaucer associates this particular

---

[8] Quoted by Robert S. Cohen, "Editorial Preface," in Zambelli, *Speculum Astronomiae*, p. x.

[9] William Langland, *Piers Plowman: The A Version*, ed. George Kane (London: Athlone Press, 1960), XI.155.

[10] John Gower, *Confessio Amantis*, in *The Complete Works of John Gower*, vol. 3, ed. G. C. Macaulay (Oxford: Clarendon Press, 1901), Book VII, p. 250, between lines 632 and 633. Hereafter I cite line numbers parenthetically.

[11] According to Edward Grant, even astrology's most vigorous opponents agreed that "the motions and natures of celestial bodies affected the behavior of sublunar animate and inanimate bodies" (p. 288). The "major sources of terrestrial effects" in the heavens were "motion, light, and 'influence' (*influentia*)" (p. 289). See his "Cosmology," in *Science in the Middle Ages*, ed. David C. Lindberg (Chicago: University of Chicago Press, 1978), pp. 265–302.

[12] Dante, *The Banquet*, trans. Christopher Ryan (Saratoga, Calif.: ANMA Libri, 1989), II.xiii, p. 70.

division of knowledge especially with the nobility, whose privileged status and tenuous good fortune dispose them to make anxious inquiry into the celestial motions that turn Fortune's "false wheel" (I.925).[13] Not only does Chaucer assign to the Knight the most overtly astrological and chivalric of the tales; but he also portrays the Theban princes as acutely sensitive in suffering and action to planetary control. In addition, he introduces Duke Theseus as the architect of an amphitheatre containing zodiacal oratories, one of them ornamented with an astrological "image" in the technical sense of geomancy (an occult art in which both Richard II and Henry V's brother, Humphrey, duke of Gloucester, showed keen interest).[14]

Exemplifying the astrological *quaestiones*, "The Knight's Tale" deals overtly with the themes of "destinee" (I.1663), "purveiaunce" (I.1665), "prescience" (I.1313), divine "governance" (I.1313), planetary control, "necessitee" (I.3041), and the chain that binds the elements, descending through the planetary spheres from the unmoved "Firste Movere" (I.2987) whose immutable decree firmly establishes "Certeyne dayes and duracioun / To al that is engendred in this place" (I.2996–97). The only freedom it ambiguously allows is to "maken vertu of necessitee" (I.3041).

As many have noted, the tales of the Miller, Reeve, and Cook respond to "The Knight's Tale." Whereas the Knight offers a pagan model of the universe that exceeds the cosmology of Albert the Great in its necessary order, symmetrical proportions, astral determinism, and admission of horoscopy and geomancy, "The Miller's Tale" limits its explorations of "Goddes pryvetee" (I.3164, 3454, 3558) to the generally accepted practice of meteorological interrogations; mocks gullible fools like John, who give too ready credence to astrologers like Nicholas; and points to the "privee" science of Alison's private parts as a more accessible domain of knowledge. In "The Reeve's Tale," astrological science is reduced to arithmetical measurement

---

[13]   In a treatise of seven chapters, the *divisio* of which is "perhaps an unconscious recognition of planetary influence," Oresme launched a societal attack on "the excessive devotion of princes to astrology and divination," in which he pointed to its dire consequences for them and their subjects. See Thorndike, *History of Magic and Experimental Science*, 3:400–401.

[14]   See Vincent J. DiMarco's note on line 2045 of "The Knight's Tale" in *The Riverside Chaucer*, ed. Larry D. Benson, 3d ed. (Boston: Houghton Mifflin, 1987), pp. 836–37; Jeanne E. Krochalis, "The Books and Reading of Henry V and His Circle," *Chaucer Review* 23 (1988): 56, 58–59.

and, as E. D. Blodgett has observed, what is "privee" there is only what is stealthily stolen—flour and sex; in "The Cook's Tale," finally, "pryvetee" becomes paradoxically public, accessible, and for sale, because prostituted.[15]

The Town and Gown contests in the tales of the Miller and Reeve pit the "lerned" against the "lewed" and thus internalize their tellers' quarrel with the Knight's esoteric metaphysics. John the Carpenter fears that Nicholas's preoccupation "with his astromye" (I.3451) and inquiry into divine secrets have driven him mad, and he considers himself fortunate to be "a lewed man / That noght but oonly his bileve kan!" (I.3455–56). Nicholas, on the other hand, confidently employs his Oxfordian astrolabe and clerical wiles to "bigyle" (I.3300) the carpenter, who becomes in the end the village laughing-stock, "For every clerk anonright heeld with oother" (I.3847). In "The Reeve's Tale," the "lewed" miller takes the initiative to trick the "sely clerkes" (I.1490) of Cambridge, quoting the proverb: " 'the gretteste clerkes been noght wisest men' " (I.4054). When the miller challenges John and Aleyn to employ scholastic "argumentes" in order to transform his "streit hous" (I.4122) into a more spacious place, he does not foresee that their *disputatio* with him will, in fact, find sufficient "places" for rebuttal, and that his "argument of herbergage" will have, as the Cook says, a "sharp conclusion" (I.4328–29). The technical terminology used by the miller and the Cook explicitly likens the Reeve's plot of clerical entry into, and exit from, a "hous" to the mathematical calculation of planetary movement and domicile.[16]

The possible *determinatio* of truth, even proverbial truth, from these dramatized disputations is, however, increasingly undermined as the fragment descends to the Cook's oxymoronic "sooth pley, quaad pley" (I.4357). Although the three fabliaux substitute cunning and chaotic action for the contemplative mood and restricted order of the Knight's epic romance, they are, as we shall see, also under the plan-

---

[15]   E. D. Blodgett, "Chaucerian *Pryvetee* and the Opposition to Time," *Speculum* 51.3 (1976): 477–93.

[16]   Chaucer uses the word "herberwe" in an astronomical sense in "The Franklin's Tale" (V.1035); Gower uses the word "herbergage" to speak of Saturn's domicile in Aquarius (*Confessio Amantis* VII.1187–89). Chaucer uses the word "argumentis" in the sense of astronomical calculation in *A Treatise on the Astrolabe, Supplementary Propositions* 44, *Riverside Chaucer*, p. 682.

etary influence of Chaucer's scheme of descent from Saturn to the Sun—a larger context that undermines the apparent freedom they represent and raises troubling epistemological issues about what is and remains "derne": divinity, planetary influence, adultery, fraud, a host of hidden or unconscious motives, and all the remote causes of things.

Saturn and "The Knight's Tale"

Chaucer's Knight incorporates into his narrative the planetary deities of all seven spheres, although not all of them figure in Chaucer's sources. Most notably, Saturn, the superior planet in the scheme outlined by Macrobius and his sources, appears only in Chaucer's version of this story. In addition to the well-known roles assumed by Saturn, Jupiter, Venus, Mars, and Diana (representing the Moon), Mercury also takes part, appearing to the semi-delirious Arcite with the urgent command: "To Atthenes shaltou wende, / Ther is thee shapen of thy wo an ende" (I.1391–2), and fiery Phoebus announces the first of May, the day of the heated battle between Palamon and Arcite in the forest, with streams of light (I.1493–96). Mercury's role in inciting Arcite to return to Athens is also unique to Chaucer, suggesting a deliberate effort on his part to provide roles for all the planetary deities of the Ptolemaic system. As Lois Roney observes, moreover, "These are the only gods who actually appear in the tale."[17] Thus, the first tale in the *Canterbury Tales* stands as a kind of introduction to the planetary themes that Chaucer will explore in more detail in subsequent tales, even as it gives first place to Saturn as the first of the gods and the most distant planet.[18]

In dealing with the sphere of Saturn as a symbolic location, Chaucer faced the same challenge that confronted Dante in the *Paradiso*. As the most distant planet from the earth, "it was closest to God, and hence most godlike"; whereas, from the point of view of the astrologers, "it was the worst of all planets—the great malefic."[19] As Richard

---

[17]   Lois Roney, *Chaucer's Knight's Tale and Theories of Scholastic Psychology* (Tampa: University of South Florida Press, 1990), p. 81.

[18]   This paragraph draws upon one in Colleen Reilly's seminar paper.

[19]   Richard Kay, *Dante's Christian Astrology* (Philadelphia: University of Pennsylvania Press, 1994), p. 218.

Kay has brilliantly argued, Dante resolved this quandary through a "simple inversion of values," whereby the worldly misfortunes associated with Saturn—"exile, famine, impotence, and poverty"—become the ascetic virtues of monks who leave the world to embrace "a life of fasting, chastity, and apostolic poverty."[20] In a monastic environment, cruel Saturn becomes the kindly god of a Golden Age, "that dear king whose rule undid all evil" (*Par.* 21.27).[21]

In assigning an explicitly Saturnine tale to the virtuous Knight, Chaucer imitates this Dantean strategy of inversion. Following the lead of Saint Bernard, the High Middle Ages had, after all, closely assimilated the monastic and chivalric ideals in the form of knightly orders, such as the Knights Templar, and generally viewed the hardships of the crusades as opportunities for the laity to embrace a penitential practice akin to that of the monks.[22] As Jill Mann has suggested, the Knight's many mortal battles fought "for oure feith" and against the "hethen" (GP 62, 66), his love of "trouthe and honour, fredom and curteisie" (GP 46), his maidenly gentleness, and his ascetical attire imbue his figure with what Jean Leclercq has called the "Crusader mystique."[23] Furthermore, as Robert Kaske has demonstrated, the asceticism of Chaucer's Knight offers a blatant contrast to the worldiness of the "outridere" Monk (GP 166), whose portrait echoes his.[24] The figure of the monkish Knight, like the "reule of Seint Maure or of Seint Beneit" (GP 173), thus provides a standard for the judging the Monk's conduct, even as the speeches of Dante's monastic saints, Peter Damian and St. Benedict, call to task the corrupt monks for whom Benedict's "Rule is left to waste the paper it was written on" (*Par.* 22.74–75).

The distant, military expeditions of the Knight, who has "riden, no man ferre, / As wel in cristendom as in hethenesse" (GP 48–49),

---

[20] Ibid.

[21] I quote from *Paradiso: The Divine Comedy of Dante Alighieri*, trans. Allen Mandelbaum (New York: Bantam, 1986).

[22] See my *Job, Boethius, and Epic Truth* (Ithaca: Cornell University Press, 1994), pp. 165–72.

[23] Jill Mann, *Chaucer and Medieval Estates Satire* (Cambridge: Cambridge University Press, 1973), pp. 108–15; Jean Leclercq, "Saint Bernard's Attitude toward War," *Studies in Medieval Cistercian History* 2, ed. John R. Sommerfeldt (Kalamazoo: Cistercian Publications, 1976), pp. 31–32.

[24] Robert E. Kaske, "The Knight's Interruption of the Monk's Tale," *ELH* 24 (1957): 249–68.

associate him, moreover, with both Christian pilgrimage and the mythical exile of Kronos-Saturn, whose "planet indicated long journeys from home."[25] As one of the older, authoritative pilgrims, and the only father traveling with his son, the Knight is markedly Saturnine in his piety, given the commonplace astrological connection between Saturn and "elders, especially in familial relationships."[26] The Knight, moreover, explicitly images himself as a farmer, and thus as a Saturnine narrator: "I have, God woot, a large feeld to ere, / And wayke been the oxen in my plough" (I.886–87).[27]

Unlike Dante's Saturnine cantos (*Par.* 21–22), however, Chaucer's "Knight's Tale" comes at the beginning, not the end of his fictive journey. Starting at Saturn's height, Chaucer does not conclude a pattern of ascent, but rather initiates a pattern of descent.[28] Whereas Dante's *Paradiso* uses Jacob's Ladder as an emblem for the monastic saints climbing the *scala perfectionis*, whom the Pilgrim encounters in Saturn's sphere, Chaucer's "Knight's Tale" introduces the Neoplatonic "faire cheyne of love" (I.2988) as an emblem for the order of being, "descendynge so til it be corrumpable" (I.3010).[29]

As what Joseph Westlund has called "an impetus for pilgrimage," the Saturnine "Knight's Tale" functions as a starting point for both the linear, literal pilgrimage to Canterbury and the circular, planetary journey into and out of the world.[30] Reconciling these two opposed itineraries requires Chaucer simultaneously to identify and disassociate the points of origin and destination. He accomplishes this in "The

---

[25]   Kay, *Dante's Christian Astrology*, pp. 219, 241.

[26]   Ibid., p. 228.

[27]   On the basis of his chivalric function, J. D. North tentatively describes the Knight as a Martian, rather than a Saturnine, figure, but he admits that the "Christian chivalric tradition of Chaucer's England was . . . difficult to fit perfectly with the ethos of the countries of origin of the astrological writings Chaucer was using, and we must tacitly assume similar qualifications to our analogy generally" (*Chaucer's Universe* [Oxford: Clarendon Press, 1988], p. 506). North's treatment of the horoscopes of the pilgrims (pp. 506–12) is frequently slightly off the mark because he fails to relate the General Prologue portraits of the pilgrims to their respective tales and links.

[28]   As Blodgett has noted, "The sense of order that Theseus provides . . . is vertical, and the view is downward," even as "the series of descents that conclude the *Knight's Tale*" initiates a pattern of unbroken descent throughout the first fragment. See "Chaucerian *Pryvetee*," pp. 485, 489. Dante provides a summary, retrospective view of the seven planets, as seen from above, in *Par.* 22.139–47.

[29]   For a treatment of Dante's use of Jacob's Ladder, see Kay, *Dante's Christian Astrology*, p. 219.

[30]   Joseph Westlund, "The *Knight's Tale* as an Impetus for Pilgrimage," *PQ* 43.4 (1964): 526–37.

Knight's Tale" by assigning to the Christian Knight a lofty, pagan romance, whose melancholy speeches and Saturnine images of imprisonment, exile, stonework, and wilderness, support a rational, philosophical inquiry into the causes of things, divine and human, that falls short of Christian revelation. Chaucer, in short, begins his tale collection with the highest planet and Aristotelian "first philosophy," but he does so in a way that implies the impossibility of ending there. The Macrobian attribute of *logistikon*, which "The Knight's Tale" exemplifies in repeated attempts to mediate rationally between the forces of concupiscence and wrath, love and strife, yields alternatively to the chaos of the one or the other, even as "The Knight's Tale" as a whole is succeeded by the Miller's and the Reeve's.

Recent scholarship has called attention to the pervasive Saturnine coloring of "The Knight's Tale." There the influences of the other planet-gods are all systematically subordinated to that of Saturn, whose "cours, that hath so wyde for to turne, / Hath moore power than woot any man" (I.2454–55). J. D. North has shown that all of Chaucer's astrological additions to, and alterations of, his source reflect "the need for a totally new form of astrological consistency" that attributes power over particular events to Saturn, whose "chilling speech must be counted the astrological centre of the entire poem."[31] Similarly, Peter Brown and Andrew Butcher call Saturn's speech "a key to the mechanisms of the tale," wherein "Saturn is revealed as the controlling force."[32]

Chaucer must have found the *Teseida* especially amendable in its basic elements of plot and setting to a Saturnine revisioning. As Kay reminds us, the myth of Kronos-Saturn included his exile and imprisonment, even as Saturnians were prone to repeat his suffering.[33] The Theban princes held captive by Theseus in Athens clearly endure both these torments, which Arcite explicitly attributes to "som wikke aspect or disposicioun / Of Saturne" (I.1087–88). Later Arcite is released from prison, but exiled from Athens, and the division of Saturnine fates between the cousins intensifies their rivalrous obsession over Emelye.

---

[31] North, *Chaucer's Universe*, pp. 409, 412.

[32] Peter Brown and Andrew Butcher, *The Age of Saturn: Literature and History in the "Canterbury Tales"* (Oxford: Basil Blackwell, 1991), pp. 212–13. See pp. 212–23 for a discussion of Saturn's comprehensive influence in the tale.

[33] Kay, *Dante's Christian Astrology*, pp. 219, 226.

As V. A. Kolve has eloquently demonstrated, through Chaucer's artistry the juxtaposition of two scenes—Emelye in the garden and the princes imprisoned in the tower above her—becomes a controlling image for the tale as a whole in its exploration of Boethian themes. Through what Kolve calls the "grave and beautiful metamorphosis" of the prison/garden,[34] the garden is transformed into the wild and wooded grove, where the princes duel; the bestial grove becomes, in turn, the walled amphitheatre of civilized tournament; the stony amphitheatre then becomes the passage back into the oaken grove for Arcite's burial; and finally, that same grove resumes gardenlike features when Palamon, still garbed in the "blacke clothes" (I.2978) of mourning, is betrothed to Emelye. These symbolic locations are all Saturnine. According to Kay, "Prisons . . . had long been associated with Saturn because of Kronos' legendary imprisonment, and by extension many astrologers mention other forms of captivity as well, such as physical restraint by shackles, manacles, and chains."[35] Chaucer's Saturn himself declares, "Myn is the prison in the derke cote" (I.2457). The other sites most frequently linked to Saturn as an agricultural deity were "wild and savage landscape[s]," on the one hand, and tilled and fruitful fields and gardens, on the other.[36]

The tale's protagonists, moreover, exhibit various Saturnine qualities. In speech after speech, Arcite and Palamon show themselves to be genuine Saturnians, who are, as Kay relates, "at least inclined to be gloomy and habitually unhappy (tristis), if they are not reduced to actual sorrow (dolor) and lamentation."[37] As Brown and Butcher emphasize, however, Arcite's melancholy affliction with "the loveris maladye" (I.1373) singles him out as Saturn's special victim long before his actual death due to specifically Saturnine causes.[38] The servile status to which Arcite is reduced in Theseus's household is also a Saturnine fate, according to Kay.[39] As Walter Clyde Curry noted long ago, the infection that takes Arcite's life is attributable to Saturn, and

[34] V. A. Kolve, *Chaucer and the Imagery of Narrative: The First Five Canterbury Tales* (Stanford: Stanford University Press, 1984), p. 86. Kolve discusses Saturn's influence in the tale on pp. 123–26.

[35] Kay, *Dante's Christian Astrology*, p. 226.

[36] Ibid., p. 225.

[37] Ibid., p. 222.

[38] Brown and Butcher, *Age of Saturn*, pp. 221–23.

[39] Kay, *Dante's Christian Astrology*, pp. 227–28.

Lycurgus, Palamon's ally, exhibits Saturnine features in his appearance.[40] Egeus, the "olde fader" of Theseus, represents the planet-god's age and gloomy wisdom, declaring, "Deeth is an ende of every worldly soore" (I.2849). The Amazonian chastity of Hypolita, Emelye's chastity, and the long-suffering chastity of her princely lovers are also appropriately Saturnine, given the planet's reputed frigidity and the god's mythological castration.[41]

Chaucer's "Knight's Tale," however, reserves to Theseus and Saturn himself the Saturnine attributes deriving from a specifically Neoplatonic tradition. Like Dante, who associates monastic contemplatives with Saturn, Chaucer follows Macrobius and the astrologers in identifying Saturn's sphere with *logistikon*, the power to think ("cogitationis vis"), to reason, and to search into "things that are hidden or concealed," especially "God's secret reasons for predestination."[42]

This Neoplatonic tradition, which gains expression in Macrobius, Chalcidius, Remigius of Auxerre, Hugh of St. Victor, and others, associates passage through the first three planetary spheres with the unfolding of the tripartite soul, as it extends itself from its "simple essence, symbolized by the monad, . . . into a virtual threeness, in which it desires one thing through concupiscence, detests another through wrath, and judges between these two by reason."[43] The quality of reason, *logistikon*, descends from the divine Mind itself, and thus belongs to the first and highest sphere, Saturn's.

In "The Knight's Tale," the godlike Theseus exemplifies this rational quality on the human level as he repeatedly takes counsel within "his gentil herte" (I.1772) to determine the best course of action. He mediates between the forces of love and hate, represented first in the plight of the grieving Theban women and then in the bitter quarrel between Arcite and Palamon, both of whom are in love with Emelye. On the divine level, Saturn himself mediates between the claims of Mars and Venus, the archetypal representatives of wrath and concupiscence and the patrons of the opposed princes.

---

[40]   Walter Clyde Curry, *Chaucer and the Mediaeval Sciences*, rev. ed. (1926; New York: Barnes and Noble, 1960), pp. 134–37, 139–46.

[41]   Kay, *Dante's Christian Astrology*, p. 231.

[42]   Ibid., p. 239.

[43]   Hugh of St. Victor, *Didascalicon*, trans. Jerome Taylor (New York: Columbia University Press, 1961, repr. 1991), II.4, pp. 64–65. See also p. 200 n29.

In the end, not action but Saturnian logic, in the limited sense of the literal fulfillment of prayers and promises, governs all the outcomes in the tale. There is something perversely Stoic in the identification of the *logos* of the universe with a cruel linguistic logic whereby, on the one hand, all prayers are perfectly answered, and on the other, as Arcite laments, "We witen nat what thing we preyen heere" (I.1260). Unlike the Father of the Gospels, who does not give a scorpion to the son who asks for an egg, nor a snake to the child who asks for a fish (Luke 11:11–12), Saturn gives bad, but nominally justified, gifts, thus proving himself supreme among the "crueel goddes" that govern the world with the fatal binding of a "word eterne" (I.1303–4).

In order to still the conflict between Venus and Mars, Saturn must allow them to keep their promises to their proteges. In order to reconcile the requests of the knights and the promises of their deities, Saturn must discover the way in which all that has been asked and promised is completely compatible. As a result of the contradictions or omissions in the pleas of both knights, Saturn is able to fit the two seemingly opposing requests together in one scenario, which in strictly logical terms fulfills all the stated requirements. Saturn thus resolves the conflict between the planetary deities and determines a proper earthly outcome, one which follows a higher order and neither precisely conforms to, nor blatantly violates, the earthly order arranged by Theseus. Arcite wins the contest, is almost immediately killed, and gives Emelye over to Palamon just before he dies. The gods apparently are pleased with this outcome, and the people, though disturbed, attribute the resolution to a higher order that is inconceivable to them.[44]

Although Theseus attributes final causality to a stable "Firste Moevere" (I.2987), whom he calls "Juppiter, the kyng" (I.3035), there is, as Blodgett asserts, "no proof in the tale that the Knight's world is anything other than Saturn's."[45] Even if there is a divine mover behind Saturn (as astrological theology affirms), that leaves open both the problem of the virtual identification of the First Cause with the malignant, secondary cause (and thus, of divine benevolence) and the related issues of limited human knowledge and freedom. As Kolve

---

[44]   The language of this paragraph echoes Colleen Reilly's seminar paper.
[45]   Blodgett, "Chaucerian *Pryvetee*," p. 487.

aptly puts it, "In 'The Knight's Tale,' 'Jupiter' is not a name for the Christian God."[46] The tale achieves an ordered universe, but only at the cost of imposing a pervasive "necessitee" on gods and human beings alike, even when they are apparently free and unaware of their control by causes prior to themselves.

Jupiter in "The Miller's Tale"

Jovian causality in "The Miller's Tale" is more veiled than Saturn's in "The Knight's Tale." The god Jupiter does not appear as a protagonist; rather, the distant but overarching influence of the planet Jupiter is evidenced allusively in the tale through an analogy between the Miller's requital of the Knight and the god Jupiter's usurpation of Saturn; parallels between the Miller's portrait and traditional portraits of Jupiter; the pervasive, absent presence of the flood; and the emphasis in plot and characterization on a handiness correspondent to Jovian *praktikon* in Macrobius's descending scheme. Finally, the general sense of hilarity and poetic justice, which are so pervasive in "The Miller's Tale," also links it with the planet Jupiter's traditional influence and effect.

As countless scholars have noted, the Miller includes in his "noble tale" (I.3126) elements in plot, language, and theme so similar to those in the Knight's "noble storie" (I.3111) that "The Miller's Tale" serves as the Miller's churlish requital of the narrative and ideology of his social superior, the Knight.[47] The Miller does more than simply tell a humorous story; he insinuates that the Knight's cleverly constructed romance conceals the earthy motives underlying his characters' behavior: the desires for sex and ownership that result in jealous competition between young men. Indeed, the bum-burning fabliau of "The Miller's Tale" may be said to castrate the epic romance of "The Knight's Tale" symbolically by cutting away its powerfully decorous trappings and civilized, chaos-ordering artifice.

[46]   Kolve, *Chaucer and the Imagery of Narrative*, p. 150.
[47]   As Peggy Knapp observes, "It is a critical commonplace that the Miller's tale requites the Knight's by replicating its formula—a woman under the guardianship of an older man sought by two young lovers—but debasing its tone and direction" (*Chaucer and the Social Contest* [New York: Routledge, 1990], p. 34). See p. 41 for echoes of "The Knight's Tale" in "The Miller's Tale." I thank Colleen Reilly for this note.

Chaucer disposes his clerical readers to anticipate the Miller's Jovian challenge to the sovereignty of the Knight's Saturn through ambiguous references to Jupiter in "The Knight's Tale." Despite Saturn's actual control over all the action, the humans in that tale mistakenly view Jupiter as the ruler of the universe. Deficient in his understanding of the celestial realm, Theseus calls Jupiter "the kyng, / That is prince and cause of alle thyng" (I.3035–36). Although Theseus's conception of Jupiter conforms to traditional views of the god's power, Jupiter's real influence over the outcome "of alle thyng" in "The Knight's Tale" is almost nonexistent. The narrator only describes Jupiter directly one time, when Jupiter attempts unsuccessfully to end the dispute between Venus and Mars: "swich strif ther is bigonne . . . That Juppiter was bisy it to stente" (I.2437–42). In "The Knight's Tale" Saturn succeeds where Jupiter fails.[48]

Chaucer was certainly familiar (through the *Romance of the Rose*, lines 6270–75) with the mythic, father-son rivalry between Saturn and Jupiter, which led to Saturn's castration.[49] Casting the usurpatious Miller comically in the role of Jupiter, Chaucer portrays him in a manner that departs significantly from, even as it recalls, earlier Jovian portraits. Chaucer's Miller, in short, numbers among those imaginary figures whom Jean Seznec has called the "hybrid descendants" of classical originals.[50]

As Kay indicates, the mythological and astrological association of Jupiter with air (aër = Hera), "which the Greeks understood to be composed of the qualities of wetness and hotness," tended to link him with musical instruments, among which Dante, in his Jovian cantos, mentions the bagpipe and the lute in particular (*Par.* 20.22–27, 142–43).[51] The Miller is described as bagpipe player (GP 565), a musician of sorts, and his hero Nicholas plays "a gay sautrie" (I.3213), just as the Jupiter of Martianus's *Marriage of Philology and Mercury* is a musician who plays a nine-stringed lyre.[52]

[48] For this and the following paragraph, I am indebted to Colleen Reilly.

[49] See Jean Seznec, *The Survival of the Pagan Gods: The Mythological Tradition and Its Place in Renaissance Humanism and Art*, trans. Barbara F. Sessions (New York: Pantheon Books, 1953), p. 236.

[50] Ibid., p. 238. See also Ernest H. Wilkins, "Descriptions of Pagan Divinities From Petrarch to Chaucer," *Speculum* 32.3 (1957): 511–22.

[51] Kay, *Dante's Christian Astrology*, pp. 189, 197.

[52] See *Martianus Capella and the Seven Liberal Arts: The Marriage of Philology and Mercury*, vol. 2, trans. William H. Stahl and Richard Johnson (New York: Columbia University

Jovian air, heat, and wetness, moreover, traditionally linked both the god and the planet with thunderstorms and floods. Not unlike "Jupiter, that maketh the thondre rynge" (*TC* 2.233), the Miller speaks loudly in "Pilates voys" (I.3124), and his hero Nicholas lets "fle a fart, / As greet as it had been a thonder-dent" in answer to Absolon's romantic plea, "Spek, sweete bryd" (I.3805–7).

Much more important to "The Miller's Tale" than the Jovian attribute of thunder, however, is the god's association with flood waters. Kay notes that "Jupiter's wetness is acknowledged by extensive water imagery" in Dante's Jovian cantos, and that "the most notable water image" (found in *Par.* 19.58–63) "compares divine justice to the sea," the depths of which "are beyond human knowing."[53] Chaucer's "Miller's Tale" similarly connects the theme of our limited human knowledge of "Goddes pryvetee" (I.3558) with images of "reyn," "shour," drowning, and deep waters "walwynge as the see" (I.3517, 3520, 3616)—even as it comically foregrounds John's ignorance of the "ful privee" (I.3201) amorous plots and activity of Nicholas and Alison.

The impending recurrence of "Nowelis flood" (I.3818), which hangs over the action of Chaucer's tale, recalls an equally destructive flood in classical myth and effects a virtual identification between Jupiter, that flood's divine originator, and the Judeo-Christian God who began the biblical flood.[54] In Ovid's *Metamorphoses*, Jupiter desires to destroy all humankind for their sins and chooses a flood, rather than fire, as his destructive means: "He preferred a different punishment, to destroy the human race beneath the waves and to send down rain from every quarter of the sky."[55] Similarly, in "The Miller's Tale," the Lord God warns that "al the world with water sholde be lorn" (I.3536).

Although Nicholas cites "Cristes conseil" (I.3508) as the origin of

---

Press, 1977), p. 25. For a treatment of musical elements in the tale, see Robert Boenig, "Absolon's Musical Instruments," *ELN* 28 (1990): 7–15.

[53] Kay, *Dante's Christian Astrology*, pp. 188–89.

[54] The association of the two floods was common. As Zambelli notes, Albertus Magnus compares the floods of Noah and Deucalion under the heading of "universal deluges" in *De causis proprietatum elementorum*, a treatise concerned with astrometeorology and meteorological interrogations of the sort Nicholas practiced. See *Speculum astronomiae*, p. 98.

[55] Ovid, *Metamorphoses*, trans. Frank Miller, Loeb Classical Library (London: Heinemann; Cambridge: Harvard University Press, 1921), I.260–61, p. 21.

his information about the flood, he also states that he has "yfounde" the information "in myn astrologye" (I.3514). Nicholas thus invents a flood which, by his own account, has both Christian and celestial origins. Employing his "astrelabie, longynge for his art" (I.3209) to self-serving ends, Nicholas points to the planetary heavens as the book wherein he reads the secrets he imparts to John the Carpenter. Indeed, the opening lines of the tale emphasize "astrologye" (I.3192), the forecast of "droghte or elles shoures" (I.3196) and the prediction of other events, in a way that encourages a clerical interpretation of the tale as a whole from a planetary perspective.

Interpreted as a tale exemplifying the spiritual influence exerted upon the soul as it descends through the sphere of Jupiter, "The Miller's Tale" is remarkable in both plot and characterization for its emphasis (in Macrobian terms) on "the power to act, called *praktikon*" (I.xii.14, p. 136). As Charles Muscatine reminds us, "The Miller's Tale" displays the generic "preference for action" typical of the fabliau to such an extent that "the fabliau's preference for physical action becomes an ethical imperative."[56]

The oft-repeated epithet "hende Nicholas" (I.3199, 3272, 3386, 3397, 3401, 3462, 3487, 3526), applied to its chief protagonist, encapsulates the tale's active emphasis. Plotting and planning in the body of the tale are followed by immediate action, not the negotiation and compromise which controls the action in "The Knight's Tale." For example, the reader of "The Miller's Tale" first learns of Nicholas's attraction to and his desire for Alison through his direct physical advances toward her. "Hendy" Nicholas handles his desire first through decisive action (I.3274: "And prively he caughte hire by the queynte") and then through some token verbal persuasion (I.3288: "This Nicholas gan mercy for to cry")—active strategies that Palamon and Arcite would never even dream of employing. Having gained Alison's adulterous consent, ". . . right anon, withouten wordes mo, / This Nicholas no lenger wolde tarie" (I.3409–10), but rather he immediately goes up to his chamber to enact his plan to trick John. In the end, confronted by Nicholas's success and Alison's mockery, even the love-sick Absolon acts and reacts. In response to the unsavory kiss he has received from Alison, he immediately puts aside his obsessive

---

[56] Charles Muscatine, *Chaucer and the French Tradition: A Study in Style and Meaning* (Berkeley: University of California Press, 1957), p. 224.

love for her and directly puts into action a plan to "quite" Alison by going to the smith Gerveys, obtaining the "hoote kultour," and returning to Alison's window to take his revenge (I.3746–89).[57]

The predominance of poetic justice in "The Miller's Tale" corresponds to Jupiter's traditional connection with justice for humankind. Dante's Jovian cantos feature the imperative "DILIGITE IUSTITIAM" (*Par.* 18.91)—a command that is, as Kay indicates, astrologically appropriate to Jupiter as " 'the star of judges' and 'judgments,' " and the patron of "judges, lawyers, notaries, and rulers at every level of society."[58] All portraits of Jupiter, beginning with that in Homer's *Iliad*, focus in some way on Jupiter's scales of justice as one of his major accouterments, just as portraits of millers, such as that contained within "The Reeve's Tale," typically depict millers together with their scales.[59]

A Jovian character, Chaucer's pilgrim Miller, too, has his scales and displays a keen delight in meting out appropriate rewards and punishments to his characters. Old John suffers public humiliation due to his foolish "fantasye" (I.3840) and ends up having shared with Nicholas the young wife he had jealously kept for himself. As a punishment for his amorous presumption and too persistent courtship, "Absolon hath kist hir nether ye" (I.3852). And Nicholas, for his lechery, dishonesty, and arrogance, is "scalded in the towte" (I.3853). Thus all the men in the tale are punished in relatively fitting ways, and the pilgrims' response to the tale accords with the joviality of Jove: "for the moore part they loughe and pleyde" (I.3858).[60]

Mars in "The Reeve's Tale"

Like the soul in its planetary descent, the subject matter of the first fragment of the *Canterbury Tales* passes from the sphere of Jupiter into

---

[57] This paragraph and the one preceding it derive from Colleen Reilly's seminar paper and appear here with her kind permission.

[58] Kay, *Dante's Christian Astrology*, pp. 200–201.

[59] Bernard Silvestris, for example, describes Jupiter as follows: "Seated in his council chamber, Jove shone in regal majesty, wielding in his right hand a scepter, and suspending from his left a scale, in the balance of which he determined the affairs, now of men, now of the higher powers" (*The Cosmographia of Bernard Silvestris*, trans. Winthrop Wetherbee [New York: Columbia University Press, 1973], p. 100).

[60] For the *hilaritas* of Jupiter, see Kay, *Dante's Christian Astrology*, pp. 191–92.

the sphere of Mars in "The Reeve's Tale." As Kay explains, astrologers accepted the commonplace identification of Mars as the god of war "and constructed their interpretation of the planet around it."[61] A fiery planet, due to its proximity to the Sun, Mars became the place where Mars "holds sway, prolific in wrath, sowing the seeds of war, thirsty for disputes, thirstier still for our blood, banishing peace, wiping out treaties."[62] One of the *bellicosi* under Martian influence, the Reeve is portrayed as possessing many malignant, Martian traits—constant thirst, lechery, destructive wrath, and deceitfulness—just as the story he tells can easily be shown to reflect in its plot and characterization notable Martian qualities, especially the boldness (*thymikon* or *audacia*) which the sphere of Mars, according to Macrobius and the astrologers, bestows upon the traveling soul.

The Reeve's "colerik" (GP 587) nature is conspicuously Martian. According to *The Seven Planets*, a person who is born on Tuesday (and therefore, "vnder Mars") "schall be colerycke, strong and wrethefull, covetyse, a mansleer, a traytor, and ryche."[63] Even as the fiery planet Mars signified to the astrologers "all kinds of burning up (*combustio*)," the choleric person was by definition dry, thirsty, and thus easily ignited.[64] In the words of the Middle English *Secreta secretorum*, "The colerike (man) by kynde he sholde be lene of body; his body is light and drye, and he shal be sumwhat rogh; and lyght to wrethe and lyght to peyse; of sharpe witt, wyse and of good memorie, a greete entremyttere; he louyth hasty wengeaunce; desyrous of company of women moore than hym nedyth."[65]

The Reeve closely matches this choleric and Martian description. The Reeve's own words connect him imagistically with the dryness of hay, fire, and thirst. His "gras tyme is doon," he says, and his "fodder is now forage" (I.3868). "Foure gleedes" of fire—boasting, lying, anger, and covetousness—continue to burn in the Reeve's ashes (I.3882–85), even as "the derke ymaginyng" of "crueel Ire, reed as

---

[61] Ibid., p. 151.
[62] Alan de Lille, *Anticlaudianus*, trans. James J. Sheridan (Toronto: Pontifical Institute of Medieval Studies, 1973), p. 133.
[63] *The Seven Planets*, ed. Peter Brown, in *Popular and Practical Science of Medieval England*, ed. Lister M. Matheson (East Lansing, Mich.: Colleagues Press, 1994), p. 18.
[64] Kay, *Dante's Christian Astrology*, p. 150.
[65] *Three Prose Versions of the "Secreta Secretorum,"* ed. Robert Steele, EETS e.s. 74 (London: Kegan Paul, Trench & Trübner, 1898), p. 220; quoted by Walter Clyde Curry, *Chaucer and the Mediaeval Sciences*, p. 72. I thank Colleen Reilly for this reference.

any gleede" (I.1995, 1997) decorates the Knight's temple of Mars. Having "an hoor heed and a grene tayl" (I.3878), the thirsty Reeve is tormented by lustful desires which he cannot fulfill, since "the tonne" of his life, long ago tapped and running, is almost empty (I.3890–98).

Easily aroused to anger, the Reeve displays an "affinity for abusive language (*maledictiones*), insults (*contumeliae*), derision, and the like," which is, according to Kay, typical of Martians.[66] Stirred to "ire" (I.3862) by the Miller's supposed slight, the Reeve vows to "quite" him twice in only 44 lines of direct speech (I.3864, 3916) and joins promise with increasingly violent threats. By the end of the prologue to his tale, the Reeve desires not only to shame the Miller by speaking in "cherles termes" about a miller, but also to see him dead: "I pray to God his nekke mote to-breke" (I.3917–18).

According to Kay, "the Martian proclivity for contradiction is so strong that it often takes the form of denying the truth," with the result that "the Martian tends to be a liar," makes false accusations, and "is often involved in transactions that are fraudulent."[67] According to the General Prologue portrait, the Reeve is notoriously dishonest and, not unlike the malevolent god and planet, "crueel Mars" (II.301), he strikes fear in the hearts of those with whom he deals: "Ther nas baillif, ne hierde, nor oother hyne, / That he ne knew his sleighte and his covyne; / They were adrad of hym as of the deeth" (GP 603–5).

Emanating from such a choleric and Martian pilgrim, "The Reeve's Tale" is an appropriately aggressive, bold, lecherous, and vengeful narrative, designed in its characterization and plot to "quite" the Miller mercilessly. In his effort to insult and defame the Miller, the Reeve paradoxically attributes to Symkin typically Martian faults—pride, fraudulence, a foolish sense of security, and vengeful wrath—and he does so in a story whose plot evokes Martian astrological myths.

According to Kay, astrologers single out "wrath, envy and pride" among the seven deadly sins as vices to which Martians are especially prone; because of the association of Mars with blood, moreover, Martians tend to take particular pride in their lineage.[68] In keeping with

[66]   Kay, *Dante's Christian Astrology*, p. 167.
[67]   Ibid., p. 157.
[68]   Ibid., pp. 162–65.

this Martian convention, the Reeve's miller is as "proud and gay" as "any pecok" (I.3926); takes foolish pride in possessing a wife "of noble kyn" (I.3942); and hopes to marry his daughter "into som worthy blood of auncetrye" (I.3982), appropriate to the "hooly blood" (I.3985) of his father-in-law and to his own "estaat of yoman-rye" (I.3949). His wife, in turn, is "proud, and pert as is a pye" (I.3950) and insists on being called "dame" (I.3956), even though she "was as digne as water in a ditch" (I.3964).

Chaucer's emphasis on family pride in "The Reeve's Tale" dram-atizes a possible misreading of Dante's treatment of that subject in his Martian cantos. There Cacciaguida, Dante's great great grandfather, speaking in Latin, greets his descendant Dante with the words: "O sanguis meus, o superinfusa gratia Dei" (*Par.* 15.28–29), a greeting which Chaucer playfully (mis)translates into the "hooly chirches blood" (I.3984) of the parson and his illegitimate daughter.[69] Dante endeavors to distinguish between virtuous and vicious ancestral pride, placing Alighieri I among the Prideful in Purgatory (*Par.* 15.91–93) and allowing Cacciaguida to speak at length about the rise and fall of formerly important, dynastic families. Even in heaven, however, Cac-ciaguida and Dante the pilgrim take obvious pride in their own an-cestry (*Par.* 16.1: "nostra nobiltà di sangue"), and Chaucer submits that ambiguity to a thorough examination.

Looking back to a Florentine Golden Age, Cacciaguida recalls a time when "no daughter's birth brought fear unto her father, for age and dowry then did not imbalance" (*Par.* 15.103–4), a time when happy and virtuous wives worked "at spindle and at spools" and "watched with loving care the cradle" of their infants (*Par.* 15.117, 121). In "The Reeve's Tale," Chaucer turns precisely these domestic concerns into the miller's anxiety over finding a suitable match for his daughter and into the miller's wife's misguided search for "the cradel" of her sleeping child (I.4214, 4221, 4224), and he uses them to "quite" not only the Miller as a tale-teller, but also Dante.

Infamous for his pride, the Reeve's miller is also feared in the vil-lage for his pugnacity and known to be "a theef" (I.3939). In order to steal half a bushel of flour from his customers, the vigilant young clerks from Cambridge, Symkin turns loose their horse and sends

---

[69]   In a single breath, as it were, Cacciaguida actually first addresses Dante and then apostrophizes the divine favor that has brought him to Paradise before his death.

them on a memorable horse-chase toward "the fen, ther wilde mares renne" (I.4065). The fast-paced escapade is astrologically appropriate to Mars in several ways. As Kay notes, according to a medieval commonplace inherited from Greek astrology, "Mars signifies mobility (*mobilitatem*) in all things," and "Mars causes men to be 'agile' and to go 'nimbly and swiftly.' "[70] Such a description certainly applies to the horse, who ran "as faste as he may go" (I.4081) and to the "sely clerkes" who "rennen up and doun," calling breathlessly after him (I.4100).

As V. A. Kolve has argued, moreover, given the common cultural association of uncontrolled horses with unbridled passions, the vivid description of the horse-chase stands as a central memorial image that encapsulates the meaning of the tale.[71] Kolve rightly emphasizes the Platonic myth of the soul-chariot in *Phaedrus* 246–56, but that myth has its Ovidian double in the story of Apollo's son, Phaëthon, who could not control the horses of the sun. Kay observes that Beatrice fittingly compares Dante to Phaëthon in the sphere of Mars (*Par.* 17.1–6), because Phaëthon's inept driving "has the effects that astrologers attribute to Mars: rivers dry up, vegetation burns, and the very mountains are set ablaze."[72] Similarly, the effect of the riotous horse-chase on the clerks is to render them "combustible" in the Martian sense, angry, and eager for revenge.

The miller, for his part, exhibits the "false and foolish sense of security," which Kay terms characteristic of Martians.[73] He invites the two young men, whom he has robbed, to spend the night in the same room with himself, his wife, and his daughter. He drinks himself drunk, moreover, and serves his guests "strong ale atte beste" (I.4147), which heightens in them the Martian boldness or *audacia* that spurs them to act vengefully in accord with the proverb, "Unhardy is unseely" (I.4210).

Aleyn justifies his rape of Symkin's sleeping daughter with the typically Martian "lawe that says thus: / That gif a man in a point be agreved, / That in another he sal be releved" (I.4181–83). John takes

---

[70] Ibid., pp. 174–75.
[71] See V. A. Kolve, *Chaucer and the Imagery of Narrative*, pp. 237–48. Kolve calls special attention to the horses representing the five senses in Alan de Lille's *Anticlaudianus* IV.
[72] Kay, *Dante's Christian Astrology*, p. 151. The stated reason for comparing Dante to Phaëthon is their common interest in their fathers.
[73] Ibid., p. 166.

the miller's wife unaware in a similar spirit of vengeance against Symkin, pricking her "harde and depe as he were mad" (I.4231). The miller responds to their crimes in a equally violent manner, bloodying and throttling Aleyn and threatening to kill him: "Thow shalt be deed, by Goddes dignitee!" (I.4270).

In "The Reeve's Tale" Symkin's discovery of his daughter's deflowering and his wife's rape in his own bedroom distantly recalls the classical myth of Mars's adultery with Venus, in which the trapped lovers face public humiliation at the hands of Vulcan. According to Kay, the myth led to a general association of the planet Mars with captivity, daylight disclosure, and flight.[74] All of these plot elements are relevant to the conclusion of the tale. In rapid sequence the miller learns what has happened, and the miller's wife, taking advantage of "a litel shymeryng of a light" (I.4297), accidentally strikes her husband as he is fighting with Aleyn, which allows for the clerks' hasty escape "in the dawenynge" (I.4234).

In the Vicinity of the Sun: The Cook, "The Cook's Tale," and "The Manciple's Tale"

As we have seen, Neoplatonic theory associates the first three planets—Saturn, Jupiter, and Mars—with the unfolding of the tripartite soul. The influence of the solar sphere, on the other hand, imbues the soul with attributes linked to the body: namely, sense perception (*aisthetikon*) and imagination (*phantastikon*). The Sun thus represents a major new beginning in the soul's development, and the descending approach to the Sun (prior to bodily conception), like the exit from the solar sphere (in the soul's ascent after bodily death), was understood to be an important and traumatic transitional phase.[75] As Macrobius explains, "So long as the souls heading downwards still remain in Cancer, they are considered in the company of the gods,

---

[74] Ibid., pp. 154–55, 176. As Colleen Reilly pointed out to me, an example of this extended meaning can be found in *Fulgentius the Mythographer*, trans. Leslie George Whitbread (Columbus: Ohio State University Press, 1971), pp. 60–61.

[75] J. D. North has argued that the structure of Dante's *Inferno* also mirrors that of the heavens, and that Dante employs the image of a castle wall to mark the solar midpoint of the planetary sequence. See his *Stars, Minds, and Fate: Essays in Ancient and Modern Cosmology* (London: Hambledon Press, 1989), pp. 187–94. I thank Colleen Reilly for this reference.

since in that position, they have not yet left the Milky Way. But when in their descent they have reached Leo, they enter upon the first stages of their future condition" (I.xii.4, p. 134). The Sun, as Kay indicates, bears "a special astrological relation to the zodiacal sign of Leo," for he rules that sign "both by day and night."[76] In this solar region, the soul experiences a kind of intoxication and loss of orientation:

> When the soul is being drawn towards a body in this first protraction of itself it begins to experience a tumultuous influx of matter rushing upon it. This is what Plato alludes to when he speaks in the *Phaedo* of a soul suddenly staggering as if drunk as it is being drawn into the body; he wishes to imply the recent draught of onrushing matter by which the soul, defiled and weighted down, is pressed earthwards. (I.xii.7, p. 135)

Chaucer's choice of the Cook to exemplify this solar transition is astrologically appropriate in several ways. Kay has demonstrated that astrologers accorded to the Sun, as a source of light and heat, a special influence on two bodily organs, the head and the heart. The Sun thus affected also the parts of the head: the face, the mouth and the eyes— a solar association that encouraged Dante to use gustatory and ocular imagery in his cantos of the Sun.[77] Chaucer, too, links the approach to the Sun with the palate through the figure of the Cook, who uses heat to "boille" (GP 380), to "rooste, and sethe, and broille, and frye" (GP 383), and who prepares tasty pies.

The Cook, moreover, exhibits a conspicuously drunken behavior that matches the Neoplatonic description of the soul's intoxication in the vicinity of the Sun. His portrait in the General Prologue mentions specifically that "wel koude he knowe a draughte of Londoun ale" (GP 382). Furthermore, his boisterous interjections following "The Reeve's Tale" could certainly represent drunken behavior, for he yells impetuously such things as "Ha! ha!" (I.4327) and "by my fey!" (I.4356). More importantly, when the Cook resurfaces in the Manciple's Prologue, he is too drunk even to begin to tell a tale. Harry Bailly sees him nodding and fears that "he wol falle fro his hors atones" (IX.10). The Manciple describes his eyes as "daswen"

[76]   Kay, *Dante's Christian Astrology*, p. 109.
[77]   Ibid., pp. 112–13.

(IX.31); his breath as "soure" (IX.32), stinking and "cursed" (IX.39); his body as "hevy" and "dronken" (IX.67). Then we see the Cook imbibing eagerly from the Manciple's proffered gourd of wine, even though he has drunk "ynough biforn" (IX.89). The Cook's inebriation is, in fact, so extreme that the Manciple calls him ape-drunk (IX.44)—inarticulate, barely conscious, close to sleep or death.

The brevity of the unfinished "Cook's Tale" in Fragment I makes sense, moreover, as the necessary outcome of a sequential analogy, according to which the size of a planet's orbit measures both the power of its deity and the length of the tale that exemplifies it. Even as the orbits of the higher planetary spheres, beginning with Saturn's as the largest "cours," are successively smaller and faster to complete, the tales in the first fragment display a reeling pattern of accelerating brevity. According to the calculation of Martianus Capella, Saturn, the slowest of the planets, completes its great orbit in 30 years; Jupiter in 12 years; Mars in 2 years; and the Sun in 365 ¼ days.[78] Similarly, "The Knight's Tale" is 2,249 lines; "The Miller's Tale," counting the prologue, 746 lines; "The Reeve's Tale," 469 lines; and "The Cook's Tale," only 57 lines.[79]

The Ellesmere order, moreover, twice connects the figure of the drunken Cook with the Sun. First of all, it continues the pattern of planetary descent initiated in Fragment I by moving from the fragmentary "Cook's Tale" to the Prologue to the Man of Law's Tale, which begins with an elaborated solar reference: "Oure Hooste saugh wel that the brighte sonne / The ark of his artificial day hath ronne / The ferthe part" (II.1–3). Second, it mirrors the pattern of descent in the first part of the *Tales* with an ascending pattern in the latter half that reaches a climax in the Manciple's Prologue and Tale. There the exit from the solar sphere links the depiction of the Bacchic Cook in the Prologue with a tale in which Apollo, god of the Sun, figures as a major protagonist.

This kind of solar patterning allows Chaucer to bring his tale-telling to a symbolic conclusion in "The Manciple's Tale" not only through the breaking of Apollo's harp, but also through a planetary movement away from the realm of sense perception and imagination, the Macrobian *phantastikon* on which the art of poetry depends. Thus Chau-

---

[78] *The Marriage of Philology and Mercury*, vol. 2, VIII, pp. 339–43.
[79] This paragraph echoes Colleen Reilly's seminar paper.

cer does not merely answer the Cook's Bacchus with the Manciple's Apollo, opposing sensual indulgence to reasoned control; but rather, he draws the two together as part of a continuum in which thought itself, even the brightest thought, remains imagistic, fantastical, body-linked, and therefore clouded.

As others have noticed, by reintroducing the figures of the Cook and the Manciple in Fragment IX, Chaucer establishes a literal connection between Fragment I and IX that the Ellesmere order recognizes and affirms within an extended chiasmus.[80] Mirroring the first story-block, "The Manciple's Tale" combines within itself a generic mixture of romance and fabliau and reiterates the plot elements of a lovers' triangle. From a thematic perspective, it highlights the theme of proper naming that "The Reeve's Tale" previously brought to the fore ("Dame" vs. bastard, "lady" vs. "lemman"), and the tale as a whole offers an extended commentary on the Cook's proverbial "sooth pley, quaad pley" (I.4357).

Supported by an allusory structure of planetary pilgrimage and scientific *divisio*, however, the Manciple's Prologue and Tale do more. They answer to the epistemological issues raised in Fragment I—issues for which the Cook's intoxication is a philosophical emblem. Speculative science, after all (especially an astrological metaphysics), aims at the knowledge of "Goddes pryvetee" and all the principles of causation governing creation. That same science, however (at least to the extent that it is Neoplatonist), also places severe limits on the power of sense-bound creatures to know spiritual realities, to grasp the truth of things behind the world of appearances.

The Cook of London aims at telling the "sooth" (I.4356–57) about a "hostileer" (I.4360) at Harry Bailly's expense, and he threatens a similar retaliation against the Manciple. In each case, he fails. Too drunk to perceive and tell the "sooth," or even to remember it, the figure of the Cook symbolically calls into question the truth of other supposedly true assertions. The crow's confident "I saugh" (IX.256) and the Manciple's "he saugh" (IX.261) attempt to separate the realms of knowledge and fiction, truth and poetry, whereas a grief-stricken Apollo struggles to hold them together, defending the mem-

---

[80] The only manciple besides the pilgrim Manciple to appear in the *Tales* is the sick "maunciple" for whom John and Aleyn run their errand in "The Reeve's Tale" (I.3993).

ory of his beautiful, "gilteles" (IX.280) wife and lamenting the "fals suspecion" (IX.281) that moved him to kill her.

In the end, the Manciple succeeds in silencing the Cook, even as his tale of the truth-telling crow puts an end to Apollo's (and Chaucer's) fictions and the crow's nightingale-like song.[81] The Bacchic Cook's unfinished and untold tales remain, however, in the Ellesmere *Tales* as an absent presence, offering a silent comment on the limits of speculative knowledge in all its forms, from the lofty wisdom of the Knight's Theseus to the "I saugh" (IX.256) of the Manciple's crow.

Chaucer's Ellesmere *Tales* thus leave Apollo's solar sphere in much the same way that Dante's *Paradiso* departs from the fourth heaven. At that important juncture, Thomas Aquinas himself contrasts the wisdom of Solomon with the self-aggrandizing intellectual speculation that seeks to resolve such questions as the exact number of angels, whether motion is possible without an efficient cause (*si est dare primum motum esse*), and whether only a right-angled triangle can be drawn within a semicircle (*Par.* 13.94–102). Pointing to a host of great intellectuals—Parmenides, Melissus, Bryson, Sabellius, and Arius—whose too-confident assertions have since been refuted, Aquinas cautions the pilgrim Dante to beware of rash judgments and to move slowly "to *yes* or *no* when you do not see (*vedi*) clearly" (*Par.* 13.114). Aquinas, in fact, plays with images of mistaken vision, concave mirrors, and ocular proof throughout his speech, using various forms of the verb "to see": *vedi* (13.114) *venduto* (13.133), *vidi* (13.136), *per vedere* (13.140). He concludes by turning from the academic arguments of philosophers to the vulgar proofs of gossip, urging ordinary folk to avoid judging their neighbors when (they think) "they see one rob and . . . another who donates," since God's insight and counsel frequently differ from ours: "the last may fall, the other may be saved" (13.141–42). Thus not only the philosophy of Theseus but also the eyewitness report of the Manciple's crow may be wrong, since they both judge by the appearance of things. On earth, after all, we all remain in the intoxicating vicinity of the senses and the Sun.

[81]   Chaucer's use of Apollo as a poetic emblem at the end of his fictions (see pp. 24–25 of the "Introduction" to this book) offers a complex response to Dante the poet, who invokes Apollo as his muse at the start of the *Paradiso* (1.13–36), and to Dante the pilgrim, who begins his eagle-flight through the spheres by gazing with Beatrice at the sun.

And . . . [the sonne] causeth yit
A man to be soubtil of wit
To worche in gold, and to be wys,
In every thing which is of pris.
                    —John Gower

Love is the wise man's stone.
                    —Angelus Silesius

4

SOLAR ALCHEMY IN

FRAGMENTS II AND VIII

The notion of a two-way planetary pilgrimage helps to explain the evident similarities between Fragments II and VIII, which the Ellesmere order pairs within an extended chiasmus. Whereas "The Cook's Tale" and "The Manciple's Tale" exemplify the entrance to, and exit from, the solar sphere, the tales in these fragments are firmly under the influence of the Sun. The Host subordinates the Man of Law's tale-telling to the "ark" of "the brighte sonne" and warns the pilgrims against the "ydelnesse" that results in the "los of tyme," which is more valuable "than gold in cofre" (II.1–2, 32, 28, 26). Similarly, the Second Nun invokes the Virgin Mary as "the sonne of excellence," deplores "ydelnesse," and points to Saint Cecilia as " 'hevenes lilie,' " whose example of "bisy . . . good werkynge" is as "swift and round and eek brennynge" as the "sonne" in the heavens above (VIII.52, 17, 87, 116, 108). Both Cecilia and Custance are instrumental in the solar cure of blindness.[1] Furthermore, as Joseph Grennen and Bruce Rosenberg have shown, "The Second

---

[1] On a day when "bright was the sonne" (II.554), Custance, Hermengild, and the Constable encounter a "blinde Britoun" (II.561) who asks the newly christened Hermengild to cure him. She does so when "Custance made hire boold, and bad hire wirche / The wyl of Crist" (II.566–67). As a result, the Constable too converts. Cecilia's very name is glossed as " 'the wey to blynde' " (VIII.92).

Nun's Tale" is replete with alchemical imagery, which is accentuated by its close pairing with the Canon's Yeoman's tales (autobiographical and fictional) of quests for the ellusive gold that is the Sun's metal: "Sol gold is" (VIII.826).[2] As we shall see, the language of alchemy by extension also illumines the Man of Law's tale of saintly Custance, who, like Cecilia, converts the pagans around her to Christianity through her (first and second) marriage to a heathen husband.

Interpreted as fragments both occupying the same heaven, Fragments II and VIII strikingly recall Dante's treatment of the solar sphere in *Paradiso* 10–14. As Richard Kay has shown, the astrologers associated the Sun with the salvation of the soul (*salus animae*), and Dante accordingly peoples this sphere with the doctors and good shepherds of the Church, chief among them, the mendicant founders, Saints Francis and Dominic, whose characterization exemplifies respectively the sun's ardent heat and sapient light.[3] Dante draws an extended parallel between Francis's legendary spiritual marriage to Lady Poverty and Dominic's to Lady Faith and emphasizes the zealous apostolic work of both saints. Following the astrologers, who associate flowers and roses in particular with the sun, Dante depicts the saints in this sphere as forming "two garlands of those sempiternal roses" (*Par.* 12.19) and makes extensive use of roseate imagery throughout the solar cantos.[4] Dante, moreover, explicitly contrasts the true wisdom, zeal, and inner wealth of the Sun-saints with the false wisdom of ambitious lawyers, whose worldly busyness and *leges* do not coincide with the laws of God and nature.[5]

Chaucer's juxtaposition of Custance and Cecilia as saints mirrors Dante's contrastive pairing of Francis and Dominic in important ways. There is, in short, a structural as well as a stylistic basis for Glending Olson's impression that "listening to the *Second Nun's Tale* is like listening to the lives of St. Francis and St. Dominic in the *Paradiso*."[6]

---

[2] See especially Joseph Grennen, "Saint Cecilia's 'Chemical Wedding': The Unity of the *Canterbury Tales* Fragment VIII," *JEGP* 65 (1966): 466–81; Bruce A. Rosenberg, "The Contrary Tales of the Second Nun and the Canon's Yeoman," *Chaucer Review* 2 (1967–68): 278–91.

[3] Richard Kay, *Dante's Christian Astrology* (Philadelphia: University of Pennsylvania Press, 1994), pp. 99–100, 127–28; John Freccero, *Dante: The Poetics of Conversion*, ed. Rachel Jacoff (Cambridge: Harvard University Press, 1986), p. 243. For a general study of the Sun as a symbol of Christ, see Franz Dölger, *Sol Salutis* (Münster: Aschendorff, 1925).

[4] Kay, *Dante's Christian Astrology*, p. 108. Here and throughout I use Dante Alighieri, *Paradiso*, trans. Allen Mandelbaum (New York: Bantam Books, 1986).

[5] Kay, *Dante's Christian Astrology*, p. 126. See *Par.* 11.4–5; 12.82–84.

[6] Glending Olson, "Chaucer, Dante, and the Structure of Fragment VIII (G) of the

Chaucer's women share with the mendicants a tremendous power to effect conversion. For the sake of Custance, the Sultan and his subjects accept Christianity; in Northumbria, Custance's prayers bring about the conversions of Hermengild, the constable, the king, "and many another in that place" (II.685). Similarly, Cecilia brings to Christ first Valerian, then Tiburce, Maximus, the ministers of Almachius, and others.

Like Francis and Dominic, both women are espoused. Whereas Custance—widowed, dispossessed, exiled, nameless, and disowned—resembles Lady Poverty, Cecilia in her marriage to Valerian resembles the Lady Faith whom St. Dominic weds (*Par.* 13.61–63). Like Dante's Dominic, she is outstanding for her "sapience and for hire thewes cleere" (VIII.101); she converts others through "hir wise loore" (VIII.414); she preaches actively and is outspoken in her Christian witness before pagan judges. Her tale emphasizes faith, assent to the creed, belief in unseen realities, and miracles. The symbolism of light, roses, lilies, and garlands abounds in Chaucer's descriptions of her.[7]

Custance, on the other hand, like St. Francis's Lady Poverty, is twice-married. Like Lady Poverty, whose first husband, Christ, is violently put to death (*Par.* 11.64–66), Custance is widowed on her wedding day and later remarries. Like Francis, who preached to the Sultan and whose native "Assisi" (*Ascesi*) means "Orient" (*Par.* 11.100–2, 52–54), Custance goes as a missionary to her Sultan-husband in Syria.[8] Custance shares, moreover, in the "costance" (*Par.* 11.70) that Lady Poverty exhibits in the multiple trials that she endures in union with the persecuted and crucified Christ and the stigmatized Francis. Even as Francis is especially close to Christ in his infancy and passion, Custance weeps for her innocent baby, whom she likens to Mary's "child ... on a croys yrent" (II.844), and she hails the "hooly croys" (II.451) as the means of salvation. Whereas Dante's Aquinas praises

---

Canterbury Tales," Chaucer Review 16 (1982): 222–36. Olson's essay emphasizes the Dantean pattern of examples of vice and virtue in the *Purgatorio*. Chaucer points to Dante directly by paraphrasing *Par.* 30.1–39 in VIII.36–56.

[7] As many others have noted, the imagery of roses and lilies also abounds in alchemical treatises, which aimed, after all, at the production of the sun's metal, gold. According to Lynn Thorndike, "many *Rosaries* and other flowery titles cluster around the name of Arnald of Villanova," and "such floral titles were extended from the rose to the lily." See *A History of Magic and Experimental Science*, History of Science Society Publications, n.s. 4 (New York: Columbia University Press, 1934), 3:55, 62.

[8] Kay points to the astrological association of the Sun with Babylon, sultans, and Saracens (*Dante's Christian Astrology*, pp. 119–20). "The Man of Law's Tale" is the only tale in the *Canterbury Tales* that includes Islamic figures.

Franciscan poverty apostrophically (*Par.* 11.82: "O wealth unknown! O good that is fruitful!"), alludes to Francis's rejection by his merchant father Bernardone, and condemns lawyers (*Par.* 12.82–83), Chaucer's wise-seeming Man of Law uses apostrophe to condemn poverty (II.99: "O hateful harm, condicion of poverte!"), praises merchants (II.122–33), and promotes his own gain as he tells Custance's story.[9]

The contrast between spiritual wealth and worldly lucre implicit in the teller-tale relationship in Fragment II becomes explicit in Chaucer's pairing of tales of religious conversion and alchemical change in Fragment VIII. Once again Chaucer fashions a fiction that answers Dante's in his representation of the alchemist as a man who "semeth a Salomon" (VIII.961). In the heaven of the sun, the pilgrim Dante encounters Solomon as the fifth and fairest light in the first garland of souls. Aquinas praises Solomon as possessing an unsurpassed wisdom (*Par.* 10.112–14)—a praise that puzzles Dante, whose doubt is only resolved much later, when Aquinas explains that he was referring specifically to Solomon's "kingly prudence" when he spoke of his "matchless vision" (*Par.* 13.103). The biblical Solomon had, after all, asked God for a discerning heart, rather than for riches or for a long life for himself or for power over his enemies (1 Kings 3:5–12).

By contrast, the quest for riches and for long life notoriously motivated the alchemists, who searched for "the philosophres stoon, / Elixir clept" (VIII.862–63), which had the power to turn base metals into gold and (in some traditions) to bestow immortality. Like Aquinas, who praises Solomon, the Yeoman first describes his master as "a man of heigh discrecioun," who is "gretter than a clerk" (VIII.613, 617). Later he explains his words, significantly qualifying their meaning to the point of ironic inversion. His master is "to wys" and possesses "over-greet a wit" (VIII.644, 648). In "seven yeer" he has been unable to teach his apprentice anything of his "slidynge science" (VIII.720,732). His master's faults, moreover, are shared by alchemists in general, who "semen wonder wise, / Oure termes been so clergial and so queynte" (VIII.751–52), but who can neither understand nor convey the books they vainly read in "lernyng of this elvysshe nyce loore" (VIII.842).[10] The "secree of secrees" they pursue is by defi-

9   See my "Apostrophe, Prayer, and the Structure of Satire in the Man of Law's Tale," *SAC* 13 (1991): 81–97; repr. and rev. in *Job, Boethius, and Epic Truth* (Ithaca: Cornell University Press, 1994), pp. 108–25.
10   For a discussion of the densities of alchemical language, see Lee Patterson, "Per-

nition "*ignotum,*" even as their method is "*per ignocius*" (VIII.1446, 1457).

If the Yeoman's master is Solomon's antitype by virtue of his foolish wisdom, the canon and the priest in "The Canon's Yeoman's Tale" are Solomonic antitypes through their greed for gold. Unlike the Yeoman and his master, who are always borrowing gold for their experiments and thus in debt beyond their power to repay, the fraudulent canon of *pars secunda* actually makes money. His "feendly . . . doublenesse" (VIII.1300, 1303) enables him to dupe the priest into giving him forty pounds in payment for his alchemical recipe. The priest, for his part, is destroyed through the charlatan's deceit and his own "coveitise" for wealth and occult knowledge, which impels him to attempt to produce gold and thus "to wexe a philosofre" through his practice of alchemical art (VIII.1077, 1122).

The Yeoman's trickster alchemist deceives the priest by involving him in an experiment which requires him "coles for to couchen" (VIII.1152). The language and action of the tale focuses attention relentlessly on the burning coals (VIII.1157, 1160, 1176, 1180, 1181, 1189, 1192, 1196, 1202, 1268, 1278), which the priest tends and in which the canon hides silver filings. Chaucer's "Canon's Yeoman's Tale" thus repositions in a striking way the central image of Solomon's speech in Dante's *Paradiso.*

Solomon, whose silent presence haunts the solar sphere from Aquinas's first introduction of him in Canto 10 to Aquinas's meditation on his wisdom in Canto 13, speaks only once. His modest voice, which sounds in Dante's ear like Gabriel's speaking to Mary (*Par.* 14.34–36), is the last voice heard in the fourth heaven. Beatrice poses Dante's unspoken question, asking whether the exceedingly bright light that invests the bodiless souls will remain undimmed at the Resurrection of the Body, and if so, whether the embodied souls will be able "to see such light and not be harmed" (*Par.* 14.18). In answer, Solomon declares that the "glorified and sanctified . . . flesh" (*Par.* 14.43) will not diminish, but rather enhance, both the soul's light and its vision. The brightness of the "reborn flesh" will actually outshine "the brightness that envelopes" it, even as a glowing coal ("carbon") burns with a greater

---

petual Motion: Alchemy and the Technology of the Self," *SAC* 15 (1993): 25–57, esp. pp. 39–54. Patterson provides an excellent review of scholarship on "The Canon's Yeoman's Tale."

intensity than the flame it feeds (*Par.* 14.52–57). The faculties of
the transfigured body will, moreover, be able to sustain that intensity of vision without tiring. Solomon thus echoes the teaching of
Aquinas,[11] and the blessed souls respond with an "Amen" that expresses "how they longed for their dead bodies" (*Par.* 14.63).

At first sight, Solomon's topic—although certainly not his image of
the burning coal—seems far removed from alchemy. Chaucer, however, apparently saw in Solomon's closing speech (and in Aquinas's
earlier one about the "defective work" of Nature and art as opposed
to the "perfection" wrought by God alone [*Par.* 13.61–87]) a pointed
Dantean response to specific alchemical issues. Chaucer's solar tales,
at any rate, make explicit a series of alchemical connections that Dante's cantos leave implicit,[12] and they do so in a way that directly engages Solomon's closing topic of the relationship between the body
and the soul.

In linking the tales of the Second Nun and the Canon's Yeoman,
Chaucer places emphasis on spiritual change and metallic metamorphosis as analogous processes—an emphasis that raises and exemplifies key issues in contemporary academic debates in the field of
physics. From a clerical perspective, he does so fittingly in the sphere
of the Sun. There, as we have seen, the soul is imbued with the sense
perception (*aisthetikon*) that allows it to probe experimentally into the
science of matter; to learn the "Physique," which, as Gower's Genius
explains, includes "sondri knowlechinges / Upon the bodiliche
thinges / Of man, of beste, of herbe, of ston, / Of fissch, of foughl,
of everychon" (VII.137–40);[13] and ultimately to grasp what Hugh
of St. Victor terms the "invisible causes of visible things."[14] In the
Convivio, Dante himself likens the Sun to Arithmetic, especially

---

[11]   See Brian Davies, *The Thought of Thomas Aquinas* (Oxford: Clarendon Press, 1992;
repr. 1993), pp. 215–20.

[12]   Kay remarks on the absence of images of things "of great value, such as gold,
tapestries, perfumes, etc." in Dante's solar heaven, and explains that "by a sort of poetic
alchemy he [Dante] transmutes them from material to spiritual objects" (*Dante's Christian Astrology*, pp. 104–5). Dante's alchemists appear instead in the tenth bolgia of the
eighth circle where falsifiers are punished (*Inferno* 29–30).

[13]   Here and elsewhere I use John Gower, *Confessio Amantis*, in *The Complete Works of John
Gower*, vols. 2 and 3, ed. G. C. Macaulay (Oxford: Clarendon Press, 1901), citing book
and line numbers parenthetically.

[14]   Hugh of St. Victor, *Didascalicon*, trans. Jerome Taylor, (New York: Columbia University Press, 1961, repr. 1991), appendix A, p. 153.

in its application to natural science, which "concentrates primarily on the study of the fundamental constitutive principles of natural things, of which there are three, namely, matter, privation, and form."[15]

The Elements of Body and Soul

As the Aristotelian *libri naturales* taught the Middle Ages, natural science (*physis*) addresses the sensible world in its evident mutability and properly concerns itself with the potential and actual causes of material change. Aristotle defined "change" broadly to include changes "with respect to substance or to quantity or to quality or to place."[16] More specifically, in keeping with the axiom that "every thing that comes to be comes into being from a contrary and some substrate, and passes away likewise,"[17] he explained physical change in terms of the constant generation of the four earthly elements—earth, water, air, and fire—into and out of one another through the energetic interplay of their contrary qualities: hot/cold, wet/dry, heavy/light, coarse/fine.

Aristotle distinguised, moreover, between the mutable earthly realm and the heavenly spheres of both the fixed stars, where "no change appears to have taken place," and the planets, where the rotating bodies exhibit an "unnatural" circular motion that precludes the "natural" qualities of heaviness and lightness responsible for falling and rising motions.[18] Aristotle held that since the heavens were "divine," "eternal . . . unaging and unalterable and unmodified,"[19] they must be constituted by "something else beyond earth, fire, air, and water."[20] He understood this superior fifth element to be lacking the contrary qualities characteristic of earthly matter, and he followed ear-

---

[15] Dante, *The Banquet*, trans. Christopher Ryan (Saratoga, Calif.: ANMA Libri, 1989), II.xiii, p. 69.

[16] Aristotle, *Physics*, trans. R. P. Hardie and R. K. Gaye, in *The Complete Works of Aristotle*, ed. Jonathan Barnes, Bollingen Series 71.2 (Princeton: Princeton University Press, 1984), vol. 1, III.1, p. 342.

[17] Aristotle, "On the Heavens," trans. J. L. Stocks, in *The Complete Works of Aristotle*, vol. 1, I.3, p. 450.

[18] Ibid., I.3, p. 451; I.2–3, p. 449.

[19] Ibid., I.3, p. 450.

[20] Ibid., I.3, p. 451.

lier philosophers in calling it "*aether,* derived from the fact that it 'runs always' for an eternity of time."[21]

In introducing ether as a fifth element, Aristotle upheld more than one kind of matter and attributed materiality to eternal and divine things, whereas Genesis speaks of only one kind of matter and sharply distinguishes the materiality of the body from the immateriality of the soul. Not surprisingly, the recovery of Aristotle precipitated a heated debate among theologians and physicists over the meaning of "substantial forms" and the possibility of different kinds of matter, spiritual and corporeal.[22] At stake was the fundamental relationship between the "visible things" in the middle realm accessible to sensory experience and the "invisible causes" that impinged upon them from "below" (as elements and *minima*) and "above" (as ethereal emanations and divine forms).

Aristotle's delineation of multiple causes (efficient, final, material, formal, immediate, and remote) led to an ever more complicated analytical scheme, which tried to harmonize the material and formal causes of the individual elements and their contrary qualities, on the one hand, with the material and formal causes of more complex entities, on the other. As Robert P. Multhauf relates, Saint Boniface (1221–74), for instance, held that "every being assumes as many forms as it has different properties" and that each thing, therefore, has "a multiplicity of forms,"[23] whereas Saint Thomas Aquinas argued that every thing per se possesses a single substantial form and a multiplicity of accidents.

A special focus of the debate concerned the nature of the soul. Aristotle's own treatment of the subject in *De anima* acknowledges its difficulty and surveys a wide range of positions, paying particular attention to the familiar argument that the soul is cognitive and therefore must be corporeal, since "like . . . is known by like."[24] Aristotle exemplifies this view by referring (among many others) to Empedocles, who held that the soul was composed of all the elements:

21   Ibid.
22   See Robert P. Multhauf, "The Science of Matter," in *Science in the Middle Ages,* ed. David C. Lindberg (Chicago: University of Chicago Press, 1978), pp. 369–90, esp. 382–85.
23   Ibid., p. 385.
24   Aristotle, "On the Soul," trans. J. A. Smith, in *The Complete Works of Aristotle,* vol. 1, I.2, p. 646.

"For tis by Earth we see Earth; by Water, Water; / By Ether, Ether divine; by Fire, destructive Fire; / By Love, Love; and Hate by cruel Hate."[25] Although Aristotle goes on to maintain that the human soul is best understood in formal, rather than elemental, terms, he nevertheless concludes that "the soul is inseparable from the body, or at any rate that certain parts of it are (if it has parts)."[26] Aristotle thus leaves as open questions both the ethereal substance of the higher part of the soul (*nous*) and the precise relation of matter and form.

In answer to issues raised by Aristotle's hylomorphism, Aquinas took several positions that were much contested and even condemned outright by some of his contemporaries, who differed from him in embracing the extremes of Materialism or Dualism.[27] On the one hand, Aquinas refuted the cognitive argument for the materiality of the soul on the grounds that a potential, rather than actual, likeness is sufficient for the soul's knowledge of corporeal things.[28] Similarly, he refuted the argument that the soul must be material because it "moves" the body, maintaining instead (with Aristotle) that the soul is motionless in its substance, but moving and moved in its attributes.[29]

Against the materialists, Aquinas held that the human soul, as "the principle of intellectual operation," is necessarily "incorporeal and subsistent."[30] Against those who argued that the soul is constituted by a mixture of matter and form, Aquinas held that "the soul has no matter" and is therefore "incorruptible."[31] Even granting the remote

---

[25]   Ibid., I.2, p. 645.

[26]   Ibid., II.1, p. 657. Aristotle's mention of "parts" refers to Plato's doctrine of the tripartite soul: rational, irascible, and appetitive (*Timaeus* 69d–72b; *Phaedo* 80b; *Republic* 4.444b). At issue was the separability of the rational soul.

[27]   Several Thomistic positions were condemned in March 1277, in Paris (by Étienne Tempier) and at Oxford (by Robert Kilwardby). Following Avicenna, St. Boniface and his school held that the soul is a composite of spiritual matter and form, that the body and soul each have an individual substantiality, and that there is a natural bond (*colligantia naturalis*) between the body and the soul. Following Averroës, others maintained with Aristotle that the soul is the form of the body, but that it is completely immersed in matter and inseparable from matter. Aquinas took a middle position between these two extremes, arguing against Boniface that the soul is the form of the body (and not "spiritual matter" or a mixture of matter and form), but also arguing against the Averroists that the human soul is an immaterial intellectual substance, separable from the body.

[28]   St. Thomas Aquinas, *Summa theologica*, in *Basic Writings of Saint Thomas Aquinas*, ed. Anton C. Pegis (New York: Random House, 1945), vol. 1, Q. 75, Art.1, p. 684.

[29]   Ibid., Q. 75, Art. 1, pp. 683–84.

[30]   Ibid., Q. 75, Art. 2, p. 685.

[31]   Ibid., Q. 75, Art. 5, p. 689; Q. 75, Art. 6, p. 692.

possibility that the soul might be "composed of matter and form" (a view he did not share), Aquinas still argued for the incorruptibility of the soul on the basis of the ethereal quality of heavenly (as opposed to earthly) bodies.[32] Scripture, moreover, attests that "the human soul is produced by God," and not by "some power of the body."[33]

The human being, however, is to be identified neither with the soul nor with the body alone, but with their union. In answer to the dualists, Aquinas firmly maintained with Augustine that "man is not a soul, but something composed of body and soul"—the basic teaching that underlies the Thomistic view of the personal afterlife, which is echoed by Dante's Solomon.[34] In his view, every individual human being is constituted by a specific form numerically matched to its own specific matter. Since, moreover, "the difference which constitutes man is *rational,*" the soul as the form of the human body must be singular, not plural: "The sensitive soul, the intellectual soul and the nutritive soul are in man numerically one and the same soul."[35]

Book VII of Gower's *Confessio Amantis* demonstrates a lay man's understanding of these complicated issues. In his discussion of "physique," Genius speaks of a primordial "matiere universal" called "Ylem," out of which the four earthly "elementz ben mad and formed" (VII.215–16, 218). Although these elements "ben diverse" (VII.222), they share a common *materia prima* and can be transmuted one into the other through qualitative changes. Through "diverse impressions / Of moist and ek of drye" (VII.270–71), for instance, air can become "myst" or "moiste dropes of the reyn" (VII.281, 286)—that is, water—and rain, in turn, can be turned into wet earth. Genius goes on to relate the "foure elementz" to the "complexions foure" of the bodily humors (VII.385, 88) and the four temperaments.

Immediately thereafter he discusses the human soul, whose passionate "motions" are body-linked (and therefore the proper subject of "physique"), but which, "as the clerkes ous enforme" (VII.495), is directly created by God and joined to matter as a divine "forme" (VII.496). The soul thus is both mutable and immutable, its wits "conjoint" with the corruptible body and its "hyh noblesse" partaking of

---

[32] Ibid., Q. 75, Art. 6, p. 692.
[33] Ibid.
[34] Ibid., Q. 75, Art. 4, p. 688. See Davies, *The Thought of Thomas Aquinas*, pp. 215–20.
[35] Ibid., Q. 76, Art. 3, p. 706.

the eternal (VII.502, 498). Genius concludes with a brief discussion of Aristotle's enigmatic fifth element, which, unlike the four earthly elements, is immutable and "set of the hihe goddes yifte" (VII.612) above the other elements to enclose them like an eggshell. Gower thus suggestively associates the soul as a heavenly "forme" with the fixed stars and ether (which he calls "orbis"), even as he links the passionate soul to the humors and the earthly elements.

Alchemical "Physique"

In this panoply of physical and metaphysical concerns, alchemy as a science had a particularly problematic status. Whereas the physicists posited a *materia prima* (hyle) underlying the four elements, which could be transmuted one into the other, the alchemists held analogously that a single substance (mercury and sulphur or simply mercury) stood behind the seven, apparently discrete metals, all of which could be reduced to the same thing.[36] They spoke of the catalytic "elixer" or "philosopher's stone" in terms as mysterious as those surrounding Aristotle's divine element, ether. Indeed, according to F. Sherwood Taylor, many alchemists explicitly identified the mysterious stone with "a *quinta essentia*, a fifth being, over and above the four elements."[37] The influence of the philosopher's stone upon base metals, which supposedly led to their ennoblement as gold, was thus similar to (and, in some sense, identical with) the favorable *influentia* of the heavens upon the earthly elements. Such a view was consistent with the identification of gold as the metal of the Sun, whose central, life-giving position in the cosmos represented the mystical site of the *anima mundi*.[38]

---

[36] The close linkage of these alchemical and physical doctrines is evident in the twelfth-century treatise of Marius. See his *On the Elements*, ed. and trans. Richard C. Dales (Berkeley: University of California Press, 1976), esp. pp. 152–54. Thorndike reports a shift in fourteenth-century alchemical theory away from the earlier emphasis on sulphur and mercury toward a focus on mercury alone. See "Alchemy of the Later Middle Ages," in *A History of Magic and Experimental Science*, 3:39–51.

[37] F. Sherwood Taylor, *The Alchemists: Founders of Modern Chemistry* (New York: Schuman, 1949), pp. 116–17. See, for example, John of Rupescissa, *The Book of Quinte Essence*, ed. F. J. Furnivall, EETS o.s., vol. 16 (London: Trübner, 1856).

[38] See Freccero, *Dante: The Poetics of Conversion*, p. 239; Tullio Gregory, *Anima Mundi* (Florence: Sansoni, 1955).

As Robert P. Multhauf has suggested, the marked analogies between alchemy and physics led Roger Bacon and Albertus Magnus to distinguish "two kinds of alchemy, one concerned with gold-making and the other with changes in 'things' as a general problem."[39] In their view, alchemy, broadly defined as a speculative science, deals with the "generation of all things from the elements" and is thus virtually identical with physics, whereas alchemy, narrowly defined as an operative science, concerns itself specifically with the generation of gold from the baser metals.[40]

Perhaps because practical alchemy and experimental physics were dangerously alike, and the fraud and failure of alchemists tended to discredit the physical theory that alchemy mirrored, others were intent on disassociating the two.[41] In 1323 the Dominican Chapter General at Barcelona responded to a widespread series of "perilous scandals" by forbidding members of the Order to "study, or take lessons, operate or have operated" in the art of alchemy and commanding them to "destroy and burn" writings on that topic.[42] A few years earlier, Pope John XXII issued the decretal *Spondent quas non exhibent* (c. 1317) prohibiting "alchemies" and requiring counterfeiters and alchemists to "forfeit to the public treasury for the benefit of the poor as much genuine gold and silver as they have manufactured of the false or adulterate metal."[43] Lynn Thorndike reports that, according to the inquisitor Eymeric (late fourteenth century), that decretal resulted from a conference at which the pope "assembled as many natural scientists and alchemists as he could to determine whether the art had any basis in nature."[44] In answer to the pope's question, the assembled physicists supposedly repudiated alchemy.

The contest remained alive, however. In his *Pretiosa margarita novella*

---

[39]   Multhauf, "Science of Matter," p. 378.
[40]   Ibid., p. 379.
[41]   See Patterson, "Perpetual Motion," pp. 52–53. For a study of the various reactions to alchemy, see Will H. L. Ogrince, "Western Society and Alchemy, 1200–1500," *Journal of Medieval History* 6 (1980): 103–32.
[42]   "Chartularium universitatis Parisiensis, II, 271," in *University Records and Life in the Middle Ages*, ed. Lynn Thorndike (New York: Columbia University Press, 1944), p. 168.
[43]   James J. Walsh, *The Popes and Science: A History of the Papal Relations to Science during the Middle Ages and down to Our Day* (New York: Fordham University Press, 1908), p. 125. Walsh provides a full translation of the decree and appends the Latin text (p. 414).
[44]   Thorndike, *History of Magic and Experimental Science*, 3:32.

(1330), for instance, the Lombard physician Petrus Bonus contends that alchemy is comprehended under natural philosophy and enumerates (and attempts to refute) twenty-six arguments to the contrary. As Petrus Bonus relates, in addition to those who object to alchemy because of the moral and religious scandals associated with its malpractice, the art unfortunately has scientific opponents who will not agree that the metals differ only in their accidents and not in species, who reject the evolutionary notion of metallic ennoblement, who object to the alchemical evaluation of all other metals as imperfect in contrast to the perfection of gold, and who deny that alchemists possess sufficient knowledge of the complexities of natural processes to imitate or even to assist Nature by their Art.[45]

In defending alchemy against these and other charges, Petrus Bonus shared the stage with several prominent fourteenth-century canon lawyers. Oldrado da Ponte (d. 1335), a consistorial advocate during the papacy of John XXII, wrote an influential *consilium* in which he refuted anti-alchemical arguments that the art is not only not conducive to piety, but also illegal, given the canonical decrees forbidding the transmutation of species and the decoction of gold. In reply, Oldrado compared alchemists as public benefactors to miners and maintained that their art does not aim at the changing of species, but rather merely imitates and accelerates the natural process whereby base metals evolve into gold "as silk is produced from worms."[46] Oldrado's defense was later seconded by such lawyers as John Andrea (d. 1348), Andrea de Rampinis of Isernia (d. 1353), and Alberico da Rosciate of Bergamo (d. 1354).[47]

As Thorndike indicates, the controversy was fueled by "a great burst of alchemical literature in the first half of the fourteenth century."[48] Circulating beside the *Speculum naturale* of Vincent of Beauvais and the *De mineralibus* of Albert the Great were the *Turba philosophorum* and a host of other new alchemical treatises attributed to such revered masters of the art as Arnald of Villanova (d.1311), Ortolanus or Hortulanus, Rosarius, and (later) Raymond Lull. The authority of still other works was enhanced by assigning their authorship variously

---

[45] See Thorndike, *A History of Magic and Experimental Science*, 3:147–62.
[46] Ibid., pp. 48–49.
[47] Ibid., pp. 49–50.
[48] Ibid., p. 47.

(and falsely) to Pope Innocent III, Roger Bacon, Albert the Great, Thomas Aquinas, Solomon, and a host of others.[49]

Commenting on the proliferation, popularity, and nonintelligibility of these texts, Gower's Genius remarks that "fewe understonde" them, "Bot yit to put hem in assai / Ther ben full manye now aday" (IV.2613–16). As Lee Patterson has astutely argued, the wide dissemination of alchemical texts and their vernacular translations, combined with ecclesiastical efforts to expel alchemy from the university, paradoxically "undermined the clerical monopoly upon learning" by offering lay clerks "a way to be an intellectual."[50] As the Yeoman's duplicitous alchemist tells the too-gullible priest, it is possible for him to "wexe a philosofre" (VIII.1122) by embracing the art.[51] Judging by "The Canon's Yeoman's Tale," Chaucer was one of the scholarly lay men who studied the plentiful "bokes . . . / Upon this craft" (CA IV.2613–14), appropriated its science, and converted its dark and learned language into his poetry.[52]

Late-medieval alchemical treatises typically exhibit two contrastive, but closely related tendencies, which are explicable in terms of not only alchemy's ancient origins, but also the ongoing scholastic debate over the physics of the soul.[53] These tendencies define two subgenres, as it were. The first kind of treatise, as Titus Burkhardt notes, "is predominantly artisanal in nature," seeks its legitimacy in experimental science, foregrounds professional activity, and mentions the so-called inward work only "occasionally and incidentally," whereas the

[49] See Patterson, "Perpetual Motion," pp. 46–47. Some alchemical treatises and sayings (including those that Chaucer attributes in the Yeoman's closing dialogue to Plato) are ascribed to Solomon as one of the many supposed ancient masters of the art—no doubt because of his reputation for wealth, wisdom, and allegorical expression, and because the superlative title of his Song of Songs recalls the "Secree of Secrees."
[50] Ibid., p. 54.
[51] Compare the Yeoman's own invitation to the would-be alchemist: "Lat hym appiere, and wexe a philosophre" (VIII.837).
[52] For Chaucer's knowledge of alchemical literature, see Pauline Aiken, "Vincent of Beauvais and Chaucer's Knowledge of Alchemy," SP 41 (1944): 371–89; Joseph Grennen, "Chaucer and the Commonplaces of Alchemy," C&M 26 (1965): 306–33; and especially Edgar H. Duncan, "The Literature of Alchemy and Chaucer's Canon's Yeoman's Tale: Framework, Theme, and Characters," Speculum 43 (1968): 633–56; See John Reidy's note concerning Chaucer's connection to William Shuchirch, a canon of the King's Chapel at Windsor, reputed to be an alchemist (The Riverside Chaucer, ed. Larry D. Benson, 3d ed. [Boston: Houghton Mifflin, 1987], p. 946).
[53] See Mircea Eliade, The Forge and the Crucible, trans. Stephen Corrin, 2d ed. (1956; Chicago: University of Chicago Press, 1978), pp. 19, 147–49. I thank Mary Olson for this and the following reference.

second "makes use of metallurgical processes [almost] exclusively as analogies" for the salvific process in souls.[54]

As "a natural mirror for revealed truths," the alchemical elements and processes afforded an allegory of salvation history.[55] Thus Petrus Bonus likens belief in the philosopher's stone to belief in the miracles of Christianity, and the writings attributed to Arnald of Villanova draw extensive analogies between the incarnation, passion, and resurrection of Christ and the alchemical process.[56] These analogies proved to be two-edged, however, working either to confirm alchemical truth or to arouse suspicions of blasphemy and nigromancy.[57]

By linking the tale of the Canon's Yeoman to the Second Nun's (and, by solar extension, to the Man of Law's), Chaucer himself draws a similar analogy between religious conversion and metallic change, even as he undercuts it in two directions. On the one hand, "The Second Nun's Tale" emphasizes the separate existence and incorporeality of the soul; on the other, "The Canon's Yeoman's Tale" explores the vexed array of *quaestiones* concerning the moral probity of alchemical practice and the legitimacy of alchemy as a physical science. "The Canon's Yeoman's Tale" may be said to exemplify the artisanal current in alchemical texts; the tales of Cecilia and Custance, its mystical counterpart. In opposition, however, to the pronounced tendency in alchemical treatises virtually to identify the conversions of spiritual and material substances within the framework of what Patterson rightly calls "a radically monist view of the world,"[58] Chaucer's juxtaposition of narratives in Fragment VIII separates the two processes as widely as possible. The rank materialism of "The Canon's Yeoman's Tale" is answered by the body/soul dualism of "The Second Nun's Tale," and these two tales, in turn, stand opposed to both Chaucer's tale of Custance and Solomon's celestial image of the burning coal within the flame.

---

[54] Titus Burkhardt, *Alchemy: Science of the Cosmos, Science of the Soul,* trans. William Stoddart (1960; Baltimore: Penguin, 1972), p. 17.

[55] Ibid., p. 18.

[56] See Thorndike, *A History of Magic and Experimental Science,* 3:76–77, 152, 159.

[57] William Langland's Dame Studie associates "Experimenȝ of Alkenamye" with "Nigromancie and perimancie" in *Piers Plowman: The B Text,* ed. George Kane and E. Talbot Donaldson [(London: Athlone Press, 1975), Passus X, lines 217–18. See Joseph Grennen, "The Canon's Yeoman's Alchemical 'Mass,' " *SP* 62 (1965): 546–60, and the articles cited in note 61 below.

[58] Patterson, "Perpetual Motion," p. 42.

Chaucer's Solar Tales and the Alchemical Quaestiones

In many ways, the fictive argument of "The Canon's Yeoman's Tale" resembles the structure of Petrus Bonus's *Pretiosa margarita novella*, which begins (in the manner of a scholastic *quaestio*) with a long and candid listing of the objections against alchemy and ends with a series of *responsiones* in its favor. The debt-ridden Yeoman and his poorly clad, "sluttish" master (VIII.636) embody the charge levelled against alchemists in Pope John XXII's 1317 decretal: "Poor themselves, the alchemists promise riches which are not forthcoming."[59] Their seven years of fruitless labor, like the vain quest of "many ancient Sages, as well as kings and princes, who had hundreds of profound scholars at their beck and call," confirm the objection recorded by Petrus Bonus that gold-making is "one of Nature's own secrets, and the Art of Alchemy must . . . be pronounced not only unknowable, but utterly impossible."[60] The technical language rehearsed by the Yeoman, who admits to understanding virtually none of it, exemplifies the commonplace objection that "the books of the so-called Alchemistic Sages are full of obscurities and wantonly perplexing phraseology" (p. 59). The canon's frequently broken (albeit tempered) pots, which fail to withstand the heat of the fire and the "greet violence" (VIII.908) of the metals within, validate the objection that "glass, stone, and earthenware jars and vessels can never take the place of the natural womb of metals in the bosom of the earth" (p. 56). Even more serious are the moral and religious objections to alchemy raised by the argument of the Yeoman's tales, both of which are replete with infernal and diabolic imagery.[61]

The tale's *responsio* to these multiple objections is considerably weaker and more ambiguous than that offered by Petrus Bonus. After

[59] *De crimine falsi* (*Spondent quas non exhibent*), in Walsh, *The Popes and Science*, p. 125. Compare Gower's comment in the *Confessio* on the poverty of alchemists: "To gete a pound thei spenden fyve" (IV.2591).

[60] Petrus Bonus, *The New Pearl of Great Price*, trans. Arthur Edward Waite (1894; London: Vincent Stuart, 1963), pp. 59, 54. Hereafter page numbers are parenthetical. I thank Mary Olson for introducing me to this work.

[61] See K. Michael Olmert, "The *Canon's Yeoman's Tale*: An Interpretation," *Annuale Mediaevale* 8 (1967): 70–94; Lawrence V. Ryan, "The Canon's Yeoman's Desperate Confession," *Chaucer Review* 8.4 (1974): 297–310; Joseph Grennen, "The Canon's Yeoman and the Cosmic Furnace: Language and Meaning in the 'Canon's Yeoman's Tale,' " *Criticism* 4 (1962): 225–40; Bruce A. Rosenberg, "Swindling Alchemist, Antichrist," *Centennial Review of Arts and Sciences* 6 (1962): 566–80.

summarizing all the arguments against alchemy (VIII.1388–1425) and exhorting practicing alchemists to abandon the art, the Yeoman allows the alchemical "philosophres" to refute his conclusion: "Lo, thus seith Arnold of the Newe Toun, / As his Rosarie maketh mencioun" (VIII.1427–29).[62] The alchemists he cites, however, only seem to confirm his reasons. Arnald of Villanova first quotes an occult passage from Hermes Trismegistus and then discourages anyone from attempting the art "But if that he th'entencioun and speche / Of philosophres understonde kan" (VIII.1443–44). A dialogue between Plato and his disciple "Senior" confirms that the stone is by definition a secret that none of the philosophers may reveal. The true object of alchemical search is, in fact, "so lief and deere" to Christ that God has reserved to himself the right to reveal it directly to those whom he chooses to inspire (VIII.1467–71).

The brief words of Plato that represent the obscurity of alchemy as divinely ordained to protect the secret from profanation recall a commonplace defence of the art.[63] Although the Yeoman is quick to conclude that alchemical practice is "contrarie" to God's will (VIII.1477), Plato's closing words, Christlike details in the portrait of the Yeoman's long-suffering and now betrayed master, significant analogies between "The Canon's Yeoman's Tale" and "The Second Nun's Tale," and the possibility of latter-day miracles all combine to leave the *quaestio* open. Like Gower, who criticizes practical aspects of alchemy but who nevertheless maintains that "the science of himself is trewe / Upon the forme as it was founded" (*CA* IV.2598–99), Chaucer declines in the end to condemn alchemy. The idolatrous "stoon" to which Saint Cecilia draws insistent attention (VIII.500, 501, 503) may or may not be the "stoon" of the alchemists, just as there is more than one "canon" in the Yeoman's tales—one of them a falsifier, the other a dedicated artisan who speaks no word in his own defense.

The artisanal cast of "The Canon's Yeoman's Tale" places the material elements, metals, equipment, practitioners, and procedures of alchemy in the foreground, even as it alludes only distantly and oc-

[62]   See Edgar H. Duncan, "Chaucer and 'Arnold of the Newe Toun,' " *MLN* 57 (1942): 31–33.
[63]   See Joseph Grennen, "Chaucer's 'Secree of Secrees': An Alchemical 'Topic,' " *PQ* 42 (1963): 562–66; Dorothee Finkelstein, "The Code of Chaucer's 'Secree of Secrees': Arabic Alchemical Terminology in 'The Canon's Yeoman's Tale,' " *Archiv für das Studium der neueren Sprachen und Literaturen* 207 (1970): 260–76.

casionally to God and the soul. The materiality of the narrative is, in fact, so pronounced that it virtually catalogs the cosmos from the "elementes foure" to the "foure spirites and the bodies sevene" to countless herbal ingredients and "poudres diverse, asshes, donge, pisse, and cley" (VIII.1460, 820, 807). Much of the Yeoman's long tale in two parts consists of lists of concrete things, both familiar and exotic.

One effect of this plenum is a representation of God and the soul too in material terms. The bodies of the Yeoman and his Canon are physically assimilated to and affected by their alchemical practice. When the pair arrive on horseback, the Canon (like their horses) is sweating hard: "His forhead dropped as a stillatorie / Were ful of plantayne and of paritorie" (VIII.580–81). The Yeoman's "chaunged" face is "discoloured" with "a leden hewe" (VIII.667, 664, 728) and his eye is "blered" (VIII.730) as an apparent result of his habitual closeness to fire and heated metals. The Canon smells of "brymstoon" (VIII.885).

As others have noted, these physical properties are, in turn, emblematic of the total condition of the alchemists, for whom the human soul tends to be as material as the "foure spirits" whose "ascensioun" (VIII.820, 778) they effect and to whom the devil's presence is indicated by stench, heat, and explosion. In the Canon's workshop, the repeated breaking of pots and the scattering of their contents leads in an immediate, elemental fashion to fiendish "rancour" and "greet strif" (VIII.919, 931) among the Canon's apprentices. Sometimes the Yeoman represents his contract with his lord as a pact with the devil; at other times, he virtually identifies God with the "philosophres stoon" (VIII.861). In a confused speech, the Yeoman leaves it ambiguous whether God is withholding the stone from them despite all their labors, expenses, and sorrows (as the speech of Plato later suggests), or whether it is the stone itself that "wol nat come us to" (VIII.867). The same passage also leaves it unclear whether God inspires within them the "good hope" (VIII.870) that impels them to continue their search, or whether it is the alluring influence of the stone itself.

This kind of alchemical pan-materialism figures prominently in the objections raised against alchemy. The five pseudo-Aristotelian objections recorded by Petrus Bonus (Reasons 20–26) emphasize that the change in accidents affected by alchemical experimentation is not substantial change, and that our physical senses cannot afford us access to the "inward and essential nature" of metals (pp. 70–71). More pointedly, Reason 15 objects that

> the Sages represent the Stone as bearing the same relation to the metals which is borne by form to substance, or, soul to body: hence it cannot be extracted from such gross things as metals.... Nor can so highly spiritual a substance as the Philosopher's Stone is represented [to be] be obtained from the metallic spirits. (Pp. 61–62)

By pairing the materialistic view of "The Canon's Yeoman's Tale" with the dualistic stance of "The Second Nun's Tale" and interweaving the two tales through echoic, alchemical language, Chaucer exemplifies the ongoing academic debate concerning *quaestiones* about the materiality of the soul, its existence as substance, its kinds and parts, its faculties, and its separability or inseparability as a form from the body.[64] Unlike the alchemists, for whom all spirits are somehow corporeal, the Second Nun understands the soul to be decidedly incorporeal.

As countless readers have noted, the Second Nun and her Cecilia exhibit a radical dualism that verges upon the Manichaean. The Nun begs illumination for her "soule in prison," which is troubled by "the contagioun / Of [hir] body" (VIII.71–73).[65] Her heroine chastises her flesh, wearing a hairshirt "under hir robe of gold" (VIII.132). She abstains from sex even in marriage in order to keep her body "unwemmed" like that of the "Virgine wemmelees" (VIII.137, 47). She and her fellow Christians court martyrdom for the sake of "bettre lif in oother place, / That nevere shal be lost" (VIII.323–24). In an emblematic separation of body and soul, earth and heaven, Valerian and Tiburce both lose "hir hevedes in the place" of execution, while their souls journey upward and homeward "to the kyng of grace" (VIII.398–99).

More importantly, Cecilia's experience and that of her fellow Chris-

---

[64] See especially Grennen, "St. Ceilia's 'Chemical Wedding,' " and Rosenberg, "Contrary Tales."

[65] In her notes on lines 71–74 in *The Riverside Chaucer*, Florence H. Ridley indicates that Chaucer's use of the word "contagion" is "the earliest use of the word in this sense in English" (p. 944). It apparently translates Macrobius's "contagione corporis." The passage as a whole echoes Macrobius, *Commentary on the Dream of Scipio*, trans. William H. Stahl, (1952; New York: Columbia University Press, 1990), I.x.9, I.xi.2–4, and I.xi.11, pp. 128, 130–33.

tians affirms the "soothnesse" of supernatural realities, in comparison with which earthly realities are only "dremes" (VIII.261–63).[66] Belief and baptism afford them access to another plane of existence where they can see and commune with angels and wear heavenly crowns (invisible to the uninitiated) "of roses and of lilie," whose flowers shall never decay nor "lese hir soote savour" (VIII.220, 228–29). The sensual appeal of this higher plane is paradoxically both incorporeal (in that it leads to a rejection of the world of ordinary sense-experience), and corporeal (in its evocation of a fifth, ethereal essence, above the elements of this world).

The concrete things of heaven—the sight of angels, the vision of the man holding "a book with lettre of gold" (VIII.202), and the smell of the floral garlands—affect the ethereal soul in its elemental thingness in a manner that directly parallels the effect of physical things on the lower, material soul. As Tiburce remarks, "The sweete smel that in myn herte I fynde / Hath chaunged me al in another kynde" (VIII.251–52). Cecilia herself exhibits qualities of "another kynde" when her body, placed in a "bath of flambes red" (VIII.515) withstands the heat without harm and without perspiring even "a drope" of sweat (VIII.522).

As the story unfolds, Cecilia's supernatural qualities and zealous "good werkynge" (VIII.116) in word and deed bring about conversion after conversion, beginning with Valerian, who changes from being "lyk a fiers leoun" to being "as meke as evere was any lomb" (VIII.198–99) in his embrace of Christian belief.[67] As Patterson observes, in the case of Cecilia, Christ's own "conversionary power passes unimpeded through a saint uncontaminated by either sexual attachments or psychological complexity."[68] Unchanging herself, Cecilia like the philosopher's stone powerfully changes the world around her.

---

[66] Sherry Reames has argued that Chaucer's version of Cecilia's legend uses abridgement to emphasize faith, miracles, and supernatural agency at the expense of human reason and natural psychological processes. See "The Cecilia Legend as Chaucer Inherited It and Retold It: The Disappearance of an Augustinian Ideal," *Speculum* 55.1 (1980): 38–57, but also "A Recent Discovery Concerning the Sources of the 'Second Nun's Tale,' " *MP* 87 (1990): 337–61.

[67] This particular conversion is typically solar. As Kay observes, "the Sun bears a special astrological relation to the zodiacal signs of Leo and Aries," and hence with images of lions, sheep, and rams (*Dante's Christian Astrology*, p. 109).

[68] Patterson, "Perpetual Motion," p. 31.

In her power to effect conversion, Cecilia resembles Custance, whose constancy under trial likens her, too, to the miraculous stone and whose journeys are marked by the working of miracles. Custance's story begins with the Syrian merchants, whose report of her beauty and virtue causes the Sultan to fall in love with her. The negotiations that follow in Syria and Rome end, on the one hand, in the Sultan's decision to be baptized a Christian in order to overcome any legal barrier to their marriage on the grounds of *disparitas cultus*; on the other, in the joint decision of the Roman Emperor, the Pope, and "al the chirche, and al the chivalrie" (II.235) to assent to the Sultan's marriage proposal "in destruccioun of mawmettrie, / And in encrees of Cristes lawe deere" (II.236–37).

The complicated legal counsel, "tretys and embassadrie" (II.233) surrounding Custance's marriage accord with the Sultan would have recalled to Chaucer's audience the conditions rendering licit and/or valid a Christian's marriage to a non-Christian.[69] The tale's initial narrative emphasis on the conversion of a non-Christian king to Christianity through his marriage to a Christian spouse is underscored later when "by Custances mediacioun" (VIII.684) the king of Northumbria first converts to Christianity and then marries her.

Although both the Sultan and Alla are baptized prior to their marriage with Custance, unlike Valerian, who is christened after his wedding to Cecilia, all three husbands are converted through the Christian woman whom they espouse. As Sharon Farmer has shown, successive commentators on 1 Corinthians 7:14 translated the verse in ways that strengthened its force. Whereas Augustine and the early Church Fathers, following Saint Paul, endorsed mixed marriages on the grounds that "the unbelieving husband is consecrated [*sanctificatus*] through his the believing wife," later commentators spoke of the husband being "saved" (*potest salvari, salvabitur*) or "converted" (*possit convertere, convertitur*) through his wife and thus accorded to the Christian woman an active role of increased responsibility and power.[70] Encouraged by 1 Peter 3:1–7, thirteenth-century clerics such as Thomas Chobham extended the application of the verse, moreover, to apply to the wifely conversion of not only non-Christian husbands

[69] See Paul E. Beichner, "Chaucer's Man of Law and *Disparitas Cultus*," *Speculum* 23 (1948): 70–75.

[70] Sharon Farmer, "Persuasive Voices: Clerical Images of Medieval Wives," *Speculum* 61.3 (1986): 517–43, esp. pp. 527–30.

but also sinful Christian ones—plunderers, usurers, oppressors of the poor—through their good example and alluring speech: "because no priest is able to soften the heart of a man the way his wife can."[71]

In the various commentaries on 1 Corinthians 7:14, Cecilia figures prominently among the examples of saintly wives who effected their husbands' conversions.[72] Indeed, Cecilia's archetypal stature was such that the story of any Christian woman who effected her husband's conversion to Christianity would have recalled hers. Interpreted from a clerical perspective, therefore, Chaucer's chiastic pairing of the tales of Custance and Cecilia is perfectly appropriate.

Custance's legend, moreover, complements Cecilia's in important ways. Both women are virtuous and associated with gold. Like Cecilia, who wears a "robe of gold" (VIII.132) on her wedding day, Custance is given in marriage to the Sultan, along with "certein gold, I noot what quantitee" (II.242). Cecilia is tried by fire and Custance by water, the two elements essential to alchemical purification. As Rosenberg and others have observed, the lighter elements of air and fire predominate in Cecilia's story of fragrance, music, light, and flames.[73] In "The Man of Law's Tale," on the other hand, the heavier elements of wind, water, and shore predominate. As the narrator prays when the hapless Custance is set again to sea, "For wynd and weder almyghty God purchase, / And brynge hire hoom!" (II.873–74). Her watery circulation is, moreover, appropriate to the solar sphere, because the Sun, as Kay has demonstrated, was understood by astrologers and physicists alike to be responsible for the motion of water and air.[74]

More importantly, however, the tales of Custance and Cecilia provide different models for the relationship between body and soul. As we have seen, in the case of the Second Nun and her protagonist, the body is the soul's "prison" (VIII.71) from which it is released. Although the bodies of martyred "seintes" like Valerian, Tiburce, and Cecilia may become relics buried "under the stoon" (VIII.548–49, 409), and Cecilia's own empty "hous" may be "halwed" as a

---

[71] Ibid., p. 517.
[72] Ibid., pp. 532–33, 536. Farmer mentions, in addition to Cecilia, Augustine's mother, Monica; Queen Clotilda; and Ethelbert's wife, Bertha.
[73] Rosenberg, "Contrary Tales," p. 280.
[74] Kay, *Dante's Christian Astrology*, pp. 103–4.

"chirche" (VIII.546–51), the body in the Nun's story is something the soul easily leaves behind. The soul itself is so substantial, ethereal, and separable that it has no real need of the body. The soul has its own sights, sounds, smells, even its own angelic lovers, and these are all of "another kynde" from those of the body.

Custance's story, on the other hand, envisions the body/soul relationship repeatedly as the sea voyage of a woman in a ship. V. A. Kolve's brilliant iconographic study of the tale has taught us that Custance's three voyages (from Rome to Syria, from Syria to Northumbria, from Northumbria back to Rome) evoke three different levels of interpretation for the image of the ship at sea. Custance's "second journey brings into prominence a new symbolic meaning, that of the individual soul journeying through the sea of this world, subject to the changes of fortune and the temptations of sin," whereas her third journey in a rudderless ship suggests "the journey the soul makes after death."[75] Both journeys associate the ship with the body as the soul's companion and shelter and emphasize the soul's dependence upon and near-inseparability from the body.

The very meaning of Custance's name and the unfolding of her destiny point to a close body/soul relationship. As "constancy" she represents the eternity of the soul; as "long suffering" she combines that perdurance with an affliction that is felt with the body and the soul's bodily-linked affections. Unlike Cecilia's ethereal body of "another kynde," which resists heat and flame and only yields (after three blows and several days) to the sword, Custance's body is vulnerable. Unlike Cecilia, who seemingly feels no grief, Custance meets her fate bravely but "with a deedly pale face" (II.822), and her words express her suffering at her baby's plight and her husband's inexplicably cruel disownment. Indeed, Custance's manifest suffering unites her martyrdom closely and explicitly to Christ's passion and death, whereas Cecilia's trial is the trial of a saint already somehow past death, beyond the body, and eager to leave the world behind.

Cecilia's audacious "werkynge," which sets everything around her into motion, likens her to the soul of the Platonist philosophers, which is so divinized that it both moves itself and the body it inhabits.

---

[75] V. A. Kolve, *Chaucer and the Imagery of Narrative: The First Five Canterbury Tales* (Stanford: Stanford University Press, 1984), pp. 325, 340.

Custance's passive long-suffering, on the other hand, causes her to resemble the soul as Aristotle and Aquinas describe it, that is, as unmoved in its substance, but moved and moving in its attributes.[76] Repeatedly being sent from place to place, she welcomes "Goddes sonde" (II.523,826) as it comes to her through changing circumstances beyond her control. Her emotional responses are sensitive, but her basic attitude of a freely given, instrumental assent to God's Will remains constant. Custance's understanding of the divine "firste moevyng" (II.295) differs radically from the materialistic view of the lawyer who narrates her story, with the result that she, like the Unmoved Mover, is constant herself and a cause of conversion for those to whom she is sent.

Custance's marriage, too, contrasts with Cecilia's and mirrors a body/soul relationship unlike hers. Cecilia's marriage to Valerian is unconsummated and radically virginal—a non-marriage that leaves the spouses side by side, joined only by the commingled fragrance of their invisible garlands, bearing fruit only in spiritual children. Custance's marriage to Alla, on the other hand, is physically consummated and fertile. Although the Man of Law interposes a tasteless, snickering comment about what happens when Custance and Alla "goon to bedde" (II.708) on their wedding night, there is no indication on Custance's part of an aversion to marital relations, and there are strong signs that she loves both her baby and her "housbonde routhelees" (II.863), and that Alla cares deeply about "his wyf and his child" (II.878).

If Kolve is right in thinking that Custance's third sea voyage powerfully evokes the imagery of the soul-journey after death (and I believe he is), and that Custance's safe homecoming to Rome mirrors the soul's arrival at the heavenly *patria*, then we may also discover in Custance's blissful reunion with her "giltelees" (II.1073) husband an image of the soul's reunion with the body.[77] The narrator suggests as much when he declares:

---

[76]   Chaucer would have been familiar with the terms of this debate from Macrobius, *Commentary on the Dream of Scipio*, II.xiii–xvi (pp. 225–43 in Stahl). There Macrobius at great length argues for the Platonic position of the self-moved soul against the Aristotelian view of the soul as an unmoved mover. Lines 71–74 of "The Second Nun's Tale" offer proof that Chaucer was drawing on Macrobius in his characterization of Cecilia. See n. 65 above. For Chaucerian references to the unmoved Mover, see *Boece* III.pr.2.194–99 and Theseus's speech in "The Knight's Tale" (I.3004).

[77]   The Christian association of the marriage between man and woman and the rela-

> I trowe an hundred tymes been they kist,
> And swich a blisse is ther bitwix hem two,
> That, save the joye that lasteth everemo,
> Ther is noon lyk that any creature
> Hath seyn or shal, whil that the world may dure.
>
> (II.1074–78)

Their reunion resembles that for which Dante's disembodied souls are longing, as they await the restoration of their own bodies, and desire bodies "not only for themselves, perhaps, but for / their mothers, fathers, and for others dear / to them before they were eternal flames" (*Par.* 14.64–66).

In "The Man of Law's Tale" Chaucer fittingly responds with the story of a married saint to the epithalamium of Dante's fifth and fairest flame, Solomon, whose Song of Songs "breathes forth such love that all the world below / hungers for tidings of it" (*Par.* 10.110–11). At another level, the Ellesmere arrangement of solar tales opposes "The Man of Law's Tale" to the extreme positions of materialism and dualism represented respectively in "The Canon Yeoman's Tale" and "The Second Nun's Tale." Like Solomon's closing speech as the pilgrim Dante prepares to leave the heaven of the Sun, the tale of Custance uses none of alchemy's technical language, but its symbolic patterns—like Solomon's image of the glowing coal enfolded in flame—speak of miraculous conversions effected through an alchemy of love that is neither materialistic nor dualistic, but rather incarnational (in a Franciscan sense), composite (in a way evocative of Aquinas), and marital (in the manner of Solomon's mystical Song).

In the Ellesmere *Tales*, however, even that word is not the last in the *quaestio*. Rather, the Ellesmere order of solar tales—Custance, Cecilia, and the Canon's Yeoman—exactly parallels that of Dante, who first tells the story of Saint Francis and Lady Poverty, then that of Saint Dominic and Lady Faith, and ends with Solomon's speech. If "The

---

tionship between the body and the soul gains classic expression in Saint Paul's counsel that "husbands ought to love their wives just as they love their own bodies" (Ephesians 5:28) and in biblical commentaries on Solomon's Song of Songs. See my *Song of Songs in the Middle Ages* (Ithaca: Cornell University Press, 1990), esp. pp. 30–32.

Man of Law's Tale" intimates Solomon's true teaching, "The Canon's Yeoman's Tale" represents the alchemical wisdom of seeming Solomons, for whom the burning coal symbolizes an earthly, not a heavenly, secret of secrets.

Mercurius hathe significacion of tidyngis, eloquens, & disputacions & computacions. . . . Venus enclyneth men to lust & love.

—On the Elections of Times

5

MERCURIAL MARRIAGE IN FRAGMENTS

III–IV–V:

PHILOSOPHIC MISOGAMY AND

THE TRIVIUM OF WOMAN'S KNOWLEDGE

Unlike the Dante of the *Paradiso,* whose pilgrim travels upward from the sphere of the Moon first to the sphere of Mercury and thence to that of Venus, the Ellesmere Chaucer charts a more complex astrological and educational course for his pilgrims, who first descend to, and then ascend from, a sublunar center. Also unlike Dante, who keeps the spheres of Mercury and Venus distinct, Chaucer capitalizes on the criss-crossing orbits of the two planets which, as both Macrobius and Martianus Capella record, encircle the sun and vary in their respective distance from the earth: "When both planets have a position above the sun, Mercury is closer to the earth; when they are below the sun, Venus is closer, inasmuch as it has a broader and more sweeping orbit."[1]

Whereas the Dante of the *Convivio* associates Mercury with Dialectic and Venus with Rhetoric, the Dante of the *Paradiso* subordinates references to these verbal arts to the themes of empire and love, respectively.[2] Unlike Dante, who deals with each planetary sphere separately,

---

[1] *Martianus Capella and the Seven Liberal Arts: The Marriage of Philology and Mercury,* vol. 2, trans. William H. Stahl and Richard Johnson (New York: Columbia University Press, 1977), VIII, p. 333. See also Macrobius, *Commentary on the Dream of Scipio,* trans. William H. Stahl (New York: Columbia University Press, 1952, repr. 1990), I.xix.1–5, pp. 162–63.

[2] See Dante, *The Banquet,* trans. Christopher Ryan (Saratoga, Calif.: ANMA Libri,

Chaucer discovers in the close pairing and criss-crossing of the planetary orbits an astrological image for a literal, dramatic rivalry among the pilgrims—a rivalry that adumbrates both the rising social tension between the sexes and the closely related (because gendered) academic turf-fighting among the teachers and practitioners of the verbal arts. As Alisoun of Bath explains in a passage that provides an astrological heading for the story blocks that follow, because "Venus falleth ther Mercurie is reysed" (III.705), the "children of Mercurie and of Venus / Been in hir wirkyng ful contrarius; / Mercurie loveth wysdam and science, / And Venus loveth ryot and dispence" (III.697–700).

When Dante the pilgrim enters the sphere of Venus, Charles Martel recites for him the opening line of Dante's own canzone, "Voi che 'ntendendo il terzo ciel movete" (*Par.* 8.37: "You who, through understanding, move the third heaven").[3] In the *Convivio* Dante interprets that canzone to refer literally to the *donna gentile* who comforted him at the time of Beatrice's death; allegorically to Lady Philosophy herself.[4] Dante goes on to compare Venus, "the third heaven," to Rhetoric, "for Rhetoric is sweeter than all the other sciences,"[5] even as love is the inspirer of poetry. Recited in the *Paradiso*, the canzone retains all of these earlier associations, even as it takes on a new meaning in relation to the heavenly Beatrice and the poetry of *caritas*.

Dante provides a kind of (lesser) double for the *donna gentile* and for Beatrice in the person of the Venusian saint, Cunizza da Romano, who was the beloved of the troubador Sordello, and who alludes to the love-poet (and later Cistercian) Folquet as a fellow Venusian. Chaucer, in turn, creates a double for Cunizza in Alisoun of Bath. Both women have been married five times and have had clerkly husbands.[6] Like Alisoun, who justifies her "al Venerien" (III.609) conduct through her birth-horoscope, Cunizza finds "the reason for

---

1989), II.xiii, p. 68. On the special association of both dialectic and clerks with Mercury, see also Gustavo Costa, "Dialectic and Mercury (Education, Magic, and Religion in Dante)," in *The "Divine Comedy" and the Encyclopedia of Arts and Sciences*, ed. Giuseppe Di Scipio and Aldo Scaglione (Philadelphia: John Benjamins, 1988), pp. 43–64.

[3] Here and throughout I use Dante Alighieri, *Paradiso*, trans. Allen Mandelbaum (New York: Bantam, 1986).

[4] See Dante, *The Banquet*, II.ii, p. 44; II.xii, p. 66.

[5] Ibid., II.xiii, p. 68.

[6] Fourteenth-century commentators on Dante's *Paradiso* were fascinated by Cunizza. Jacopo della Lana, for instance, remarks that "she was a woman in love in all her ages, and so generous in her love she would have counted it great villainy to refuse it to any man who sought it courteously." See the notes to lines 31–36 by Anthony Oldcorn and Daniel Feldman, with Giuseppe Di Scipio, in *Paradiso*, p. 341.

[her] fate" in Venusian influence: "This planet's radiance conquered me" (*Par.* 9.33–34). Dante's Cunizza does not regret her amorous destiny, which has brought her to heaven, but she admits that "vulgar minds may find this hard to see" (*Par.* 9.34–36). Chaucer seizes upon this admission and entertains the vulgar doubts that Dante suppresses by allowing the Wife of Bath, as an *altera Cunizza,* to tell her own story and defend her views at length.

Through the mediation of Cunizza, the Wife's erudite treatment of "scole-matere" (III.1272) ultimately answers to the philosophical discourses of Dante's bluestocking Beatrice. Indeed, Chaucer uses the Wife and the story-sequence initiated by her Prologue and Tale to give an extended comment on the role of *eros* in both the educational process and philosophical poetry. As Alastair J. Minnis has shown, late-medieval vernacular writers had to deal with the "issue of whether *amor* can be reconciled with *auctoritas*," of whether a lover can be a philosopher.[7] Gower gave a partial "yes" to the question, identifying "John Gower" as Amans, but he does so only retrospectively, naming himself for the first time in the closing lines of the *Confessio* when the lover is finally cured of his afflictive, inordinate attachment to his lady (*CA* VIII.2908). Dante answered in the affirmative, dedicating love-poetry to Lady Philosophy and praising the Beatrice of Paradise in what Minnis terms a "calculated attempt to elevate vernacular poetry through the appropriation (and adaptation, of course)" of scholasticism.[8] Boccaccio found it difficult, however, to reconcile Dante's authorial status with his persistent "lust" (*lussuria*) for Beatrice,[9] and Chaucer, too, evidently had strong misgivings. In his earlier poems, Chaucer never casts himself unequivocally in the Dantean role of a lover-philosopher, and in the "Marriage Group" of the *Canterbury Tales,* he dramatizes the this-worldly incompatibility of *amours* and academics. In so doing, he becomes the poet of both, but in a way than differs radically from Dante's.

Whereas Dante celebrates a rhetorical common ground between the children of Mercury and Venus,[10] Chaucer turns that common

[7]   Alastair J. Minnis, "Authors in Love: The Exegesis of Late-Medieval Love-Poets," in *The Uses of Manuscripts in Literary Studies: Essays in Memory of Judson Boyce Allen,* ed. Charlotte C. Morse, Penelope R. Doob, and Marjorie C. Woods (Kalamazoo, Mich.: Medieval Institute Publications, 1992), p. 183.

[8]   Ibid., p. 185.

[9]   Ibid., pp. 181–83.

[10]   See Richard Kay, *Dante's Christian Astrology* (Philadelphia: University of Pennsylvania Press, 1994), p. 83.

ground into a battlefield of the verbal arts that pits Mercurial clerks against Venusian wives, and wives against clerks, within a larger scheme of social and scientific division. Contrary to a commonplace critical understanding, the "marriage group" of tales in Fragments III–IV–V is constituted not merely by the pilgrims' dramatized responses to the Wife's "preamble" (III.831) and "preambulacioun" (III.837), nor by the presentation of divergent positions on marital "maisterie."[11] The series of fragments has a complex intertextual relationship to the varieties of clerical literature on marriage. The three fragments not only abound in explicit references to and echoes of the misogamous and antigamous literature current in the universities; they also systematically recall the literary tradition of pedagogical epithalamia in order to oppose clerical wisdom to the wiles of women in an ordered exposé of woman's rhetoric, logic, and grammar.

The Universities and the Battle of the Sexes

The rise of the universities in the thirteenth and fourteenth centuries created a celibate male enclave with access to knowledge that was largely denied to women. As Alan B. Cobban explains, the authorities at the English universities supported the view that students were espoused to Wisdom by endeavoring to keep women as far apart from the universities as possible. They severely restricted the on-campus visits of women, and "many sets of college statutes . . . declared that all servants were to be males, because the proximity of women might provoke sexual immorality."[12] On the other hand, the repressive official attitude toward not only contact with women, but also the enjoyment of music, games, pets, sports and all forms of distractions from study, backfired in the "excesses of drunkenness, gam-

---

[11] First proposed by George Lyman Kittredge, the idea of a "Marriage Group" has excited considerable discussion, chiefly among critics concerned with issues of framing. Recent criticism has questioned the very existence of the "Marriage Group." For pertinent studies, see George Lyman Kittredge, "Chaucer's Discussion of Marriage," *MP* 9 (1912): 435–67, repr. in *Chaucer Criticism*, vol. 1, ed. Richard J. Schoeck and Jerome Taylor (Notre Dame: University of Notre Dame Press, 1960, repr. 1975), pp. 130–59, esp. 158n1.

[12] Alan B. Cobban, *The Medieval English Universities: Oxford and Cambridge to circa. 1500* (Berkeley: University of California Press, 1988), p. 378. Subsequent citations are parenthetical.

bling, immorality, disorder and crime that were common to all medieval universities" (p. 363). Prostitution, in particular, was "a perennial problem in the university towns, and repeated legislative attempts were made to drive prostitutes out of Oxford and Cambridge" (p. 364). Chaucer's students are generally more notable for their *amours* than for their studies, and the reputation of the universities was in fact so bad that John Gower's *Vox Clamantis* laments the passing of a former age when scholars wedded themselves to true Wisdom and heralds instead a new age when clerks attend the universities for less noble reasons: sexual license, a life of ease, and careerist hopes of advancement.[13]

A threefold stream of matrimonial literature attended and supported the obligatory celibacy of medieval scholars. At the positive pole, a series of epithalamic, pedagogical works celebrated in allegorical terms the bliss of learning and thus persuaded the cleric to dedicate himself undividedly to the pursuit of Wisdom as a surrogate spouse. At the negative pole, a notorious body of misogamous (and frequently misogynist) texts maligned marriage to flesh-and-blood women on the grounds of the incompatibility of scholarship with the married state. Clerical misogamy thus did not exist in isolation, but rather in creative tension with its opposite, the advocated marriage of Mercury to Philology. A third stream supported celibacy, but not virginity. It drew inspiration from, and participated in, the antigamous literature of courtly love to allow amorous clerks the pleasures of furtive, often adulterous sex without the loss of their clerical status.[14]

The philosophic misogamy attendant on the rise of the universities found its classical formulation in the short "Golden Book" attributed by Saint Jerome to Theophrastus. In answer to the question "whether the wise man marries," Theophrastus concludes that "a wise man therefore must not take a wife," because "the study of philosophy will

[13]   See John Gower, *Vox Clamantis* III, chapters 28–29, in *The Major Latin Works*, trans. Eric W. Stockton (Seattle: University of Washington Press, 1962), pp. 162–64.
[14]   I am indebted to Katharina M. Wilson and Elizabeth M. Makowski (*Wykked Wyves and the Woes of Marriage: Misogamous Literature from Juvenal to Chaucer* [Albany: State University of New York Press, 1990]) for the useful distinctions they make between and among misogyny, misogamy (ascetic, philosophical, and general), and antigamy. They do not offer a parallel treatment of pedagogical epithalamia. For a different attempt to explore the Chaucerian link between the patristic and courtly views of women, see Daniel M. Murtaugh, "Women and Geoffrey Chaucer," *ELH* 38.4 (1971): 473–92.

be hindered, and it is impossible for anyone to attend to his books and his wife at the same time" ("Non est ergo uxor ducenda sapienti. Primum enim impediri studia Philosophiae; nec posse quemquam libris et uxori pariter inservire").[15] Theophrastus goes on to enumerate the cost of women's clothes, the patience required to endure their nightly prattle and nagging complaints, the anxiety husbands suffer over their wives' fidelity, and the discomfort caused by the physical and temperamental defects of women. Jerome, who contextualizes Theophrastus's work within his own *Epistola adversus Jovinianum*, uses the example of Socrates' troubled marriage to Xanthippe, as well as the authority of Cicero, to corroborate Theophrastus's conclusion about the incompatibility of a wife and books in a philosopher's life: "When Cicero after divorcing Terentia was requested by Hirtius to marry his sister, he put the matter altogether aside and said that he could not possibly devote himself to a wife and to philosophy" (PL 23, c278: "non posse se uxori et philosophiae pariter operam dare").[16]

As Robert A. Pratt, Katharina Wilson, Elizabeth Makowski, and others have shown, beginning in the twelfth century the texts of Theophrastus and Jerome became a rich seedbed for the philosophic misogamy of a new intellectual elite. Peter Abelard's *Theologia Christiana* and John of Salisbury's *De molestis et oneribus coniugiorum* (1159) both give prominence to Theophrastus and Jerome. Abelard's *Historia calamitatum* (c. 1132) records Héloïse's famous argument against their marriage—a *dissuasio* later summarized in Jean de Meun's *Roman de la Rose* and alluded to in the Wife of Bath's Prologue (III.677–78). In it Héloïse echoes Theophrastus, Jerome, Cicero, and Seneca to elaborate on the theme of the incompatibility of marriage and childbearing with philosophical pursuits, and she begs Abelard, the *philosophus mundi*, not to betray his high calling by binding himself to one woman.[17] Also dating from the twelfth century, Walter Map's *Dissuasio*

---

[15]   I quote from the translation of Theophrastus that appears in *Woman Defamed and Woman Defended: An Anthology of Medieval Texts*, ed. Alcuin Blamires with Karen Pratt and C. W. Marx (Oxford: Clarendon Press, 1992), p. 70. For the Latin text, see PL 23, c276–78. For a study of the influence of Theophrastus, see Charles B. Schmitt, "Theophrastus in the Middle Ages," *Viator* 2 (1971): 251–70.

[16]   *Woman Defamed, Woman Defended*, p. 70.

[17]   See Betty Radice, trans., *The Letters of Abelard and Heloïse* (New York: Penguin Books, 1974), esp. pp. 70–74. For the Latin text, see J. T. Muckle, ed., "Abelard's Letter of Consolation to a Friend (*Historia calamitatum*)," *Mediaeval Studies* 12 (1950): 163–213.

Valerii ad Ruffinum philosophum ne uxorem ducat records Valerius's arguments against marriage addressed to Rufinus, "a friend . . . of philosophic life" who has fallen victim to the disease of love-sickness. After echoing Jerome and Theophrastus, Map's Valerius concludes with echoes of Martianus's *De nuptiis* and Solomon's Song of Songs: "I would not have you be the husband of Venus, but of Pallas. She will deck you with precious necklaces, will clothe you in a wedding garment. Those espousals will be brilliant with Apollo for groomsman; this bridal song will Stilbon the married [i.e., Mercury] teach to the cedars of Lebanon."[18]

As Map's conclusion makes abundantly clear, misogamous tracts in the clerical tradition are closely related to—and, in dialogic terms, inseparable from—the opposed literary genre which persuades them toward an alternative marriage with a personified Wisdom. An enduring allegorical tradition had, of course, associated the themes of education with epithalamia. Fulgentius's fifth-century *Mitologiae* allegorizes the wedding of Orpheus and Eurydice as a failed attempt to join voice and judgment, expression and insight, practical and theoretical knowledge.[19] Martianus Capella's influential *De nuptiis Philologiae et Mercurii* (early fifth century) celebrates the allegorical union of word and wisdom in a celestial wedding feast attended by personifications of the seven liberal arts. Bernard Sylvestris's twelfth-century commentary on Virgil's *Aeneid* associates Aeneas's progress toward Italy with his mastery of the liberal arts and the three philosophies. In this scheme Aeneas's marriage to Lavinia and his renunciation of Dido represent his free choice of the spiritual and intellectual *labores* belonging to his homeward journey.[20] The *Anticlaudianus* of Alan de Lille represents the seven liberal arts as sisters working together to assist Prudence's flight toward God under the supervision of Concord who "entwines interchanges, bonds, ties, pacts, friendship, peace."[21]

---

[18] Walter Map, *Dissuasio Valerii ad Ruffinum*, in *De nugis curialium*, ed. and trans. M. R. James, rev. C. N. L. Brooke and R. A. B. Mynors (Oxford: Clarendon Press, 1983), pp. 287, 309.
[19] See *Fulgentius the Mythographer*, trans. Leslie George Whitbread (Columbus: Ohio State University Press, 1971), pp. 96–97.
[20] See Earl G. Schreiber and Thomas E. Maresca, Introduction to Bernardus Silvestris, *The Commentary on the First Six Books of Virgil's "Aeneid,"* trans. Schreiber and Maresca (Lincoln: University of Nebraska Press, 1979), p. xxviii.
[21] Alan of Lille, *Anticlaudianus*, trans. James J. Sheridan (Toronto: Pontifical Institute of Mediaeval Studies, 1973), II, p. 74.

Finally, John of Salisbury echoes Cicero, Martianus, Saint Augustine, and Matthew 19:6 when he celebrates in his *Metalogicon*

> this delightful and fruitful copulation of reason and speech which has given birth to so many outstanding cities, has made friends and allies of so many kingdoms, and has unified and knit together in bonds of love so many peoples. Whoever tries to 'thrust asunder what God has joined together' for the common good, should rightly be judged a public enemy. One who would eliminate the teaching of eloquence from philosophical studies, begrudges Mercury his possession of Philology, and wrests from Philology's arms her beloved Mercury.[22]

Chaucer and the Literature of Clerical Marriage and Misogamy

Like John of Salisbury, Chaucer makes explicit reference to Martianus Capella's *De nuptiis*. As we have emphasized elsewhere, a memorable passage in the *House of Fame* depicts Geoffrey supported by eagle's wings like the "fetheres of Philosophye," thinking of "Boece," "Marcian / And eke on Anteclaudian," as he makes his comic ascent to "Fames Hous" (II.974, 972, 985–86, 1027), the goal of his life's journey as a poet. A second double reference to *De nuptiis* occurs in "The Merchant's Tale" when Venus first laughs to see her knight January wed May, and the narrator proceeds to apostrophize "thou poete Marcian, / That writest us that ilke wedding murie / Of hire Philologie and him Mercurie, / And of the songes that the Muses songe!" (IV.1723–26, 1732–35).

The importance of Boethius, Alan de Lille, and Martianus as poetic models, the encyclopedic impulse evident in the Ellesmere *Tales* from its cosmological opening to its treatiselike conclusion, the explicit reference to *De nuptiis* in "The Merchant's Tale," the density of misogamous and antigamous citations, and the marked coincidence of marital concerns and "scole-matere" (III.1272) in Fragments III–IV–V urge us to find in the vivid images of Chaucer's "Marriage Group" a figural, misogamist, and antigamous representation of the *artes* to rival the allegorical representations of an earlier, Realist age. Chaucer not only, as Nicholas Orme has observed, includes "discussion of ed-

---

[22] *The Metalogicon of John of Salisbury*, trans. Daniel D. McGarry (Berkeley: University of California Press, 1955), I.1, p. 11. Subsequent citations are parenthetical.

ucation both on a large scale and in a serious way" in the "Marriage Group";[23] he also answers his predecessors in the tradition of pedagogical epithalamia by reliteralizing and inverting their terms.

In Martianus's syncretic *De nuptiis*, on the other hand, a pleasure-loving Epicurus, Venus, and Voluptas can contribute with little difficulty to the marriage of Mercury and Philology; indeed, their numinous powers of attraction are vitally necessary to consummate the union of reasoning and eloquence, thought and expression.[24] In Chaucer's "Marriage Group," on the other hand, "Mercurie loveth wysdam and science" (III.699), even as Martianus's Mercury loves Philology, but "the children of Mercurie" (III.697)—especially clerks and merchants—are markedly unhappy in marriages presided over by Venus. In Chaucer's "Marriage Group" the love of women and the love of books are set at odds; women's knowledge overturns clerical science; and the followers of Venus, Voluptas, and Epicurus continually pervert and forestall the fruitful copulation of reason and speech, theory and practice, in their application of the *artes*.

The action and interaction of tellers and tales thus allow Chaucer to explore not only the problematic marriage between wisdom and eloquence to which the educational process aspires, but also the difficulty of representing philosophical synthesis in nuptial terms, given what Emerson Brown, Jr., has called the "conflict between the classroom and the bedroom"[25]—a conflict especially evident among medieval clerks, who were ostensibly married to Athena, virulently misogamous in their theory, and too often antigamous in their social practice.

The Wife of Bath, whose "experience" confirms what clerical authorities attest about the "wo that is in marriage" (III.1–3), certainly encourages this kind of cultural and literary contextualization. First

---

[23]   Nicholas Orme, "Chaucer and Education," *Chaucer Review* 16 (1981): 55.
[24]   In *De nuptiis* II.213, an Epicurus "carrying roses mixed with violets and all the allurements of pleasure" ("Epicurus vero mixtas violis rosas et totas apportabat illecebras voluptatum") appears next to an Aristotle "seeking Entelechia." For the Latin text, see *Martianus Capella*, ed. James Willis (Leipzig: Teubner, 1983), p. 56. As Emerson Brown, Jr., observes, "Epicurus and his companions inhabit . . . the Paradise of the Intellectuals," and Epicurus brings "to the heavenly wedding tokens of sexual pleasure that appear often enough in *De nuptiis* to be read as a continuing motif" ("Epicurus and Voluptas in Late Antiquity: The Curious Testimony of Martianus Capella," *Traditio* 38 [1982]: 77, 100).
[25]   Brown, "Epicurus and Voluptas," p. 98.

of all, she states her opinions and relates her life story in a manner that echoes the "book of wikked wyves" (III.685) read nightly by her fifth husband, Jankyn, who was "som tyme . . . a clerk of Oxenford" (III.527), and she specifies its contents: "Valerie and Theofraste," Saint Jerome's "book agayn Jovinianum," the "Parables of Salomon," "Ovides Art," "Tertulan, Crisippus, Trotula, and Helowys," and other "bookes many on" filled with the stories of "wikked wyves," beginning with Eve (III.671–81).

Alisoun thus indicates the principle works in the clerical misogamous tradition, among them, Theophrastus's brief *De nuptiis*, which was preserved in Jerome's fourth-century *Epistola adversus Jovinianum*, and Walter Map's *Dissuasio Valerii ad Ruffinum philosophum ne uxorem ducat* (c.1180)—all of which, according to Robert A. Pratt, belonged to the rich store of "celibate propaganda [that] flourished in the university in the late Middle Ages."[26] Map's *Dissuasio Valerii*, in particular, was widely known in Oxford, where in the early fourteenth century "it became the subject of two long and learned commentaries, one by Nicholas Trevet, the other by John Ridewall."[27] The manuscript evidence, in short, supports Alisoun's claim that "it is an impossible / that any clerk wol speke good of wyves" (III.688–89).

The Pardoner, as Wilson and Makowski have observed, immediately recognizes in the Wife's Prologue the authorities regularly cited in the disputations staged at the universities on the canonical question "whether a wise man ought to marry" ("An vir sapiens ducat uxorem") and applies it to himself: "I was aboute to wedde a wyf; allas!" (III.166).[28] The same question figures at the beginning of "The Clerk's Tale," when the people beg the "discreet" marquis, Walter, to marry: "Chese yow a wyf" (IV.75, 130). The Merchant reintroduces the *quaestio* in the pseudo-debate about whether the "wys" knight, January, ought to marry and, if so, to whom: "Diverse men diversely hym tolde / Of mariage manye ensamples olde" (IV.1469–70). While old January's inclination is to "Deffie Theofraste" (IV.1310) and the

---

[26]   Robert A. Pratt, "Jankyn's Book of Wikked Wyves: Medieval Antimatrimonial Propaganda in the Universities," *Annuale Mediaevale* 3 (1962): 5.

[27]   Ibid., p. 20.

[28]   See Wilson and Makowski, *Wykked Wyves*, p. 153. Citing Quintilian (1st c.) and Boethius (6th c.), they observe that the indefinite topos, *an vir ducat uxorem*, and the limited topos, *an vir sapiens ducat uxorem*, were regular topics for debate in the schoolrooms of antiquity and the Middle Ages (p. 3).

clerks who share his misogamous stance, the Merchant himself in his "wepyng and waylyng" (IV.1213) echoes not only the Clerk's "Lenvoy Chaucer," but also the *Lamentations of Matheolus* as he regrets his own choice to marry: "Were I unbounden, also moot I thee / I wolde nevere eft comen in the snare" (IV.1126–27). The long complaint of Dorigen in "The Franklin's Tale" (V.1355–1456) summarizes the six chapters of Jerome's *Adversus Jovinianum* that precede the "Golden Book" of Theophrastus and thus harkens back to the Wife's Prologue to complete the circuit of misogamous intertextual reference.[29] The pattern of citation of authorities and *exempla* throughout the "Marriage Group" thus marks it, in the words of Wilson and Makowski, as "a traditionally developed *altercatio* on the subject of marriage."[30]

When the Wife of Bath in her Prologue first spins the web of misogamous citation that unifies the fragments, she corroborates her account of clerical practice astrologically by pointing to the heavens and the humours, to a fundamental opposition between Venus and Mercury and the kinds of marriages into which they enter. Astronomy and Physics, as theoretical sciences, thus confirm and explain her experience. "No womman of no clerk is preysed," she says, because "Venus falleth ther Mercurie is reysed" (III.705–6).

In the Wife's Prologue the allegorical antagonism between Venus and Mercury expresses itself finally, however, as analogy, Venusian "ryot" and chaos turning into symmetry, when Alisoun appropriates clerical status for herself: "Of fyve husbondes scoleiyng am I" (III.44f). She sets the wisdom of wives in competition with the clerical wisdom epitomized in "the wise kyng, daun Salomon" (III.35) when she affirms that "wise wyves" (III.225) master three arts. They know how to speak either shrewishly or sweetly to their husbands, how to confound their reasoning (III.231–34), and how to secure "maisterie" for themselves: "This knoweth every womman that is wys" (III.524). As we shall see, the Wife's threefold definition of womanly wisdom defines a trivium of female rhetoric, logic, and grammar and provides a general heading for the *distinctio* of topics developed in the "Marriage Group" of tales.

In the Ellesmere *Tales* the close relationship between Fragments

---

[29]   See Robert A. Pratt, "Saint Jerome in Jankyn's Book of Wikked Wyves," *Criticism* 5.4 (1963): 316–22. According to Pratt, "the Jerome materials in the Franklin's Tale answer the Jerome materials in the Wife of Bath's Prologue" (p. 321).

[30]   Wilson and Makowski, *Wykked Wyves*, p. 152.

III–IV–V raises a question of *divisio* that is characteristically medieval. As Judson Boyce Allen has insisted, "the crucial act of medieval criticism . . . is division," because division "exposes the *forma tractatus*" as a literal ordering of parts and thus makes possible the discovery of an analogous, pretextual (because conceptual) outline of topics. To the extent that *divisio* discriminates "an array of parts of a whole," it indicates *distinctio*, that is, the "single name, topic, concept, or thing" being defined additively, according to the number of its kinds.[31] If we can number the parts and name a single *partitio* correctly, we can discover the whole, the subject that has been subdivided logically into discursive units.

As a work composed in fragments, the *Canterbury Tales* as we know it has strongly marked divisions that point to Chaucer's practice of unitary composition, his building with story-blocks in accord with a developing plan for the collection as a whole. Internal evidence—especially the envoy sung "for the Wyves love of Bathe" (IV.1178) and the reference in "The Merchant's Tale" to the Wife's previous discussion of marriage (IV.1685–88)—and the combined witness of the Ellesmere and the Hengwrt manuscripts isolate Fragments III–IV–V as what Dolores W. Frese has termed "an obviously intended, poetically explicated sequence" of seven tales divided into three story groups, the first of these groups headed by the Wife's Prologue and Tale, the second by the Clerk's, the third by the Squire's.[32] Assuming that these divisions are meaningful, how are we to name these *partitiones*, and what, if anything, does the theme of marriage contribute to the definition of the combined story groups in Chaucer's overall outline?

John Alford recently provided us with a key in a brilliant argument about the rivalry between the Clerk and the Wife of Bath. Observing that the quarrel between them "is implicit already in the General Prologue" in the "degree of sustained contrast in their respective portraits," Alford goes on to show that the portraits "come directly from the tradition of the allegorized liberal arts. The Clerk has not merely gone 'unto logyk'; he is Logic personified. The Wife is not only one of the most rhetorical of the storytellers; she is Dame Rhet-

[31] Judson Boyce Allen, *The Ethical Poetic of the Later Middle Ages: A Decorum of Convenient Distinction* (Toronto: University of Toronto Press, 1982), pp. 126, 142.
[32] Dolores Warwick Frese, *An "Ars Legendi" for Chaucer's "Canterbury Tales": A Reconstructive Reading* (Gainesville: University of Florida Press, 1991), p. 203.

oric herself." In a final move, Alford argues that "the tales of the Wife and the Clerk are the formal expression of the rival arts of discourse which these two figures personify."[33]

This chapter extends Alford's thesis in application to the "Marriage Group" as a whole to argue that the three fragments with their seven tales recall the trivium in relation to the seven liberal arts. In this referential frame, three key figures—the Wife, the Clerk, and the Squire—represent personified *artes*, while the tales of the Wife, Friar, and Summoner exemplify rhetoric; of the Clerk and Merchant, logic; of the Squire and Franklin, grammar. Chaucer's "Marriage Group" thus typifies the practice of the arts under the figurative headings of the pilgrims who represent them and entails an ordered survey of the discursive *artes* in relation to one another. The tales, in short, participate in the allegorical tradition of pedagogical epithalamia. They do so, however, by placing into the foreground its cultural and literary opposite: the misogamous and antigamous propaganda of the clerks, which represents the trivium of woman's knowledge as shrewish and seductive talk, irrational "logic," and the grammatical inversion of social *regimen.*

The Trivium of Woman's Knowledge

The Wife's rhetorical theory and practice sets the rhetoric of a "wyse womman" against the Ciceronian rhetoric taught in the schools. The Wife's "scoleiyng" in the "diverse scoles" of five husbands has made her a "parfyt clerk" with a well-trained tongue (III.44c–f). As Alisoun relates, her first three husbands "were ful glad" when she "spak to hem faire / For, God it woot, I chidde hem spitously" (III.222–23). She sets herself up as a model for all "wise wyves"—"Thus shulde ye speke"—on the grounds that "half so boldely kan ther no man / Swere and lyen, as a womman kan" (III.225–28). In recognition of the peculiarly female rhetoric mastered by the Wife of Bath and others of her "secte," the Clerk recites "Lenvoy de Chaucer" to declare in her praise: "For though thyn housbonde

[33] John A. Alford, "The Wife of Bath versus the Clerk of Oxford: What Their Rivalry Means," *Chaucer Review* 21.2 (1986): 109, 110, 122.

armed be in maille, / The arwes of thy crabbed eloquence / Shal perce his brest and eek his aventaille" (IV.1202–4).

The Wife's "crabbed eloquence," as the all-too-effective antitype of clerical eloquence, gives expression to a commonplace of philosophical misogamy. In Gregory the Great's *Moralia*, for instance, we read that even as Eve's tongue misled Adam, the wife of holy Job tempted him to the point of despair with seductive and shrewish words "of a bad persuasion"; and such rhetoric is typical of foolish women.[34] Among classical sources, Juvenal's Satire VI abounds in warnings against female rhetoric. There the wife caught in adultery silences her husband and brazenly defends herself with a rhetoric superior to his: "Speak, speak, Quintilian, give me one of your colours!" (VI.280). Woman's rhetoric is, in fact, so potent that the satirist advises his friend Postumus: "Let not the wife of your bosom / possess a special style [*dicendi genus*] of her own; let her not hurl at you in whirling speech the crooked enthymeme!" (VI.449–50). Indeed, a fast-talking woman wields such verbal force that "the grammarians make way before her; the rhetoricians give in; the whole crowd is silenced; no lawyer, no auctioneer will get a word in" (VI.438–39).[35]

In this misogamist tradition, female rhetoric is, of course, closely tied to female (il)logic. As Chaucer's Pandarus attests, the practical intelligence and wisdom of women in "short avysement" (*TC* IV.936) was commonly held to surpass that of men. Taking that innate resourcefulness as a given, the Wife of Bath challenges every "wys wyf" to convice her husband that "the cow is wood" (III.231–32) through arguments that lead him to discount what he has previously seen and heard. "For al swich wit," she says, "is yeven us in oure byrthe; / Deceite, wepyng, spynnyng God hath yive / To wommen kyndely" (III.400–401). As the one-time clerk Matheolus complains in his *Lamentations* about his wife, "She is always armed with arguments which torture me terribly."[36] He prefaces his multiple examples of the "lin-

---

[34] See my "Job's Wife, Walter's Wife, and the Wife of Bath," in *Old Testament Women in Western Literature*, ed. Raymond-Jean Frontain and Jan Wojcik (Conway: University of Central Arkansas Press, 1991), pp. 92–107.

[35] Juvenal, *Satire VI*, in *Juvenal and Persius*, ed. and trans. G. G. Ramsey, Loeb Classical Library (Cambridge: Harvard University Press, 1918, rev. and repr. 1950), pp. 105, 121, 119.

[36] *The Lamentations of Matheolus*, in *Woman Defamed, Woman Defended*, p. 181. Subsequent citations are parenthetical. For a comment on Matheolus and the trivium, see R. Howard Bloch, "Medieval Misogyny," *Representations* 20 (1987): 1–24, esp. p. 17.

guistic sophistry" of women with the scholarly observation: "In addition to using arguments and disputes, a woman can lead her man to false conclusions by means of five different types of sophism" (p. 179).

Nor does any amount of education protect a man from being outwitted by women. The root cause of the "perpetual confusion" endured by male "practitioners of the liberal arts" when confronted by female rhetoric, logic, and grammar is, according to Matheolus, the "unnatural act" whereby Phyllis, the courtesan of Alexander the Great, playfully seduced Aristotle, the philosopher *per eminentiam*, and humiliated him by riding on his back as he crawled on all fours to indulge her whim:

> Women can sing to more than one tune. What good were the *Perihermeneias*, the *Elenchi*, divided into several branches, the *Prior* and *Posterior Analytics*, logic, or the mathematical sciences to Aristotle? For a woman surmounted all of these in mounting him and conquered the master of logic. She placed a bit and headstall on his head, and he was dragged into solecism, barbastoma, and barbarism.... The governor was governed and the role of the sexes reversed, for she was active and he passive, willing to neigh under her. Thus the natural order of things was turned upside down.... Thus was grammar betrayed and logic sorely dismayed. (p. 180)

Like Alexander's Phyllis, the Wife of Bath and every woman of her "secte" knows how to be "the whippe" (III.175) and metaphorically ride the rider through the pathetic force of words and quick-witted replies—a female repertoire of rhetorical and logical strategies that leads ultimately to the imposition of an inverted female grammar whereby the male "predicate" (as the active, verbal element) becomes the passive "subject" of the female subject within the social syntax of marriage. Like the hermaphrodite of Alan de Lille's *De Planctu Naturae*, such a man becomes a woman ("femina vir factus"), at once masculine and feminine, predicate and subject: "Praedicat et subjicit."[37] As Matheolus laments, "If a husband is forced to be his wife's serf, it is a terrible calamity, for he ought to be the boss. The natural

---

[37] Alan de Lille, *De Planctu Naturae*, PL 210, c431, Metr. 1.15–24.

order of things has been overturned by women and their madness"
(p. 178).

As Paul Lehman, Jan Ziolkowski, and John Alford have shown, the
varied use of grammatical puns and metaphors to describe the relationship between the sexes was widespread among clerks during the
Middle Ages. The use of grammatical terms ranged in complexity
from amorous wordplay on double-meaning Latin words such as *con-
iunctio, declinatio, casus, conjugatio, figura, genitivus, dativus, ablatus, vo-
cativus, copula,* and *interiectio* to serious analogies in theological and
political discussions. In every case the underlying assumption, in Alford's words, is that "social and linguistic order meet in the grammatical concept" of right relation or (to use a Modistic term) *regimen,*
"each constituent part observing its proper relation to the others:
adjectives must be governed by nouns; pronouns must be ruled by
their antecedents; there must be agreement in number, gender, and
case."[38] Analogously, kings should be governed by God, subjects by
kings, wives by their husbands. To attempt to invert any of these relations of *regimen* is to violate the grammar of creation.

Epicurean Education

In this broad context, the trivium of woman's wiles, with its peculiarly crooked rhetoric, logic, and grammar, extends itself into the
discursive (mal)practice of men as well as women and aligns itself in
Chaucer's tales with the lawlessness of a distinctively Epicurean social
curriculum. Fragments III–IV–V are virtually populated by Epicureans.
Alisoun of Bath quotes Jerome's *Epistola adversus Jovinianum* as an authoritative text to confirm the experiential woes of marriage, but she
herself takes a definite, libertarian, pro-marriage stance like that of
Jovinian, whom Jerome denounces repeatedly as a "Christian Epicurus."[39] Both the Friar and the Summoner are pleasure-seeking, lech-

[38] John A. Alford, "The Grammatical Metaphor: A Survey of Its Use in the Middle
Ages," *Speculum* 57 (1982): 756. See also Jan Ziolkowski, *Alan of Lille's Grammar of Sex:
The Meaning of Grammar to a Twelfth-Century Intellectual* (Cambridge, Mass.: Medieval Acad-
emy of America, 1985); Paul Lehmann, *Die Parodie im Mittelalter* (Stuttgart: Anton Hier-
semann, 1963), esp. pp. 49–54, 223–24; and my "*Translatio* of Chaucer's Pardoner,"
Exemplaria 4.2 (1991): 411–28.
[39] See Brown, "Epicurus and Voluptas," p. 82; Howard Jones, *The Epicurean Tradition*
(London: Routledge, 1989), pp. 109–13.

erous, and prone to gluttony. The Clerk's Walter pays attention only
to his "lust present" and seeks to maintain his absolute liberty
through a tyrannous marriage. The Merchant's January endeavors "to
lyve ful deliciously" (IV.2025) and builds a garden of sexual pleasure
for himself in keeping with the Epicurean stance of "somme clerkes"
who "holden that felicitee / Stant in delit" (2021–22). The Franklin's
Dorigen and Aurelius both gravitate toward pleasure gardens, while
the Franklin himself, according to his portrayal in the General Prologue, is "Epicurus owene sone" (GP 336).

The marked emphasis on Epicurus in the "Marriage Group" makes
sense from a pedagogical perspective, given the late-antique and medieval branding of Epicurus as an enemy of true philosophy. In Chaucer's *Boece* Lady Philosophy appears in a wonderful but torn dress,
embroidered with symbols of the practical and theoretical *artes*, the
Greek letters Pi and Theta joined by "seyn degrees nobly ywrought
in manere of laddres" (I.p1.34–35). She complains that "the peple
of Epycuriens and Stoyciens" (I.p3.32–33) have "torven and torente"
the clothes that she had woven with her own hands (39–41), appro-
priating for themselves bits and pieces of her seamless garment, so
that others mistake them for her true familiars. Later she specifies the
error of Epicurus, who wrongly "juggid and establissyde that delyt is
the soverayn good" (III.p2.78–80), mistaking the outward forms of
human happiness—"rychesse, honours, power, glorie, and delitz"
(76–77)—for its true substance.

Isidore of Seville, who followed Boethius in his summary of Epicurean doctrine, emphasizes that true philosophers, pagan and Christian, have called Epicurus a lover of vanity, not wisdom ("amatore
vanitatis, non sapientiae"), because he held bodily pleasure to be the
highest good ("voluptatem corporis summum bonum asseruit"), attributed the origin of things to the chance configuration of atoms,
denied divine providence, and asserted the materiality and mortality
of the soul: "animam nihil aliud esse quam corpus."[40]

In the *Policraticus* John of Salisbury associates the four rivers watering "the garden of the Epicureans" with the outward forms of human
happiness named by Boethius as partial goods subject to Fortune.
Streaming from the single source of "lust," Epicurean desires mani-

---

[40]   Isidore of Seville, *Etymologiae* VII.vi.15–16, PL 82, c306–07. See also Jones, *The Epicurean Tradition*, pp. 139–41.

fest themselves in avarice, "self-indulgence," the potentially tyrannical impulse to "protect [one's own] natural liberty" against any infringement, and the striving for celebrity and human respect.[41] Imprisoned in this Epicurean garden, one cannot hope to reach the *hortus deliciarum* in which the liberal arts lead a person upward, step by step, toward metaphysics and theology. Thus, in the *Metalogicon* John of Salisbury assails his satirical target, Cornificius, for "wallowing in carnal excesses which would shame even an Epicurean pig" (*Met.* I.2, p. 13) and for denying any common ground between eloquence and philosophy, words and wisdom (I.6, p. 25).

Having denied the fundamental body-soul distinction and its implicit hierarchy of spirit over matter, the Epicurean takes a symbolic position inimical to the pedagogical hierarchies assumed and maintained in a systematic course of study directed anagogically toward the metaphysical knowledge of God and creatures. As the antitype of the true philosopher, the lover of wisdom, Epicurus is, as Robert Miller observes, the "classical example of the 'error' which mistakes ends for means, temporal for immutable good,"[42] and thus the enemy of the educational system which represents itself in Boethian terms as an ascending ladder of seven degrees, as trivium and quadrivium. At the same time, the close association of Epicurus with Venus allies him with the "secte" of the Wife of Bath as she rivals Athena in her battle for "maisterie" over Mercurial clerks.

Representing the Liberal Arts

In the "Marriage Group" Chaucer's Epicurean rhetors, logicians, and grammarians enter into a series of unhappy (dis)unions that represent the battle of the liberal arts as a battle of the sexes in which the male and female discursive *artes* contend with each other at the very brink of divorce, their conflict played out against the literary background of harmonious encyclopedic nuptials, like those of Martianus Capella and Alan de Lille. In so doing, Chaucer employs three

---

[41] John of Salisbury, *Policraticus* VIII.xvi, trans. Joseph B. Pike, in *Frivolities of Courtiers and Footprints of Philosophers* (Minneapolis: University of Minnesota Press, 1938), pp. 346–47.

[42] Robert P. Miller, "The Epicurean Homily on Marriage by Chaucer's Franklin," *Mediaevalia* 6 (1980): 154.

different modes of representation which, as Adolf Katzenellenbogen has shown, were common to pictorial treatments of the liberal arts.[43] First of all, Chaucer's General Prologue portraits and link portrayals of the Wife, the Clerk, and the Squire correspond to the representations of the trivium in decorative miniatures. Second, the "Marriage Group" stories told by the pilgrims resemble the biblical scenes carved on candelabra to exemplify the (mal)practice of the different *artes*. Third, the "Marriage Group" functions within the Ellesmere *Tales* as a whole in a manner parallel to the iconographic inclusion of the *artes* within a universal scheme of things, as they appeared on church facades.

Book illuminations of the individual *artes* take various forms. As Katzenellenbogen observes, they "illustrate the practice of the Arts. They portray the masters who were instrumental in originating them, and they represent the personifications of the Liberal Arts themselves," adapting "attributes for the Liberal Arts from those mentioned by Martianus Capella" and "other literary sources," and even "invent[ing] attributes wherever it seemed desirable."[44]

Chaucer's portraits of the Wife, the Clerk, and the Squire belong to this tradition. As John Alford has shown, the Wife as a representation of Rhetorica is copious in her words, colorful in her dress, broad-hipped and full-figured. A weaver of cloth and words, she bases her reasoning on circumstantial "experience" in accord with the inductive method characteristic of rhetorical hypothesis. Signed by Mars and Venus, Alisoun alternates between threats and blandishments in her speech and uses her words skillfully to control her husbands and captivate her fellow pilgrims.[45] An expert in insinuation, she establishes a misogynist common ground with her opponents, only to shift that ground in her own favor.

---

[43] See Adolf Katzenellenbogen, "The Representation of the Seven Liberal Arts," in Marshall Clagett, Gaines Post, and Robert Reynolds, eds., *Twelfth-Century Europe and the Foundations of Modern Society* (Madison: University of Wisconsin Press, 1961), pp. 39–55.
[44] Ibid., p. 41.
[45] See Alford, "The Wife of Bath versus the Clerk," esp. pp. 117–18, 120–22. As John T. Kirby has shown, the word "persuasion," and its personification in the Greek goddess Peitho, consistently appear in presocratic texts in semantic clusters with the words for "violent force" (*bia*) and "seduction" (*eros*). See "The 'Great Triangle' in Early Greek Rhetoric and Poetics," *Rhetorica* 8.3 (1990): 213–27. Lee Patterson explores the close alignment of the poet's voice with that of women in " 'For the Wyves love of Bathe': Feminine Rhetoric and Poetic Resolution in the *Roman de la Rose* and the *Canterbury Tales*," *Speculum* 58 (1983): 656–95.

The Clerk from Oxenford, on the other hand, as a representation of Logic, speaks "noght o word . . . moore than was neede" (GP 305), with syllogistic shortness, exactitude, and truthfulness. His body and even his horse are lean, his demeanor sober, his clothes plain and "thredbare" (GP 209). His discourse is didactic; his teaching, "moral vertu" (GP 307); his favorite bedtime reading, the works of Aristotle.[46] Taken individually and as a contrastive pair, the detailed portraits of the Wife and the Clerk thus reflect and develop the attributes of Rhetoric and Logic in the allegories of Martianus and Alan de Lille.

Similarly, the portrait of the Squire singles him out as a representative of Grammatica.[47] He is "yong" (GP 79)—indeed, as Derek Pearsall notes, "the only young man on the pilgrimage"[48]—and childlike in his service to his father, even as grammatical study, "the cradle of all philosophy, and . . . the first nurse of the whole study of letters" (Met. I.13, p. 37), "the starting point of the liberal arts,"[49] belongs especially to little children and youth. He wears a short gown, like the short-gowned, unmarried Mercury, whose adolescent nakedness—as an emblem of "nude eloquence" (Met. IV.29, p. 246)—provokes Venus to peals of laughter in Martianus's De nuptiis I.5. His clothes are "embrouded . . . as it were a meede / Al ful of fresshe flowers, whyte and reede" (GP 89–90), in a manner that recalls (both to Chaucer's Franklin and to us) the so-called colors and flowers of rhetoric that were the partial object of grammatical study. Finally, the Squire, like Chaucer the pilgrim, is a poet—indeed, as Helen Cooper observes, "the only pilgrim with literary pretensions."[50] He "koude songes make and wel endite / . . . and weel purtreye and write" (GP 95–96)—arts of imitation and invention belonging to the enarratio poetarum traditionally subsumed by the discipline of grammar.[51] As Orme

[46] See Alford, "The Wife of Bath versus the Clerk," esp. pp. 116, 119–20.

[47] In both Martianus and Alan, Grammatica combines fatherly and motherly, corrective and nurturing functions and features. Alan's Grammatica "teaches infants to speak, looses tied tongues, and shapes words in the proper mould" (Anticlaudianus II, p. 85). For depictions of Grammar, see Katzenellenbogen, "Representation," and Rudolf Wittkower, " 'Grammatica': From Martianus Capella to Hogarth," Journal of the Warburg and Courtauld Institutes 2 (1938): 82–84. Wittkower attaches importance to the image of planting and gardening and insists that "the watering of the flower became the chief motive of the allegory" (p. 84).

[48] Derek Pearsall, "The Squire as Story-Teller," UTQ 34 (1964): 82.

[49] This phrase, quoted by John of Salisbury, goes back to Isidore of Seville, Ety. 1.5.

[50] Helen Cooper, The Structure of the "Canterbury Tales" (London: Duckworth, 1983), p. 72.

[51] See James J. Murphy, Rhetoric in the Middle Ages: A History of Rhetorical Theory from Saint Augustine to the Renaissance (Berkeley: University of California Press, 1974, repr. 1990),

insists, Chaucer takes "the curriculum as a frame of reference" in the Squire's portrait, making him literally the product of his education.[52]

Under the heading of these three portraits—the Wife's, the Clerk's, and the Squire's—the tales in Fragments III–IV–V become exemplary of the arts of the trivium. The technique is similar to that used in the Milan cathedral candelabrum (late twelfth-century) where the word "Rhetorica" appears above the temptation scene from Genesis, "Logica" over the depictions of Noah and the Ark and Abraham's sacrifice of Isaac.[53] In Chaucer's "Marriage Group," however, the trivium of woman's wiles stands in the foreground, over and against the clerical *artes* of the universities. The wommanish, Epicurean rhetoric exemplified in Fragment III emphasizes the carnal power of words to seduce, deceive, and enthrall, as "glossing" appropriates to its own ends the letter of patristic, legal, and biblical texts. The allegorical logic exemplified in Fragment IV is similarly overturned by female (il)logic and the Epicurean impulse to discover in things only what one wishes (oneself and others) to see and believe to be true. Finally, Fragment V illustrates the ungrammatical, antigamous grammar whereby the lord becomes the servant of his lady, the female subject becomes the predicate, and clerks become as "gentil" as courtly lovers.

Rhetorica

The Wife exemplifies the practice of rhetoric first in the "scolematere" of her own Prologue, then in the Old Hag's conversion of her newlywed husband, attaching the latter to a traditional rhetorical *locus*, the trial scene in a courtroom. As we have seen, in her Prologue the Wife associates herself in theory and practice with the infamous, Eve-like shrews and temptresses who figure in Jankyn's "book of wykked wyves." The Friar observes that she has touched upon scholarly concerns of "greet difficultee" (III.1272) in her discourse and advises her to leave the citation of patristic and scriptural authorities to preachers and "scoles of clergye" (III.1277). The Wife's rejoinder

---

pp. 135–93. In Alan's *Anticlaudianus* Grammar's gift to the New Man includes the ability "to join words in metrical feet and compose a poem in pleasing rhythm" (VII, p. 181). In the *Metalogicon* John of Salisbury warns, "Either poetry will remain a part of grammar, or it will be dropped from the roll of liberal studies" (p. 52).

52 Orme, "Chaucer and Education," p. 43.

53 See Katzenellenbogen, "Representation," p. 53.

insinuates that the seductive talk and sophistic preaching of friars liken them to incubi, and she accepts the challenge to compete with them in her own tale, where a shape-changing Hag persuasively cites multiple authorities—Valerius Maximus, Tullius Hostillius, Seneca, Boethius, Juvenal, Dante, and Jesus—to win sexual and moral "maisterie" over her reluctant marital partner.

The other two tellers and tales in Fragment III share the Wife's rhetorical emphasis. The pilgrim Summoner's own characteristic vocabulary—"Ay 'Questio quid iuris' wolde he crie" (GP 646)—shows his superficial knowledge of the *ars dictaminis*, the practical rhetorical art associated with medieval legal studies: "A fewe termes hadde he, two or thre, / That he had lerned out of som decree" (GP 639–40). In his tale, the Friar mocks the clerical pretensions of the Summoner through the multiple *quaestiones* of the crooked summoner, who is "evere enqueryng upon every thyng" (III.1409)—in particular, about the nature of fiends; who enters into a contractual, brotherly relationship with the devil himself, the archsophist; and who is destined to know through hellish experience "more than a master of dyvynytee" (III.1638).

Friar Hubert's assault then prompts the pilgrim Summoner to retaliate by fictionalizing the fraudulent preaching of a friar within an elaborate parody of Pentecost, the gift of tongues, and Christ's original commission of the apostles as preachers.[54] The friar in the tale boasts, " 'in prechyng is my diligence, / And studie in Petres wordes and in Poules' " (III.1818–19)—a predilection that likens him to the medicant pilgrim, who specializes in the *ars praedicandi*, the rhetoric of preaching: "In alle the ordres foure is noon that kan / So muchel of daliaunce and fair langage" (GP 210–11). The preaching of both friars, however, is a deceptive preaching that "glosses" Scripture in a self-interested way, translating it into a praise of friars and an exhortation to give them money and meals, not to mention other favors.

Fragment III thus represents the three rhetorical, public forums of the Middle Ages—scholastic disputation, the courtroom, and the pulpit—and renders thematic the keeping of "trouthe" in a sophistic

---

[54] See Penn R. Szittya, "The Friar as False Apostle: Antifraternal Exegesis and the *Summoner's Tale*," *SP* 71 (1974): 19–46; Bernard Levy, "Biblical Parody in the *Summoner's Tale*," *Tennessee Studies in Literature* 11 (1966): 45–60. For a general study of the biblical origins and medieval development of the *ars praedicandi*, see Murphy, *Rhetoric in the Middle Ages*, pp. 269–355.

sense that subordinates words and things to the speaker's intent with his audience, as a means to an end. Epicurean rhetors like the Wife, the Summoner, and the Friar use words; they do not by choice "keep" them, and the marriage of word and deed in their tales inevitably takes the imagistic form not of marriage but of rape. Thus the Old Hag rapes her rapist husband by forcing him to marry her; the Green Yeoman carries off the Summoner to hell; and the friar "gropes" Thomas beneath his buttocks.

Chaucer places the tales of the Summoner and Friar parallel to the Wife's tale and under the heading of her Rhetorica, even as John Gower in *Vox Clamantis* places on the lips of a carnal cleric the same words Chaucer ascribes to the Wife of Bath. "Decretals and sacred theology are not a bit to [the] liking" of Gower's collegiate rector, who relies on his "natural knowledge" and "study with a female companion" to teach him the meaning of scriptural passages, especially the command in Genesis to "multiply" and "bear fruit"—the same "gentil text" that Alisoun of Bath claims to understand well (III.29).[55] Giving "to Venus the tithe which ought to be God's," Gower's profligate scholar becomes "like a layman," and indeed, like his concubine, having learned from her everything she knows: "Ask a question, and being answerable for it, he has an answer for everything." The rightful bride of the curate languishes meanwhile, for the womanizing clerk has deserted "the virtue of study" to apply his studies "vigilantly to vices," learning from association with women only what belongs to a wommanish curriculum.

Logica

As a dedicated student (GP 303: "Of studie tooke he moost cure and moost heede") and a skilled logician, Chaucer's Clerk stands opposed to the Epicurean rhetoric exemplified by Alisoun, the Friar, and the Summoner. His thoughtful silence leads Harry Bailly to surmise in the headlink to his tale that he is studying "aboute som sophyme" (IV.5). The tale the Clerk tells is, moreover, emphatically a clerk's tale, one he "lerned at Padowe of a worthy clerk": "Frraunceys

---

[55] John Gower, *Vox Clamantis* III.17, in *The Major Latin Works*, pp. 148–49. See also Stockton's comment, pp. 44–45.

Petrak, the lauriat poete, / Highte this clerk, whos rethorike sweete / Enlumyned al Ytaille of poetrie" (IV.27, 31–33).

The Clerk's argumentative logic sets the rhetoric of Petrarch against the rhetoric of the Wife's "secte" and confuses it in the process. Unlike the tales in Fragment III, whose rhetorical effectiveness depends upon their being taken literally, the Clerk's tale only instructs its auditors if they read it allegorically to discover a universal truth behind the veil of its impossible particulars. The lesson of the tale is not, the Clerk emphasizes, "that wyves sholde / Folwen Grisilde as in humylitee," but rather that "every wight, in his degree, / Sholde be constant in adversitee" (IV.1142–43, 1145–46).

The Clerk, even more than Petrarch, stresses the literal impossibility of the tale. Walter's decision to take a wife entails a series of conditions, demands that Walter places upon his people and Griselda in order to ensure his absolute autocracy even in marriage. In this matter Walter resembles Theophrastus who, in response to the question "An ducat vir sapiens uxorem" answers with an initial "yes," provided "that the wife . . . be fair, of good character and honest parentage, the husband in good health and of ample means."[56] Since, however, "all these conditions are seldom satisfied in marriage," Theophrastus reverses his judgment to conclude: "A wise man therefore must not take a wife." In the person of Griselda, Chaucer's Clerk presents an image of the perfect wife for a clerk or a king. She is beautiful, virtuous, devoted to her father and husband, fertile but without children to rear, compliant, silent, and unopposing. Her fictive perfection, however, is monstrous enough and "of swich mervaille" (IV.1186) to demonstrate her literal nonexistence—"Grisilde is deed" (IV.1177)—and to warrant the opposite conclusion: "A wise man therefore must not marry." The Clerk stops short of spelling out this misogamous conclusion—"lat us stynte of ernestful matere" (IV.1175)—but his gleeful recitation of an envoy "for the Wyves love of Bathe" exhorts Alisoun and her "secte" to be and do precisely what disqualifies them for clerical approbation: to follow "Ekko, that holdeth no silence" (IV.1170, 1189), to contradict and disobey their husbands, to rule over them, to parade about in public, and to flirt with other men.

---

[56] Theophrastus, "Golden Book," in *Woman Defamed, Woman Defended*, p. 70; PL 23, c276.

The Clerk's logic allows him through the "impossible" case of Griselda to do what Alisoun has termed "an impossible" for a Clerk: to "speke good of wyves" (III.688–89). Understood as a contrary-to-fact condition, Griselda opposes the Wife's carnal conclusions about the marriage of clerks, even as she—as a typological allegory—supports the celibate marriage of clerks to Wisdom, Virtue, and the Church. As many have noted, Chaucer's version of the tale, unlike Petrarch's, introduces into the narrative a series of biblical and Christological allusions that liken Griselda to Mary at the Annunciation, Nativity, Crucifixion, Resurrection, Assumption, and Coronation. As such, Griselda points beyond herself to the true bride of Christian scholars.[57]

The Clerk establishes Griselda as the Marian antitype of Eve-like Alisoun in part by demonizing Walter, whose lust for marital "maisterie" parallels Alisoun's. Condemning Walter for his cruelty allows the Clerk-narrator to censure indirectly the Wife's analogous torture of her husbands. As John Alford insists, the tale does resemble a sopheme in its extreme testing of the proposition of wifely submission and is, in fact, an a fortiori argument against the Wife of Bath's position in its advocacy of "maisterie." Jerome Taylor similarly characterizes "The Clerk's Tale" as an *argumentum e contrario* that refutes the Wife's sophistical refutation of truth by reducing it to absurdity.[58]

To the extent, however, that the Clerk accommodates the logic of his tale to the Wife's in an attempt to answer her, the analogies he draws become contaminated, complex, and self-contradictory. The Clerk preserves Petrarch's moralization of the tale, which likens Griselda's husband to the benevolent but inscrutable God of Stoic providence; at the same time the Clerk's own Christian allegory reverses the relationship, likening Walter not to God but to Satan, and making Griselda a type of Christ rather than humankind per se. As a final complication, Walter's "impossible" marriage to Griselda causes him to resemble, on the one hand, the whip-bearing Wife of Bath; and, on the other, the clerk espoused to no earthly woman, but rather

---

[57] Others have emphasized ways in which the Clerk resembles Griselda. See Elaine Tuttle Hansen, *Chaucer and the Fictions of Gender* (Berkeley: University of California Press, 1992), p. 203; Carolyn Dinshaw, *Chaucer's Sexual Poetics* (Madison: University of Wisconsin Press, 1989), pp. 135–37.

[58] See Alford, "The Wife of Bath Versus the Clerk"; Jerome Taylor, "Fraunceys Petrak and the Logyk of Chaucer's Clerk," pp. 364–83 in Aldo Scaglione, ed., *Francis Petrarch, Six Centuries Later: A Symposium* (Chapel Hill: Department of Romance Languages, University of North Carolina Press, 1975).

Wisdom and Virtue. The Clerk's logic in the tale of Griselda's martyrdom is, in short, fraught with contradictions not unlike those in
Beatrice's Mercurial argument (in answer to Dante's question) over
the justice and injustice of Christ's Crucifixion, in which she affirms
both (*Par.* 7).

Given the possibility of multiple and contradictory interpretations,
the logic of the Clerk's argument cannot by any means be termed
deductive. "On the face of it," as Alford concedes, "the story of patient Griselda hardly seems to typify logical discourse."[59] Indeed, as
Taylor observes, "the tale patently contains no passages of abstract
reasoning, is no vehicle for Aristotelian philosophy, not even Aristotelian ethics, and is generally considered a masterpiece of illogicality
as fiction."[60] The "logyk" that subsumes both the Clerk's tale and the
Merchant's is not primarily Aristotelian and syllogistic, but analogi-
cal—the same logic under which biblical exegesis classed the Song of
Songs—a text to which both tales allude and whose allegorical status
they approximate.

In its broadest meaning, as Martianus's Dialectic insists, "whatever
the other Arts propound," including the precepts of Grammar, is
entirely under the authority of Logic.[61] The grammatical work of interpreting texts and discerning the meaning of speech depends in
particular upon logic for the definition of the proper and transferred
sense of words.[62] Logic thus provides the key for the disclosure of
allegory, whether by similarity or contrariety; is indispensable for the
correct understanding of figurative texts, among which the biblical
epithalamium, the Song of Songs, is a prime example; and is essential
to allegorical commentary. As Earl Schreiber and Thomas Maresca
have observed in another context, "Allegory is simply the rhetorical
mode which embodies the dialectical mode of analogy. . . . the rhetorical structure of allegory reproduces the logical structure of analogy."[63]

Beginning with Origen, biblical commentators classified the three
books of Solomon—Proverbs, Ecclesiastes, and Canticles—under the
respective headings of the three Platonic philosophies: ethics, physics,

59 Alford, "The Wife of Bath Versus the Clerk," p. 125.
60 Taylor, "Fraunceys Petrak," p. 365.
61 Martianus, *The Marriage*, p. 110.
62 Ibid., pp. 111, 117–18.
63 Schreiber and Maresca, Introduction to *The Commentary on the First Six Books*, p. xxiii.

and logic, and found in the *ordo* of Solomon's writings a progressive course of study leading to true wisdom.[64] Even as Proverbs teaches good morals, and Ecclesiastes the transitory nature of things, the Song of Songs teaches spiritual union with God under the figure of the bride and bridegroom. As an inspired allegory composed entirely of figures and enigmas, the Song of Songs cannot be read without the logic that perceives analogies and detects the proper meanings of speech beneath their literal veil. Indeed, it stands as the classical biblical example of a book that requires dialectical reading—the kind of reading and reasoning that distinguishes between the letter and the spirit of the text, resolves literal contradictions, and extends literal meaning by inferences based on similarity and contrareity, consequence and comparative degree.[65]

Whereas the Logic of Alan de Lille appears in the *Anticlaudianus* with a two-edged sword that "cuts down the false, refusing to allow falsehood to be hidden beneath the appearance of truth" (III, p. 92), the logic of the exegetes typically separates the kernel from the husk, wheat from chaff, allegorical meaning from literal expression. When Honorius of Autun, for instance, explains how "logic" subsumes the Song of Songs, he cites as a proof text Canticles 8:6: "Fortis est ut mors dilectio"—a verse whose literal comparison of love to death keys in the overriding allegory of Christian charity and redemption.[66]

The Clerk's Griselda echoes that same verse from Canticles in her

---

[64] Origen comments that the rational discipline that the Greeks call "logic" (PG 13, c73: "apud Graecos, logicen") is that discipline through which the "meanings of speech" are discerned (PG 13, c74: "per quam doctrina verborum dictorumque significantiae discernuntur"). He argues that logic, therefore, belongs to both ethics and physics, as well as enoptics (to which he assigns the Song of Songs), but that logic is especially necessary in the case of figurative, enigmatic expression. See "The Prologue to the Commentary on the Song of Songs," in *Origen*, trans. Rowan A. Greer (New York: Paulist Press, 1979), pp. 231–36. See also my *Song of Songs in the Middle Ages* (Ithaca: Cornell University Press, 1990), p. 26.

[65] Compare the treatments of dialectical proof-texts in Cicero (*De inventione* I.17), Pseudo-Cicero (*Ad Herennium* I.xi.19–xii.21), Martianus (*De nuptiis* V.463–65, pp. 172–73 in William Harris Stahl's translation), Cassiodorus (*Institutiones* II.2.6), and Isidore of Seville (*Etymologiae* II.5.9).

[66] Honorius of Autun, *Expositio in Cantica Canticorum*, PL 172, c548. Honorius goes on to explain that even as death conquers all things, so does love (c481: "sicut mors omnia vincit, ita dilectio omnia vincit"); and even as death leaves the body insensible, so too true love renders the soul insensible to worldly desires (c482: "sicut mors corpus interimit, et insensibile reddit, ita vera dilectio animam concupiscentiis mundi perimit"). Origen glosses the same verse from the Song of Songs with the celebration of all-enduring love in 1 Corinth. 13:7.

double-voiced response to Walter. When he demands the life of their second child, Griselda expresses her own willingness to die at his command, saying, "Deth may noght make no comparisoun / Unto youre love" (IV.666–67).[67] Her words pay tribute to the exceeding value of his love, even as they liken it to a fate much worse than death. Walter must interpret her speech, distinguishing between its literal and allegorical senses, to discover the truth of their marital relationship, even as the readers of "The Clerk's Tale" are directed to find a true meaning underlying Walter's meaningless testings of his saintly wife.

The Merchant's tale, closely joined to the Clerk's, also echoes the Song of Songs and comments on the exegetical logic required for the right reading of carnal texts. The tale itself approaches allegory overtly in the personifying names of its characters: January, May, Justinus, and Placebo, and in the allusive comparison of January's pleasure garden to other gardens, biblical and secular: Eden, Susannah's garden, Solomon's *hortus conclusus*, Guillaume de Lorris's garden of the rose, and Dante's celestial paradise. Unlike the Clerk, however, whose dialectical reading of his own tale strains the limits of its letter, the Merchant and his Epicurean protagonist, January, are incapable of spiritual understanding. January hears and sees what he wishes to hear and see, reduces sacramental marriage to legally sanctioned fornication, and recites the Song of Songs to summon May for sexual play (IV.2138: "Rys up, my wyf, my love, my lady free!"), while the Merchant joins him in his carnal understanding of the biblical allegory: "Swiche olde lewed wordes used he" (IV.2149).

January's defiance of "Theofraste" (IV.1310) and the ready credence he gives to Epicurean clerks who "holden that felicitee / Stant in delit" (IV.2021–22) makes his marriage to May the antitype of "that ilke weddyng murie" (IV.1733) of Mercury and Philology. January rejects marriage to one of the "olde wydwes" on the grounds that a "womman of manye scoles half a clerk is" (IV.1432, 1428), but he underestimates the innate wiles of women. Despite his jealous

---

[67]   Alfred L. Kellogg notes the echo of Song of Songs 8:6 ("Love is strong as death") in both Petrarch's and Chaucer's versions of the Griselda story and suggests a common source in the thirteenth-century *Omelia de Maria Magdalene*, a popular work attributed to Origen which, according to the F Prologue to *The Legend of Good Women*, Chaucer entitled "Orygenes upon the Maudeleyne" and translated (see lines 427–28). See "The Evolution of the Clerk's Tale," in *Chaucer, Langland, and Arthur: Essays in Middle English Literature* (New Brunswick, N.J.: Rutgers University Press, 1972), pp. 287–88.

guardianship, May not only manages to copulate with her lover Damian; in a classic exercise of women's logic and rhetoric she convinces January that he did not see what he thought he saw. The gift of Proserpina endows May and every woman with the ability to excuse herself and contradict her accusors, so that "For lak of answere noon of hem shal dyen" (IV.2271). As Proserpina boasts to Pluto, "Al hadde man seyn a thynge with bothe his yen, / Yit shul we wommen visage it hardily, / And wepe, and swere, and shyde subtilly, / So that ye men shul been as lewed as gees" (IV.2272–75). Although the moral blindness of a lecherous old fool like January may seem a small victory for women in the battle of the sexes, Proserpina likens it to the downfall of Solomon, the wisest of men—a downfall that seriously undermines all clerical authority, especially misogynist texts like Chapter 25 of *Ecclesiasticus*, and attests to the all-conquering force of the female *artes.*

Accepting May's explanation as the true meaning of the pear tree episode (and Damian's child as his own?), January highlights the subjective nature of the discovery of truth: we answer the question we ask, find what we are looking for, hear what we are disposed to hear. Attaching Petrarch's allegory to his own tale, the Clerk too calls attention to the need for a logic of interpretation. The Merchant's tale can thus be paired with the Clerk's in much the same way that their portraits adjoin in the General Prologue. Both are sons of Mercury, the god of eloquence and merchants—the Merchant solemnly speaking "his resouns" (GP 274) to sow the increase of his profit, the Clerk sowing his words "in moral vertu" (GP 307).[68] Both depend on the translative power of words, telling particular tales to cloak universally valid lessons, the worldly cynicism of the Merchant standing beside the idealism of the Clerk as opposed avenues to the truth of things behind the veil of appearances.

Grammatica

Whereas the sophistic rhetoric of the Wife, Friar, and Summoner emphasizes the speaker's intent and uses words to attain ends, the

---

[68] For Mercury as the god of merchants, see Bernard Silvestris, *The Commentary on the First Six Books*, pp. 26, 70, 84.

truth-seeking logic of the Clerk and Merchant stresses the things to which words point, the analogues they disclose. In contrast, the grammar typified in Fragment V as the *ars recte loquendi* insists upon the value of words in themselves. In this final fragment, as in the previous fragments of "The Marriage Group," the trivium of woman's knowledge intrudes once more—this time in the form of a female, Epicurean grammatical *regimen* especially associated with the antigamous inversions of courtly love.

Under the emblematic heading of the Squire's portrait, the linked tales of the fragment call attention to the art of grammar and its devices. When the Squire, therefore, denies being "a rhetor excellent" (V.38)—"I am noon swich" (V.41)—his disclaimer remains an expression of elegant humility while assuming a literal force that distinguishes the Squire's *grammatica* from the Wife's *rhetorica*. Critics, following the lead of John Matthews Manly, have often noted the Squire's self-conscious use of *descriptio, diminutio, occupatio, digressio, paranomasia, quaestio,* and personification and termed these devices "rhetorical."[69] James Murphy has demonstrated, however, that "medieval rhetoricians and grammarians alike set forth the same *exornationes,* or decorative devices" and Chaucer's use of verbal figures most probably derives not from Cicero, but "from the ordinary grammar texts" of his time—Donatus, Priscian, and the *Graecismus* of Eberhard of Bethune.[70] The Squire, in short, tells his tale "as an extension of [his] . . . portrait in the *GP*,"[71] as an exemplification of grammatical, not rhetorical practice. This reading supports the view of John P. McCall and others who compare the Squire's tale-telling to "the first performance of a fairly good student in Freshman Composition," citing not only obvious narrative mismanagement but also actual ungrammaticalities, especially in Part II.[72]

---

[69] See Robert S. Haller, "Chaucer's *Squire's Tale* and the Uses of Rhetoric," *MP* 62 (1965): 285–95; Robert P. Miller, "Chaucer's Rhetorical Rendition of Mind: *The Squire's Tale,*" in Leigh A. Arrathoon, ed., *Chaucer and the Craft of Fiction* (Rochester, Mich.: Scolaris Press, 1986), pp. 219–40; Joyce E. Peterson, "The Finished Fragment: A Reassessment of the *Squire's Tale,*" *Chaucer Review* 5 (1970): 62–74; John M. Manley, "Chaucer and the Rhetoricians," *Proceedings of the British Academy* 12 (1926): 95–113; repr. *Chaucer Criticism*, vol. 1, ed. Richard Schoeck and Jerome Taylor (Notre Dame: University of Notre Dame Press, 1960), pp. 268–90.

[70] James J. Murphy, "A New Look at Chaucer and the Rhetoricians," *Review of English Studies* n.s. 15 (1964): 17.

[71] Orme, "Chaucer and Education," p. 56.

[72] John P. McCall, "The Squire in Wonderland," *Chaucer Review* 1 (1966): 108. See

The Franklin, like the Squire, emphatically disavows knowledge of rhetoric—"I lerned nevere rethorik, certeyn"—disassociates himself from "Marcus Tullius Scithero," and insists, "Colours of rethoryk been to me queynte" (V.719, 722, 726). The Franklin's self-important use of *digressio, sententia, repetitio, circumlocutio, exclamatio,* and twenty-two *exempla,* however, point to his excellent grammatical training, even as the "greet deyntee" (V.681) he takes in the Squire's "gentil" speech and "feeling" of eloquence indicates his strong association of social class with proper speech.[73] As he himself observes, "to comune" with nobility, to speak their language, is to "lerne gentilesse aright" (V.693–94). To "talken with a page" (V.692), on the other hand, is to commit a social as well as a grammatical *barbarismus.*[74]

The efforts of both the Squire (as a knightly aspirant) and the Franklin (as a member of the rising middle class) to speak the language of the "gentils" lead them into the social ungrammaticalities of courtly love and female *regimen.* The General Prologue portrait of the Squire prepares us for the error exemplified in his tale. There we are told that his chivalric adventures are motivated by his "hope to stonden in his lady grace" (GP 88), as are his continual composition and singing of songs, so that, like the lusty nightingale, he sleeps little at night: "So hoote he lovede" (GP 97). The service of ladies, to which the Squire has committed himself, makes a "subject" of the male "predicate." It not only confuses the social hierarchy and syntax of the sexes; it also provides an (adulterous) alternative for the relationship between husband and wife that is proper to marriage as an institution.

The "knotte" (V.401) of "The Squire's Tale," therefore, focuses on a symbolic ungrammaticality: the lamentatious speech of a talking bird, a falcon whose language ("leden") Canacee, "the faire kynges doghter" (V.431), can both understand and speak through the power of her "queynte ryng" (V.433)—a magical gift with clear sexual im-

---

also Donald C. Baker, ed., *The Squire's Tale,* Variorum Edition (Norman: University of Oklahoma Press, 1990), pp. 62–63, 236–37. Baker calls attention to the grammatical and stylistic observations of Thomas R. Lounsbury, *Studies in Chaucer,* 3 vols. (New York: Harper, 1892), 3:317–18.
[73] Cf. A. C. Spearing, ed., *The Franklin's Prologue and Tale* (Cambridge: Cambridge University Press, 1966), pp. 17–22.
[74] According to the *OED,* by the mid-fifteenth century the word "barbarism" marked incorrect English usage, not just an error in Greek or Latin, and signaled a person's lack of education and social standing.

plications in Chaucer's narrative vocabulary.[75] Like Canacee, the falcon is "a kynges doghter trewe" in whose "gentil herte" sentiments of pity easily flow (V.465, 452, 479). She has, she says, accepted the chivalric "service" of a male falcon who wooed her for "many a year" until she, in answer to his complaints, "graunted hym love" (V.524, 529) upon the usual courtly condition that he protect her honor publicly and privately. The grammatical inconsistency between her honored name as a lady and her actual love-granting as a mistress has opened the way for another violation of speech: his breaking of his oath of fidelity to her as he deserts her for another "woman." While the falcon's lament decries her double-talking lover, the history as a whole indites them both as guilty of a typically "gentil" error: the inversion of social grammar through a seductive courtly subterfuge.

The Franklin's tale, like the Squire's, depicts the inverse *regimen* of courtly love. The Breton knight Arveragus, we are told, takes "his payne / To serve a lady" (V.730–31), until she, highborn and beautiful, observing his suffering, "worthynesse," and "meke obeysaunce" (V.738–39), has pity on him and accepts him "for hir housbonde and hir lord" (V.742). He, however, forswears any "maisterie" over her, vows to remain in obedience to her and to follow her will "as any lovere to his lady shal" (V.750), covering his actual status as her servant "for shame of his degree" (V.752) with the "name of soveraynetee" (V.751) proper to a husband. The end result is an ungrammatical marriage where the male is subjected to the female subject, at once the "servant" and "lord" of a woman who is simultaneously his "lady" and his "wyf" (V.792–97).

Dorigen, for her part, continues to play the role of a courtly lady after her marriage. When Aurelius, another "servant to Venus" (V.937), makes his amorous suit, she answers both a wifely "no" and a courtly "yes" to him and imposes on him, as an expression of courtly service, the impossible task of removing all the coastal rocks. The ungrammaticality of Dorigen's reply, which is simultaneously a denial and a promise, "fynal" (V.987) and open-ended, indicative and subjunctive, active and passive, prepares the way for Aurelius's true and false claim that "the rokkes been aweye" (V.1338), his demand that she keep her ambiguous "trouthe" (V.1328), and finally,

---

[75] See *Troilus and Criseyde* II.585 and the Wife's repeated euphemistic use of "queynte" (III.332, 444, 516).

Arveragus's decision to support Dorigen in her ladylike fulfillment of the adulterous pledge, provided she maintain his public reputation as her husband and tell no one that he is a cuckold.

The last word in the Franklin's (un)grammatical tale belongs, appropriately enough, to a university student, the "philosophre" (V.1585) of Orléans, whose study in books "of magyk natureel" (V.1125) enables him to create the "apparence" (V.1157) that the rocks of Brittany have disappeared. This clerk, who speaks Latin and whose house is magically as well supplied as the Franklin's own country estate—"Hem lakked no vitaille that myghte hem plese" (V.1186)—specializes in the substitution of illusion for reality, the creation of superficial, false, and pleasurable impressions. When he cancels the debt Aurelius owes him for his services, he claims as a clerk to have acted as "gentilly" (V.1608) as have the squire and the knight, and the Franklin applies to all three figures the aristocratic adjective "fre" (V.1622).

"The Franklin's Tale" thus typifies both a female grammar, in which predicates become subjects, and an allied Epicurean *grammatica* in which words constitute reality. As R. A. Shoaf has insisted, the tale is "an exposure or penetration of literalism," the kind of literalism that Dante associates with the sect of the Epicureans and the petrifying glance of the Medusa.[76] In the world of "The Franklin's Tale," language assumes an echoic, narcissistic self-referentiality that excludes reality itself—so much so that anything is permissible if one can find an acceptable name for it and maintain the proper appearances. Thus "adultery" becomes "keeping trouthe," and sharing one's wife with another lover is "fredom," "franchise," and "gentilesse."

If, as John of Salisbury observes, deceit is an abuse of language, it nonetheless eludes mere grammatical detection, because grammar *per se* concerns itself only with correctness, not truth.[77] The conciliatory

[76] R. A. Shoaf, " *The Franklin's Tale*: Chaucer and Medusa," *Chaucer Review* 21 (1986): 276. See also John Freccero, *Dante: The Poetics of Conversion*, ed. Rachel Jacoff (Cambridge: Harvard University Press, 1986), pp. 119–35. In Martianus Capella's *De nuptiis*, Dialectica and Geometria both invoke the Medusa (IV.333 and VI.572) over whom Athena, goddess of Wisdom, has triumphed.

[77] John of Salisbury observes, "Manifestly there are two kinds of faults in speech: lying, and violating the established usages of language." "Grammatical rules," however, "do not censure lying"; nor does Grammar "presume to constitute itself a judge of truth" (*Met.* I.15, pp. 43–45).

Franklin, therefore, speaks the last word in the "Marriage Group," but it is only a word—grammatically, even politically correct within the pilgrim circle, but not necessarily true. Thus Chaucer's troubled review of the trivium ends, rather than begins, with grammar, giving the last word to would-be courtly poets, but his unsettling appeal "back to basics" reminds us that even the childhood *ars recte loquendi* inhabits a speculative and disputatious ground when the verbal *artes* of Mercurial clerks meet their contentious match in the trivium of woman's knowledge.[78]

[78] For discussions of the influence of speculative grammar on Chaucer, see Piero Boitani, *Chaucer and the Imaginary World of Fame* (Cambridge: D. S. Brewer, 1984), pp. 212–15; Peter W. Travis, "The *Nun's Priest's Tale* as Grammar-School Primer," *SAC* Proceedings 1 (1984): 81–91; Holly Wallace Boucher, "Nominalism: The Difference for Chaucer and Boccaccio," *Chaucer Review* 20.3 (1986): 213–20. See also G. L. Bursill-Hall, *Speculative Grammars of the Middle Ages: The Doctrine of "Partes Orationis" of the Modistae* (The Hague: Mouton, 1971).

But goth now rather awey, ye mermaydenes, whiche that ben swete til it be at the laste, and suffreth this man to ben cured and heeled by myne muses (*that is to seyn, by noteful sciences*).

—Lady Philosophy in *Boece*

6

CHAUCER'S MERCURIAL MUSE:

FRAGMENT VII AND THE

CAUSES OF BOOKS

On the basis of pronouns suggesting a married female speaker (VII.12, 14, 18, 19), Chaucerians agree that "The Shipman's Tale," which heads Fragment VII, may have been originally assigned to the Wife of Bath.[1] This chapter argues that the tales of the Shipman and the Wife occupy the same heaven, that of Mercury and Venus; that Fragment VII, comprised of six tales, balances Fragments III–IV–V, which comprises a total of seven tales (one of them incomplete), within an extended chiasmus of narratives centered on Fragment VI; and that the two groupings share a common concern with the exemplification of the verbal arts. Whereas the "Marriage Group" of tales ends with a focus on grammar, the "Literature Group" begins precisely there and launches into a systematic exploration of the making of poetry.

Modern readers often confront a medieval text as if it were a Chinese encyclopedia which exhibits, as Michel Foucault puts it, "the exotic charm of another system of thought," even as it exposes "the limitation of our own."[2] The one-after-anotherness of things seems strange to us

[1] See the explanatory notes to "The Shipman's Tale" by J. A. Burrow and V. J. Scattergood in *The Riverside Chaucer*, ed. Larry D. Benson, 3d ed. (Boston: Houghton Mifflin, 1987), p. 910.
[2] Michel Foucault, *The Order of Things: An Archeology of the Human Sciences* (New York: Pantheon, 1970), p. xv.

because we have lost the categorical grid that names the hidden relationships prescribing their order. Fragment VII of the *Canterbury Tales,* for instance—a story-group that links together the tales of the Shipman, the Prioress, the pilgrim Chaucer, the Monk, and the Nun's Priest—is notoriously problematic. F. N. Robinson observes that "there seems to be no principle of arrangement save that of contrast or variety."[3] Larry D. Benson, the most recent editor of Chaucer's works, notes that "Fragment VII is the longest and most varied of the fragments and lacks any very clear unifying theme."[4] The Fragment, in short, like Jorge L. Borges's Chinese encyclopedia, has eluded our powers of classification; its underlying conceptual code has largely remained undeciphered.

Concentrating on the evidence of the links, Alan T. Gaylord suggested two decades ago that the Fragment is "controlled by a single, though admittedly very broad subject: *the art of storytelling.*"[5] Gaylord's tentative designation of Fragment VII as "the literature group" has gained fresh (albeit indirect) support recently in the growing awareness that Chaucer's work, taken as a whole, exhibits an "undisguised self-consciousness about the making of make-believe"[6] and represents, as Robert Edwards puts it, "a sustained reflection on the nature and devices of art."[7] Not only does Chaucer fictionalize himself as a writer in the dreamer-*persona* of the early poems, the narrator of *Troilus and Criseyde,* the accused (and penalized) poet of the *Legend of Good Women,* and Chaucer the Pilgrim; he creates in each of the pilgrims a different *persona* of himself as artist.[8] As Alfred David affirms, "each teller shows some new face of the poet's strumpet Muse."[9]

[3]　F. N. Robinson, ed., *The Works of Geoffrey Chaucer,* 2d ed. (Cambridge, Mass.: Houghton Mifflin, 1957), p. 11.

[4]　Larry D. Benson, ed., *The Riverside Chaucer,* p. 910. This edition will be used throughout, with subsequent citations given parenthetically.

[5]　Alan T. Gaylord, "*Sentence* and *Solaas* in Fragment VII of the *Canterbury Tales*: Harry Bailly as Horseback Editor," *PMLA* 82.2 (1967): 226.

[6]　Robert M. Jordan, *Chaucer's Poetics and the Modern Reader* (Berkeley: University of California Press, 1987), p. 21.

[7]　Robert R. Edwards, *The Dream of Chaucer: Representation and Reflection in the Early Narratives* (Durham, N.C.: Duke University Press, 1989), p. xvi.

[8]　Carol Ann Martin points to the figure of Mercury as an emblem of Chaucer's art and distinguishes Mercurial attributes in the pilgrims. See her "Mercurial Haeresis: Chaucer's Hermeneutical Po-Et(h)ics" (Ph.D. diss., University of Notre Dame, 1993).

[9]　Alfred David, *The Strumpet Muse: Art and Morals in Chaucer's Poetry* (Bloomington: Indiana University Press, 1976), p. 7.

While this heightened critical awareness of Chaucer's self-reflexivity broadly extends the term "literature group" to his whole oeuvre, it continues to encourage a particular focus on Fragment VII where Chaucer explicitly represents himself in the tales told by Chaucer the pilgrim. Lee Patterson has argued that Chaucer plays the part of a minstrel in "The Tale of Sir Thopas," that of a courtly counselor in "The Tale of Melibee," to dramatize (and partly resolve) the problem of authorial self-definition.[10] C. David Benson calls attention to the same two tales as tales of *solaas* and *sentence* that play with the Horatian definition of literary purpose and thus fictionalize, in the center of Fragment VII, Chaucer the poet's efforts to delight and instruct.[11] The question, however, remains: do the other tales in the fragment participate in the same kind of literary self-reference and, if so, does a meta-literary conceptual frame determine the specific structure of Fragment VII?

Following the dictum of Judson B. Allen that *divisio* meaningfully discriminates "an array of parts of a whole,"[12] I will argue that the tales of Thopas and Melibee provide a key that unlocks the whole structure of the fragment as a systematic exploration of the four Aristotelian causes of books. "To teach and to delight" is, of course, the classical definition of the *causa finalis* of poetry—a formulation that applies to the contrastive tales of Chaucer the pilgrim.[13] Once we have identified the tales of Thopas and Melibee as *exempla* of the final cause, we can recognize in the remaining tales of Fragment VII *divisiones* corresponding to the other three causes and enabling their exemplification. The *causa efficiens*—the poet himself in his twofold

---

[10]   See Lee Patterson, " 'What Man Artow?': Authorial Self-Definition in *The Tale of Sir Thopas* and *The Tale of Melibee*," *SAC* 11 (1989): 117–75. Patterson closely aligns the "childish frivolity" of *Sir Thopas* with the comedic attributes evident in the *Tales* as a whole and observes that the tales of Fragment VII "are particularly focused upon the question of childhood" (p. 162) and the child-*persona* favored by Chaucer the poet in self-representation.

[11]   See C. David Benson, "Their Telling Difference: Chaucer the Pilgrim and His Two Contrasting Tales," *Chaucer Review* 18 (1983): 61–76.

[12]   Judson Boyce Allen, *The Ethical Poetic of the Later Middle Ages: A Decorum of Convenient Distinction* (Toronto: University of Toronto Press, 1982), p. 142.

[13]   Horace formulates it as such in *Ars poetica*: "aut prodesse volunt aut delectare poetae, / aut simul et iucunda et idonea dicere vitae" (lines 333–34) / The poet's aim is either to profit or to please, or to blend in one the delightful and the useful. See *Horace on the Art of Poetry*, ed. and trans. Edward Henry Blakeney (London: Scholartis Press, 1928), p. 54.

representation as a well-trained craftsman and a channel of inspired utterance—determines the linkage of the tales of the Shipman and the Prioress at the beginning of the fragment. The *causa materialis* gains expression in the Monk's collection of tragic histories. Finally, the *causa formalis* finds its exemplification in "The Nun's Priest's Tale" as a fable veiling doctrine.

Throughout the fragment, Chaucer focuses, as Gaylord suggested long ago, upon the struggle to tell tales, but he does so through the tales themselves, not just in the links, and he does it systematically through the topics of the Aristotelian *accessus*. If it was difficult to tell tales properly, that difficulty sprang from the multiple, metaphysically defined causes of books, addressed singly and taken as a whole. As Allen has stated in another context, "one must presume that the Aristotelian causes in fact were causes—did make things happen."[14] In this case, the causes constituted Fragment VII as a story-group by predetermining Chaucer's conceptual approach to the problem of literary production.

The magisterial scholarship of A. J. Minnis has made us aware that, beginning in the thirteenth century, the Aristotelian causes provided the standard outline for introductory lectures on the works of classical authors, as well as expository prologues to the books of the Bible. In Dante's letter to Can Grande, for instance, he mentions that six things need to be asked concerning any literary work: "what is its subject, its form, its agent, its end, the title of the book, and its branch of philosophy."[15] The first four topics—subject, form, agent, end—correspond to the Aristotelian causes of books: *materialis, formalis, efficiens,* and *finalis*—while the last two address concerns important in the earlier, prescholastic style of *accessus ad auctores*.[16] In Aristotelian prologues, as Minnis notes, discussions of the *causa efficiens* deal with the immediate and remote authorship of a work—that is, both the human *auctor* who wrote it and, especially in scriptural cases, the divine *auctor* who inspired him. Treatments of the *causa materialis* designate "the

---

[14]   Allen, *Ethical Poetic,* p. 106.

[15]   Dante, "The Letter to Can Grande," in *Literary Criticism of Dante Alighieri,* trans. and ed. Robert S. Haller (Lincoln: University of Nebraska Press, 1973), p. 98.

[16]   For a classic study of the *accessus* topics, see Edward A. Quain, S.J., "The Medieval *Accessus Ad Auctores,*" *Traditio* 3 (1945): 215–64.

literary materials which were the writer's sources." Expositions of the formal cause call attention to "the pattern imposed by the *auctor* on his materials"—both the overt ordering of parts and the style of approach (*modus agendi*). Naming the final cause of a work justifies it in terms of the rhetorical end or objective the writer hoped to accomplish, "the particular good . . . he had intended to bring about,"[17] and invites the audience's cooperation with that intent.

As David Burnley has observed, the Latin tradition of naming literary causes contributes heavily "both to the vocabulary in which [Chaucer] discusses his authorial role and the way in which he visualizes it."[18] Chaucer's common use of the terms *matere, fyn, ende, conclusioun, fruyt, purpos*, and *entente* affirms his familiarity with the *accessus* tradition, while "The Tale of Melibee" makes explicit its philosophical background in an elaborate exposition of the Aristotelian causes. In that tale, Prudence analyzes Melibee's misfortune from the perspective of "certeine causes, / which that clerkes clepen *Oriens* and *Efficiens*, and *Causa longinqua* and *Causa propinqua*" (VII.1395). While the "neer cause" (VII.1397) or agent of Melibee's distress is his three enemies, the remote *causa efficiens* is God himself. The wounds of his daughter constitute the "cause material" (VII.1399). The "cause formal" is the "manere" of the attackers' "werkynge" (VII.1400). The "cause final" or intent of the enemies was "to sle" (VII.1401) Melibee's daughter, while the providential aim of God was to purify and convert Melibee (see VII.1409, 1425).

The use of the four causes in "The Tale of Melibee" does not, of course, constitute a *literary* exposition. Melibee's grief is not a book, only the partial subject of one. Prudence's instruction, however, would have recalled analogous lectures in the schools which introduced the works of classical *auctores* according to a similar outline.[19] The appearance of such a discussion virtually at the center of Fragment VII suggests, as I hope to show, that the outline of the causes is the underlying *distinctio* determining the order and treatment of the stories in that tale-group.

[17] A. J. Minnis, *Medieval Theory of Authorship: Scholastic Literary Attitudes in the Later Middle Ages*, 2d ed. (Philadelphia: University of Pennsylvania Press, 1988), pp. 28–29.
[18] David Burnley, *A Guide to Chaucer's Language* (Norman: University of Oklahoma Press, 1983), p. 221.
[19] See Minnis, *Medieval Theory of Authorship*, pp. 9–39.

The Artist as Efficient Cause: By Craft or Inspiration?

The fragment calls attention, first of all, to the *causa efficiens*. As I have already noted, this cause was subdivided into two causes, "fer" and "neer," human and divine—a division especially proper to sacred scripture but reflecting the analogous, ancient debate about the priority of inborn talent or acquired skill, nature or nurture, inspiration by a Muse or practiced method, ecstasy or conscious craft on the part of the poet. While "The Prioress's Tale" emphasizes the "fer cause" of divine inspiration, "The Shipman's Tale" stresses the "neer cause" of human skill, presenting the act of tale-telling as craft and craftiness, as an art to be cleverly and profitably managed in the keeping of appearances.

The images controlling "The Shipman's Tale" make it a fitting *exemplum* of efficient causality. As Gerhard Joseph notes, Chaucer elsewhere uses navigational imagery to comment on the difficult task of narration—a commonplace comparison, rooted in the etymological association of "book" (Latin *liber*) with "bark." As "a sea-traveller between nations," the Shipman "is the suitable artist-figure for the story he tells"—a story that marks the English literary reception (and conversion) of a foreign form, the French fabliau.[20]

The merchant-hero and victim of the tale is also a traveler, journeying back and forth from Seint-Denys to Bruges to Flaunders to Paris. Indeed, he describes himself as a chapman who weathers the stormy vicissitudes "Of hap and fortune" (VII.238) by maintaining the outward appearances of success, security, and control:

> We may wel make chiere and good visage,
> And dryve forth the world as it may be,
> And kepen oure estaat in privetee,
> Til we be deed, or elles that we pleye
> A pilgrymage, or goon out of the weye.
>
> (VII.230–34)

His craft, in short, rivals that of the Shipman who knows "of his craft to rekene wel his tydes, / His stremes, and his daungers him bisides" (GP 401–2) and, by implication, that of Chaucer's Merchant-Pilgrim

---

[20] Gerhard Joseph, "Chaucer's Coinage: Foreign Exchange and the Puns of the *Shipman's Tale*," *Chaucer Review* 17.4 (1983): 342–43.

and Chaucer himself, the poet who skillfully "plays" a pilgrimage in the earnest game of the *Canterbury Tales*.

As V. J. Scattergood has shown, the "chiere and good visage" (VII.230) maintained by the merchant as a security for credit incorporate a number of outward signs associated with the bourgeois mercantile ethos.[21] The narrative emphasizes the merchant's heavy investment in: (1) the arrangement and maintenance of his "worthy hous" (VII.20) and (2) his wife's costly clothes. The first fifty lines of the tale use the word "hous" four times (VII.20, 31, 44, 47) and treat it as a symbol of the merchant's wealth, fiscal wisdom, and social status. The wife's fairness and rich array reflect similarly upon the merchant's "owene worshipe" (VII.13) and "honour" (VII.179). Her need for a hundred franks "[herself] for to arraye" (VII.179) precipitates her assignation with the monk and sets into motion the monetary exchange between her husband and her lover. The deceptive civility covering up the betrayals parallels the outward facade of house and clothes with its power to belie bankruptcy.[22]

Like the imagistic linkage of sailing and traveling with narration, the images of house and dress recall commonplace metaphors for the poet's craft. As Charles Sears Baldwin maintains, the Second Sophistic of late antiquity "reduced rhetoric to style," confused rhetoric with poetic, and "confirmed the tendency to conceive poetry itself as an art of decoration." Medieval handbooks influenced by this tradition— Matthew de Vendôme's *Ars versificatoria*, Geoffrey de Vinsauf's *Poetria nova*, and John of Garland's *Poetria*—all define *poetria* essentially as "the study of style, and specifically the study of stylistic decoration."[23] In these handbooks poetry as craft, as a mechanical art, provides the superficial, outward forms of expression—a function rendered metaphorically in images of verbal encasement, covering, housing, and feminine adornment.[24]

---

[21]   See V. J. Scattergood, "The Originality of the *Shipman's Tale*," *Chaucer Review* 11.3 (1977): 210–31.

[22]   Unfortunately, as Scattergood observes, the merchant's trusting dependence on "chiere and good visage" (VII.230) encourages him to see others as he wishes to be seen. Taking things "at their face value" (Scattergood, p. 226) makes him vulnerable to cozenage by his false "cosyn" (VII.149), the monk.

[23]   Charles Sears Baldwin, *Medieval Rhetoric and Poetic (to 1400)* (Gloucester: Peter Smith, 1959), pp. 39–40, 195.

[24]   Geoffrey of Vinsauf, for instance, invites the art of poetry to come "to clothe the matter with words" (line 61: "Materiam verbis veniat vestire poesis"). Later he images

The merchant himself identifies the "chiere and good visage" (VII.230) he maintains through the status symbols of a well-furnished house and a well-dressed wife with language: "We may creaunce whil we have a name" (VII.289). The "name" the merchant acquires through conspicuous consumption and "largesse" (VII.22), his reputation as a successful businessman, enables him to borrow the money he needs and keep his true "estaat in pryvetee" (VII.232). One currency—the verbal exchange involved in naming—parallels, and participates in, the analogous fiscal currency of borrowing, buying, and trading: "goldlees for to be, it is no game" (VII.290).

At another level, respectable "naming" in the tale allows for sexual commerce between the monk and the wife, who manage to contract their assignation using decorous circumlocutions in the garden. As Gerhard Joseph has shown, the ubiquitous punning in the tale "that conflates the imagery of commercial and sexual exchange"[25] in almost every passage of dialogue calls attention to language itself as a medium of exchange in which one word replaces another, substituting meaning for meaning.

The parallel between the merchant, sequestered with his books in the counting house, and the poet, locked in the tower with his, must have been especially acute for Chaucer—himself both a poet and an accountant, in fact, the Controller of Customs. Indeed, the tale, in its emphasis on the verbal and monetary financing of a pleasant, bourgeois facade, evokes the same archetypal pattern of associations that make Mercury the god of trade and the master of eloquence, linked to both the commerce of goods and the flow of words, profit and poetry, lucre and lies, fiscal increase and verbal *amplificatio*. Chaucer himself underscores the correspondence between the tale's action and the poet's craft by ending the Shipman's narrative with an unusual pun that links the monetary and sexual tallying of the monk and the merchant to the

---

this act of clothing ("vestire") as the dressing of a woman: "Let a noble sentiment be graced by a noble expression, lest a well-born matron blush to be dressed in shabby garments" (lines 759–60: "Dives honoretur sententia divite verbo, / Ne rubeat matrona potens in paupere panno"). See Ernest Gallo, ed. and trans., The *"Poetria Nova" and Its Sources in Early Rhetorical Doctrine* (The Hague and Paris: Mouton, 1971), pp. 16–17, 54–55.

[25] Joseph, "Chaucer's Coinage," p. 349. The most extensive study of the analogy between fiscal and verbal exchange in medieval thought is R. A. Shoaf's *Dante, Chaucer, and the Currency of the Word: Money, Images, and Reference in Late Medieval Poetry* (Norman, Okla.: Pilgrim Books, 1983).

"taillyng" of the story-teller: "Thus endeth my tale, and God us sende / Taillynge ynough unto oure lyves ende" (VII.433–34).[26]

If such a definition of the poet is reductive, valorizing style over substance, sophistic show over and against content, the second approach to the *causa efficiens* is equally fraught with problems. Plato posed the issue early on in the *Ion* when he has Socrates assert that the poet sings, not by art, "but by power divine," uttering what he does not know "while bereft of reason," possessed by God in ecstasy as an oracular channel.[27] The Platonic idea of the divine inspirer as a remote efficient cause was a familiar one to the Middle Ages. Boccaccio, for instance, declares that the gift of poetry proceeds "from the bosom of God" to be received by a few chosen ones who are then affected by a sublime fury that compels them to think and write unheard of things.[28] He quotes Cicero who calls on the authority of the ancient philosophers to insist that "poetry . . . is infused with a strange supernal inspiration" (Osgood, p. 41).

"The Prioress's Tale" demonstrates the shortcomings of this model when taken in isolation. Proceeding on the assumption that poetry comes "from the bosom of God," the Prioress places her mouth metaphorically "on the brest soukynge" (VII.458) and depicts herself as an infant "of twelf month oold or lesse" (VII.484), weak in understanding ("my konnyng is so wayk, o blisful Queene" [VII.483]), who "kan unnethes any word expresse" (VII.485). When the Prioress asks the Virgin Mary to inspire the song she herself cannot understand, she places herself in a position parallel to the little clergeon who sings the Latin anthem first by rote, and then with a cut throat under a miraculous compulsion. God's "laude" is "parfourned" by both the Prioress and the boy, "by mouth of innocentz" (VII.608) and "by the mouth of children" (VII.457).

Chaucer plays with the model of the inspired poet in "The Prioress's Tale" in two ways. First of all, he has the Prioress tell her story as a "song" (VII.487) of praise. She adopts an appropriately ecstatic

---

[26] The fact that it *is* a pun and was recognized by Chaucer's contemporaries as such is evident in the substitution of the rare word "talyng" for "taillynge" in several manuscripts.

[27] See *Ion* in *The Dialogues of Plato*, vol. 1, trans. Benjamin Jowett (New York: Random House, 1892, 1937), p. 289.

[28] Boccaccio, "Genealogy of the Gods: XIV," in *Boccaccio on Poetry*, trans. Charles G. Osgood, 2d ed. (New York: The Liberal Arts Press, 1956), p. 39. Subsequent references to Osgood's translation will be given parenthetically.

posture, which gains expression in (1) *apostrophe and prayer:* "O mooder mayde, O mayde mooder" (VII.467), "O Lord, oure Lord" (VII.453), "O cursed folk of Herodes" (VII.574), "O martir sowded to virginitee" (VII.579), "O grete God" (VII.607), "O yonge Hugh of Lyncoln" (VII.684); (2) *anaphora:* "Lady, thy bountee, thy magnificence, / Thy vertu, and thy grete humylitee" (VII.474–75); (3) *echoic epithets,* such as "litel" (a word repeated in lines 495, 503, 509, 516, 552, 587, 596, 667, and 682) and "cursed" (lines 574, 599, 631); and (4) *repetition,* such as the triple use of the word "mercy" in her concluding petition (lines 688–89).

Chaucer then couples this kind of ecstatic utterance with avowals and demonstrations of the speaker's ignorance. Not only does the Prioress openly declare her lack of "konnyng" (VII.483); she explicitly compares herself as narrator to the child as singer, thus underscoring her lack of understanding with his: "Noght wiste he what this Latyn was to seye" (VII.523). Indeed, she characterizes the child as a reedlike channel of utterance. "Twies a day" the anthem "passed thurgh his throte" (VII.548) and, after the murderous attack, "he with throte ykorven lay upright" (VII.611), still singing words beyond his ken. His prophetic possession—symbolized by the mysterious grain placed upon his tongue—parallels the Prioress's own inspiration as narrator, and his final silence occasions hers as the tale draws to a close.

In the end, the Prioress's personal lack of understanding of the song she sings, the tale she tells, exposes her unfitness as a prophet of mercy and makes her naivete macabre, her pity cruel. After extolling the "torment" and "shameful death" (VII.628) inflicted on the Jews, her prayer for mercy on "synful folk" (VII.687) sounds absurdly incongruous. She can translate the moral import of *Alma Redemptoris* no better than the boy can explicate its Latin. Her ignorance thus undercuts her *ethos* as much as the cunning of the "taillynge" narrator undermines his. Like Plato's Ion, whose mindless inspiration ill equips him to be an interpreter of what he sings, the Prioress needs instruction in what she purports to teach.

The Final Cause: To Delight and to Instruct

The next two tales, as we have already indicated, take up the classical *causa finalis* of poetry—the Horatian aim to delight and to instruct. Bailly's request for a tale "in which ther be som murthe or som doctryne" (VII.935) separates the two ends of poetry, even as it seems to associate them with opposite kinds of poems. In "The Tale of Sir Thopas" Chaucer assumes the role of a minstrel telling "a tale of myrthe" (VII.706); in the "Melibee," that of a teacher imparting *sententiae* through a moral "tretys" (VII.957). In both the storyteller fails to realize his intent. Instead of entertaining Harry Bailly with his clever parody, Chaucer succeeds only in annoying him. Bailly complains of his "verray lewednesse" (VII.921), his "drasty speche" (VII.923), and "drasty rymyng" (VII.930). Nor does Bailly learn anything from the providential wisdom of "The Tale of Melibee." The only sentence that the Host derives from it applies, not to himself, but to his vengeful, big-armed wife: "I hadde levere than a barel ale, / That Goodelief, my wyf, hadde herd this tale!" (VII.1893–94).

Prudence, the teacher within the tale, is almost equally unsuccessful in her efforts to instruct Melibee. Her husband shows a marked propensity to learn only what he wishes to learn, assembling to his counsel "straunge folk, yonge folk, false flatereres, and enemys reconsiled, and folk that doon [him] reverence withouten love" (VII.1245). When good advice is given him, he misinterprets it. Prudence's twice-repeated question—"I wolde fayn knowe how that ye understonde thilke wordes and what is youre sentence" (VII.1332 and 1278)—invariably evokes an incorrect response.[29] Melibee's inability to derive the correct *sententia* in a tale full of sentences and proverbs dramatizes the difficulty of the pilgrim poet who seeks to convey "the sentence of this tretys lyte" (VII.963) and thus achieve his final cause. As Judith Ferster has observed, "Prudence is a figure for the author and demonstrates the perils of narration. No matter how she tries to determine the meaning of her words, she cannot control Melibee's interpretation of them."[30]

Paradoxically, the *causa finalis* in these two tales seems to remain unrealized precisely because it has completely subjugated the subject matter, thus eliminating all artistic indirection. "The Tale of Melibee" endeavors to teach, to convey "sentence" (a word repeated four times in the headlink, at lines 947, 952, 961, and 963). Accordingly, it mul-

---

[29] Cf. Patterson, " 'What Man Artow?' " p. 158.
[30] Judith Ferster, *Chaucer on Interpretation* (Cambridge: Cambridge University Press, 1985), p. 21.

tiplies *sententiae*. As Chaucer remarks to his auditors, "I telle somwhat moore / Of proverbes than ye han herd bifoore" (VII.955–56). Counsel constitutes the plot of the tale, beginning with the "conseil" (VII.1004) of Prudence and the "conseillyng" (VII.1002) of the "greet congregacioun of folk" (VII.1004) who advise Melibee. All of Melibee's instructors quote, in turn, the sentences of other counselors—Ovid, Seneca, Solomon, Petrus Alphonsus, Cicero, Cassiodorus, Cato, Gratian, Caecilius Balbus, Saints Peter, Paul, James, Jerome, and Augustine. The sheer multiplication of *sententiae* leaves Melibee unable to "governe" himself "after hire sentence" (VII.1002), not knowing whether to wage spiritual war against his foes (allegorized as the world, the flesh, and the devil) or to be reconciled with them. Submitting to Prudence's "wise informaciouns and techynges" (VII.1870), he finally renders a merciful "sentence and juggement" (VII.1831) on his enemies, but the tale itself teaches no single lesson beyond the necessity of *sententia*: "Werk alle thy thinges by conseil" (VII.1003). The failure of instruction dramatized in the tale raises, as Lee Patterson observes, "probing questions about the kind of pedagogy in which *Melibee* engages"[31] and, indeed, about the poet's role as princely advisor.

If "The Tale of Melibee" is a tale about teaching that fails to instruct, "The Tale of Thopas" similarly subverts its end of delighting by confusing ends and means: "And I will telle verrayment / Of myrthe and of solas" (VII.713–14). Chaucer, as it were, laughs so hard at his own joke—"joye it was to heere" (VII.768)—that the joke itself is lost on Harry Bailly who fails to recognize the parodic nature of Chaucer's "deyntee thyng" (VII.711). The final cause is, in fact, so immediate, so identified with the matter and form of the tale, that when Bailly cuts it short—"Namoore of this, for Goddes dignitee" (VII.919)—"Thopas" has already reached (or failed to reach) its end, substituting a jest for a "geeste" (VII.933).

The Material Cause: "Olde Bookes"

Following the two tales of Chaucer the pilgrim, "The Monk's Tale" calls attention to the intrinsic problems of the *causa materialis*. The

---

[31] Patterson, " 'What Man Artow?' " p. 156.

Monk has plenty of "olde bookes" (VII.1974)—a hundred tragedies, he tells us, in his monastery cell (see VII.1971–72). From them he draws the seventeen plot summaries that constitute his tale as a collection of tales. His recitation, like that of Chaucer's, is interrupted—first by the Knight, who objects to his preoccupation with the fall of nobles; then by the Host, who declares, "Youre tale anoyeth al this compaignye" (VII.2789). Bailly complains, in particular, of boredom, announcing that he would have fallen asleep long ago, were it not for the clinking of the bells on the Monk's bridle. The Monk has lost his audience because his "thing" is not "wel reported" (VII.2804). It is mere substance without style; content without form; the raw, undeveloped *materia* of art.

Chaucer carefully weds the Monk's reduction of art to *materia* with the materialistic philosophy he espouses.[32] He bewails "in manere of tragedie / The harm of hem that stoode in heigh degree" (VII.1991–92), chronicling every form of "meschaunce" (VII.2014). In doing so, he focuses on losses that Boethius identifies explicitly with the body, not the soul; with matter, not the spirit. Lady Philosophy negates the power of tyrants "over a free corage" (*Boece* II.Pr.6.49–50), asking, "wher schal men fynden any man that mai exercen or haunten any ryght upon another man, but oonly on his body, or elles upon thynges that been lowere than the body, the whiche I clepe fortunous possessiouns" (*Boece* II.Pr.6.44–48).

Not only the subject but also the method of the Monk's storytelling exemplifies material causality. First of all, his tale consists of an aggregate of tales, unlinked and atomistic. As an artist, the Monk resembles destiny itself, which "departeth and ordeyneth alle thinges singulerly and devyded in moevynges in places, in formes, in tymes" (*Boece* IV.Pr.6.70–72)—not providence, which "embraceth alle thinges to-hepe, althoghe that thei been diverse" (*Boece* IV.Pr.6.67–69). Secondly, the Monk's tragedies are unmotivated by any sense of human choice or divine purpose; instead they underscore the mechanical turning of Fortune's wheel, the "cours" of which no one can

---

[32] Scholars typically regard the Monk's philosophy to be unsound. See R. E. Kaske, "The Knight's Interruption of the *Monk's Tale*," *ELH* 24 (1957): 252–67; Jack B. Oruch, "Chaucer's Worldly Monk," *Criticism* 8 (1966): 280–88; David E. Berndt, "Monastic *Acedia* and Chaucer's Characterization of Daun Piers," *SP* 68.4 (1971): 435–50. For a contrastive view, see Douglas L. Lepley, "The Monk's Boethian Tale," *Chaucer Review* 12.3 (1978): 162–70.

"withholde" (VII.1996). As a narrator, the Monk is as blind as the prisoner Boethius to "the hidde causes of thinges," unable "to discovere . . . the resouns covered with derknes" (*Boece* IV.Pr.6.1–4). For him there is no final cause, no intentionality, only formless *materia*.

The Formal Cause: Truth under a Veil

In "The Nun's Priest's Tale" Chaucer focuses on the formal causation absent in "The Monk's Tale."[33] As a beast fable including a prophetic dream, the story of Chauntecleer dramatizes the "modus poeticus" in its pure form, classically understood as a concealment of truth under fiction.[34] As Boccaccio expresses it, "Whatever is composed as under a veil is poetry and poetry alone" (Osgood, p. 42).[35] The poet writes "sub velamento" and "sub figmento," making use of the integument (*involucrum*, *integumentum*) of a tale to convey a deeper meaning that becomes obvious once the husk has been removed ("amoto cortice"), the chaff discarded. Boccaccio enumerates four types of such fictions in *Genealogiae Deorum* XIV, beginning with the purest type of allegory: "The first superficially lacks all appearance of truth; for example, when brutes or inanimate things converse" (Osgood, p. 48).[36] To this class belongs the beast fables of Aesop, as well as Chaucer's tale "of a cok" (VII.3252). As the narrator insists in his concluding comment:

> But ye that holden this tale a folye,
> As of a fox, or of a cok and hen,

[33]   The progression from a consideration of the material cause to the formal cause is a logical one. Allen cites a commentary on Ovid's *Metamorphoses* (Oxford, Bodleian Library, ms Canon, misc. 457, f10v) that approaches the opening lines of Book II (a description of the palace of the Sun) in a similar fashion: "primo describit eam materialiter, secundo formaliter" / first he describes it in terms of material, second in terms of form (*Ethical Poetic*, p. 139).

[34]   Cf. Minnis's treatment of Ulrich of Strassburg's *Liber de summo bono* (circa 1262), in which Ulrich characterizes the scriptural "modus poeticus" according to the Aristotelian definition of poetry (in *Metaphysics* I) as a representation of truth "under fictional garments" (*Medieval Theory of Authorship*, p. 140).

[35]   The Latin reads: "Mera poesis est, quicquid sub velamento componimus et exquiritur exquisite" (Boccaccio, *In Defence of Poetry: Genealogiae Deorum gentilium liber XIV*, ed. Jeremiah Reedy [Toronto: Pontifical Institute of Mediaeval Studies, 1978], p. 36).

[36]   "Prima omnimo veritate caret in cortice, ut puta, quando animalia bruta aut eciam insensata inter se loquencia inducimus" (Reedy, p. 41).

> Taketh the moralite, goode men.
> For Seint Paul seith that al that writen is,
> To oure doctrine it is ywrite, ywis;
> Taketh the fruyt, and lat the chaf be stille.
>
> (VII.3438–43)

The *causa formalis* of poetry, thus understood, also has its limitations—as the tale itself comically dramatizes. A veiled truth tends to remain buried. Often the auditor lacks either the necessary exegetical skill or the will to accept it. Chaucer illustrates both of these possibilities in the paired responses of Pertelote and Chauntecleer to the cock's dream. Pertelote fails to penetrate the underlying truth of the dream and dismisses it as "vanitee" (VII.2922). Her carnal reading of the dream as a product of excessive "rede colera" (VII.2928) prompts her urging that Chauntecleer "purge" (VII.2947) himself by taking a laxative. Chauntecleer, on the other hand, correctly interprets the dream as a "significacioun" (VII.2979) of impending danger, citing Cicero and Macrobius as authorities and recalling appropriate *exempla*. He, however, lacks the will to accept the dream as a *memento mori*. Distracted by "the beautee" (VII.3160) of Pertelote's face, he defies "both sweven and dreem" (VII.3171). Indeed, his ability to overwhelm Pertelote with his exegesis awakens an analogous desire to tread and feather her—so much so that his combined interpretive and sexual power over her makes him "dredeless" of dreams: "Real he was, he was namoore aferd" (VII.3176).[37]

The link between Chauntecleer's responses to the dream and to Pertelote evokes a long tradition associating feminine figures with the pleasurable, and therefore perilous, attractions of poetry. Poetry veils truth, but the literal veil is itself a seductive siren song, distracting in its sensory appeal, dangerous in its indirection. In order to exemplify the negative potential of the *causa formalis*, the tale absorbs a series of images linking song with seduction. Chauntecleer, "the clear singer," is himself a figure of the poet: "In al the land, of crowyng nas his peer" (VII.2850).[38] Entrapped in the beauty of his own utterance,

---

[37] Cf. Ian Bishop, "*The Nun's Priest's Tale* and the Liberal Arts," *Review of English Studies*, n.s. 30 (1979): 266; Larry Scanlon, "The Authority of Fable: Allegory and Irony in the *Nun's Priest's Tale*," *Exemplaria* 1 (1989): 59.

[38] The identification of Chauntecleer with the poet gains support from Dolores Warwick Frese's suggestion that the name "Chauntecleer" is an anagram for Chaucer's own

Chauntecleer is self-tempted and therefore vulnerable to nearly fatal
flattery by the fox who begs to hear him sing: "For trewely, ye have
as myrie a stevene / As any aungel hath that is in hevene" (VII.3291–
92).

When Pertelote and the other hens bathe themselves, they provide
an emblem for Chauntecleer's own mermaidish qualities:

> Faire in the soond, to bathe hire myrily,
> Lith Pertelote, and alle hire sustres by,
> Agayn the sonne, and Chauntecleer so free
> Soong murier than the mermayde in the see
> (For Phisiologus seith sikerly
> How that they syngen wel and myrily).
>
> (VII.3267–72)

The mermaid or siren is, of course, a classical image for the seduction
of poetry. The ironic reference to *Physiologus* conveys what remains
unstated: that the marvelous singing of the mermaids causes the ship-
wreck of sailors and brings them to mortal danger.[39] To hear their
music without yielding to its attractions requires the fortitude of Ulysses, who had himself bound to the mast, lest he succumb. Thus, in
the *Polycraticus* of John of Salisbury, Ulysses stands as an exemplum—
first of all, for the poet who must note vices without teaching them;
secondly, for the reader who must pass through the dangers of textual
seduction in order to make room for virtue.[40] Boccaccio, too, uses the
example of Ulysses to confront readers who object to poetry as in-
herently alluring: "Well may the wretches blush and revise their mad
counsel, considering how Ulysses, noble soul, spurned the sound, not
of songs read in the closet, but the dulcet music of the Sirens, whom
he passed by for fear of harm at their hands" (Osgood, p. 77).[41]

---

name. See "The *Nun's Priest's Tale*: Chaucer's Identified Masterpiece?" *Chaucer Review*
16 (1982): 330–43.

[39] See Richard J. Schrader, "Chauntecleer, the Mermaid, and Daun Burnel," *Chaucer
Review* 4.4 (1970): 286. He quotes from *Physiologus: A Metrical Bestiary of Twelve Chapters
by Bishop Theobald* (Printed in Cologne, 1492), ed. and trans. Alan W. Rendell (London,
1928).

[40] See John of Salisbury, *Polycraticus* VII.ix, PL 199, C 656.

[41] "Erubescant igitur miseri, et in melius insanum suum reforment consilium, pros-
pectentque Ulixem, gentilem hominem, non mutorum carminum set mellifluos syren-

In the end, "The Nun's Priest's Tale" offers little hope for that kind of heroic resistance to poetic images. After remarking about the transitoriness of "worldly joye" (VII.3206), the narrator compares the truth of his tale to that of "the book of Launcelot de Lake / That wommen holde in ful greet reverence" (VII.3212–13). The Old French prose *Lancelot* records the adultery of Launcelot and Guinevere—a story held in "reverence," as Dante demonstrates, only at the risk of damnation. Paolo and Francesca were reading that romance, after all, when they yielded to the passions that condemned them (see *Inf.* 5.117–38). The book itself became for them a Gallehault, a go-between, mediating their mutual seduction.

Chauntecleer treading Pertelote, of course, provides a comic parallel to the tragic union of the Arthurian lovers, but the comedy nevertheless serves to underscore the formal parallel between the book and the tale. If the truth of "The Nun's Priest's Tale" is comparable to that of an adulterous fiction, it is because it too pretends to teach and thus precipitates learning—without, however, exercising any real control over *what* people learn. It panders to the audience, presenting a multitude of possible *sententiae*, expecting us to hear what we want to hear. Indeed, Chaucer's *modus agendi* in the tale seems to rest on the uncomfortable conviction "that the meaning of a work resides not so much in the writing as in the reading."[42] At the close of the tale, Chauntecleer learns one lesson, the Fox another, but the moral of the tale itself remains elusive and teasing, undisclosed and undiscoverable, flattering and frustrating our ability to interpret.[43]

---

arum cantus spreuisse tamquam nocuos atque transisse" (Reedy, p. 67). In the allegorical tradition, Ulysses' adventures come to symbolize the wise man's battles against many forms of temptation. See Hugo Rahner, "Odysseus at the Mast," in *Greek Myths and Christian Mystery*, trans. Brian Battershaw (London: Burns and Oates, 1963), pp. 328–86. For a discussion of Dante's use of Ulysses as an image of his own unredeemed self, see David Thompson, *Dante's Epic Journeys* (Baltimore: Johns Hopkins University Press, 1974), esp. pp. 69–73.

[42] Karla Taylor, "The Text and Its Afterlife," *Comparative Literature* 35.1 (1983): 19. Taylor compares the attitudes of Dante and Chaucer regarding "the social effect of literature" (p. 9) and concludes that Chaucer is more pessimistic about the possibility of controlling reader response. Cf. Judith Ferster's comment on Chaucer's "anxiety about his influence on his audience's spiritual health" (*Chaucer on Interpretation*, p. 11).

[43] See Scanlon for an insightful discussion of the political consequences of the secular appropriation of the teaching function ascribed to sacred scripture. The tale, according to Scanlon, teaches only that "all writing is doctrinal," and "the polemical power" of that claim "lies precisely in its open-endedness" ("Authority of Fable," p. 54).

The Cause of Reception

Dramatizing the fable's failure to reveal the truth it claims to conceal effectually breaks the fourfold frame of the Aristotelian causes, even as Chaucer completes it, by introducing yet another cause: that of reception. In the end, the "menynge" of the poet—whatever his authorial intent—is not necessarily the meaning of the poem as it is received by its audience. The veiled moral of "The Nun's Priest's Tale" threatens to become as many morals as the tale has auditors. Thus, when the narrator attempts to justify his secular fable by invoking the Pauline dictum in Romans 15:4 that "al that writen is, / To oure doctrine it is ywrite, ywis" (VII.3441–42), he shifts the ethical burden from the teller to the listener with a double imperative: "Taketh the moralite, goode men. . . . Taketh the fruyt" (VII.3440, 3443). The veiled truth must be taken because it has not been, and cannot be, given.

The insistence on the ethical responsibility of the auditor is a familiar Chaucerian stance, reminiscent of the *apologia* in the General Prologue where Chaucer compares his plain rehearsal of the pilgrims' rough-and-ready talk to Christ's "ful brode" (GP 739) speech "in hooly writ." To the ears of a properly disposed listener, it is "no vileynye" (GP 740). The apology in the Miller's prologue similarly insists upon the narrator's good intent in repeating what he has heard and the auditor's responsibility to follow the dictates of personal conscience in choosing a "storial thing": "Blameth nat me if that ye chese amys" (I.3181). The listener is responsible for what he or she learns.

When the words of Saint Paul about textual doctrine (quoted by the Nun's Priest in his epilogue) are repeated in the context of the "retracciouns" (X.1085), however, Chaucer seems much less confident of his own impunity.[44] He begins, on the one hand, by asserting his good will: "For oure book seith, 'All that is writen is writen for

[44] Douglas Wurtele ("The Penitence of Geoffrey Chaucer," *Viator* 11 [1980]: 335–59) has argued that lines 1081–84 and 1090–92 of the Retraction are spoken by the Parson, and that lines 1085–90 are an interpolation by Chaucer, partly on the grounds that "it would have been presumptuous for Chaucer to apply St. Paul's dictum to his own profane work" (p. 341). The use of the same text (Romans 15:4: "Quaecumque enim scripta sunt, ad nostram doctrinam scripta sunt") by the Nun's Priest in reference to the fable of Chauntecleer, however, clearly indicates that Chaucer did apply the scriptural principle to his secular tales.

oure doctrine,' and that is myn entente" (X.1083). Whatever his conscious intent, however, he bears and accepts responsibility for the actual consequences of his writings in the lives of his listeners. His acknowledged "giltes" (X.1084) include the writing of many a "leccherous lay" (X. 1087) and the "enditynges of worldly vanitees" (X.1084), among which he numbers "the tales of Caunterbury, thilke that sownen into synne" (X.1086). Indeed, the actual words of the Retraction express much the same sentiment evident in the grimmer death-bed lament attributed to Chaucer by Thomas Gascoigne (1403–58): "Woe to me, woe to me, because I can neither revoke nor destroy those things I have wickedly written about the sinful and shameful lust of men for women, and now they will be passed on from man to man."[45]

Confronted by the afterlife of his writings, the immoral doctrine actually learned, whether or not it has been willfully taught, Chaucer finds himself powerless in the face of causes that impinge upon the Aristotelian four, defining them, as it were, by their limits and limitations. The limit of the *causa formalis*, in particular, is its seductive cortex, the chaff which, as a bad, substitute seed, can inspire sin.

Chaucer and the Multiplicity of Causes

As an exemplum of formal causality in poetry, Chaucer's tale of Chauntecleer brings to an end the array of possible causes co-determining texts. It looks forward in its doctrinal concern, as we have seen, to the Retraction written at the end of Chaucer's life. At the same time, the thoroughgoing investigation of the problem of writing in Fragment VII has its clear foreshadowing in Chaucer's early works. In the *Book of the Duchess*, for instance, the dream and the poem have their identifiable material cause in the Ovidian fable of Alcyone and Ceys, the "romaunce" (*BD* 48) the sleepless narrator reads. The *Parliament of Fowls*, too, begins with the reading of a book: "Tullyus of the Dreme of Scipioun" (*PF.* 31). The *House of*

---

[45] "Vae mihi, vae mihi quia revocare / nec destruere iam potero illa quae male scripsi de malo et turpissimo amore hominum ad mulieres sed iam de homine in hominem continuabuntur." Quoted by Wurtele, p. 356. Translation mine.

Fame calls attention to the person of the poet ("Geffrey," *HF* 729) as an efficient cause, elected to follow the poets of old. All the early dream visions concern themselves, in one way or another, with the "causa formalis" of poetry as a mixture of truth and fable, as a sign requiring interpretation.

Chaucer, however, reserves the systematic unfolding of artistic causality for his later works. The array of causes in Fragment VII has, in fact, its closest analogue in the G Prologue to the *Legend of Good Women*. There the poet, who finds himself on trial for publishing the inconstancy of women in love, must defend himself (and be defended by Alceste) by pleading the limitations of his causes. First of all, the Queen points to the *causa materialis* and represents Chaucer to the god of Love as a mere translator who conveys into English the matter of other writers: "He may translate a thyng in no malyce, / But for he useth bokes for to make, / And taketh non hed of what matere he take, / Therefore he wrot the Rose and ek Crisseyde / Of innocence" (G 341–45). Second, Alceste raises the issue of agency, or efficient causality, substituting for the impelling force of divine inspiration the compulsion of a tyrannical human patron: "Or hym was boden make thilke tweye / Of som persone, and durste it not withseye" (G 346–47). As a third defense, Chaucer calls attention to the final cause that motivated him:

> what so myn auctour mente,
> Algate, God wot, it was myn entente
> To forthere trouthe in love and it cheryce,
> And to be war fro falsnesse and fro vice
> By swich ensaumple; this was my menynge.
> (G 460–64)

If he has failed to realize that intent, the failure stems in part from the nature of poetry itself, which makes its point indirectly through the "other speaking" of symbol and irony. Alceste herself, veiled under the figure of the "dayesye," represents the capacity of fables and legends to conceal the metamorphosized truth they are meant to convey. When, therefore, the god of Love commands Chaucer to "let be the chaf, and writ wel of the corn" (G 529), he imposes an impossible constraint—one of several in the Prologue—on the poet by divorcing

him from the "causa formalis" of poetry itself which, by its very nature, compels him to write "sub velamento."[46]

In the *Legend*'s Prologue G and in Fragment VII of the *Tales*, then,
Chaucer explores the multiple causality of art and the contradictory
claims it makes upon the poet who must be a mechanically competent
versifier and an inspired, spontaneous oracle; ingenious in sophistic
ornamentation and, at the same time, artlessly ingenuous; absolutely
true to his sources but equally creative with them; an instructor who
teaches indirectly and thus has little guarantee that his true intent will
be realized by his audience; an entertainer whose success in delighting
endangers his didactic purpose as much or more as does his failure
to please.

Fragment VII, like the *Legend*, offers us a remarkable, composite
"portrait of the artist,"[47] and it does so from the comic perspective
of Chaucer's maturity when he has learned to triumph, even in his
failure, by dramatizing the struggle of storytelling. The Retraction at
the end of the *Tales* gives a more somber, retrospective picture of
Chaucer's life as an artist, but it too is comic in its invocation of divine
mercy and final causality. Chaucer's authorial failure precipitates his
repentance and thus his redemption: "so that I may been oon of hem
at the day of doom that shulle be saved" (X.1092). However much
the divine "fer cause" acts initially to inspire human authorship,
in the end it proves its power in the form of providential polishing
and revision, cleansing what has been blotted, righting what has been
written.

---

[46] Chaucer's Parson embraces this option, rejecting "fables" and "draf" in favor of
the "whete" of "moralitee and vertuous mateere" (X.34–36).
[47] See Donald W. Rowe, *Through Nature to Eternity: Chaucer's "Legend of Good Women"*
(Lincoln: University of Nebraska Press, 1988), p. 11.

Bot what man under his pouer
Is Bore, he schal his places change
And seche manye londes strange:
And as of this condicion
The Mones disposicion
Upon the lond of Alemaigne
Is set, and ek upon Bretaigne,
Which nou is cleped Engelond.

—John Gower

7

LUNAR "PRACTIQUE":

LAW, MEDICINE, AND THEOLOGY

IN FRAGMENTS VI AND X

Confronted at the start of "The Physician's Tale" with "a hodgepodge of what amounts to digressions, disconnected and incompatible in feeling," many critics have recoiled from accepting Daniel Kempton's claim that the horrific tale "typifies Canterbury fiction."[1] Nevertheless, as a compilation of multiple, disjunctive units of discourse, it exhibits in a condensed way the paratactic fragmentariness of the *Canterbury Tales* as a whole, and it does so at the very center of the chiastic Ellesmere ordering.

This chapter argues that Chaucer's selection and handling of material in "The Physician's Tale" and in Fragment VI as a whole is guided by his overall plan of planetary pilgrimage and, in particular, by his attempt to represent as under lunar influence the divisions of clerkly practitioners most directly responsible for social governance: physicians, lawyers, and pastors.[2] Like the encyclopedic Gower of Book VII of *Confessio Amantis*, Chaucer begins with "Theorique" (in Frag-

---

[1] Daniel Kempton, "The *Physician's Tale*: The Doctor of Physic's Diplomatic 'Cure,'" *Chaucer Review* 19.1 (1984): 24–25.
[2] For an integrated approach to medieval law, medicine, and theology, see John Alford, "Literature and Law in Medieval England," *PMLA* 92 (1977): 941–51; "Medicine in the Middle Ages: The Theory of a Profession," *Centennial Review* 23 (1979): 377–96.

ments I and II), proceeds to "Rhetorique" (in Fragments III–IV–V), and ends with "Practique" (in Fragments VI and X). Like Dante, Chaucer associates the Moon with the theme of "fals justise" (VI.289; *Par.* 4.66: "ingiusta . . . giustizia") and uses its position, as lowest in the planetary sequence, to offset, at the highest point, the heavenly New Jerusalem and its divine order.[3] Indeed, Fragments VI and X are best understood as a complex and detailed response to Dantean lunarity.

The sudden appearance of Nature at the beginning of "The Physician's Tale" locates the tales about to be told securely in the sphere of the Moon, where she is traditionally understood to exercise her dominion. As Nature herself declares, "ech thyng in my cure is / Under the moone, that may wane and waxe" (VI.22–23). Nature's speech and action in creating Virginia not only recall Alan de Lille's *De Planctu Naturae* and *Anticlaudianus* and thus contextualize Fragment VI within that didascalic tradition; but her declaration of perfect obedience to God as his "vicaire" (VI.20) and artisan (VI.25: "My lord and I been ful of oon accord") also sounds the theme of ordered love that prevails in Dante's lunar cantos and to which Chaucer responds.[4] As Piccarda explains to Dante, "In His will there is our peace" (*Par.* 3.85). As I hope to show, the intertextual relationships between Chaucer's Fragment VI and the works of Dante and Alan (among others) are directed by a series of lunar *topoi* that serve to advance Chaucer's planetary and philosophical pilgrimage.

Virginity and Childhood

In the sphere of the Moon, Dante meets only two identified figures, Piccarda Donati and Costanza, wife of the Swabian emperor Henry VI (1165–1197). Both women had taken the religious vows of poverty,

---

For a study emphasizing Chaucer's legal interests, see Joseph Hornsby, *Chaucer and the Law* (Norman: Pilgrims Books, 1988).

[3] Here and throughout I use Dante Alighieri, *Paradiso*, trans. Allen Mandelbaum (New York: Bantam, 1986); *The Riverside Chaucer*, ed. Larry D. Benson, 3d ed. (Boston: Houghton Mifflin, 1987).

[4] See Jay Ruud, "Natural Law and Chaucer's *Physician's Tale*," *Journal of the Rocky Mountain Medieval and Renaissance Association* 9 (1988): 29–45.

chastity, and obedience in their youth, only to be taken violently from their cloisters and compelled to marry. They are the only nuns whom Dante meets in the *Paradiso*. As Piccarda explains, "I was a nun, a virgin" (*Par.* 3.46). Later, her own brother Corso abducted her and forced her to marry his henchman, Rossellino della Torso. Similarly, Costanza was a sister until "against her will, against all honest practice" (*Par.* 3.116) she was forcibly taken from the convent to the court. The fate of both women thus contrasts with that of Saint Clare, to whom Piccarda refers, who successfully resisted a comparable attempt by her male relatives to drag her from the convent walls within which she had enclosed herself, and who thus succeeded in keeping her vows and meriting a higher place in heaven. As Richard Kay observes, "since an attachment to virginity is the constant factor" in the careers of these women, "anyone conversant with ancient mythology could detect some evidence of Lunar influence, inasmuch as Diana, goddess of the Moon, was the patronness of virgins."[5]

Chaucer's "Physician's Tale" features not a pair of religious sisters, but rather a daughter and a father whose very names evoke the virginity that is the peculiar province of the Moon. Like Dante's sisters, who vow virginity in their youth, Chaucer's Virginia is a child of twelve, whose perfect physical beauty is only surpassed by her virtue: "As wel in goost as body chast was she, / For which she floured in virginitee" (VI.43–44). The long list of her virtues recalls not only the moral giftedness of Alan de Lille's "New Man," but also the Ambrosian virtues regarded as especially appropriate for consecrated virgins.[6]

"The Physician's Tale" presents Virginia as the masterpiece of both Nature and nurture, even as Diana is the goddess of both virginity and childbirth. As Kay indicates, the astrologers associated the Moon with "pregnant women, mothers, nurses, and matrons" and with "child rearing" in general (pp. 28, 33). Appropriately, then, Chaucer's lunar "Physician's Tale" (unlike *Roman de la Rose* 5589–5658) emphasizes Virginia's status as a child in relation to her parents and guardians. The long digression (VI.72–104) in which the narrator exhorts governesses, fathers, and mothers to the proper "gover-

[5]   Richard Kay, *Dante's Christian Astrology* (Philadelphia: University of Pennsylvania Press, 1994), p. 21. Hereafter citations are parenthetical by page.
[6]   See Karl Young, "The Maidenly Virtues of Chaucer's Virginia," *Speculum* 16 (1941): 340–49.

naunce" (VI.73, 75, 96) of the children entrusted to them not only connects the household rule of Virginia's parents with the civic policy of Apius as "governour" (VI.122) of the region, in keeping with the *divisiones* of Aristotelian practical philosophy;[7] it also marks the story and its teller as Lunarian. Similarly, the imagery of "sheep and lamb" (VI.102), which, as Kay has shown, is prominent in both Chaucer's tale and Dante's lunar cantos (*Par.* 4.4–6, 5.82–84), reflects both the whiteness of the Moon and its association with all those in real or metaphoric need of a shepherd's care and protection (p. 34).

The plot of Apius and his henchman Claudius to force Virginius to yield his freeborn, virginal daughter to them as their "thral" and sex-slave, "in lecherie to lyven" (VI.202, 206), grimly recalls the word of astrologers like Omar, whom Kay quotes as indicating that "the Lunar type of slave dealer is one who traffics in virgins" (p. 290 n11). More importantly, it sets the enclosure of Virginius's house parallel to Dante's cloister and establishes an analogy between Virginia's persecutors and the "men more used to malice than to good" (*Par.* 3.106) who carried Piccarda away against her will. Chaucer's much discussed departure from his sources in absenting Virginia from the courtroom and staging the final encounter between her and her father instead within a familial and domestic space, at "hoom" and "in his halle" (VI.207), enforces such a parallel and complicates the issue of unjust justice with which both Dante and Chaucer deal.

Lunarian Piety and Unjust Justice

In Dante the question of "ingiusta . . . giustizia" (*Par.* 4.67) directly concerns God's assignment to Piccarda and Costanza of the lowest place in the Empyrean when, as we have been told, they broke their vows unwillingly and under duress. What blame can be theirs? In a lengthy explanation, Beatrice explores the complicity of the victims in the actions of their oppressors and the degree to which their resistance to evil has "abetted force" and "yielded much or little" out of love for their relatives and the fearful desire "to flee menace" to

---

[7]   Gower gives the threefold, Aristotelian scheme of practical philosophy in *Confessio Amantis* VII.1649–98 and uses the story of Virginia (VII.5130–5306) under that heading to exemplify chastity, one of the five points of policy. See *The Complete Works of John Gower*, ed. G. C. Macaulay (Oxford: Clarendon Press, 1901), vol. 3.

themselves and others (*Par.* 4.79–80, 101). Even though the "absolute will does not concur in wrong," the contingent will nevertheless consents to it "through fear that its resistance might bring greater harm" (*Par.* 4.109–11). Their will thus mingles with the sinful will of another and becomes tainted by it.

Beatrice draws a shocking parallel between the contingent (and therefore culpable) consent of the nuns to marry and the guilty piety of Alcmaeon, who killed his mother "to meet the wishes of his father": "not to fail in filial piety, he acted ruthlessly" (*Par.* 4.103–5). The *pietas* that is typical of Lunarians as children obedient to their parents, as sheep following their shepherd, and conversely, as guardians caring for others, thus becomes, in Kay's words, a "morally ambiguous" virtue in a world where the will of those in positions of power and authority frequently differs from the will of God, whose deputies and representatives they are called to be (p. 27).

Lest she be misunderstood in her insistence on the absolute keeping of vows, Beatrice goes on to draw a sharp contrast between the religious vows of the nuns, for which no other "matter" can be substituted, and the rash vow of Jephthah, which he first made foolishly and then fulfilled with shocking impiety, when he took the life of his own daughter as a sacrificial offering (*Par.* 5.69–72).

Chaucer's treatment of the issues raised by these *exempla* offers a complex rejoinder to Dante. At the literal level, Chaucer shifts attention away from God's seemingly "unjust justice" to the indisputably *false* justice of a corrupt earthly judge. Prompted by "the feend" (VI.130), Apius plots and enacts a heinous miscarriage of justice in the courtroom that rightly earns him the epithets of "false juge," "cursed juge," and "fals justise" (VI.154, 158, 161, 196, 289).

Like Dante and unlike Jean de Meun, Chaucer alludes to the biblical story of "Jepte" (VI.240), but he makes no mention of Jephthah's foolish vow;[8] rather, he focuses on both the piety and the impiety of Virginius's act in beheading his own child. The "fadres pitee" that wounds his heart and moves his "pitous hand" (VI.211, 226) is both pity and piety. Given the choice of death or shame for his beloved daughter, he chooses what he perceives to be the lesser of two evils. In so doing, however, his contingent will becomes con-

---

[8] See Richard L. Hoffman, "Jephthah's Daughter and Chaucer's Virginia," *Chaucer Review* 2 (1967): 20–31.

joint with that of the evil Apius, and he, like Apius, becomes a false judge, condemning an innocent person who is undeserving of death: "Take thou thy deeth, for this is my sentence" (VI.224).

Virginia's response, on the other hand, more closely approaches the absolute resistance to evil that Beatrice illustrates with the examples of Saint Lawrence and Mucius (*Par.* 4.82–84). Like Mucius, who, condemned to death at the stake, thrusts his own hand into the fire, Virginia chooses virginity and a martyr's death: "Yif me my deeth, er that I have a shame" (VI.249). She does so, moreover, as an act of piety that aligns her father not with the evil Apius, but with God, and herself with him/Him: "Dooth with youre child youre wyl, a Goddes name" (VI.250).

Chaucer's treatment of Virginia's death makes her, in fact, so Christlike that "The Physician's Tale" returns, at an allegorical level, to the Dantean question of God's unjust justice—this time, however, with respect to the sacrifice of Christ, the innocent Lamb of God, on the cross.[9] Like Dante's Beatrice, but in terms less direct than hers, Chaucer affirms that divine "justice seems unjust" to mortal eyes, but also that this paradox "should serve as evidence for faith" (*Par.* 4.67–69). Although the Physician's moralization of the tale threatens sinners with punishment, and capital offenders with death, his story calls attention less to the deservedly bad ends of Apius and Claudius than to the death of the guiltless Virginia—a death for which there is "no remedye" (VI.236) and which powerfully represents the mystery of evil in a fallen world where all people, good and evil alike, must die, if not through human betrayal and violence, then through some other "pestilence" (VI.91).

Medicine and the Plague

As Kay teaches us, according to the astrologer Albumasar, the Lunarian is conspicuously "concerned about the health of the body" (p. 27). This doctrine applies especially to physicians, all the more so because ancient and medieval medicine took its theoretical bearings from astronomy. As Laura Braswell reports, "a survey of medieval

---

[9] For the patristic Christological allegorization of the story of Jephthah, see Hoffman, "Jephthah's Daughter," pp. 29–31.

medical manuscripts . . . indicates a central orientation within the position and nature of the moon as a basis for medical practice, principally with reference to Galenic humoral theory."[10] Any practitioner
of medicine looked to Luna, the Moon, in order to determine the
"*cur, quando, quam,* 'why,' 'when,' and 'how' " of treatment.[11] Appropriately then, Chaucer's Physician, who is a "verray, parfit praktisour,"
well-versed in humoral theory and "grounded in astronomye" (GP
422, 414), tells his tale in the sphere of the Moon.

As Beryl Rowland has shown, "The Physician's Tale" (unlike Gower's rendition of the same story in *Confessio Amantis* VII.5131–5306)
indicts corrupt lawyers and judges, not kings, and thus participates in
the ancient feud between law and medicine that continued to rage in
the late-medieval universities.[12] It does so, however, in a way that simultaneously suggests the terrible limits of medicine itself in dealing
with disease and preserving life.[13] As Harry Bailly observes, the cause
of Virginia's death is twofold. On the one hand, wicked "juges and
hire advocatz" (VI.291) stand responsible; on the other, Virginia's
beauty and goodness are to blame: "Hire beautee was hire deth" (VI.
297).

The Nature whom the Physician invokes at the start of his tale is
beneficent and powerful; her laws are divine, her gifts are good, and
Virginia is her masterpiece.[14] Virginia, moreover, lives according to a
healthful regimen, avoiding wine and carousing and observing instead
"abstinence," "attemperaunce," and "mesure" (VI.45–47), much
like the Physician himself, whose "diete mesurable" (GP 435) is exemplary for his patients. Virginia dies, nevertheless, and Harry Bailly
regards the death of the Physician's heroine as a failure of his art,
both medical and artistic. The Physician's "pitous tale" (VI.302) fails
to save Virginia's life; casts doubt on the efficacy of the doctor's "uryn-

---

[10]   Laura Braswell, "The Moon and Medicine in Chaucer's Time," *SAC* 8 (1986): 145.
[11]   Ibid., p. 147.
[12]   Beryl Rowland, "The Physician's 'Historial Thyng Notable' and the Man of Law,"
ELH 40 (1973): 165–78.
[13]   Cf. Kempton, "The Doctor of Physic's Diplomatic 'Cure'." For general studies of
medical education, see Huling E. Ussery, *Chaucer's Physician* (New Orleans: Tulane University Press, 1971); Nancy G. Siraisi, *Medieval and Early Renaissance Medicine: An Introduction to Knowledge and Practice* (Chicago: University of Chicago Press, 1990).
[14]   See George Economou, *The Goddess Natura in Medieval Literature* (Cambridge: Harvard University Press, 1972), esp. pp. 26–27.

als," "jurdones," "ypocras," and "galiones" (VI.305–6); and succeeds in making Bailly ill: "But wel I woot thou doost myn herte to
erme, / That I almoost have caught a cardynacle" (VI.312–13). Bailly
is, in fact, so sickened by the story that he begs to hear a "myrie tale"
as a "triacle" (VI.314, 316).

The Host's response, which links hearing a tale to physical health
or "unheele," points to the common notion that a physician, like a
priest, should be skillful in tale-telling and well versed in "gode
prouerbeȝ pertenyng to his crafte in counfortyng of pacientez."[15] As
John Arderne, the respected physician in attendance on John of
Gaunt, remarks in one of his treatises on fistula, "it spedeth þat a
leche kunne talke of gode taleȝ and of honest that may make þe
pacientes to laugh, as wele of the biblee . . . and any othir þingis of
which it is noȝt to charge whileȝ þat þey make or induce a liȝt hert
to þe pacient or þe sike man."[16] Arderne explains this principle, quoting "Boecius" on the importance of applying spiritual remedies in
the promotion of a patient's total health: "ffor gret hert makeþ a man
hardy and strong to suffre sharp þingis and greuous."[17]

In the face of the plague, medieval physicians had little more than
tales and proverbs to offer their patients, and more often than not
they were lacking even in these. The official pronouncement made
by the members of the College of Physicians at the University of Paris
in 1348, at the first outbreak of the Black Death, is consonant with
the views of Chaucer's university-trained "doctour of phisik" (GP
411) in its emphasis on Nature's benevolence, astronomy, and dietary
control. Endeavoring "to make known the causes of this pestilence,"
the physicians cited astral and atmospheric disturbances and the
spread of contaminated vapors. Being "of the opinion that the constellations, with the aid of Nature, strive, by virtue of their divine
might, to protect and heal the human race," they predicted that an
unusually heavy rain in July, followed by days of sunshine, would eventually serve to purge the air. In the meantime, they urged dietary

[15] John Arderne, *Treatises of Fistula in Ano*, ed. D'Arcy Power, EETS 139 (London:
Kegan Paul, 1910), p. 7. On the medieval medical justification for literature, see Glending Olson, *Literature as Recreation in the Later Middle Ages* (Ithaca: Cornell University
Press, 1982).
[16] Arderne, *Fistula*, p. 8.
[17] Ibid., p. 7.

regulations, prescribed chastity, and counseled the avoidance of night air and rain water.[18]

Not surprisingly, given the inadequacy of these directives, medieval physicians found themselves helpless in 1348–49 and in successive outbreaks of the epidemic in 1361, 1368–69, 1371, 1375, 1390, and 1405. As the French physician Gui de Chauliac wrote, "The plague was shameful for the physicians, who could give no help at all, especially as, out of fear of infection, they hesitated to visit the sick. Even if they did, they achieved nothing . . . for all those who caught the plague died, except for a few towards the end of the epidemic."[19] Those few medical men who survived may have prospered financially, like Chaucer's Physician, who "kepte that he wan in pestilence," but that gold was a "cordial" (GP 442–43) that carried with it the memory of incurable disease, terrible death, and mass burials.

Bitterly disappointed in the efficacy of the largely preventive medicine of the physicians, people sought supernatural rather than natural remedies, flocking to the altars and pillars of the Virgin Mary and of other thaumaturgic saints, like Saints Sebastian, Roch, Job, and Thomas of Kent.[20] Chaucer represents this turn in the links between the tales of the Physician and the Pardoner, when Harry Bailly's list of medical instruments is transformed into the Pardoner's catalog of supposedly curative "relikes," holy "cloutes," and "bones" (VI.348–49).[21]

St. Thomas, in particular, had an extraordinary and enduring reputation for physical healings of all kinds. As a fifteenth-century sermon relates, as a result of his intercession "some recouerd he[r] yȝen, some here preuy membres, the whiche they hadde lost by the justices

---

[18]   The text of the pronouncement appears in George Deaux, *The Black Death, 1347* (London: Hamish Hamilton, 1969), pp. 52–53. See also Philip Ziegler, *The Black Death* (New York: Harper and Row, 1969), pp. 63–83.

[19]   Ziegler, *Black Death*, p. 71.

[20]   See Johannes Nohl, *The Black Death: A Chronicle of the Plague Compiled from Contemporary Sources*, trans. C. H. Clarke (London: Unwin, 1961), pp. 84–88.

[21]   For a discussion of "the religious and ethical questions commonly associated with medicine," see Nancy Siraisi, "Dante and the Art and Science of Medicine," in *The "Divine Comedy" and the Encyclopedia of Arts and Sciences*, ed. Giuseppe Di Scipio and Aldo Scaglione (Philadelphia: John Benjamins, 1988), pp. 223–45. See also Katherine B. Trower, "Spiritual Sickness in the Physician's and Pardoner's Tales: Thematic Unity in Fragment VI of the *Canterbury Tales*," *American Benedictine Review* 29 (1978): 67–86.

of the kynges. And ded men he reysid fro deth to lyue, lepre men he clensed, and did manye other myracles that are innumerable."[22] To Becket, then, the people prayed; and, according to J. D. Hall, in 1350, "the year following the worst devastation of the Black Death," the offerings given in gratitude by plague-survivors at Canterbury reached the enormous sum of about £700.[23]

Chaucer's company of pilgrims is following in the footsteps of these historical believers to the shrine of the "hooly blisful martir . . . / That hem hath holpen whan that they were seeke" (GP 18). Therefore, as Melvin Storm has brilliantly shown, the Pardoner's display of bogus relics, preaching against sin, and promise of absolution offer "a meretricious surrogate for what the other pilgrims seek at Becket's shrine."[24] The Pardoner of Rouncival thus "endangers the pilgrimage realistically as well as symbolically" by providing an alternative end point halfway on the journey from London to Canterbury.[25] Similarly, from the point of view of Chaucer's planetary pilgrimage, the descent from Saturn to the sublunar earth could end precisely here, in Fragment VI, or it could continue upward in a returning ascent beyond the stars.

The Pardoner's Lunarity: Nutrition, Revelation, Inconstancy, Fratricide, Forgetfulness, and Sexuality

Chaucer's characterization of the Pardoner is riddled with notorious *cruces*, all of which can be explained (at least in part) astrologically, when we see him as a Lunarian. The Pardoner, for instance, is the only pilgrim who stops to eat and drink before he tells his story: " 'But first,' quod he, 'heere at this alestake / I wol bothe drynke and eten of a cake' " (VI.321–22). He grants the pilgrims' wish to hear

[22] *Speculum sacerdotale*, ed. Edward H. Weatherly, EETS 200 (London: Oxford University Press, 1936), p. 15.
[23] D. J. Hall, *English Mediaeval Pilgrimage* (London: Routledge and Kegan Paul, 1965), p. 155.
[24] Melvin Storm, "The Pardoner's Invitation: Quaester's Bag or Becket's Shrine?" *PMLA* 97.5 (1982): 810.
[25] Ibid. For articles of related interest, see David K. Maxfield, "St. Mary Rouncivale, Charing Cross: The Hospital of Chaucer's Pardoner," *Chaucer Review* 28.2 (1993): 148–63; Siegfried Wenzel, "Chaucer's Pardoner and His Relics," *SAC* 11 (1989): 37–41.

"som moral thyng," but insists that he must first " 'thynke / Upon som honest thyng' " while he drinks " 'a draughte of corny ale' " (VI.325, 327–28, 456). This curious pause for nourishment parodies Dante's heavenly banqueting in the *Paradiso*. The lunar cantos, as Kay notes, give prominence to the imagery of food and drink, as Dante hungers for, consumes, and digests the "food" of Beatrice's explanations. She tells him, "You need to sit at table somewhat longer" (*Par.* 5.37). Commenting on this passage, Kay explains that, through a process of generalization, the Moon's influence had been extended from childbirth to child-rearing, and thus from mothers to nurses (*nutrices*); "by generalizing the nurse's function, the Moon had also come to be associated with nutrition (*nutritura*)" (p. 33).

As the Pardoner lingers over his cake and ale, he shocks the pilgrim company with a long, boastful disclosure of his own fraud, hypocrisy, and avarice (among other sins). This "confession" has frequently been discussed in psychological and generic terms, but its strangely simple lunarity has gone unnoticed.[26] Kay, commenting on the "cumulative mass" of revelations that Beatrice herself makes to Dante in the sphere of the Moon, cites the astrologer Guido Bonatti, who explains that "the Moon promotes the concealment of secrets when Luna herself is concealed by the Sun, whereas the reverse is true when, passing from conjunction to opposition, she is fully revealed to sight" (p. 31). Like the full moon, the Pardoner stands momentarily and crazily exposed to light, but the qualitative difference between what he confesses and what Beatrice reveals could not be greater.

The sins to which the Pardoner confesses, both directly in his prologue and indirectly in his tale, also betray lunar influence. Not surprisingly, as Kay relates, the "earliest astrologers had associated the Moon with change because of its rapid monthly revolution through the zodiac and its attendant and readily observed changes of phase," and thus, by extension, the Moon became linked with the Goddess of Fortune, falsehood, and infidelity (pp. 24, 25, 30).

The mysterious, despairing Old Man, who wanders everywhere as a "restelees kaityf" (VI.728), seeking someone willing to exchange his

---

[26] See especially Lee W. Patterson, "Chaucerian Confession: Penitential Literature and the Pardoner," *Medievalia et Humanistica* 7 (1976): 153–74, and "The Subject of Confession: The Pardoner and the Rhetoric of Penance," in *Chaucer and the Subject of History* (Madison: University of Wisconsin Press, 1991), pp. 376–421.

youth for his old age, virtually personifies the Moon's instability and capacity for change.[27] As Gower's Genius says, describing the child of the Moon: "Bot what man under his pouer / Is Bore, he schal his places change / And seche manye londes strange" (*CA* VII.746–48). As Gerhard Joseph and others have noted, "The Pardoner's Tale" focuses particular attention on the "yiftes of Fortune" (VI.295, 779) and the consequences of an avaricious attachment to them.[28] The Pardoner's admitted hypocrisy, fraud, and "false japes" (VI.394) encompass multiple forms of falsehood. The Pardoner illustrates infidelity, moreover, with a tale of broken vows of brotherhood and thus answers to Dante's exempla of broken religious vows of sisterhood in the cases of Piccarda and Costanza.

The fratricide finally committed by the young rioters recalls yet another sin that Dante associates with the Moon, when he questions a bemused Beatrice about the popular belief that Cain is imprisoned there as the proverbial "man in the moon" (Cf. *Par.* 2.49–51). "The Parson's Tale" suggests that Cain lives instead on earth. Responding to Physician's "letuarie" (VI.307) and brotherly collusion with apothecaries (GP 425–27), the Pardoner makes "a pothecarie" (VI.852) the accomplice of his young murderer, substitutes poison for medicine, and cites "Avycen" (VI.889), one of the Physician's own authorities (GP 432), as a witness to the terrible "signes of empoisonyng" (VI.891) that convulse the young men's bodies as they die.

Whereas "The Physician's Tale" emphasizes the Diana of virgins and childbirth, "The Pardoner's Tale" stresses the third face of the moon goddess, that of Hecate, whom Emelye invokes in Diana's temple as "Queene of the regne of Pluto derk and lowe" (I.2299), the goddess of death and the underworld. In the realm over which Nature has sway, things both "waxe and wane" (Cf. VI.23–24), live and die, but in "The Pardoner's Tale" that general mortality becomes particularized in the plague and personifed in "a privee theef men clepeth

---

[27] The Man has been identified variously as Death, Old Age, the Wandering Jew, a Wisdom figure, Despair, the Pauline *vetus homo*, and Avarice. For a helpful review of scholarship, see Elizabeth R. Hatcher, "Life without Death: The Old Man in Chaucer's *Pardoner's Tale*," *Chaucer Review* 9 (1975): 246–52.

[28] See Gerhard Joseph, "The Gifts of Nature, Fortune, and Grace in the *Physician's, Pardoner's*, and *Parson's Tales*," *Chaucer Review* 9 (1975): 237–45.

Deeth" (VI.675), who, as the boy tells the three rioters, "hath a thousand slayn this pestilence" (VI.679).[29]

Although the Pardoner's young men eventually leave the tavern they frequent in order to go in search of Death, many others fled from Death's approach into "riot, stywes, and tavernes" (VI.465), seeking to forget the plague's horrors through the pleasures of dance, dice, drink, and debauchery. There the deadly tavern sins, against which the Pardoner preaches, threatened to destroy the life of their souls through another, worse form of pestilence. Others, like the youthful band of Boccaccio's Decameron, escaped into the countryside and a world of sensual make-believe.[30]

As historians of the plague have noted, the Black Death promoted hedonism, crime, and general demoralization throughout Europe.[31] Paradoxically, then, the epidemic, which was held by ecclesiastics like Archbishop Zouche of York and Bishop Edynton of Winchester to be a divine "chastisement" for "the sins of men who, made callous by prosperity, neglect to remember the benefits of the Supreme Giver," occasioned worse sin,[32] even as it inspired hard-pressed clergy to recall in their sermons both the plagues that moved Pharoah to repent and the confession of King David that ended the "grett pestilence" sent into the kingdom as a punishment for David's sin.[33]

In the impassioned conclusion of his tale, the Pardoner calls his pilgrim congregation to a repentance like David's and offers them pardon and absolution. His audacity in doing so, his much-discussed forgetfulness about his supply of relics (VI.919: "O word forgat I in my tale"), and his apparent loss of memory about his earlier revelations to his listeners, expose him to the wrath of Harry Bailly. The Pardoner thus becomes a victim of his own lunarity, for, according to Kay, lapses of memory are "proper to the Moon, which Albumasar,

---

[29] See Peter G. Beidler, "The Plague and Chaucer's Pardoner," Chaucer Review 16.3 (1982): 257–69.

[30] The "Preface to the Ladies" that introduces Boccaccio's Decameron is generally regarded as a grim but accurate description of the plague in Florence. For a critical study, see Aldo S. Bernardo, "The Plague as Key to Meaning in Boccaccio's Decameron," in The Black Death: The Impact of the Fourteenth-Century Plague, ed. Daniel Williman (Binghamton: SUNY Center for Medieval and Early Renaissance Studies, 1982), pp. 39–64.

[31] See Deaux, Black Death, 1347, pp. 145–75; Ziegler, Black Death, pp. 270–77.

[32] The 1348 letters of Zouche and Edyngton to their clergy are quoted in Deaux, The Black Death, 1347, pp. 129, 138–39.

[33] Middle English Sermons, ed. Woodburn O. Ross, EETS o.s. 209 (London: Oxford University Press, 1940, repr. 1960), pp. 310, 312.

Ibn Ezra, and Scot agreed was responsible for human forgetfulness" (p. 31).[34]

The Pardoner is, of course, a child of the Moon in a still more humiliating way, to which Harry Bailly rudely refers when he substitutes the Pardoner's "coillons" for his "relikes" (VI.952–53). His eyes, we are told, are "glarynge . . . as an hare" (GP 684), an animal of hermaphroditic repute that was believed to sleep with its eyes open.[35] At night, then, the rabbit's eyes were the earthly counterpart of the maculated Moon, which Beatrice compares (as Kay puts it) "to a great eye turned earthward" in *Par.* 2.142–44 (p. 36). Like that of Narcissus, whom Dante invokes when he first sees faces in the watery, mirrorlike vicinity of the Moon (*Par.* 3.16–18), the Pardoner's gaze manifests a self-love that cannot easily be defined as heterosexual. Beardless, high-voiced, and long-haired, the Pardoner travels with "his freend and his compeer" (GP 670), the Summoner, with whom he sings love songs. Under the strong influence of a feminine planet, the Pardoner's sexual identity is *in translatio*, leaving the pilgrim Chaucer (and generations of Chaucerians) to wonder whether he is "a geldyng or a mare" (GP 691) and thus the symbol (in Alan de Lille's terms) of a Nature in tragic disarray.[36]

The Parson's Lunar Remedia

As we mentioned earlier, the legend of Saint Clare forms part of the story of Piccarda in Dante's first heaven. As Piccarda says, "Still young, I fled the world to follow her; and, in her order's habit, I enclosed myself and promised my life to her rule" (*Par.* 3.103–5). A consecrated virgin, Clare somehow belongs, like Piccarda, to the

---

[34] Dante twice suffers from forgetfulness in the lunar sphere. See *Par.* 3.7–9 and 3.34–63, where he fails to recognize Piccarda.

[35] Edward C. Schweitzer, Jr., "Chaucer's Pardoner and the Hare," *ELN* 4 (1966–67): 247–50.

[36] See Walter Clyde Curry, "The Secret of Chaucer's Pardoner," *JEGP* 18 (1919): 593–606; Robert P. Miller, "Chaucer's Pardoner, the Scriptural Eunuch, and the *Pardoner's Tale*," *Speculum* 30 (1955): 180–99; Beryl Rowland, "Chaucer's Idea of the Pardoner," *Chaucer Review* 14 (1979): 140–54; Monica E. McAlpine, "The Pardoner's Homosexuality and How It Matters," *PMLA* 95 (1980): 8–22; and my "*Translatio* of Chaucer's Pardoner," *Exemplaria* 4.2 (1992): 411–28. See also Nature's complaint about homosexuality in Alan of Lille, *The Plaint of Nature*, trans. James J. Sheridan (Toronto: Pontifical Institute of Medieval Studies, 1980), VIII.pr.4, pp. 131–37.

Moon, but Dante does not find her there. Rather, as Piccarda explains, Clare's "perfect life," "high merit," and unbroken vows have earned for her a place in an unnamed higher heaven, "up above" (*Par.* 3.97–98). Clare, in short, both is and is not in the Moon, even as the faithful Christian is in the world, but not of the world (Cf. John 17:14–18). Kay proposes the monastic sphere of Saturn as an appropriate place for her and suggests that Dante thus uses Clare to link and oppose "the first and last of Dante's planetary heavens" (p. 23).

Chaucer employs a parallel strategy in the antithetical relationship he establishes between the Pardoner and the Parson and thus, by extension, between Fragments VI and X. The General Prologue both associates the two (as clerical practitioners with pastoral duties) and distances them from one another morally. We are told that whenever the Pardoner finds "a povre person dwellynge upon lond," he makes more money in a single day than the parson gains "in monthes tweye" (GP 702–4). Indeed, he usurps the parson's position in the pulpit and makes "the person and the peple his apes" (GP 706) through his forged bulls and avaricious preaching. The "poure Persoun of a Toun" (GP 478), on the other hand, uses the pulpit for teaching, the collection money for almsgiving.

This initial opposition is sustained in the respective prologues to the tales of the Pardoner and the Parson. The pilgrims beg for "som moral thyng" from the Pardoner, and they offer him the conditional promise: "thanne wol we gladly heere" (VI.325–26). By way of contrast, the pilgrims assent unconditionally to the Parson's offer of "Moralitee and vertuous mateere": "Sey what you list, and we wol gladly heere" (X.38, 73). The Pardoner, moreover, boasts about captivating his auditors with "false japes," "ensamples many oon," and "tales olde" (VI.394, 435, 437), whereas the Parson emphatically rejects the telling of "fables and swich wrecchednesse" (X.34). In his prologue the Pardoner admits to a fundamental gap between his moral preaching and his practice: "I preche agayn that same vice / Which that I use" (VI.427–28). The Parson, on the other hand, is known to practice what he preaches: "He taughte; but first he folwed it hymselve" (GP 528).

"The Pardoner's Tale" stands at the structural center of the Ellesmere order; "The Parson's Tale," at its end. The tale order thus reverses the order of the portraits in the General Prologue, where the

Parson stands (roughly speaking) in the middle; the Pardoner, last. The Pardoner and the Parson are, moreover, the only two pilgrims whose tales simulate sermons and who speak on the topic of the deadly sins.[37] Despite these obvious points of similarity, "The Pardoner's Tale" and "The Parson's Tale" have seldom been compared, perhaps because of equally obvious differences.[38] "The Parson's Tale," after all, is a long penitential treatise in prose,[39] whereas "The Pardoner's Tale" is a gripping exemplum of only 452 lines (excluding the epilogue), related in verse. "The Parson's Tale," moreover, serves "to knytte up al this feeste" (X.47), and thus responds to all the preceding tales, not just the Pardoner's.

There are, however, at least two clear pivot points to support a particular relationship between, and enable a closer comparison of, Fragments VI and X. The first focuses on their respective treatments of avarice and its *remedia*; the second, on the Parson's treatment of pride and its remedy in relation to the gifts of Nature, Fortune, and Grace. As Morton Bloomfield and others have shown, moral theologians developed different lists and orderings of the deadly sins.[40] Chaucer's Pardoner displays in his rhetoric the late-medieval tendency to put avarice first as the scriptural *radix malorum* (1 Timothy 6:10), whereas the Parson follows a rival, Gregorian tradition in giving first place to pride as a motive for the original disobedience of Adam and Eve.[41] The difference is a telling one.

In his treatment of avarice, the Parson, like the Pardoner, begins by quoting Saint Paul's epistle to Timothy: "the roote of alle harmes is Coveitise" (X.738). Also like the Pardoner, the Parson recognizes

[37] The degree to which the tales resemble contemporary sermons has been much discussed. See Alan J. Fletcher, "The Preaching of the Pardoner," *SAC* 11 (1989): 15–35; Nancy H. Owen, "The Pardoner's Introduction, Prologue, and Tale: Sermon and *Fabliau*," *JEGP* 66 (1967): 541–49.

[38] For an exception to this rule, see Tita French Baumlin, "Theology and Discourse in the *Pardoner's Tale*, the *Parson's Tale*, and the *Retraction*," *Renascence* 41.3 (1989): 127–42.

[39] On the question of the genre of "The Parson's Tale," see Lee Patterson, "The 'Parson's Tale' and the Quitting of the *Canterbury Tales*," *Traditio* 34 (1978): 331–80.

[40] Morton W. Bloomfield, *The Seven Deadly Sins* (Lansing: Michigan State College Press, 1952). See also T. K. Seung, "The Metaphysics of the *Commedia*," in *The "Divine Comedy" and the Encyclopedia of the Arts and Sciences*, ed. Giuseppe Di Scipio and Aldo Scaglione (Philadelphia: John Benjamins, 1988), pp. 181–222. Seung points out that St. Thomas Aquinas gave at least three different orderings of the seven sins.

[41] On the question of pride or avarice as the root sin, see Bloomfield, *Seven Deadly Sins*, esp. pp. 77, 88.

that avarice leads to the "tavern sins": "Now comth hasardrie with
his apurtenaunces, as tables and rafles, of which comth deceite, false
othes, chidynges, and alle ravynes, blasphemynge and reneiynge of
God, and hate of his neighebores, wast of goodes, mysspendynge of
tyme, and somtyme manslaughtre" (X.792). Unlike the Pardoner,
however, who simply begins with avarice and shows its consequences
symptomatically, the Parson offers a diagnosis that points to accidie
(sloth and despair) as the underlying cause of avarice: "For soothly,
whan the herte of a man is confounded in itself and troubled, and
that soule hath lost the confort of God, thanne seketh he an ydel solas
of worldly thynges" (X.739). Constructing what Siegfried Wenzel
aptly calls "a psychological concatenation between the deadly sins,"[42]
the Parson indicates that a desperate spiritual emptiness stands behind the "likerousnesse in herte to have erthely thinges" (X.740) that
all too easily becomes a form of idolatry for the greedy person: "For
certes, every floryn in his cofre is his mawmet" (X.748).

Even as the Parson's understanding of avarice reaches behind its
most superficial manifestation in the lust for money to its underlying
causes, so too the principal remedy he proposes is not the usual one
of largesse, but rather mercy and pity—virtues of compassion that fill
the empty heart and move a person from within to perform "chari-
table werkes of misericorde" (X.806). Indeed, unlike the Pardoner
who urges his listeners to detach themselves from their goods and
"yeven hir pens" (VI.402) to him, the Parson counsels firmly against
"fool-largesse" (X.812).[43]

"The Parson's Tale" thus offers a corrective to "The Pardoner's
Tale" by pointing to deeper causes and cures. To find the root cause
and cure of avarice, however, one must follow the pattern of concatenation not merely back to accidie but all the way back to pride, "the
general roote of alle harmes" (X.387). That Chaucer intends a special
connection between Fragment VI and "De Superbia" is made obvious
by the Parson's lengthy discussion of the goods of Nature, Fortune,
and Grace (X.449–73).[44] Harry Bailly's reference to the "yiftes of For-

---

[42]   Siegfried Wenzel, "Notes on the *Parson's Tale*," *Chaucer Review* 16 (1982): 246.

[43]   The passage on "fool-largesse" does not appear in *Postquam*, one of Chaucer's
known sources for the "Parson's Tale." See Siegfried Wenzel, "The Source for the
'Remedia' of the Parson's Tale," *Traditio* 27 (1971): 436, 445.

[44]   According to Siegfried Wenzel, "the discussion of the causes of Pride based on the
three goods . . . are fairly closely paralleled by Peraldus" (p. 362) in what must be con-

tune and of Nature" (VI.295) not only offers what Gerhard Joseph calls a "thematic hinge" to bridge the disparate tales of the Physician and the Pardoner;[45] but it also bridges the distance between them and "The Parson's Tale." Whereas the Host treats the gifts of Nature and Fortune as the "cause of deeth" (VI.296), the Parson discusses them as the potential sources of pride. He does so at the end of a long treatment of the various branches and "twigges" of pride: "disobedience, auauntynge, ypocrisie, despit, arrogance, inpudence, swellynge of herte . . . and many another twig" (X.391).

As the most basic form of pride, disobedience to the "commandementz of God" (X.392) recalls the Original Sin of Adam, "by whom synne entred into this world, whan he brak the commaundementz of God" (X.322). That "original synne," which is immediately contracted by Adam's descendants "whan the soule is put in oure body" (X.333), brings a fundamental disorder into the life of every human being and into the world of their relationships. That disorder has both physical and spiritual consequences. It means that every one "moste nedes dye, wheither he wolde or noon" (X.323), and that he suffers, while he lives, the "peyne" of concupiscence, which, wrongly directed, "maketh hym coveite, by coveitise of flessh, flesshly synne . . . and eek coveitise of hynesse by pride of herte" (X.335).

The Parson thus traces the origins of the Pardoner's *cupiditas* back to original disobedience as an expression of pride. In so doing, he establishes a theological background for the whole of Fragment VI, where there is "no remedye" for pestilence and death and "no grace," and where disobedience takes the forms of "fals justise" (VI.236, 289) and violent crime. There the "yiftes of Fortune and of Nature / Been cause of deeth to many a creature" (VI.295–96) who possesses or desires them. As the Parson explains, however, God wills the opposite: namely, that the gifts of Nature, Fortune, and Grace—precisely because they are gifts that come from God—should increase our love for him and for one another and our consciousness of our "gentrie" and "gentillesse" as children "of o fader and of o mooder," as "Cristes child" (X.460, 461–62).

---

sidered Chaucer's "ultimate source," Peraldus's *Summa in vitiis,* but it is absent in Chaucer's more immediate "source," *Quoniam.* See Wenzel, "The Source of Chaucer's Seven Deadly Sins," *Traditio* 30 (1974): 351–78.

[45]   Joseph, "The Gifts of Nature, Fortune, and Grace," p. 237.

A hypocrite, the Pardoner lacks this sense of his own identity as a child of God. According to the Parson, a hypocrite "is he that hideth to shewe hym swich as he is and sheweth hym swich as he noght is" (X.393). The Pardoner has admitted that he preaches in order "to been avaunced by ypocrisye" and that he spits out his "venym under hewe / Of hoolynesse, to semen hooly and trewe" (VI.421–22). As Lee Patterson has ably shown, however, his hypocrisy is exceedingly problematic, because admitted.[46] The Pardoner shows himself before the pilgrims to be the hypocrite that he is, but even in that boastful "confessioun of mouth" (X.107) he fails to escape the hypocrisy he reveals, because he lacks the necessary "contricioun of herte." As H. Marshall Leicester, Jr., has observed, "The Pardoner's greatest self-condemnation is his moment of greatest pride," when he "posits himself as a malignant *objection* to God and his creation."[47] Unrepentant, his confession, like all his pseudo-religious acts, is false and thus participates in the same hypocrisy that keeps him from seeing himself, and allowing himself to be seen, as he is. Even (and perhaps especially) to himself, the Pardoner is always other than he is.

As a remedy for pride, disobedience, and hypocrisy, the Parson prescribes "humylitee, or mekenesse," a virtue "thurgh which a man hath verray knoweleche of hymself" (X.475–76). As Wenzel has shown, the Parson's treatment of humility and the other remedial virtues closely follows that in *Postquam,* a Latin treatise composed for preachers which, like other works in that genre, "combines a firm logical and systematic structure with a rich collection of pertinent subject matter for use in persuasive oratory."[48] As Wenzel observes, however, Chaucer was selective: "he concentrated on schemes and divisions but disregarded almost completely ... the wealth of similes which form a major part of *Postquam.*"[49]

Significantly, the extended simile in Chaucer's source that is deleted in the Parson's discussion of humility likens that virtue to the Moon, "whose eleven properties are moralized at some length (197–

---

[46] See Patterson, "Chaucerian Confession."
[47] H. Marshall Leicester, Jr., "Synne Horrible: The Pardoner's Exegesis of His Tale and Chaucer's," in *Acts of Interpretation: The Text in Its Contexts, 700–1600,* ed. Mary J. Carruthers and Elizabeth D. Kirk (Norman, Okla.: Pilgrim Books, 1982), p. 45.
[48] Siegfried Wenzel, Introduction to *Summa virtutum de remediis anime,* ed. Siegfried Wenzel, The Chaucer Library (Athens: University of Georgia Press, 1984), p. 6.
[49] Ibid., p. 27.

356)."[50] First, even as the word "moon" (from Greek *mene*) means "defect," humility "always judges itself deficient in itself and from itself." Second, just as "the moon borrows all its light from the sun," so too humility "takes everything as received from Christ and credits nothing from itself." Third, "the more light the moon receives from the sun, the more clearly appears the spot in it that comes from the earth's shadow or from its own composition"; similarly, "the more humility grows, the more clearly does it recognize its defects." The remaining comparisons of the Moon to humility call attention to the Moon (4) as a wandering star; (5) as the planet closest to the earth; (6) as a planet which, when full, "shows the image of a man"—not Cain, but the crucified Christ—"suspended in it"; (7) as a horned planet which, when it waxes, points to the east; (8) as the source of dew; (9) as a planet decreasing in size when in closer proximity to the Sun; (10) as a planet that waxes and wanes, and that (11) begins to wane "as soon as it is full."

In prescribing humility as a remedy, then, Chaucer's Parson is urging a specifically lunar virtue, a virtue that turns to the good the sublunar, earthly realities of defect, lack, instability, change, suffering, and death. True humility is without pretense before God and others; it judges itself to be as it is, matching its words to its acts. False humility or hypocrisy, on the other hand, causes a false judgment of itself "when it does one thing and shows forth another."[51] Indeed, as *Postquam* explains, the very word "hypocrisy" derives from the Greek words *hypos* and *crisis* and thus literally means "false judgement" ("falsum iudicium").[52]

In Fragment VI, then, the hypocrisy of the Pardoner appropriately complements the "fals justise" of the Physician's Apius, even as the false judgment of both one's self and others looks for its cure to the lunar humility prescribed by the Parson in Fragment X. The Parson speaks under the sign of the Moon, when "the moones exaltacioun— / I mene Libra—alwey gan ascende" (X.10–11), and he prepares the pilgrims to meet "the day of doom" and "juggement" (X.157, 160) through an examination of conscience. His lunarity, however, is the antitype of the Physician's and the Pardoner's. Like Saint Clare,

---

[50]   Ibid., p. 3. For the following comparisons of the properties of the Moon to humility, see pp. 92/93–94/95 in Wenzel's dual language edition.

[51]   Ibid., p. 94.

[52]   Ibid, pp. 94/95.

he is both in the lunar sphere and at the farthest remove from it. Obedient to "the lawe of God" that is "the love of God" (X.124) and teaching obedience to others, he stands in the midst of the pilgrims as a sign of a redeemed order, the realm of the blessed, where, as Piccarda says, "to live in love is . . . necessity" (*Par.* 3.77).

As a priest, the Parson is a cleric; but he is also a "clerk" in a second sense that bears upon Chaucer's encyclopedia of tales. As the pilgrim narrator, who emphasizes the Parson's goodness, insists, "He was also a lerned man, a clerk" (GP 481). The extent of the Parson's formal education cannot be established, but he is certainly not a "lewed man" (GP 502), and, despite his protest that he is "nat textueel" (X.57), the penitential treatise that Chaucer assigns to him as his tale is even more "scholastic" than its sources in its systematic use of definition, divisions, and authorities, and in its exclusion of rhetorical *exempla*.[53] His theoretical and practical learning is, moreover, directed toward a single goal: the authentic teaching of "Cristes gospel" (GP 481), and that orientation necessarily places theology, and moral theology in particular, at the head of the sciences.

The Parson, however, first practices what he preaches, so his knowledge is imbued with wisdom: "first he wroghte, and afterward he taughte" (GP 497). As a practitioner, then, the Parson not only can administer remedies that surpass those of the physicians, but he can also uphold the divine law on which all natural and positive law depends.[54] Indeed, at the end of Chaucer's planetary and philosophical pilgrimage, the Parson speaks in a manner not unlike Lady Philosophy herself, who, in the closing lines of *Boece*, abandons her previous compass of speculation and simply exhorts her pupil:

> Withstond thanne and eschue thou vices; worschipe and love thou vertues; areise thi corage to ryghtful hopes; yilde thou humble preieres an heye . . . syn that ye worken and don (*that is to seyn, your dedes or your werkes*) byforn the eyen of the juge that seeth and demeth alle thinges.
> (*Boece* V.pr.6.302–10)

---

[53] Ibid., pp. 6–7. According to Wenzel, *Postquam* is typical of the work of "Franciscan masters writing in the first half of the thirteenth century" and registers "the impact of the universities and the mendicant orders" on late-medieval preaching.

[54] See Elizabeth A. Dobbs, "Literary, Legal, and Last Judgments in *The Canterbury Tales*," *SAC* 14 (1992): 31–52.

CONCLUSION

Almost two decades ago, Lee Patterson observed that we know the beginning (Fragment I) and the ending of the *Canterbury Tales* (Fragment X), but that it remains for us to show

how the middle develops from the beginning and requires the end: we can go from A to Z easily enough, but how are all the other letters to be fitted in their appropriate order? To my knowledge, nobody has even attempted this kind of progressive reading of the tales; but if one is to argue that they are meaningful primarily . . . in terms of pilgrimage, then this timely and specific relevance must be demonstrated.[1]

This book has attempted precisely such an ordering, using not the letters of the alphabet but equally conventional listings in the public domain: namely, those of the seven planets and of the divisions of philosophy. Assimilated to each other in a kind of transparent overlay, these two outlines, which were frequently joined in the didascalic literature with which Chaucer was familiar, accommodate the actual structural divisions of the Ellesmere *Tales*, define the story-blocks as

---

[1] Lee W. Patterson, "The 'Parson's Tale' and the Quitting of the *Canterbury Tales*," *Traditio* 34 (1978): 372.

topical units, and show the pilgrims' progress from London to Canterbury to be simultaneously a planetary pilgrimage and a philosophical journey of the soul.

These two outlines have allowed us literally to locate and relocate Chaucer in relation to both Gower and Dante, major poets with whom he shared the relatively novel status of a "lay clerk." Like Gower's *Confessio Amantis*, the Ellesmere *Canterbury Tales* weds a social to a philosophical *summa*; offers what Judson B. Allen has called "an ordered collection of exemplary stories"[2]; displays a similar tripartite division of philosophy into theoretical, verbal, and practical branches; and accords special prominence to the exposition of the Seven Deadly Sins and their remedies. Gower's Genius, whom James Simpson identifies as Amans's imagination, is, moreover, an often unreliable, Ovidian guide-figure for the *Confessio*'s equally unreliable first-person narrator, Amans—a circumstance that links Gower's didactic poem more closely to Chaucer's *Tales* than to Dante's *Commedia* and that "involves its reader as an active participant in the construction of its meaning."[3] The similarities between the two works are, in short, much greater than we have previously recognized and confirm Chauncey Wood's suggestion that "Gower's most important influence on Chaucer was on structure rather than plot; world view or thought pattern rather than story."[4]

In his dialogue with Gower (as in his conversation with Dante), Chaucer expresses both agreement and disagreement. Whereas Gower treats the *divisio philosophiae* explicitly in an apparent digression that is actually a frame for the whole, Chaucer uses the *divisio* in a veiled way throughout to determine the *forma tractatus* of the *Tales*. Whereas Gower's disciplinary range is fairly narrow and focuses, as Simpson observes, "almost wholly on the practical sciences of ethics, economics, and politics,"[5] Chaucer's scope (like Alan's and Dante's) is much broader and gives equal attention to the speculative, verbal,

---

[2] Judson Boyce Allen, *The Ethical Poetic of the Later Middle Ages: A Decorum of Convenient Distinction* (Toronto: University of Toronto Press, 1982), p. 104.

[3] James Simpson, *Sciences and the Self in Medieval Poetry: Alan of Lille's "Anticlaudianus" and John Gower's "Confessio Amantis"* (Cambridge: Cambridge University Press, 1995), p. 138.

[4] Chauncey Wood, "Chaucer's Most 'Gowerian' Tale," in *Chaucer and Gower: Difference, Mutuality, Exchange*, ed. R. F. Yeager (Victoria: University of Victoria Press, 1991), p. 76.

[5] Simpson, *Sciences and the Self*, p. 253.

and practical sciences. More importantly, however, Chaucer and Gower disagree on the actual hierarchy of the sciences. This becomes apparent when one considers "The Parson's Tale," which Wood has rightly termed both the most and the least "Gowerian" of Chaucer's tales.

Gower, on the one hand, uses the *distinctio* of the seven sins to structure the *Confessio*, but he renders the lover's examination of conscience by Venus's priest in purely secular, ethical terms, and he ultimately subordinates ethics to politics within the theoretical framework provided in Book VII. Chaucer, on the other hand, basically reverses these relationships. In the *Canterbury Tales*, "The Parson's Tale" functions in a compendious way comparable to Gower's Book VII. In that tale, moreover, the sins are treated by the Parson in a specifically Christian and sacramental context, according to which the examination of vice and the recommendation of virtue are subsumed not by practical philosophy, but rather by pastoral theology. Whereas penitential examination serves as a means for Gower to fashion a philosopher-king in the person of Amans and the reader, Chaucer's exhaustive philosophical curriculum aims at fashioning in the end a humble Christian penitent. Gower points to ethics and politics; Chaucer, to moral theology.

In each case, as Simpson would say, "the literary form of the poem" corresponds to the "ideal form" of the reader whom the poet envisions, instructs, and helps to create.[6] Whereas Gower challenges his reader to learn by discovering the veiled connection between the ostensibly digressive Book VII and the ongoing examination of the lover's conscience (and thus between ethics and politics), Chaucer similarly poses as a question the relationship between the apparently disjunctive "Parson's Tale" and what has preceded it (and thus the connection between the human and the divine sciences, knowledge and self-knowledge, fables and "meditacioun" [X.55]).

In his impulse toward scientific comprehensiveness and in his subordination of philosophy to theology, the Chaucer of the Ellesmere *Tales* resembles Dante more closely than he resembles Gower. With the important exceptions of Winthrop Wetherbee, Karla Taylor, Richard Neuse, and Donald Rowe, however, most scholars have tended to

6   Ibid., p. 7.

detect a relatively strong Dantean influence only in the early poetry of Chaucer's "Italian period" and to limit it overall, in the words of Howard Schless, to a "few direct adaptations and translations made for the purpose of their content and [to] the many shorter images borrowed for their verbal and dramatic force."[7] A localized comparison of Chaucer's planetary pilgrimage to Dante's reveals, to the contrary, that the whole of the Ellesmere *Canterbury Tales* is structured in dialogue with Dante's *Paradiso* and represents an elaborately detailed response to the images used, and the stories related, in Dante's successive heavens.

As we have seen, the tracing of a planetary pilgrimage in the Ellesmere *Tales* depends upon, and extends from, the initial Saturnine emphasis in "The Knight's Tale."[8] It allows, in turn, for a correlation between the fragments of the *Tales* and the heavens of the *Paradiso* and provides a single, astrological, and Dantean solution to a long series of Chaucerian *cruces* that have, until now, been treated variously and in isolation. In general, Dante's "poetic influence" on Chaucer proves to be operative (in Taylor's words) "not only in local imitations of phrasing and technique, but also in the considerably more elusive realm of form," as Chaucer defines his own relationship to the tradition of philosophical poetry against the contrastive background of Dante's.[9]

Previous attempts to define "what Dante meant to Chaucer" have had little to say about the *Canterbury Tales*.[10] This book has in many

---

[7]   Howard H. Schless, *Chaucer and Dante: A Revaluation* (Norman, Okla.: Pilgrim Books, 1984), p. 246. Schless concludes that "Chaucer drew on Dante not heavily but over a long period of time" (p. 247). In opposition to this view, Winthrop Wetherbee (*Chaucer and the Poets: An Essay on "Troilus and Criseyde"* [Ithaca: Cornell University Press, 1984]), and Karla Taylor (*Chaucer Reads "The Divine Comedy"* [Stanford: Stanford University Press, 1989]), point to Dante's influence on the *Troilus;* Donald Rowe argues for a structural link between the *Inferno* and the *Legend of Good Women* (*Through Nature to Eternity* [Lincoln: University of Nebraska Press, 1988]); and, most recently, Richard Neuse has drawn a Dantean connection to the *Canterbury Tales* (*Chaucer's Dante: Allegory and Epic Theater in "The Canterbury Tales"* [Berkeley: University of California Press, 1991]).

[8]   Paradoxically, Chaucer's knowledge of and interest in astronomy and astrology have long been recognized, and his elaborate and detailed astrological references have drawn careful scholarly attention to the specific passages in which they occur, but the simple overarching planetary pattern has gone unnoticed. See Chauncey A. Wood, *Chaucer and the Country of the Stars* (Princeton: Princeton University Press, 1970), and J. D. North, *Chaucer's Universe* (Oxford: Clarendon Press, 1988).

[9]   Taylor, *Chaucer Reads "The Divine Comedy,"* p. 1.

[10]   See Piero Boitani, "What Dante Meant to Chaucer," in *Chaucer and the Italian Trecento* (Cambridge: Cambridge University Press, 1983), pp. 115–39.

ways extended and confirmed Taylor's and Neuse's perceptions of basic differences between Dante's and Chaucer's poetic vision. As Taylor has observed, both the *Tales* and the *Commedia* relate "a journey seen in retrospect" and involve a first-person narrator, but Chaucer's treatment differs from Dante's in its radical immanence, which allows for change in the people whom the pilgrim narrator meets and which renders suspect the truth-claims of all the storytellers, including those of Chaucer the pilgrim.[11]

Both Taylor and Neuse have emphasized the difference in the subjectivity of Dante and Chaucer as pilgrims. Whereas Dante, following the paradigm of Augustine's *Confessions* and Boethius's *Consolation*, fashions himself into a kind of everyman and makes his own perspective a center of consciousness for the reader,[12] Chaucer represents himself as a pilgrim among pilgrims, all of whom have their own points of view. He allows himself as a speaker to be displaced by a series of tale-tellers, whose words he ostensibly rehearses. Chaucer's "communal self" is thus very different from Dante's—centrifugal, rather than centripetal; heterogeneous, rather than homogeneous; dispersed, rather than in-gathered; intersubjective, rather than subjective.

This divergence in the authorial fictions of Chaucer and Dante makes a marked difference in the audiences their poems imply and create. As Taylor has stressed, Dante works carefully to guide the interpretations and responses of his readers from within the *Commedia* through his own affective responses and questions and through the authoritative answers of his guides. Chaucer, on the other hand, provides no unequivocally authoritative guide for his pilgrims and dramatizes in the links between tales how little control speakers and writers have over the responses of their audience. As Neuse argues, Chaucer's *Tales* "postulates for itself" a "heterogeneous audience" not unlike the pilgrims within the poem, who "collectively . . . form an open symposiastic circle in which everyone contributes to the debate but no conclusion is reached."[13]

Whereas Dante can monitor the progress of his pilgrim self (and

---

[11]   Taylor, *Chaucer Reads "The Divine Comedy,"* pp. 1–3.

[12]   In the *Convivio*, Dante explicitly justifies first-person narrative by pointing to Augustine's example. See *The Banquet*, trans. Christopher Ryan (Saratoga, Calif.: ANMA Libri, 1989), I.ii, p. 17.

[13]   Neuse, *Chaucer's Dante*, pp. 36, 7.

thus of his implied reader) in a continuous narrative that moves from one symbolic location to another and that involves a hierarchical succession of guides, Chaucer can and does offer fewer and more veiled signposts for the soul-journey of his pilgrims and his readers. The traditional signposts—astrological spheres and philosophical topics—are there, to be sure, but Chaucer recognizes that only those who read his poem "like a Clerk" are likely to see them, and that only wise readers who are willing to learn are going to be instructed by the poem he has written "for oure doctrine" (X.1083). A philosophical poet like Dante, Chaucer can chart a curriculum and provide an occasion for learning, but he, much more so than Dante, entrusts the completion of his work to his audience and, ultimately, to the mercy of God.

In bringing Dante's heavens back down to earth, Chaucer necessarily reopened what had been closed, fragmented what had been finished. The planetary pattern we have explicated in the Ellesmere arrangement explains the feature of the *Canterbury Tales* that is perhaps the most puzzling of all: its existence and apparent composition in the form of separate fragments or story-blocks, the discrete integrity of which is generally preserved in the manuscripts. If, as we have argued, Chaucer consciously modeled his horizontal pilgrimage to Canterbury after Dante's vertical pilgrimage into the Empyrean, then the very definition of his artistic project depended on its *divisio* and *ordinatio* of tales into distinct units correspondent to the Dantean heavens. As the author of *Postquam* affirms, echoing a scholastic commonplace, "Division is the way toward definition" ("diuisio est uia in diffinicionem").[14] Had Chaucer linked the tales together continuously, the structural breaks necessary for topical location, and thus for meaning, would simply have disappeared. How, if at all, Chaucer would have solved the artistic problem he posed for himself is a question none of us can resolve, but recognizing what the problem was affords us a measure for Chaucer's particular poetic achievement which we have been hitherto lacking.

What, then, are we to say about the authority of the Ellesmere manuscript? The recent tendency has been to assign a relatively late date

---

[14]   *Summa virtutum de remediis anime*, ed. Siegfried Wenzel, The Chaucer Library (Athens: University of Georgia Press, 1984), pp. 52/53.

of circa 1410 (ten years after Chaucer's death) to the manuscript and thus to separate the manuscript and its tale order both from Chaucer and his authorial intention and from the Hengwrt manuscript, which was copied by the same scribe and which contains the earliest extant version of the *Tales*.[15] Even if the Ellesmere manuscript dates from 1410, however, the high quality of its text and the expensiveness of its production argue for its close connection to Chaucer's own family. Germaine Dempster's observation still holds true, when she, following John Manly, points to the Ellesmere as "the only surviving manuscript . . . to derive its texts of most *CT* pieces from the copies in Chaucer's house at his death."[16]

To be sure, a close Chaucerian provenance does not in itself ensure that the tale order in the Ellesmere reflects Chaucer's intention. The Hengwrt manuscript, after all, presents the tales in a different order, and the extant fifteenth-century manuscripts of the *Tales* similarly evince considerable variation.[17] Chaucer may, as some argue, have devised no firm plan for the work as a whole, or he may have failed to communicate his plan (if he had one) to anyone, leaving his *magnum opus* to his literary executors as what Derek Pearsall calls "a partly assembled kit with no directions," with the result that "the order of the *Tales*, as deduced by the editors of [even the best surviving] man-

---

[15] On the scribal question, see A. I. Doyle and M. B. Parkes, Paleographical Introduction to *The Canterbury Tales, Geoffrey Chaucer: A Facsimile and Transcription of the Hengwrt Manuscript, With Variants from the Ellesmere Manuscript*, ed. Paul G. Ruggiers (Norman: University of Oklahoma Press, 1979), pp. xix–xlix; "The Production of Copies of the *Canterbury Tales* and the *Confessio Amantis* in the Early Fifteenth Century," in *Medieval Scribes, Manuscripts, and Libraries: Essays Presented to N. R. Ker*, ed. M. B. Parkes and Andrew G. Watson (London: Scolar, 1978), pp. 163–210; M. L. Samuels, "The Scribe of the Hengwrt and Ellesmere Manuscripts of *The Canterbury Tales*," *SAC* 5 (1983): 49–65.

[16] Germaine Dempster, "Manly's Conception of the Early History of the *Canterbury Tales*," *PMLA* 61 (1946): 396.

[17] Norman F. Blake has argued that all "the later orders [including that found in the Ellesmere] are developments of that in Hg," that the Hengwrt scribe "had access to Chaucer's own copy," and that "that copy was the only one in existence when the poet died." See *The Canterbury Tales by Geoffrey Chaucer, Edited from the Hengwrt Manuscript*, ed. N. F. Blake (London: Edward Arnold, 1980), pp. 10–11. Others, following Manly and Rickert, have argued that individual tales and tale-groups were in circulation among Chaucer's friends during his lifetime, and that the various attempts to collect them after his death resulted in the different orders. For a strong critique of the Manly/Rickert edition, see George Kane, "John M. Manly (1865–1940) and Edith Rickert (1871–1938)," in *Editing Chaucer: The Great Tradition*, ed. Paul G. Ruggiers (Norman, Okla.: Pilgrim Books, 1984), pp. 207–29.

uscripts, is not Chaucer's," but rather "provisional and merely pragmatic."[18]

The argument of this book, however, militates against such a conclusion. Chaucer's choice of a basic ordering principle for the *Tales* is, in fact, discoverable and matches that actually found in the Ellesmere order. As we have seen, Fragment I, which is indisputably Chaucerian and integral, initiates a pattern of planetary descent in the first three tales that is continued systematically in the Ellesmere order. Furthermore, once that pattern has been discerned, it is possible to locate a sustained series of correspondences between Chaucer's *Tales* and Dante's *Paradiso* that does not emerge unless the tales are ordered in just that sequence.

Although a very well-educated clerk may conceivably have recognized the Saturn-Jupiter-Mars triad in Fragment I and arranged the remaining tales and tale-groups accordingly, no one but Chaucer himself could have answered Dante point by point, as he did, and no one but Chaucer would have had the ability, the motive, and the daring to do so. Behind the scenes of Chaucer's dramatized story-telling contest, in short, there is another, more important poetic contest, a contest announced obliquely in the *House of Fame*: namely, that between Chaucer and Dante.

This bookish and Dantean "Ellesmere Chaucer" may not be to the liking of all Chaucerians. It is singularly appropriate, however, that the manuscript that visibly represents the *Canterbury Tales* as a (clerically oriented) social *summa*, as an encyclopedia of the arts and sciences, and as a flight of the soul, as well as a companionable story-telling contest *en route* to Canterbury, should serve as the basis for the editions of the *Tales* that are used in our classrooms today. As a *compilatio*, the *Canterbury Tales* is meant for students and teachers, for would-be clerks, questioners, debaters, and dreamers of all kinds.

---

[18] Derek Pearsall, *The Canterbury Tales* (London: George Allen and Unwin, 1985), pp. 23, xi, 19. See also Charles A. Owen, Jr., "The Alternative Reading of *The Canterbury Tales*: Chaucer's Text and the Early Manuscripts," *PMLA* 97 (1982): 237–50; "Pre-1450 Manuscripts of the *Canterbury Tales*: Relationships and Significance," Parts I and II, *Chaucer Review* 23.1 and 2 (1988): 1–29, 95–116; N. F. Blake, "On Editing the *Canterbury Tales*," in *Medieval Studies for J. A. W. Bennett*, ed. P. L. Heyworth (Oxford: Clarendon Press, 1981), pp. 101–20. For textual arguments in favor of the authority of the Ellesmere order, see Larry D. Benson, "The Order of *The Canterbury Tales*," *SAC* 3 (1981): 77–120, and Dolores W. Frese, *An Ars Legendi for Chaucer's "Canterbury Tales": Re-Constructive Reading* (Gainesville: University of Florida Press, 1991), pp. 194–233.

It offers us a bridge between our own construction of knowledge and the academic culture and pedagogy of Chaucer's own day. It puts our own academic rivalries and *disputationes* in perspective, and it allows us to see something of ourselves not only in the *speculum* of Chaucer's pilgrim-company, but also in "thilke large book / Which that men clepe the hevene" (II.190–91).

BIBLIOGRAPHY

PRIMARY SOURCES

Abélard, Peter. "Abélard's Letter of Consolation to a Friend (*Historia Calamitatum*)." Ed. J. T. Muckle. *Mediaeval Studies* 12 (1950): 163–213.
——. *The Letters of Abélard and Héloïse.* Trans. Betty Radice. New York: Penguin Books, 1974.
Alan of Lille. *Anticlaudianus.* Trans. James J. Sheridan. Toronto: Pontifical Institute of Mediaeval Studies, 1973.
——. *The Plaint of Nature.* Trans. James J. Sheridan. Toronto: Pontifical Institute of Medieval Studies, 1980.
Aquinas, Saint Thomas. *Basic Writings of Saint Thomas Aquinas.* Ed. Anton G. Pegis. New York: Random House, 1945.
——. *The Division and Methods of the Sciences: Questions V and VI of his Commentary on the "De Trinitate" of Boethius.* Trans. Armand Maurer. 4th rev. ed. Toronto: Pontifical Institute of Mediaeval Studies, 1953, repr. 1986.
Arderne, John. *Treatises of Fistula in Ano.* Ed. D'Arcy Power. EETS 139. London: Kegan Paul, 1910.
Aristotle. *On the Heavens.* Trans. J. L. Stocks. In *The Complete Works of Aristotle,* vol. 1, ed. Jonathan Barnes. Bollingen Series 71.2. Princeton: Princeton University Press, 1984.
——. *On the Soul.* Trans. J. A. Smith. In *The Complete Works of Aristotle,* vol. 1, ed. Jonathan Barnes. Bollingen Series 71.2. Princeton: Princeton University Press, 1984.
——. *Physics.* Trans. R. P. Hardie and R. K. Gaye. In *The Complete Works of*

Aristotle, vol. 1, ed. Jonathan Barnes. Bollingen Series 71.2. Princeton: Princeton University Press, 1984.

Augustine, Saint. *The City of God against the Pagans*. Trans. David S. Wiesen. Loeb Classical Library. Cambridge: Harvard University Press, 1968.

Bernard Silvestris. *The Commentary on the First Six Books of Virgil's "Aeneid."* Trans. Earl G. Schreiber and Thomas E. Maresca. Lincoln: University of Nebraska Press, 1979.

———. *The Cosmographia*. Trans. Winthrop Wetherbee. New York: Columbia University Press, 1973.

Boccacio. *Boccaccio on Poetry*. Trans. Charles G. Osgood. 2d ed. New York: Liberal Arts Press, 1956.

———. *In Defence of Poetry: Genealogiae Deorum gentilium liber XIV*. Ed. Jeremiah Reedy. Toronto Medieval Latin Texts. Toronto: Pontifical Institute of Mediaeval Studies, 1978.

Brewer, Derek, ed. *Chaucer: The Critical Heritage*. 2 vols. London: Routledge and Kegan Paul, 1978.

Brunetto Latini. *The Book of the Treasure*. Trans. Paul Barrette and Spurgeon Baldwin. Garland Library of Medieval Literature, vol. 90, Series B. New York: Garland, 1993.

———. *Li Livres dou Tresor*. Ed. Francis J. Carmody. Berkeley: University of California Press, 1948.

Capgrave, John. *John Capgrave's Abbreuiacion of Cronicles*. Ed. Peter J. Lucas. EETS 285. Oxford: Oxford University Press, 1983.

Cassiodorus. *Institutiones*. Ed. R. A. B. Mynors. Oxford: Clarendon Press, 1961.

Caxton, William. *The Prologues and Epilogues of William Caxton*. Ed. W. J. B. Crotch. EETS 176. London: Oxford University Press, 1928, repr. 1956.

Chaucer, Geoffrey. *The Riverside Chaucer*. Ed. Larry D. Benson. 3d ed. Boston: Houghton Mifflin, 1987.

———. *The Works of Geoffrey Chaucer*. Ed. F. N. Robinson. 2d ed. Boston: Houghton Mifflin, 1957.

Chaucer Life-Records. Ed. Martin M. Crow and Clair C. Olson. Austin: University of Texas Press, 1966.

Dante. *The Banquet*. Trans. Christopher Ryan. Stanford French and Italian Studies, vol. 61. Saratoga, Calif.: ANMA Libri, 1989.

———. *The Divine Comedy of Dante Alighieri*. Trans. Allen Mandelbaum. Berkeley: University of California Press, 1980–82; New York: Bantam, 1986.

———. "The Letter to Can Grande." In *Literary Criticism of Dante Alighieri*, trans. and ed. Robert S. Haller, 95–111. Lincoln: University of Nebraska Press, 1973.

Dobson, R. B., ed. *The Peasants' Revolt of 1381*. 2d ed. London: Macmillan, 1970, repr. 1980.

Fortescue, Sir John. *De laudibus legum Anglie*. Ed. S. B. Chrimes. Cambridge: Cambridge University Press, 1942, repr. 1949.

Four English Political Tracts of the Later Middle Ages. Ed. Jean-Philippe Genet. Camden Fourth Series, vol. 18. London: Royal Historical Society, 1977.

Fulgentius the Mythographer. Trans. Leslie George Whitbread. Columbus: Ohio State University Press, 1971.

Geoffrey of Vinsauf. *The "Poetria Nova" and Its Sources in Early Rhetorical Doctrine.* Ed. and trans. Ernest Gallo. The Hague and Paris: Mouton, 1971.

Godfrey of St. Victor. *The Fountain of Philosophy.* Trans. Edward A. Synan. Toronto: Pontifical Institute of Mediaeval Studies, 1972.

Gower, John. *The Complete Works of John Gower.* Ed. G. C. Macaulay. Oxford: Clarendon Press, 1902.

——. *The Major Latin Works.* Trans. Eric Stockton. Seattle: University of Washington Press, 1962.

Hoccleve's Works: The Minor Poems. Ed. Frederick J. Furnivall and I. Gollancz. Rev. Jerome Mitchell and A. I. Doyle. EETS e.s. 61 and 73. London: Oxford University Press, 1970.

Honorius of Autun. *Expositio in Cantica Canticorum.* PL 172, c347–496.

Horace on the Art of Poetry. Ed. and trans. Edward Henry Blakeney. London: Scolartis Press, 1928.

Hugh of St. Victor. *The Didascalicon.* Trans. Jerome Taylor. Records of Western Civilization. New York: Columbia University Press, 1961, repr. 1991.

Isidore of Seville. *Etymologiae.* PL 82, c73–728.

John of Rupescissa. *The Book of Quinte Essence.* Ed. F. J. Furnivall. EETS o.s. 16. London: Tübner, 1856.

John of Salisbury. *The Metalogicon.* Trans. Daniel D. McGarry. Berkeley: University of California Press, 1955.

——. *Policraticus.* In *Frivolities of Courtiers and Footprints of Philosophers,* trans. Joseph B. Pike. Minneapolis: University of Minnesota Press, 1938.

Juvenal and Persius. Ed. and trans. G. G. Ramsey. Loeb Classical Library. Rev. ed., Cambridge: Harvard University Press, 1950.

Kant, Immanuel. *The Conflict of the Faculties.* Trans. Mary J. Gregor. Lincoln: University of Nebraska Press, 1992.

Kilwardby, Robert. *De ortu scientiarum.* Ed. Albert G. Judy, O.P. Auctores Britannici Medii Aevi IV. Oxford: British Academy, and Toronto: Pontifical Institute of Mediaeval Studies, 1976.

Langland, William. *Piers Plowman: The A Version.* Ed. George Kane. London: Athlone Press, 1960.

——. *Piers Plowman: The B Version.* Ed. George Kane and E. Talbot Donaldson. London: Athlone Press, 1975.

Lydgate, John. *Lydgate's Fall of Princes.* Ed. Henry Bergen. EETS 122. London: Oxford University Press, 1924, repr. 1967.

——. *Lydgate's Troy Book.* Ed. H. Bergen. EETS e.s. 97. London: Oxford University Press, 1906.

Macrobius. *Commentary on the Dream of Scipio.* Trans. William Harris Stahl. Records of Western Civilization Series. New York: Columbia University Press, 1952, repr. 1990.

Map, Walter. *De nugis curialium.* Ed. and trans. M. R. James. Rev. C. N. L. Brooke and R. A. B. Mynors. Oxford: Clarendon Press, 1983.

Marius. *On the Elements.* Ed. and trans. Richard C. Dales. Berkeley: University of California Press, 1976.

Martianus Capella. Ed. James Willis. Leipzig: Teubner, 1983.

Martianus Capella and the Seven Liberal Arts: The Marriage of Philology and Mercury, vol. 2. Trans. William H. Stahl and Richard Johnson. Records of Western Civilization Series. New York: Columbia University Press, 1977.

Middle English Sermons. Ed. Woodburn O. Ross. EETS o.s. 209. London: Oxford University Press, 1940, repr. 1960.

Origen. *The Song of Songs: Commentary and Homilies.* Trans. R. P. Lawson. Ancient Christian Writers Series 26. London: Longmans, Green, 1957.

Ovid. *Metamorphoses.* Trans. Frank Miller. Loeb Classical Library. Cambridge: Harvard University Press, 1921.

Petrus Bonus. *The New Pearl of Great Price.* Trans. Arthur Edward Waite. 1894; London: Vincent Stuart, 1963.

Pierce the Ploughmans Crede. Ed. Walter W. Skeat. EETS o.s. 30. London: Kegan Paul, Trench, Trübner, 1867, repr. 1895.

Plato. *The Dialogues of Plato.* Vol. 1. Trans. Benjamin Jowett. New York: Random House, 1892, repr. 1937.

——. *The Republic.* Trans. Robin Waterfield. Oxford: Oxford University Press, 1993.

Polychronicon Ranulphi Higden. Ed. C. Babington and J. R. Lumby. RS 41 (1865–86).

"The Seven Planets." Ed. Peter Brown. In *Popular and Practical Science of Medieval England,* ed. Lister M. Matheson, 3–21. East Lansing, Mich.: Colleagues Press, 1994.

Speculum sacerdotale. Ed. Edward H. Weatherly. EETS 200. London: Oxford University Press, 1936.

Spurgeon, Caroline F. E., ed. *Five Hundred Years of Chaucer Criticism and Allusion, 1357–1900.* 3 vols. Cambridge: Cambridge University Press, 1925.

Summa virtutum de remediis anime. Ed. Siegfried Wenzel. The Chaucer Library. Athens: University of Georgia Press, 1984.

Three Prose Versions of the "Secreta Secretorum." Ed. Robert Steele. EETS e.s. 74. London: Kegan Paul, Trench & Trübner, 1898.

University Records and Life in the Middle Ages. Ed. Lynn Thorndike. New York: Columbia University Press, 1944.

Walsingham, Thomas. *Historia Anglicana.* Ed. Henry Thomas Riley. Rerum Britannicarum Medii Aevi Scriptores. London: Her Majesty's Stationery Office, 1863.

Wimbledon's Sermon. Ed. Ione Kemp Knight. Duquesne Studies, Philological Series, no. 9. Pittsburgh: Duquesne University Press, 1967.

Woman Defamed and Woman Defended: An Anthology of Medieval Texts. Ed. Alcuin Blamires with Karen Pratt and C. W. Marx. Oxford: Clarendon Press, 1992.

Wycliffe, John. *De officio regis.* Ed. Alfred W. Pollard and Charles Sayle. *Wyclif's Latin Works,* vol. 8. London: Trübner, 1913; repr. 1966.

——. *The English Works.* Ed. F. D. Matthew. EETS 74. London: Trübner, 1880.

——. *Opera Minora.* Ed. Johann Loserth. *Wyclif's Latin Works,* vol. 21. London: C. K. Paul, 1913; repr. 1966.

SECONDARY SOURCES

Aiken, Pauline. "Vincent of Beauvais and Chaucer's Knowledge of Alchemy." *SP* 41 (1944): 371–89.

Alford, John A. "The Grammatical Metaphor: A Survey of Its Use in the Middle Ages." *Speculum* 57 (1982): 728–60.

——. "Literature and Law in Medieval England." *PMLA* 92 (1977): 941–51.

——. "Medicine in the Middle Ages: The Theory of a Profession." *Centennial Review* 23 (1979): 377–96.

——. "The Wife of Bath Versus the Clerk of Oxford: What Their Rivalry Means." *Chaucer Review* 21.2 (1986): 108–32.

Allen, Judson Boyce. *The Ethical Poetic of the Later Middle Ages: A Decorum of Convenient Distinction.* Toronto: University of Toronto Press, 1982.

Allen, Judson Boyce, and Theresa Moritz. *A Distinction of Stories: The Medieval Unity of Chaucer's Fair Chain of Narratives for Canterbury.* Columbus: Ohio State University Press, 1981.

Astell, Ann. "Apostrophe, Prayer, and the Structure of Satire in the Man of Law's Tale." *SAC* 13 (1911): 81–97.

——. "Chaucer's 'Literature Group' and the Medieval Causes of Books." *ELH* 59 (1992): 269–87.

——. *Job, Boethius, and Epic Truth.* Ithaca: Cornell University Press, 1994.

——. "Job's Wife, Walter's Wife, and the Wife of Bath." In *Old Testament Women in Western Literature,* ed. Raymond-Jean Frontain and Jan Wojcik, 92–107. Conway: University of Central Arkansas Press, 1991.

——. "The Peasants' Revolt: Cock-crow in Gower and Chaucer." In *Four Last Things: Death, Judgment, Heaven, and Hell in the Middle Ages,* ed. Allen J. Frantzen, 53–64. Essays in Medieval Studies 10. Chicago: Illinois Medieval Association, 1994.

——. *The Song of Songs in the Middle Ages.* Ithaca: Cornell University Press, 1990, repr. 1994.

——. "The *Translatio* of Chaucer's Pardoner." *Exemplaria* 4.2 (1992): 411–28.

Baker, Donald C., ed. *The Squire's Tale: Variorum Edition.* Norman: University of Oklahoma Press, 1990.

Baldwin, Charles Sears. *Medieval Rhetoric and Poetic (to 1400).* Gloucester: Peter Smith, 1959.

Baumlin, Tita French. "Theology and Discourse in the *Pardoner's Tale,* the *Parson's Tale,* and the *Retraction.*" *Renascence* 41.3 (1989): 127–42.

Beichner, Paul E. "Chaucer's Man of Law and *Disparitas Cultus.*" *Speculum* 23 (1948): 70–75.

Beidler, Peter G. "The Plague and Chaucer's Pardoner." *Chaucer Review* 16.3 (1982): 257–69.

Bennett, J. A. W. *Chaucer at Oxford and Cambridge.* Toronto: University of Toronto Press, 1974.

——. *Chaucer's Book of Fame.* Oxford: Clarendon Press, 1968.

Benson, C. David. "Their Telling Difference: Chaucer the Pilgrim and His Two Contrasting Tales." *Chaucer Review* 18 (1983): 61–76.

Benson, Larry D. "The Order of *The Canterbury Tales.*" *SAC* 3 (1981): 77–120.

Bernardo, Aldo S. "The Plague as Key to Meaning in Boccaccio's *Decameron.*" In *The Black Death: The Impact of the Fourteenth-Century Plague,* ed. Daniel Williman, 39–64. Binghamton: SUNY Center for Medieval and Early Renaissance Studies, 1982.

Berndt, David E. "Monastic *Acedia* and Chaucer's Characterization of Daun Piers." *SP* 68.4 (1971): 435–50.

Bishop, Ian. "*The Nun's Priest's Tale* and the Liberal Arts." *Review of English Studies*, n.s. 30 (1979): 257–67.

Blake, Norman F. "Introduction." In *The Canterbury Tales by Geoffrey Chaucer, Edited From the Hengwrt Manuscript.* Ed. N. F. Blake. London: Edward Arnold, 1980.

——. "On Editing the *Canterbury Tales.*" In *Medieval Studies for J. A. W. Bennett Aetatis Suae LXX*, ed. P. L. Heyworth, 101–20. Oxford: Clarendon Press, 1981.

Bland, D. S. "Chaucer and the Inns of Court: A Reexamination." *ES* 33 (1952): 145–55.

Bloch, R. Howard. *Etymologies and Genealogies: A Literary Anthropology of the French Middle Ages.* Chicago: University of Chicago Press, 1983.

——. "Medieval Misogyny." *Representations* 20 (1987): 1–24.

Blodgett, E. D. "Chaucerian *Pryvetee* and the Opposition to Time." *Speculum* 51.3 (1976): 477–93.

Bloomfield, Morton W. *The Seven Deadly Sins.* Lansing: Michigan State College Press, 1952.

Boenig, Robert. "Absolon's Musical Instruments." *ELN* 28 (1990): 7–15.

Boitani, Piero. *Chaucer and the Imaginary World of Fame.* London: D. S. Brewer, 1984.

——. "What Dante Meant to Chaucer." In *Chaucer and the Italian Trecento*, ed. Piero Boitani, 115–39. Cambridge: Cambridge University Press, 1983.

Boucher, Holly Wallace. "Nominalism: The Difference for Chaucer and Boccaccio." *Chaucer Review* 20.3 (1986): 213–20.

Bowden, Muriel. *A Commentary on the General Prologue to the "Canterbury Tales."* 1948; New York: Columbia University Press, 1967.

Bowers, John M. "*The Tale of Berwyn* and *The Siege of Thebes*: Alternative Ideas of *The Canterbury Tales.*" *SAC* 7 (1985): 23–50.

Boyde, Patrick. *Dante: Philomythes and Philosopher.* Cambridge: Cambridge University Press, 1981.

Braswell, Laura. "The Moon and Medicine in Chaucer's Time." *SAC* 8 (1986): 145–56.

Brewer, Derek. *Chaucer in His Time.* London: Thomas Nelson, 1963.

——. "The *Reeve's Tale* and the King's Hall, Cambridge." *Chaucer Review* 5 (1971): 311–17.

Brocchieri, Mariateresa Fumagalli Beonio. "The Intellectual." In *Medieval Callings*, ed. Jacques Le Goff, 181–209. Trans. Lydia G. Cochrane. Chicago: University of Chicago Press, 1990.

Brown, Carleton. "The Evolution of the Canterbury 'Marriage Group.'" *PMLA* 48 (1938): 1041–59.

Brown, Emerson, Jr. "Epicurus and Voluptas in Late Antiquity: The Curious Testimony of Martianus Capella." *Traditio* 38 (1982): 75–106.

Brown, Peter, and Andrew Butcher. *The Age of Saturn: Literature and History in the "Canterbury Tales."* Oxford: Basil Blackwell, 1991.

Burkhardt, Titus. *Alchemy: Science of the Cosmos, Science of the Soul.* Trans. William Stoddart. Baltimore: Penguin, 1960, repr. 1972.

Burnley, David. *A Guide to Chaucer's Language.* Norman: University of Oklahoma Press, 1983.

Burrow, J. A. "The Audience of *Piers Plowman.*" *Anglia* 75 (1957): 373–84.

Bursill-Hall, G. L. *Speculative Grammars of the Middle Ages: The Doctrine of "Partes Orationes" of the Modistae.* The Hague: Mouton, 1971.

Caie, Graham D. "The Significance of the Early Chaucer Manuscript Glosses (with Special Reference to the *Wife of Bath's Prologue*)." *Chaucer Review* 10 (1975–76): 350–60.

Chenu, M.-D. *Nature, Man, and Society in the Twelfth Century.* Ed. and trans. Jerome Taylor and Lester K. Little. Chicago: University of Chicago Press, 1968, repr. 1983.

Cobban, Alan B. *The Medieval English Universities: Oxford and Cambridge to circa 1500.* Berkeley: University of California Press, 1988.

Coleman, Janet. *Medieval Readers and Writers, 1350–1400.* New York: Columbia University Press, 1981.

Cooper, Helen. *The Structure of the "Canterbury Tales."* London: Duckworth, 1983.

Costa, Gustavo. "Dialectic and Mercury (Education, Magic, and Religion in Dante)." In *The "Divine Comedy" and the Encyclopedia of Arts and Sciences,* ed. Giuseppe Di Scipio and Aldo Scaglione, 43–64. Philadelphia: John Benjamins, 1988.

Courtenay, William J. *Schools and Scholars in Fourteenth-Century England.* Princeton: Princeton University Press, 1987.

Curry, Walter Clyde. *Chaucer and the Mediaeval Sciences.* London: Oxford University Press, 1926; rev. ed. New York: Barnes and Noble, 1960.

———. "The Secret of Chaucer's Pardoner." *JEGP* 18 (1919): 593–606.

Curtius, Ernst Robert. *European Literature and the Latin Middle Ages.* Trans. Willard Trask. Bollingen Series 36. 1948; New York: Harper and Row, 1963.

David, Alfred. *The Strumpet Muse: Art and Morals in Chaucer's Poetry.* Bloomington: Indiana University Press, 1976.

Davies, Brian. *The Thought of Thomas Aquinas.* Oxford: Clarendon Press, 1992.

Deaux, George. *The Black Death, 1347.* London: Hamish Hamilton, 1969.

Delany, Sheila. *Chaucer's "House of Fame": The Poetics of Skeptical Fideism.* 1972; repr. Gainesville: University Press of Florida, 1994.

Dempster, Germaine. "Manly's Conception of the Early History of the *Canterbury Tales.*" *PMLA* 61 (1946): 379–415.

———. "A Period in the Development of the *Canterbury Tales* Marriage Group and of Blocks B2 and C." *PMLA* 68 (1953): 1142–59.

Dinshaw, Carolyn. *Chaucer's Sexual Poetics.* Madison: University of Wisconsin Press, 1989.

Dobbs, Elizabeth A. "Literary, Legal, and Last Judgments in *The Canterbury Tales.*" *SAC* 14 (1992): 31–52.

Dölger, Franz. *Sol Salutis.* Münster: Aschendorff, 1925.

Doyle, A. I., and Malcolm B. Parkes. "Paleographical Introduction." In *The Canterbury Tales, Geoffrey Chaucer: A Facsimile and Transcription of the Hengwrt*

Manuscript, With Variants from the Ellesmere Manuscript, ed. Paul G. Ruggiers, xix–xlix. Norman: University of Oklahoma Press, 1979.

——. "The Production of Copies of the *Canterbury Tales* and the *Confessio Amantis* in the Early Fifteenth Century." In *Medieval Scribes, Manuscripts, and Libraries: Essays Presented to N. R. Ker,* ed. M. B. Parkes and Andrew G. Watson, 163–210. London: Scolar, 1978.

Dronke, Peter. "Chaucer and the Medieval Latin Poets, Part A." In *Geoffrey Chaucer: Writers and Their Backgrounds,* ed. Derek Brewer, 154–72. London: G. Bell and Sons, 1974.

Duby, Georges. *The Three Orders: Feudal Society Imagined.* Trans. Arthur Goldhammer. Chicago: University of Chicago Press, 1980.

Duncan, Edgar H. "Chaucer and 'Arnold of the Newe Toun.' " *MLN* 57 (1942): 31–33.

——. "The Literature of Alchemy and Chaucer's *Canon's Yeoman's Tale:* Framework, Theme, and Characters." *Speculum* 43 (1968): 633–56.

Economou, George. *The Goddess Natura in Medieval Literature.* Cambridge: Harvard University Press, 1972.

Edwards, Robert R. *The Dream of Chaucer: Representation and Reflection in the Early Narratives.* Durham, N.C.: Duke University Press, 1989.

Eliade, Mircea. *The Forge and the Crucible.* Trans. Stephen Corrin. 2d ed. Chicago: University of Chicago Press, 1978.

Englehardt, George J. "The Lay Pilgrims of the *Canterbury Tales:* A Study in Ethology." *Mediaeval Studies* 36 (1974): 278–330.

Farmer, Sharon. "Persuasive Voices: Clerical Images of Medieval Wives." *Speculum* 61.3 (1986): 517–43.

Ferster, Judith. *Chaucer on Interpretation.* Cambridge: Cambridge University Press, 1985.

Finkelstein, Dorothee. "The Code of Chaucer's 'Secree of Secrees': Arabic Alchemical Terminology in 'The Canon's Yeoman's Tale.' " *Archiv für das Studium der neueren Sprachen und Literaturen* 207 (1970): 260–76.

Fisher, John H. *The Importance of Chaucer.* Carbondale: Southern Illinois University Press, 1992.

——. *John Gower: Moral Philosopher and Friend of Chaucer.* New York: New York University Press, 1964.

Fletcher, Alan J. "The Preaching of the Pardoner." *SAC* 11 (1989): 15–35.

Foucault, Michel. *The Archeology of Knowledge.* Trans. A. M. Sheridan Smith. New York: Pantheon, 1972.

——. *The Order of Things: An Archeology of the Human Sciences.* New York: Pantheon, 1970.

Fowler, Alastair. *Spenser and the Numbers of Time.* London: Routledge and Kegan Paul, 1964.

Freccero, John. *Dante: The Poetics of Conversion.* Ed. Rachel Jacoff. Cambridge: Harvard University Press, 1986.

Frese, Dolores W. *An Ars Legendi for Chaucer's "Canterbury Tales": Re-constructive Reading.* Gainesville: University of Florida Press, 1991.

——. "The *Nun's Priest's Tale:* Chaucer's Identified Masterpiece?" *Chaucer Review* 16 (1982): 330–43.

Fyler, John M. *Chaucer and Ovid.* New Haven: Yale University Press, 1979.

Gabel, Leona C. *Benefit of Clergy in England in the Later Middle Ages.* Smith College Series in History, vol. 14, nos. 1–4. 1928–29; New York: Octagon Books, 1969.

Galway, Margaret. "The *Troilus* Frontispiece." *MLR* 44 (1949): 161–77.

Ganim, John. *Chaucerian Theatricality.* Princeton: Princeton University Press, 1990.

Gardner, John. *The Life and Times of Chaucer.* New York: Alfred A. Knopf, 1977.

Gaylord, Alan T. "The Role of Saturn in the *Knight's Tale.*" *Chaucer Review* 8 (1974): 171–90.

——. "*Sentence* and *Solaas* in Fragment VII of the *Canterbury Tales*: Harry Bailly as Horseback Editor." *PMLA* 82.2 (1967): 226–35.

Gellrich, Jesse M. *The Idea of the Book in the Middle Ages: Language Theory, Mythology, and Fiction.* Ithaca: Cornell University Press, 1985.

Grant, Edward. "Cosmology." In *Science in the Middle Ages,* ed. David C. Lindberg, 265–302. Chicago: University of Chicago Press, 1978.

Green, Richard Firth. *Poets and Princepleasers: Literature and the English Court in the Late Middle Ages.* Toronto: University of Toronto Press, 1980.

Grennen, Joseph. "The Canon's Yeoman and the Cosmic Furnace: Language and Meaning in the 'Canon's Yeoman's Tale.' " *Criticism* 4 (1962): 225–40.

——. "Chaucer and the Commonplaces of Alchemy." *C&M* 26 (1965): 306–33.

——. "Chaucer's 'Secree of Secrees': An Alchemical 'Topic.' " *PQ* 42 (1963): 562–66.

——. "Saint Cecilia's 'Chemical Wedding': The Unity of the *Canterbury Tales* Fragment VIII." *JEGP* 65 (1966): 466–81.

Hall, D. J. *English Mediaeval Pilgrimage.* London: Routledge and Kegan Paul, 1965.

Haller, Robert S. "Chaucer's *Squire's Tale* and the Uses of Rhetoric." *MP* 62 (1965): 285–95.

Hansen, Elaine Tuttle. *Chaucer and the Fictions of Gender.* Berkeley: University of California Press, 1992.

Hatcher, Elizabeth R. "Life without Death: The Old Man in Chaucer's *Pardoner's Tale.*" *Chaucer Review* 9 (1975): 246–52.

Heer, Friedrich. "Intellectualism and the Universities." In *The Medieval World,* trans. Janet Sondheimer, 235–60. London: George Wiedenfeld and Nicolson, 1962.

Hoffman, Richard L. "Jephthah's Daughter and Chaucer's Virginia." *Chaucer Review* 2 (1967): 20–31.

Hornsby, Joseph. *Chaucer and the Law.* Norman, Okla.: Pilgrim Books, 1988.

Howard, Donald. "The *Canterbury Tales*: Memory and Form." *ELH* 38.3 (1971): 319–28.

——. *The Idea of the "Canterbury Tales."* Berkeley: University of California Press, 1967.

Ierodiakonou, Katerina. "The Stoic Division of Philosophy." *Phronesis* 38.1 (1993): 57–74.

Imbach, Ruedi. *Laien in der Philosophie des Mittelalters: Hinweise und Anregungen zu einem vernachlässigten Thema.* Amsterdam: B. R. Grüner, 1989.

Jones, Howard. *The Epicurean Tradition.* London: Routledge, 1989.

Jordan, Mark. *Ordering Wisdom: The Hierarchy of Philosophical Discourses in Aquinas.* Notre Dame: University of Notre Dame Press, 1986.

Jordan, Robert M. *Chaucer and the Shape of Creation: The Aesthetic Possibilities of Inorganic Form.* Cambridge: Harvard University Press, 1967.

———. *Chaucer's Poetics and the Modern Reader.* Berkeley: University of California Press, 1987.

Joseph, Gerhard. "Chaucer's Coinage: Foreign Exchange and the Puns of the *Shipman's Tale*." *Chaucer Review* 17.4 (1983): 341–57.

———. "The Gifts of Nature, Fortune, and Grace in the *Physician's, Pardoner's,* and *Parson's Tales*." *Chaucer Review* 9 (1975): 237–45.

Kane, George. "John M. Manly (1865–1940) and Edith Rickert (1871–1938)." In *Editing Chaucer: The Great Tradition,* 207–29, ed. Paul G. Ruggiers. Norman, Okla.: Pilgrim Books, 1984.

Kaske, Robert E. "The Knight's Interruption of the Monk's Tale." *ELH* 24 (1957): 249–68.

Katzenellenbogen, Adolf. "The Representation of the Seven Liberal Arts." In *Twelfth-Century Europe and the Foundations of Modern Society,* ed. Marshall Clagett, Gaines Post, and Robert Reynolds, 39–55. Madison: University of Wisconsin Press, 1961.

Kay, Richard. *Dante's Christian Astrology.* Philadelphia: University of Pennsylvania Press, 1994.

Kellogg, Alfred L. "The Evolution of the Clerk's Tale." In *Chaucer, Langland, and Arthur: Essays in Middle English Literature,* 287–88. New Brunswick: Rutgers University Press, 1972.

Kempton, Daniel. "The *Physician's Tale*: The Doctor of Physic's Diplomatic 'Cure.'" *Chaucer Review* 19.1 (1984): 24–38.

Kibre, Pearl, and Nancy G. Siraisi. "The Institutional Context." In *Science in the Middle Ages,* 120–44, ed. David C. Lindberg. Chicago: University of Chicago Press, 1978.

Kirby, John T. "The 'Great Triangle' in Early Greek Rhetoric and Poetics." *Rhetorica* 8.3 (1990): 213–27.

Kiser, Lisa. *Truth and Textuality in Chaucer's Poetry.* Hanover: University Press of New England, 1991.

Kittredge, George Lyman. "Chaucer's Discussion of Marriage." *MP* 9 (1912): 435–67; repr. in *Chaucer Criticism,* ed. Richard J. Schoeck and Jerome Taylor, 1:130–59. Notre Dame: University of Notre Dame Press, 1960, repr. 1975.

Knapp, Peggy. *Chaucer and the Social Contest.* New York: Routledge, 1990.

Kolve, V. A. *Chaucer and the Imagery of Narrative: The First Five Canterbury Tales.* Stanford: Stanford University Press, 1984.

Koonce, B. G. *Chaucer and the Tradition of Fame.* Princeton: Princeton University Press, 1966.

Krochalis, Jeanne. "The Books and Reading of Henry V and His Circle." *Chaucer Review* 23 (1988): 50–77.

Leclercq, Jean. "Saint Bernard's Attitude toward War." In *Studies in Medieval Cistercian History,* vol. 2, ed. John R. Sommerfeldt. Cistercian Studies Series, no. 24. Kalamazoo, Mich.: Cistercian Publications, 1976.

Lehmann, Paul. *Die Parodie im Mittelalter.* Stuttgart: Anton Hiersemann, 1963.

Leicester, H. Marshall, Jr. "Synne Horrible: The Pardoner's Exegesis of His Tale and Chaucer's." In *Acts of Interpretation: The Text in Its Contexts, 700–1600,* ed. Mary J. Carruthers and Elizabeth D. Kirk, 25–50. Norman, Okla.: Pilgrim Books, 1982.

Lenaghan, R. T. "Chaucer's Circle of Gentlemen and Clerks." *Chaucer Review* 18.1 (1983): 155–60.

Lepley, Douglas L. "The Monk's Boethian Tale." *Chaucer Review* 12.3 (1978): 162–70.

Lerer, Seth. *Chaucer and His Readers: Imagining the Author in Late-Medieval England.* Princeton: Princeton University Press, 1993.

Levy, Bernard. "Biblical Parody in the *Summoner's Tale.*" *Tennessee Studies in Literature* 11 (1966): 45–60.

Lewis, Robert E. "Glosses to the *Man of Law's Tale* from Pope Innocent III's *De Miseria Humane Conditionis.*" *SP* 64.1 (1967): 1–16.

Lindahl, Carl. *Earnest Games: Folkloric Patterns in the "Canterbury Tales."* Bloomington: Indiana University Press, 1987.

Lindberg, David C., ed. *Science in the Middle Ages.* Chicago: University of Chicago Press, 1978.

Lounsbury, Thomas R. *Studies in Chaucer.* 3 vols. 1892. New York: Russell and Russell, 1962.

Machan, Tim William. "Language Contact in *Piers Plowman.*" *Speculum* 69.2 (1994): 359–85.

Mandel, Jerome. *Geoffrey Chaucer: Building the Fragments of the "Canterbury Tales."* London: Associated University Presses, 1992.

Manly, John M. "Chaucer and the Rhetoricians." *Proceedings of the British Academy* 12 (1926): 95–113; repr. *Chaucer Criticism,* ed. Richard Schoeck and Jerome Taylor, 1:268–90. Notre Dame: University of Notre Dame Press, 1960.

———. "What Is Chaucer's *Hous of Fame?*" In *Anniversary Papers by Colleagues and Pupils of George Lyman Kittredge,* ed. Fred N. Robinson, William A. Neilson, and Edward S. Sheldon, 73–82. Boston: Ginn, 1913; repr. New York: Russell and Russell, 1967.

Mann, Jill. *Chaucer and Medieval Estates Satire.* Cambridge: Cambridge University Press, 1973.

Manzalaoui, Mahmoud A. " 'Noght in the Registre of Venus': Gower's English Mirror for Princes." In *Medieval Studies for J. A. W. Bennett Aetatis Suae LXX,* ed. P. L. Heyworth. 159–83. Oxford: Clarendon Press, 1981.

Martin, Carol Ann. "Mercurial Haeresis: Chaucer's Hermeneutical Po-Et(h)ics." Ph.D. diss., University of Notre Dame, 1993.

Maxfield, David K. "St. Mary Rouncivale, Charing Cross: The Hospital of Chaucer's Pardoner." *Chaucer Review* 28.2 (1993): 148–63.

Mazzotta, Giuseppe. *Dante's Vision and the Circle of Knowledge.* Princeton: Princeton University Press, 1993.

McAlpine, Monica E. "The Pardoner's Homosexuality and How It Matters." *PMLA* 95 (1980): 8–22.

McCall, John P. "The Squire in Wonderland." *Chaucer Review* 1 (1966): 103–9.

McFarlane, K. B. *John Wycliffe and the Beginnings of Nonconformity.* London: English Universities Press, 1952.

——. *Lancastrian Kings and Lollard Knights.* Oxford: Clarendon Press, 1972.

Middleton, Anne. "The Audience and Public of *Piers Plowman.*" In *Middle English Alliterative Poetry and Its Literary Background: Seven Essays,* ed. David Lawton, 101–23. Cambridge: Cambridge University Press, 1982.

Miller, Robert P. "Chaucer's Pardoner, the Scriptural Eunuch, and the *Pardoner's Tale.*" *Speculum* 30 (1955): 180–99.

——. "Chaucer's Rhetorical Rendition of Mind: *The Squire's Tale.*" In *Chaucer and the Craft of Fiction,* 219–40. Ed. Leigh A. Arrathoon. Rochester, Mich.: Scolaris Press, 1986.

——. "The Epicurean Homily on Marriage by Chaucer's Franklin." *Mediaevalia* 6 (1980): 151–86.

Minnis, Alastair J. "Authors in Love: The Exegesis of Late-Medieval Love-Poets." In *The Uses of Manuscripts in Literary Studies: Essays in Memory of Judson Boyce Allen,* ed. Charlotte C. Morse, Penelope R. Doob, Marjorie C. Woods, 161–92. Studies in Medieval Culture, vol. 31. Kalamazoo, Mich.: Medieval Institute Publications, 1992.

——. *Medieval Theory of Authorship: Scholastic Literary Attitudes in the Later Middle Ages.* 2d ed. London: Scolar Press, 1984. Philadelphia: University of Pennsylvania Press, 1988.

——. " 'Moral Gower' and Medieval Literary Theory." In *Gower's "Confessio Amantis": Responses and Reassessments,* ed. A. J. Minnis, 50–78. Cambridge: D. S. Brewer, 1983.

Multhauf, Robert P. "The Science of Matter." In *Science in the Middle Ages,* ed. David C. Lindberg, 369–90. Chicago: University of Chicago Press, 1978.

Murphy, James J. "John Gower's *Confessio Amantis* and the First Discussion of Rhetoric in the English Language." *PQ* 41 (1962): 401–11.

——. "A New Look at Chaucer and the Rhetoricians." *Review of English Studies* n.s. 15 (1964): 1–20.

——. *Rhetoric in the Middle Ages: A Study of Rhetorical Theory from Saint Augustine to the Renaissance.* Berkeley: University of California Press, 1974, repr. 1990.

Murtaugh, Daniel M. "Women and Geoffrey Chaucer." *ELH* 38.4 (1971): 473–92.

Muscatine, Charles. *Chaucer and the French Tradition: A Study in Style and Meaning.* Berkeley: University of California Press, 1957.

Neuse, Richard. *Chaucer's Dante: Allegory and Epic Theater in "The Canterbury Tales."* Berkeley: University of California Press, 1991.

Neville, Marie. "The Function of the *Squire's Tale* in the Canterbury Scheme." *JEGP* 50 (1951): 167–79.

Nohl, Johannes. *The Black Death: A Chronicle of the Plague Compiled from Contemporary Sources.* Trans. C. H. Clarke. London: Unwin, 1961.

North, J. D. *Chaucer's Universe.* Oxford: Clarendon Press, 1988.

——. *Stars, Minds, and Fate: Essays in Ancient and Modern Cosmology.* London: Hambledon Press, 1989.

Ogrince, Will H. L. "Western Society and Alchemy, 1200–1500." *Journal of Medieval History* 6 (1980): 103–32.

Olmert, K. Michael. "The *Canon's Yeoman's Tale*: An Interpretation." *Annuale Mediaevale* 8 (1967): 70–94.

Olson, Glending. "Chaucer, Dante, and the Structure of Fragment VIII (G) of the *Canterbury Tales*." *Chaucer Review* 16 (1982): 222–36.

——. *Literature as Recreation in the Later Middle Ages*. Ithaca: Cornell University Press, 1982.

Olson, Paul. *The "Canterbury Tales" and the Good Society*. Princeton: Princeton University Press, 1986.

Orme, Nicholas. "Chaucer and Education." *Chaucer Review* 16 (1981): 38–59.

——. *Education and Society in Medieval and Renaissance England*. London: Hambledon Press, 1989.

——. *English Schools in the Middle Ages*. London: Methuen, 1973.

——. *From Childhood to Chivalry: The Education of the English Kings and Aristocracy 1066–1530*. London: Methuen, 1984.

Oruch, Jack B. "Chaucer's Worldly Monk." *Criticism* 8 (1966): 280–88.

Owen, Charles A., Jr. "The Alternative Reading of the *Canterbury Tales*: Chaucer's Text and the Early Manuscripts." *PMLA* 97 (1982): 237–50.

——. "The *Canterbury Tales*: Early Manuscripts and Relative Popularity." *JEGP* 54 (1955): 104–10.

——. "Pre-1450 Manuscripts of the *Canterbury Tales*: Relationships and Significance," Parts I and II. *Chaucer Review* 23.1 and 2 (1988): 1–29, 95–116.

Owen, Nancy H. "The Pardoner's Introduction, Prologue, and Tale: Sermon and *Fabliau*." *JEGP* 66 (1967): 541–49.

Paetow, Louis John. *The Arts Course at Medieval Universities, With Special Reference to Grammar and Rhetoric*. University of Illinois University Studies, vol. 3, no. 7. Urbana-Champaign: University Press, 1910.

Parkes, Malcolm B. "The Influence of the Concepts of *Ordinatio* and *Compilatio* on the Development of the Book." In *Medieval Learning and Literature: Essays Presented to R. W. Hunt*, ed. J. J. G. Alexander and M. T. Gibson, 115–41. Oxford: Oxford University Press, 1976.

Patterson, Lee W. *Chaucer and the Subject of History*. Madison: University of Wisconsin Press, 1991.

——. "Chaucerian Confession: Penitential Literature and the Pardoner." *Medievalia et Humanistica* 7 (1976): 153–74.

——. " 'For the Wyves love of Bathe': Feminine Rhetoric and Poetic Resolution in the *Roman de la Rose* and the *Canterbury Tales*." *Speculum* 58 (1983): 656–95.

——. *Negotiating the Past: The Historical Understanding of Medieval Literature*. Madison: University of Wisconsin Press, 1987.

——. "The 'Parson's Tale' and the Quitting of the *Canterbury Tales*." *Traditio* 34 (1978): 331–80.

——. "Perpetual Motion: Alchemy and the Technology of the Self." *SAC* 15 (1993): 25–57.

——. " 'What Man Artow?': Authorial Self-Definition in *The Tale of Sir Thopas* and *The Tale of Melibee*." *SAC* 11 (1989): 117–75.

Payne, Robert O. *The Key of Remembrance: A Study of Chaucer's Poetics*. New Haven: Yale University Press, 1963, repr. 1964.

Pearsall, Derek. *The Canterbury Tales*. London: George Allen and Unwin, 1985.

———. "The Squire as Story-Teller." *UTQ* 34 (1964): 82–92.
———. "The *Troilus* Frontispiece and Chaucer's Audience." *YES* 7 (1977): 68–74.
Peck, Russell. "Chaucer and the Nominalist Questions." *Speculum* 53 (1978): 745–60.
———. *Kingship and Common Profit in Gower's "Confessio Amantis."* Carbondale: Southern Illinois University Press, 1978.
Pelen, Marc M. "The Manciple's 'Cosyn' to the 'Dede.' " *Chaucer Review* 25.4 (1991): 343–54.
Peterson, Joyce E. "The Finished Fragment: A Reassessment of the *Squire's Tale.*" *Chaucer Review* 5 (1970): 62–74.
Plimpton, George A. *The Education of Chaucer Illustrated from the Schoolbooks in Use in His Time.* London: Oxford University Press, 1935.
Porter, Elizabeth. "Gower's Ethical Microcosm and Political Macrocosm." In *Gower's "Confessio Amantis": Responses and Reassessments,* ed. A. J. Minnis, 135–62. London: D. S. Brewer, 1993.
Pratt, Robert A. "Jankyn's Book of Wikked Wyves: Medieval Antimatrimonial Propaganda in the Universities." *Annuale Mediaevale* 3 (1962): 5–27.
———. "Saint Jerome in Jankyn's Book of Wikked Wyves." *Criticism* 5.4 (1963): 316–22.
Quain, Edward A., S.J. "The Medieval *Accessus Ad Auctores.*" *Traditio* 3 (1945): 215–64.
Rahner, Hugo. *Greek Myths and Christian Mystery.* Trans. Brian Battershaw. London: Burns and Oates, 1963.
Rashdall, Hastings. *The Universities of Europe in the Middle Ages.* Ed. F. M. Powicke and A. B. Emden. 3 vols. Oxford: Clarendon Press, 1936.
Reames, Sherry. "The Cecilia Legend as Chaucer Inherited It and Retold It: The Disappearance of an Augustinian Ideal." *Speculum* 55.1 (1980): 38–57.
———. "A Recent Discovery Concerning the Sources of the 'Second Nun's Tale.' " *MP* 87 (1990): 337–61.
Richardson, Malcolm. "The Earliest Known Owners of *Canterbury Tales* MSS and Chaucer's Secondary Audience." *Chaucer Review* 25.1 (1990): 17–32.
———. "Hoccleve in His Social Context." *Chaucer Review* 20.4 (1986): 313–22.
Rickert, Edith. "Chaucer at School." *MP* 29 (1931–32): 257–74.
———. "Was Chaucer a Student at the Inner Temple?" In *Manly Anniversary Studies,* 20–31. Chicago: University of Chicago Press, 1923.
Roney, Lois. *Chaucer's Knight's Tale and Theories of Scholastic Psychology.* Tampa: University of South Florida Press, 1990.
Rosenberg, Bruce A. "The Contrary Tales of the Second Nun and the Canon's Yeoman." *Chaucer Review* 2 (1967–68): 278–91.
———. "Swindling Alchemist, Antichrist." *Centennial Review of Arts and Sciences* 6 (1962): 566–80.
Rouse, R. H., and M. A. "*Ordinatio* and *Compilatio* Revisited." In *Ad Litteram: Authoritative Texts and Their Medieval Readers,* ed. Mark D. Jordan and Kent Emery, Jr., 113–34. Notre Dame Conferences in Medieval Studies, vol. 3. Notre Dame: University of Notre Dame Press, 1992.
Rowe, Donald W. *Through Nature to Eternity: Chaucer's "Legend of Good Women."* Lincoln: University of Nebraska Press, 1988.

Rowland, Beryl. "Chaucer's Idea of the Pardoner." *Chaucer Review* 14 (1979): 140–54.

——. "The Physician's 'Historial Thyng Notable' and the Man of Law." *ELH* 40 (1973): 165–78.

Ruud, Jay. "Natural Law and Chaucer's *Physician's Tale*." *Journal of the Rocky Mountain Medieval and Renaissance Association* 9 (1988): 29–45.

Ryan, Lawrence V. "The Canon's Yeoman's Desperate Confession." *Chaucer Review* 8.4 (1974): 297–310.

Samuels, M. L. "The Scribe of the Hengwrt and Ellesmere Manuscripts of *The Canterbury Tales*." *SAC* 5 (1983): 49–65.

Scanlon, Larry. "The Authority of Fable: Allegory and Irony in the *Nun's Priest's Tale*." *Exemplaria* 1 (1989): 43–68.

Scattergood, V. J. "The Originality of the *Shipman's Tale*." *Chaucer Review* 11.3 (1977): 210–31.

Schless, Howard H. *Chaucer and Dante: A Revaluation*. Norman, Okla.: Pilgrim Books, 1984.

Schmidt, A. V. C. *The Clerkly Maker: Langland's Poetic Art*. Cambridge: Cambridge University Press, 1987.

Schmitt, Charles B. "Theophrastus in the Middle Ages." *Viator* 2 (1971): 251–70.

Schrader, Richard J. "Chauntecleer, the Mermaid, and Daun Burnel." *Chaucer Review* 4.4 (1970): 284–90.

Schweitzer, Edward C., Jr. "Chaucer's Pardoner and the Hare." *ELN* 4 (1967): 247–50.

Seung, T. K. "The Metaphysics of the *Commedia*." In *The "Divine Comedy" and the Encyclopedia of the Arts and Sciences*, 181–222. Ed. Giuseppe Di Scipio and Aldo Scaglione. Philadelphia: John Benjamins, 1988.

Severs, J. Burke. "Chaucer's Clerks." In *Chaucer and Middle English Studies*, ed. Beryl Rowland, 140–52. London: George Allen and Unwin, 1974.

Seznec, Jean. *The Survival of the Pagan Gods: The Mythological Tradition and Its Place in Renaissance Humanism and Art*. Trans. Barbara F. Sessions. Bollingen Series 38. New York: Pantheon Books, 1953.

Shoaf, R. A. *Dante, Chaucer, and the Currency of the Word: Money, Images, and Reference in Late Medieval Poetry*. Norman, Okla.: Pilgrim Books, 1983.

——. "*The Franklin's Tale*: Chaucer and Medusa." *Chaucer Review* 21 (1986): 274–90.

Silvia, Daniel S. "Glosses to the *Canterbury Tales* from St. Jerome's *Epistola Adversus Jovinianum*." *SP* 62 (1965): 28–39.

Simpson, James. *Sciences and the Self in Medieval Poetry: Alan of Lille's "Anticlaudianus" and John Gower's "Confessio Amantis"*. Cambridge Studies in Medieval Literature, no. 25. Cambridge: Cambridge University Press, 1995.

Siraisi, Nancy G. "Dante and the Art and Science of Medicine." In *The "Divine Comedy" and the Encyclopedia of Arts and Sciences*, ed. Giuseppe Di Scipio and Aldo Scaglione, 223–45. Philadelphia: John Benjamins, 1988.

——. *Medieval and Early Renaissance Medicine: An Introduction to Knowledge and Practice*. Chicago: University of Chicago Press, 1990.

Spearing, A. C., ed. *The Franklin's Prologue and Tale*. Cambridge: Cambridge University Press, 1966.

Steneck, Nicholas H. "A Late Medieval *Arbor Scientiarum.*" *Speculum* 50.2 (1975): 244–69.

Stevens, Martin, and Daniel Woodward, eds. *Ellesmere Chaucer: Essays in Interpretation* (Tokyo and San Marino, Calif.: Huntington Library, 1995).

Storm, Melvin. "The Pardoner's Invitation: Quaester's Bag or Becket's Shrine?" *PMLA* 97.5 (1982): 810–18.

Strohm, Paul. "Chaucer's Fifteenth-Century Audience and the Narrowing of the 'Chaucer Tradition.' " *SAC* 4 (1982): 3–32.

———. *Social Chaucer.* Cambridge: Harvard University Press, 1989.

Szittya, Penn R. "The Friar as False Apostle: Antifraternal Exegesis and the *Summoner's Tale.*" *SP* 71 (1974): 19–46.

———. "The Green Yeoman as Loathly Lady: The Friar's Parody of the Wife of Bath's Tale." *PMLA* 90.3 (1975): 386–94.

Talbot, Charles H. "Medicine." In *Science in the Middle Ages,* ed. David C. Lindberg, 391–428. Chicago: University of Chicago Press, 1978.

Tatlock, John S. P. "Chaucer and Wyclif." *MP* 14 (1916): 257–68.

Taylor, F. Sherwood. *The Alchemists: Founders of Modern Chemistry.* New York: Schuman, 1949.

Taylor, Jerome. "Fraunceys Petrak and the Logyk of Chaucer's Clerk." In *Francis Petrarch, Six Centuries Later: A Symposium,* ed. Aldo Scaglione, 364–83. North Carolina Studies in the Romance Languages and Literatures, no. 3. Chapel Hill: University of North Carolina Press, 1975.

Taylor, Karla. *Chaucer Reads "The Divine Comedy."* Stanford: Stanford University Press, 1989.

———. "The Text and Its Afterlife." *Comparative Literature* 35.1 (1983): 1–20.

Taylor, P. B. "Chaucer's *Cosyn to the Dede.*" *Speculum* 57 (1982): 315–27.

Thompson, David. *Dante's Epic Journeys.* Baltimore: Johns Hopkins University Press, 1974.

Thorndike, Lynn. *A History of Magic and Experimental Science.* 8 vols. History of Science Society Publications, n.s. 4. New York: Columbia University Press, 1934.

———. *University Records and Life in the Middle Ages.* New York: Columbia University Press, 1944.

Tout, Thomas F. *Chapters in the Administrative History of Mediaeval England.* 6 vols. 1920–33. New York: Barnes and Noble, 1967.

———. "Literature and Learning in the English Civil Service in the Fourteenth Century." *Speculum* 4 (1929): 365–89.

Travis, Peter. "The *Nun's Priest's Tale* as Grammar School Primer." *SAC* Proceedings 1 (1984): 81–91.

Trower, Katherine B. "Spiritual Sickness in the Physician's and Pardoner's Tales: Thematic Unity in Fragment VI of the *Canterbury Tales.*" *American Benedictine Review* 29 (1978): 67–86.

Tullio, Gregory. *Anima Mundi.* Florence: Sansoni, 1955.

Tupper, Frederick. "Chaucer and the Seven Deadly Sins." *PMLA* 29 (1914): 93–128.

———. "Chaucer's Sinners and Sins." *JEGP* 15 (1916): 56–106.

Uhlfelder, Myra L. "The Role of the Liberal Arts in Boethius' *Consolatio.*"

In *Boethius and the Liberal Arts: A Collection of Essays*, ed. Michael Masi, 17–34. Utah Studies in Literature and Linguistics 18. Las Vegas: Peter Lang, 1981.

Ussery, Huling E. *Chaucer's Physician*. Tulane Studies in English, no. 19. New Orleans: Tulane University Press, 1971.

Walsh, James J. *The Popes and Science: A History of the Papal Relations to Science during the Middle Ages and Down to Our Day*. New York: Fordham University Press, 1908.

Weisheipl, James A. "Classification of the Sciences in Medieval Thought." *Medieval Studies* 27 (1965): 54–90.

——. "Curriculum of the Faculty of Arts at Oxford in the Early Fourteenth Century." *Medieval Studies* 26 (1964): 143–85.

——. "The Nature, Scope, and Classification of the Sciences." In *Science in the Middle Ages*, ed. David C. Lindberg, 466–67. Chicago: University of Chicago Press, 1978.

Wenzel, Siegfried. "Chaucer's Pardoner and His Relics." *SAC* 11 (1989): 37–41.

——. "Notes on the *Parson's Tale*." *Chaucer Review* 16 (1982): 237–56.

——. "The Source for the 'Remedia' of the Parson's Tale." *Traditio* 27 (1971): 433–53.

——. "The Source of Chaucer's Seven Deadly Sins." *Traditio* 30 (1974): 351–78.

Westlund, Joseph. "The *Knight's Tale* as an Impetus for Pilgrimage." *PQ* 43.4 (1964): 526–37.

Wetherbee, Winthrop. *Chaucer and the Poets: An Essay on "Troilus and Criseyde."* Ithaca: Cornell University Press, 1984.

——. *Platonism and Poetry in the Twelfth Century: The Literary Influence of the School of Chartres*. Princeton: Princeton University Press, 1972.

Wilkins, Ernest H. "Descriptions of Pagan Divinities From Petrarch to Chaucer." *Speculum* 32.3 (1957): 511–22.

Wilson, Katharina M., and Elizabeth Makowski. *Wykked Wyves and the Woes of Marriage: Misogamous Literature from Juvenal to Chaucer*. Albany: State University of New York Press, 1990.

Wittkower, Rudolf. " 'Grammatica': From Martianus Capella to Hogarth." *Journal of the Warburg and Courtauld Institutes* 2 (1938): 82–84.

Wood, Chauncey A. *Chaucer and the Country of the Stars: Poetic Uses of Astrological Imagery*. Princeton: Princeton University Press, 1970.

——. "Chaucer's Most 'Gowerian' Tale." In *Chaucer and Gower: Difference, Mutuality, Exchange*, ed. R. F. Yeager, 75–84. English Literary Studies No. 51. Victoria: University of Victoria Press, 1991.

Wurtele, Douglas. "The Penitence of Geoffrey Chaucer." *Viator* 11 (1980): 335–59.

Yeager, R. F. *John Gower's Poetic: The Search for a New Arion*. Cambridge: D. S. Brewer, 1990.

Young, Karl. "The Maidenly Virtues of Chaucer's Virginia." *Speculum* 16 (1941): 340–49.

Zambelli, Paola. *The "Speculum Astronomiae" and Its Enigma: Astrology, Theology and Science in Albertus Magnus and His Contemporaries.* Boston Studies in the Philosophy of Science 135. Dordrecht: Kluwer Academic Publishers, 1992.

Ziegler, Philip. *The Black Death.* New York: Harper and Row, 1969.

Ziolkowski, Jan. *Alan of Lille's Grammar of Sex: The Meaning of Grammar to a Twelfth-Century Intellectual.* Speculum Anniversary Monographs 10. Cambridge, Mass.: The Medieval Academy of America, 1985.

INDEX